THE WAR
FOR AFRICA

Twelve Months that Transformed a Continent

Fred Bridgland

CASEMATE | publishers

Philadelphia & Oxford

Published in the United States of America and Great Britain in 2017 by
CASEMATE PUBLISHERS
1950 Lawrence Road, Havertown, PA 19083, USA
and
The Old Music Hall, 106–108 Cowley Road, Oxford OX4 1JE, UK

Hardcover Edition: ISBN 978-1-61200-492-1
Digital Edition: ISBN 978-1-61200-493-8

A CIP record for this book is available from the British Library

This is a revised and updated edition of *The War for Africa* (Ashanti Publishing, Gibraltar, 1990).

Typeset in India by Lapiz Digital Services, Chennai

For a complete list of Casemate titles, please contact:

CASEMATE PUBLISHERS (US)
Telephone (610) 853-9131
Fax (610) 853-9146
Email: casemate@casematepublishers.com
www.casematepublishers.com

CASEMATE PUBLISHERS (UK)
Telephone (01865) 241249
Fax (01865) 794449
Email: casemate-uk@casematepublishers.co.uk
www.casematepublishers.co.uk

THE WAR FOR AFRICA

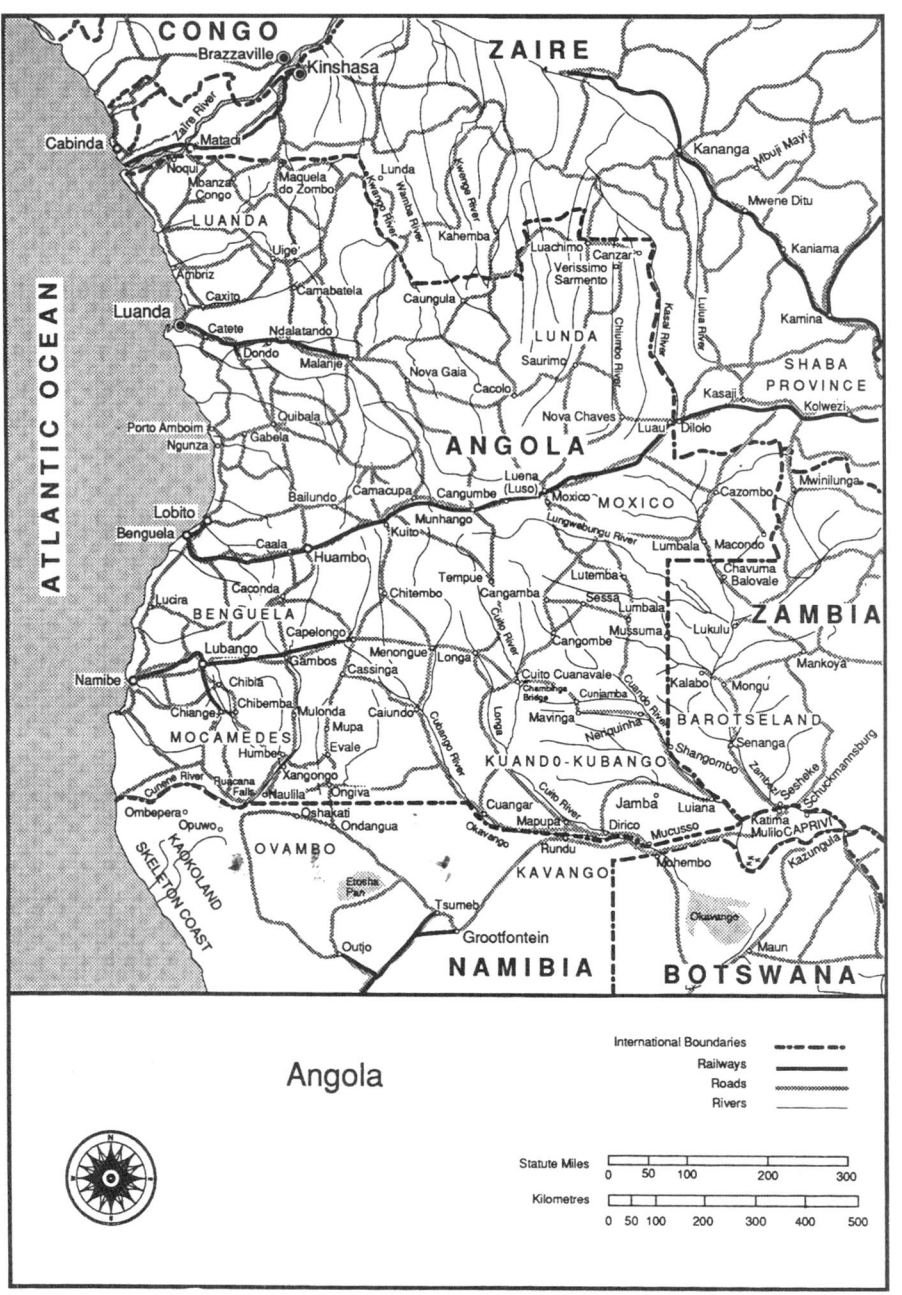

Angola

International Boundaries
Railways
Roads
Rivers

Statute Miles

0   50   100   200   300

Kilometres

0 50 100   200   300   400   500

For dear friends in Angola and South Africa
who deserve liberty, peace and prosperity

The final twelve months of the Cuban–South African conflict has been christened here 'the War for Africa' because its consequences reverberated far beyond Angola's frontiers. The war was one of the most important turning points in the history and development of the continent. It spelled the end of the last great neo-colonial attempts at African conquest, by Cuba and the former Soviet Union. It made possible the dismantling of apartheid in South Africa and a beginning of the end of one-party dictatorship in black Africa.

CONTENTS

Preface   9
Prologue   19

PART 1: GENERAL SHAGANOVITCH'S OFFENSIVE   55
1   The Prelude   57
2   The South Africans move in   65
3   Sniffing out the enemy   70
4   Fapla's advance continues   76

PART 2: THE DEFENCE   79
5   South Africa steps things up   81
6   South Africa's first disaster   86
7   Enter the Falcon   90
8   The first land battle   96
9   The Second 'Rumble on the Lomba'   103

PART 3: THE STING   117
10   Waiting and watching   119
11   Recce hardships   125
12   The Air Force gears up   128
13   War in the air   131
14   Laying the trap   140
15   Fancy tricks and dirty tricks   147
16   The Cavalry – 61 Mech – rides to the rescue   151
17   Softening up 47 Brigade   155
18   The trap closes   161
19   The destruction of 47 Brigade   168
20   Booty from the battlefield   185
21   Fapla's offensive ends   195

PART 4: THE STALEMATE   201
22   Forward beyond the Lomba   203
23   The reinforcements arrive   217

PART 5: THE COUNTER-OFFENSIVE   225
24   The attack on 16 Brigade   227
25   'Destroy the G-5S!'   245
26   Fapla's Great Escape: The Chambinga Gallop   251

PART 6: THE SIDESHOW   279
27   Begging for permission to destroy the enemy   281

PART 7: INTO 1988. OPERATION HOOPER –
        THE COUNTER-OFFENSIVE CONTINUED   293
28   The attack on 21 Brigade: 13 January 1988   295
29   Throwing something at the Cuito River Bridge   313
30   The attack on 59 Brigade: 14 February 1988   317
31   The attack on Highpoint 1251   329

PART 8: THE SIDESHOW (CONTINUED)   331
32   The attack on Menongue   333

PART 9: THE THREE BATTLES FOR THE TUMPO
        TRIANGLE   343
33   Mike Muller leads the First Tumpo Attack:
        25 February 1988   345
34   Mike Muller leads the Second Tumpo Attack:
        29 February 1988   363
35   Jaw-jaw begins to supplant war-war   369
36   Gerhard Louw leads the Third Tumpo Attack:
        23 March 1988   377

PART 10: THE DENOUEMENT   395
37   More jaw-jaw   397
38   Fidel's last hurrah!   404

Epilogue   436
Postscript: UNITA   471
Timeline   477
Glossary   481
Select Bibliography   488
Acknowledgements   492
Index   493

PREFACE

The War for Africa was written in the beginning under serious constraints. It is essential that I flag these up for this new edition, which features a new prologue and epilogue. Context in history is all-important, and new facts and insights constantly surface.

As I researched and wrote the initial account, published here unchanged from the original from page 55 onwards, I was also beginning to uncover a terrible truth about one of the important war leaders that, for reasons of life and death, I could not then reveal. Also, the young South Africans whose stories I heard and told had fought the war without knowing about historic and secret events unfolding far to the south that would transform their lives but which, at the time, were hidden from them and also from the world at large: if they had known, some of them at least might have wondered what the fight was about.

★ ★ ★

General Jannie Geldenhuys, the gentlemanly chief of the South African Defence Force, gave me unfettered access to 'ordinary' soldiers who did the fighting at the height of the Cuban-South African war in Angola in 1987–88. My wish was to write a book on the conflict seen through the eyes of those fighting men: Geldenhuys gave me freedom to interview as many of them as time, energy and money allowed. He promised there would be no interference from top levels of the military or government: there was none. I and my original publisher stipulated that there would be no question of the book being subjected to official scrutiny or censorship: there was none.

I pieced together the account that follows of the War for Africa through scores of interviews with men who were in the front line. The only officer I interviewed above the rank of colonel was General Geldenhuys.

Only now can I say that Geldenhuys would surely have withheld his permission had he known the horrific facts I had begun discovering at that time about South Africa's key wartime ally, Jonas Savimbi, leader of the Angolan rebel movement UNITA (the National Union for the Total Independence of Angola).

Thanks to my close friend, Tito Chingunji, at that time the foreign secretary of UNITA and number three in the liberation movement's hierarchy, I had begun documenting a series of truly appalling atrocities committed by Savimbi against his own people. The full story will be told in a book, as yet only part-completed, but much has already been revealed in several newspaper accounts I have written.[1]

Basically, Savimbi, at a certain point in UNITA's resistance war against Angola's ruling MPLA (Popular Movement for the Liberation of Angola), began executing some of his top officers and their wives and children in bizarre ceremonies at Jamba, his forest headquarters in southeast Angola.

On one occasion, as described to me by several eyewitnesses, Savimbi summoned the entire population of Jamba to a central clearing where the people saw a giant stack of wood and blindfolded men tied to nearby trees. Savimbi arrived with some of his senior officers, all wearing scarlet bandanas.

Savimbi rose to speak on a day that would be remembered as *Setembro vermelho* (Red September). Witches had been plaguing the movement, he said. Some would that day breathe their last and would no longer be able to retard the war effort.

An armed detachment marched towards the blindfolded men. The troops lined up, fired and the men slumped dead, still held by their ropes to the trees.

Savimbi had only just begun.

He ordered every person in the crowd, children also, to gather a twig each and cast it on the woodpile. The giant bonfire was lit. *O Mais Velho* (The Eldest One) called names of women and asked them to step forward: they, he said, were witches whom he had condemned to death. Children would die with their mothers because 'a snake's offspring is also a snake,' eyewitnesses recall Savimbi saying. One of the women who died that day was Aurora Katalayo, a paediatrician and haematologist who had trained and qualified as a doctor in Switzerland. She was the widow of a popular and outspoken guerrilla commander, Mateus Katalayo, who had been executed by Savimbi three years earlier. Aurora had resolutely refused Savimbi's invitations to sleep with him either before or after Mateus's death.

Aurora, according to several accounts, cursed Savimbi's soul aloud, called him a criminal and warned he would never win as she was frog-marched from the crowd with her four-year-old son Michel. Mother and son were pitched into the fire. Tito Chingunji said the proof Savimbi gave of Aurora's witchcraft was the 'Swissification'[2] of Michel and his 12-year-old sister M'Bimbi – but, said Tito, she really died because of her resistance to Savimbi's sexual advances.

Subsequently, my friend Tito was detained by Savimbi with his wife Raquel and their four children. As I struggled to help Tito, contacting intelligence agencies in London and Washington who had worked closely with him and urging them to act on his behalf, I received death threats from UNITA thugs who also threatened to mutilate close members of my family. My efforts failed. Tito was executed by Savimbi with his wife, children and entire extended family of about 50 people. Suddenly I knew the full meaning of bereavement, a cosmic despondency, a wrenching, terrible deprivation of a friendship that had endured amazing adventures and difficulties and had, I hoped, many rich years to run. All the efforts and subterfuges by me and others to preserve Tito's life had bitten the dust. His death must have been as lonely as that of Steve Biko.[3] His life was snuffed out callously and evilly.

The circumstance of this story in relation to the War for Africa was that thousands of UNITA soldiers fought alongside South Africans. They were the 'poor bloody infantry.'[4] Many of them riding atop South

African armoured vehicles were swept away by enemy fire like chaff in the wind. These ordinary peasant soldiers were not guilty of Savimbi's crimes, but I had no access to them as I endeavoured unsuccessfully to save Tito's life. Their role in the war deserved nevertheless to be told, so I interviewed Colonel Fred Oelschig, the senior South African Defence Force liaison officer with Savimbi throughout 1986–89, and added his analysis as a postscript to the book. Oelschig's own account appears, again unchanged, at the end of this new edition. Oelschig did not know, when I talked to him, what I had been discovering about Savimbi, and I have no idea what he knew at the time about events at the heart of the UNITA movement.

★ ★ ★

Some two years before the first shots were fired in the War for Africa, in the face of what the then South African government perceived as a 'mortal threat' to its existence, an unusual meeting took place in a Cape Town hospital. South Africa's Justice Minister Kobie Coetsee visited Nelson Mandela, the patriarch of the banned African National Congress (ANC) who was in the 22nd year of life imprisonment after being convicted on charges of sabotage and conspiring to overthrow the apartheid state.

'In my mind I had the picture of a man who was determined to seize power at all costs,' said Coetsee when recalling his thoughts before his first meeting with the man deemed one of the mortal threats to the South African state. Coetsee, however, was immediately impressed by Mandela, whom he likened to 'an old Roman citizen, with *dignitas, gravitas, honestas, simplicitas* [dignity, seriousness, integrity, openness]'. The two men struck up an unlikely friendship. Mandela, who had undergone a prostate operation, was clad in a dressing gown and immediately charmed Coetsee, who recalled: 'He acted as though we had known each other for years and this was the umpteenth time we had met. He chided me for not coming to see him sooner.'[5]

After that first encounter, Coetsee had several more meetings lasting up to three hours with Mandela, sometimes in the comfort of Coetsee's own Cape Town home where Mandela enjoyed his first alcoholic drinks in more than two decades – his favourite tipple South African medium cream sherry.[6] The ice was broken. Negotiations, no matter how tentative at first, had begun that would lead to Mandela becoming a free man and then state president within less than nine years.

Coetsee formed a special committee, which included Niël Barnard, the young head of the National Intelligence Service, and Barnard's deputy, Mike Louw, to broaden the discussions with Mandela. These detailed 'talks about talks' lasted up to seven hours at a time, and Mandela's diary notes 47 meetings in all.[7] Officials took Mandela for walks in the countryside and to fish and chip shops. On a stroll along Cape Town's crowded Sea Point beach no one recognised the man who had been hidden from the world since 1961. In a further development, Mandela was moved to Victor Verster Prison, near Paarl in the Cape winelands, where he was given his own three-bedroom house with his own chef, a butler and a swimming pool. There Mandela was able to receive up to a dozen visitors at a time, including young opponents of the National Party government, as officials sought the elusive formula for an 'honourable release'for Mandela.

'Thus for four years before the rest of the world knew anything of it, the future of South Africa was being explored in secret conversations in hospitals, prisons and a cabinet minister's home between government officials and their principal political prisoner,' observed the distinguished South African journalist Allister Sparks.[8]

Secrecy and confidentiality about these early rounds of talks were the demands of both Mandela and Coetsee. It was the stuff of an unwritten John Le Carré novel.

Meanwhile, as the talks accelerated between the government and Mandela, young men from South Africa and Angola were fighting, dying and being hideously wounded as they battled deep inside Angola. Had the white South African youths known what was happening behind closed doors in and around Cape Town, it is questionable how many would have felt motivated to wage war as hard and as courageously as they did.

The South African soldiers on the front line represented virtually the whole spectrum of young white opinion at that time, from the far right for whom there could be 'no surrender' to liberals who realised that something had to change in their own society. Many served with patriotic fervour: others did so reluctantly and with little enthusiasm.

Three thousand South African soldiers and probably about 8,000 UNITA guerillas fought in alliance against the Marxist MPLA army, Fapla (the People's Armed Forces for the Liberation of Angola), and its Cuban and Soviet allies.

A fuller story would have emerged if I been able to interview *all* the men who fought in the war, but that was of course impossible. I do regret not having met Lieutenant David Mannall, of 61 Mechanised Battalion, an armoured unit that fought the biggest and most crucial battle of the War for Africa on the banks of Angola's Lomba River, against Fapla's crack 47 Brigade on 3 October 1987. It took Mannall, then aged only 19, some twenty more years to get down all his thoughts on paper about the heat and horror of battle: his thoughts would have enhanced my account.

Mannall was just one of hundreds of thousands of white boys conscripted, at the age of 17, to compulsory National Service through the 1960s into the early 1990s in defence of homeland and border security and against communist-sponsored terrorism and a possible communist-backed takeover.

Mannall describes how many of his fellow young conscripts were mainly concerned with how to lose their virginity before they were flung into battle, and then: 'How could we know that when we lined up at Grootfontein [a forward base in Namibia] our squad would be decimated, most survivors deeply scarred – some for life. We were all destined to be casualties of war: we just didn't know it yet.'[9] Photos of the uniformed conscripts show teenagers, many of whom had not begun shaving and who look scarcely older than my own 13-year-old grandson.

Mannall's trusted driver in his Ratel anti-tank armoured car was David Corrie who 'detested being in the army and all forms of authority.' When the battle against 47 Brigade began 'the fighting was mercilessly brutal and un-fucking-flinchingly deadly! The full might of Fapla's artillery and mortar shells exploded in an almost unbroken thunder around us … At times micro-volcanic eruptions of earth being excavated by shells exploding nearby left clouds of dust hanging in the sky, sometimes reducing visibility to a few metres.' Then came the dreaded call over the communications network. Mannall's squad had taken its first fatality. A Ratel commanded by his friend, Adrian Hind, had received a direct hit from a Fapla tank. Hind, badly wounded and confused, clambered out of his armoured car and began stumbling across the field of battle between the two sides. As he lurched towards the South African line he was cut down by Fapla guns. A rifleman named Graham Green sprinted forward under intense enemy fire, reached the mortally wounded Hind and carried the near lifeless body to safety. Green was later awarded the Honoris Crux [Cross of Honour], the old South Africa's highest military award for conspicuous courage, but Adrian Hind died of his wounds before he could be airlifted out of Angola to hospital.

Soon, more South African teenagers would die and others would lose legs, arms, hands and, in at least one case, half of a face.[10] Of the return to 'normal' life, Lieutenant Mannall observed: 'Societal norms dictated we "button up" and tough it out. We were discarded, dismissed, left to find our own way. Some did OK, others less so.'

A Johannesburg psychiatrist told the London-based *New Scientist* magazine that post-traumatic stress disorder (PTSD) was commonplace among his young soldier patients until the end of the 1980s. 'Then added to the familiar symptoms of PTSD we began to see anger towards the system that had let them down,' said Dr A. At first they showed trauma resulting from the loss of friends in battle. But then they began to show signs of trauma from loss of innocence. 'They were taught that the enemy was the ANC which was equated with communism, which in turn was equated with being non-human. But suddenly [following Mandela's release in 1990 from imprisonment and a public admission of negotiations] they're seeing the "enemy" as a person with a family, who reads newspapers and speaks the same language.'[11] The re-humanisation of the enemy raised agonising questions and the spectre of self-doubt for many of the youngsters who fought in Angola.

This book never pretended to be a full account of the War for Africa. That would have required extensive research in Havana, Moscow and Luanda. I did subsequently try very hard to make a film looking at the war through the eyes of ordinary Cuban soldiers who had taken part in it, but that foundered on stultifying bureaucracy in the Cuban capital. The prologue that follows does contain parts of a long interview I conducted with Cuban General Rafael Del Pino Diaz, who commanded the Cuban Air Force in Angola before defecting to the United States.

I also met in UNITA territory a 17-year-old Cuban soldier, Private Samuel Ducentes Rodriguez, who became a prisoner-of-war of the guerrillas before he had fired a shot in anger. A cheerful and warm little man, Rodriguez became a kind of mascot to his UNITA guards. He had begun to speak Portuguese and the local Ovimbundu tribal language. Jonas Savimbi promised Rodriguez he would never be harmed.

In March 1976, with UNITA facing a Cuban blitzkrieg, Rodriguez, despite Savimbi's assurances, became one of 17 Cubans executed by a UNITA firing squad. His death stirred and depressed me greatly. It somehow crystallised all the futility of war's deaths. My wife at that time, Kathryn Kane, was also deeply upset. Although she had never met Rodriguez, I had told her about him. She wrote a poem, titled *Rodriguez,* which appears in abbreviated form before Part 7, Chapter 28 of the main narrative and which for me captures the poignancy and symbolism of the young Cuban's death.

Because my story has its limitations, as spelt out above, as a history of the conflict, readers will no doubt take them into account. I have yet to read any better warning about the dangers of as-it-happened war reporting than that in George Orwell's classic book on the Spanish Civil War, *Homage to Catalonia*, and I repeat it here: 'It is difficult to be certain about anything except what you have seen with your own eyes, and consciously or unconsciously everyone writes as a partisan. In case I have not said this earlier, I will say it now: beware of my partisanship, my mistakes of fact, and the distortion inevitably caused by my having seen only one corner of events. And beware of exactly the same thing when you read any other book on this period!'

★ ★ ★

A headache for anyone trying to get his or her head around the manifold complexities of Angola is the proliferation of acronyms that its conflicts have spawned. I have tried very hard to keep them to a minimum. The most important are the MPLA (Popular Movement for the Liberation of Angola) and UNITA (the National Union for the Total Independence of Angola). The MPLA's army during the civil war was called Fapla (the People's Armed Forces for the Liberation of Angola) and the UNITA army was called FALA (the Armed Forces for the Liberation of Angola). To avoid confusion, I refer to the MPLA army as Fapla, but I avoid the use of FALA for the UNITA guerrilla army.

Two other terms, *anhara* and *shona*, appear frequently. They are Ovimbundu and Ovambo words for open grassland. I have somewhat arbitrarily used *shona* to mean open patches of grassland within the forest away from the rivers, and *anhara* for wide strips of grass and marsh lining Angola's deep, clear and beautiful rivers. My apologies to Ovimbundu and Ovambo purists for my cavalier use of their languages.

Fred Bridgland
Edinburgh, UK
2 January 2017

Notes

1   Fred Bridgland, 'Angola's Secret Bloodbath: Jonas Savimbi and His Hidden War Against UNITA's leaders', *The Washington Post* (29 March 1992); Fred Bridgland, 'The Dragon of Death who had to be slain', *Sunday Telegraph*, London (24 February 2002); Fred Bridgland, 'The Ghost of Savimbi still hovers over Angola', *The Scotsman*, Edinburgh (22 February 2003); Craig Whitney and Jill Jolliffe, 'Ex-allies Say Angola Rebels Torture and Slay Dissenters', *New York Times* (11 March 1989); Sousa Jamba, 'A Butcher with a Ph.D.', *The Spectator*, London (18 March 1989).

2   Many of UNITA's intellectuals and medical personnel were educated at universities and colleges in Switzerland, including Savimbi himself. Savimbi seems obviously to have been accusing Aurora of having 'gone Swiss' and not returned to her African roots. It was a spurious allegation. She had resolutely refused to have sex with him, and so much of what went awry inside UNITA was down to sexual rather than ideological reasons.

3   Biko, the leader of South Africa's Black Consciousness Movement, was beaten to death by security police in September 1977.

4   British soldiers in the trenches in World War I referred to themselves as the 'poor bloody infantry'.

5   Robert Harvey, *The Fall of Apartheid: The Inside Story from Smuts to Mbeki* (Palgrave, Basingstoke, UK, 2001).

6   Allister Sparks, *Tomorrow Is Another Country: The Inside Story of South Africa's Road To Change* (Hill and Wang, New York, 1995), p.33. Sparks, who died in 2016, was for many decades one of South Africa's finest journalists and most courageous editors.

7   Sparks, *Tomorrow Is Another Country: The Inside Story of South Africa's Road To Change*, p.36.

8   Sparks, *Tomorrow Is Another Country: The Inside Story of South Africa's Road To Change*, p.36.

9   David Mannall, *Battle on the Lomba: The day a South African armoured battalion shattered Angola's last mechanised offensive* (Helion and Company, Solihull, UK), p.84.

10   It hardly needs saying but the same calamities were engulfing young Angolans and some Cubans and Soviet Russians on the other side.

11   Sue Armstrong, 'Problems faced by young whites for whom the old certainties have vanished', *New Scientist*, London (22 October 1994). Dr A requested that his full name be withheld for ethical reasons.

PROLOGUE

Conventional journalism could no more reveal this War than conventional fire-power could win it. All it could do was to take the most profound event of the decade and turn it into a communications pudding, taking its most obvious, undeniable history and making it into a secret history.

Vietnam veteran **Michael Herr,**
in his book *Dispatches.*

I stumbled upon the first and only war between Cuba and South Africa unwittingly. It was a momentous conflict whose small and largely secret beginnings I witnessed by chance and which then dragged me along with it through all its 13 long years.

Portugal's immensely rich African colony of Angola was falling uncontrollably through space in 1975 towards an independence night-mare after five centuries of rule from Lisbon. It was already clear that self-determination, scheduled for the 11th day of November, would be born in bloodshed, not brotherhood. Angola, a magnificent territory with all manner of natural resources, was becoming a pawn in the Cold War between the Soviet Union and the United States and the superpowers' various allies. There would be madness and little sanity; despair and misery, but not much hope; more cruel cynicism than good humour; and no construction, only destruction.

For many years before independence three black Angolan liberation movements had fought each other more assiduously than they had waged war against their Portuguese rulers. When independence came it was because the rightwing dictatorship in Lisbon had been overthrown in a military coup and replaced by a Marxist government which embarked upon a major decolonisation programme. At the time the Portuguese military was easily winning the conflict in Angola, although it was on the back foot in its other major African territory, Mozambique.

The precarious situations in Portugal and its colonies were ripe for exploitation by outsiders, including the veteran Soviet leader Leonid Brezhnev and the Machiavellian US Secretary of State Henry Kissinger. The Brezhnev Doctrine, which asserted that Moscow-style socialist states had obligations to intervene in similar states when socialism was threatened, had already resulted in the stamping out of Czechoslovak freedom by Soviet tanks in 1968. The Western democracies' supine response to the crushing of the Czechoslovaks encouraged Brezhnev to extend his ambitions far beyond the Soviet Union's immediate back door into the swamps and pitfalls of the Third World, full of tough and opportunistic politicians.

By the time the Portuguese flag was lowered in Angola, at midnight on 10 November 1975, Brezhnev's 'forward policy' abroad for the fulfilment of 'scientific socialism' was on a confident roll. Nearer home to Moscow, Poland, Hungary and East Germany, as well as Czechoslovakia, had been cowed into submission by drab but hard-hearted lackeys. Marxist-Leninist governments had recently been established further afield in Vietnam, Cambodia and Laos and, along with Cuba and other long-established members of the Soviet ideological empire, it seemed that little could stop them lasting for ever. The Soviet invasion of Afghanistan had yet to come: the fierce resistance it inflamed would begin to make Soviet power look less invincible. Elsewhere in the Third World 'vanguard' Marxist parties were sprouting as abundantly as shoots of corn in spring, all offering visions of utopian bliss to impoverished peoples who sought an escape route from misery.

The contradictions of Marxist-Leninist oligarchism had yet to be challenged from within with any obvious strength. It would be years before someone like the Czechoslovak author Milan Kundera felt sufficiently courageous to point out the differences between the plausible lie of socialist realism, floating boldly on the surface, and sunken, less immediately intelligible truths about Marxist miseries.

'Anyone who thinks that the Communist regimes of Central Europe are exclusively the work of criminals is overlooking a basic truth,' wrote Kundera. 'The criminal regimes were made not by criminals but by enthusiasts convinced they had discovered the only road to paradise. They defended that road so valiantly that they were forced to execute many people. Later it became clear that there was no paradise, that the enthusiasts were therefore murderers.'[1]

Brezhnev found in the Third World a willing audience of devious strongmen and naïve enthusiasts for his ideas. The weasel slogans of 'proletarian internationalism', 'power to the people', 'Proletarians of the world, unite!' and 'revolutionary consciousness' were embraced in the hope that they mapped short cuts to a sublime future. That these shallow catchphrases did not deliver the promised rewards was not widely perceived immediately by poor people, the wretched of the earth, gulled into believing that there was a simple path towards acquisition of the better things the world had to offer.

Brezhnev was aided in his forward policy by the irresolution and torpidity of the Western democracies which were flustered and panicked by the unflagging march of scientific socialist truth. After its humiliation in Vietnam, a deeply divided United States had little to give: it was too busy salving its own wounds. The Western European democracies, debilitated by oil crises and economic problems, student and trade union unrest, sapping debates about the value of NATO's deterrent weapons and guilt about their colonial pasts, had even less to offer.

The mid-1970s tussle between the Angolan parties erupted into post-independence civil war, thus providing a perfect Third World chessboard on which the Big Powers began a perilous military and ideological confrontation by proxy through local surrogates.

In this test the Soviet Union acted with strength, commitment and purpose on behalf of its client, the Marxist MPLA (Popular Movement for the Liberation of Angola). The West's support was weak, vacillating and faint-hearted for its protégés, the narrowly tribalistic FNLA (National Front for the Liberation of Angola) and the formerly Maoist

UNITA (National Union for the Total Independence of Angola), which underwent a miraculous Damascene conversion to the virtues of Western-style democracy when it realised that aid from Beijing would never match Moscow's to the MPLA. The West, whose cards were admittedly difficult to play at that time, compounded its own problems by behaving as though it had been dealt a dud poker hand, while the Soviet Union always responded with decisive forcefulness.

The Soviet leaders, unfettered by voters to whom it was answerable, acted openly and proudly in Angola while the West, subject to cantankerous electorates, skulked and acted clandestinely. Between November 1974 and February 1976 Moscow sent an estimated US$ 400 million worth of weaponry to Angola and backed the landing there, in support of the MPLA, of a Cuban military expedition force which by mid-1976 was some 11,000-strong.

The US response was to send its clients US$ 32 million worth of arms, the maximum the Central Intelligence Agency was permitted to supply by covert channels under US law. In another contribution to the war, the West plumbed deeply distasteful depths, with Britain's then Labour government playing a particularly influential role. The US, Britain and the Netherlands permitted the FNLA to recruit mercenaries in their countries with bundles of crisp new hundred-dollar banknotes. The quality of these soldiers of fortune was dismally low. They were not the tough, professional adventurers who had made the title 'white mercenary' something genuinely to be feared in the Belgian Congo of the 1960s and elsewhere in Africa. They were the new young unemployed of the mid-1970s and for the most part they were the most socially ill-equipped of their generation. Poorly educated and often from impoverished homes, they were real intellectual innocents in an African country that was fast losing its own innocence. Many had very little combat experience. Some had no military training at all, and two were London road sweepers recruited with the lure of US$ 300 a week and sent straight from their jobs to Angola. The raw and unversed mercenaries were hopelessly unable to stem the Soviet-Cuban tide. Many died. Several were captured by the Cubans and subjected by the MPLA to a nine-day show trial at which the prosecutor described them as 'professional murderers in the pay of imperialism.' Four of them, three Britons and an American, were executed by firing squad on 10 July 1976 at Granfanil military base outside Luanda, Angola's capital.

However, the West did have up its sleeve one truly substantial trick, its most secret weapon of all which went undetected for months and which almost reversed the course of history in Angola.

★ ★ ★

Everything had seemed so simple in the mid-1970s when I was posted from India to become my news organisation's Central Africa correspondent based in the capital of Zambia.

Lusaka then was home to nearly every conceivable African liberation movement. It was a young foreign correspondent's dream, a moralist's theme park and a magnet for every kind of unscrupulous adventurer. Down-at-heel men who would become their countries' presidents and ministers sat in my lounge feeding me just enough stories to keep my whisky and Drambuie flowing into their glasses. I had been a member of the Anti-Apartheid Movement, a campaigner against sports ties with South Africa, and now I fantasised about liberating white-ruled Rhodesia and South Africa through the power of my pen.

Angola, a vast country bordering Zambia to the west, took me rather by surprise. Desultory fighting broke out there in August 1975 after the Portuguese announced that in three months' time they would depart from their five-centuries-old colony. I was assigned by Reuters' international editor to cover the UNITA end of the Angola conflict from the guerrilla movement's bases in central and southern Angola. Zambia's President at that time, Kenneth Kaunda, was a passionate supporter of the energetic and highly educated leader of UNITA, Jonas Savimbi.

I usually travelled into Angola aboard either the leather-upholstered Lear jet or Hawker-Siddeley 125 executive jet which had been put at the disposal of Savimbi by the British commercial conglomerate Lonrho, whose chief executive, Roland 'Tiny' Rowland, was a close friend and financier of Kaunda. 'You can call us MI-5½,' the pilots told one reporter.

On one of my journeys, on 1 November 1975, the Hawker-Siddeley flew into Silva Porto, an exquisite little Angolan railway town whose wide streets were lined by crimson flame of the forest and mauve-flowered jacaranda trees. Ochre-tiled, Mediterranean-style villas were swathed in bougainvillea. Silva Porto [since renamed Kuito and subsequently Bie] was controlled by UNITA guerrillas wearing Mao caps and festooned with belts of cartridges for their heavy machine-guns.

I was surprised by what I saw as I stepped that day from the Lonrho jet. Two trucks crossed the airport tarmac towing armoured cars with a crowing cockerel, UNITA's symbol, painted in runny red paint on their sides.

The trucks halted. I ambled across to one of the armoured cars. A slight teenage white man with a thin, scraggy beard sat in the driving seat. When Portugal began leaving Angola many soldiers deserted and joined the different liberation movements. I assumed he was one of them, and so I greeted him in Portuguese, *Bom dia* [Good morning]. That brought no response, so I asked him what language he spoke. 'Inger-lish', he replied in a gravelly southern Africa accent. I asked him where he came from and he replied grudgingly and gutturally: 'I am from Inger-land.'

Here, some 700 kilometres deep inside Angola from the border to the south with South Africa-ruled South West Africa [now Namibia], I had begun to discover a secret South African, West-inspired, military invasion of Angola. But more work was required before I could write about it.

I sauntered to the second armoured car in which another young white occupied the driving compartment. He showed as little animation as the previous youth, and when I asked him where he came from he said: 'I am a mercenary.' OK, but from which country? – 'I cannot say.' However, the accent, obviously formed at his mother's knee somewhere south of the Orange and Limpopo Rivers, spoke for him. How long had he been in Angola? – 'Two or three weeks.'

Three other whites sat in the cabs of the trucks. A polite 'Good morning' drew from one of them a heavily Afrikaans-accented reply. Before I could ask more questions a fawn Range Rover raced up and out stepped Skip, who passed himself off as an American journalist but who, I later learned, was the CIA's liaison man with Savimbi. Skip guided a series of American military experts, most of them hardened former special force operatives in Vietnam, into UNITA's bosom and supervised the arrival of arms deliveries by strange airlines registered in tiny Caribbean states. Some of Skip's military 'advisers' were straight out of an American nightmare – for example, an unsmiling tough in his late twenties who wore a black Texan cowboy hat, high-heeled cowboy boots and studded jeans and walked with a mean swagger while his tight, sour, gum-chewing face sent the message: 'Look at me, be in awe, but don't speak to or mess with me.' Other CIA specialists stood out a mile. Posing as Men of God, they wore huge silver or wooden crosses flapping on their chests and told inquisitive reporters they were there to check on the fates of their Christian 'flocks'!

With Skip that day on the Silva Porto tarmac was a very tall, blond-haired white man in khaki shorts and blue shirt who I had never seen before. The newcomer issued crisp orders in Portuguese to a couple of black UNITA soldiers. Then, switching to English, he courteously ushered me to the Range Rover and I was driven to the palace of the former local Portuguese regional governor. Here, visiting journalists were housed in some luxury while, all around, Angola was descending into a Dark Age. The tall man's accent was South African, and I was quickly realising that the Angolan story had become more complex than any journalist had yet to discern.

Passing through Silva Porto again a week later, on 7 November 1975, I again saw the blond-haired man. This time he was with a mixed group of black and white soldiers gathered around what looked like a French-designed Panhard armoured car of a kind operated in the region only by the South African Army. It was aboard a road transporter. I was driven away to the governor's palace, but when I returned to fly on elsewhere the Panhard was on the ground and the transporter gone.

It was difficult to know how to treat my encounters with 'Inger-lishmen' in French armoured cars deep inside Angola. It was the stuff on which Evelyn Waugh-style novels on Africa are based. Brief encounters, however, with two or three armoured cars whose Inger-lish crews declined to confess they were South Africans still did not add up to enough evidence to support a story for an international news agency like Reuters, skittish about sourcing, on what I now believed to be the truth – that the most powerful military organisation on the African continent, the South African Defence Force (SADF), had secretly entered the Angolan War at the bidding not only of Western democracies who felt unable to commit their own forces but also some black African states, including Kenneth Kaunda's Zambia. Only 14 years later, in early 1990, did I learn the identity of the tall blond man who had steered me away from the Silva Porto armoured cars. His name was Willem Kaas van der Waals, an SADF paratroop brigadier. He contacted me and told me that in 1975 he had been the South African liaison officer in charge of 25 military instructors training UNITA's troops in great secrecy and responsible for making sure that UNITA's central Angola strongholds did not fall to Marxist forces.

It would require patience, persistence and a large slice of luck to pin down the facts sufficiently firmly before I could begin writing an account that would meet Reuters' exacting standards for highly controversial revelations.

One of my fellow passengers aboard the Hawker-Siddeley when I flew back from Angola to Lusaka on 9 November 1975 was British television reporter Michael Nicholson, who had just made his first short venture into Angola. Mike had established a reputation reporting from the world's trouble spots. He had gained particular celebrity the previous year during Turkey's invasion of Cyprus. His car broke down just as Turkish paratroopers were landing over his head on to the island. Mike positioned his crew beneath one of the descending heavily armed soldiers and greeted him with: 'I'm Michael Nicholson. Welcome to Cyprus.' His film was flown back to London on an RAF plane and his world scoop made the evening news the next day.

Mike was, and remains, a genial soul, the kind of colleague one trusted and shared insights with.[2] On the flight to Lusaka I told him of my encounters with mysterious South Africans claiming to be Englishmen. In Lusaka I went home to my wife and tiny daughters while Mike, away from his London base, struck up a friendship over drinks into the small hours at his hotel with the two British pilots of Savimbi's Lonrho jets. The pilots liked him and when they flew back to Angola on

10 November, the eve of independence, they invited Mike and me to stay aboard the plane for a mystery trip after they had delivered a few items to UNITA's political headquarters in Nova Lisboa, Angola's second largest city which was subsequently renamed Huambo.

There was no jet fuel in Nova Lisboa, and since the pilots had to fly Savimbi the next day on an urgent pre-independence mission to a neighbouring country they were heading somewhere else to refuel. The pilots said they would show us something that would greatly interest us as journalists and help us to understand unfolding events: the condition was that we agreed not to report the flight or anything we saw, or ask too many questions. Before we could set off into the unknown we had to persuade a famous *Newsweek* correspondent who had flown with us from Lusaka that it was essential for him to get UNITA press accreditation before he could begin reporting. No such procedure was necessary in Angola's wilds, but 'helpfully' we told him where to go and who to see, and as soon as he was gone we were off.

The plane flew due south and had covered some 700 km over the immense forests and bush of central and southern Angola before it began to descend. Now the tree cover was thinner. The trees were more stunted and their crowns no longer overlapped, exposing great stretches of sandy soil.

One of the pilots beckoned me to the flight deck and pointed to a silver river winding through the dry land. The radio crackled into life and the conversation revealed that we were crossing the Kavango River, which formed the international boundary between Angola and South Africa-ruled South West Africa. A woman spoke from the ground to the pilots in the same clipped South African English as the young men in the armoured cars at Silva Porto. She was ground control at the airport at Rundu, on the south bank of the Kavango, where the Republic of South Africa maintained a forward military headquarters for operations against guerrillas of the South West Africa People's Organisation (SWAPO), fighting for the independence of their country from bases inside Angola.

We touched down on a runway lined by machine-gun emplacements behind sandbags. Mike and I crouched on the floor of the plane for we had been told to keep our heads down and stay away from the exit door until we were back in the air. The plane taxied towards an area surrounded by a wall of sandbags some 7 metres high. It passed through a narrow entrance into a vast protected tarmacadam area, and there we saw the pot of gold at the end of Jonas Savimbi's rainbow.

We peeped over the bottom edge of the plane's small oval windows as the pilots talked on the tarmac to South African Army and Air Force officers while mechanics refuelled the plane. In the light of clues I had already picked up, I realised that we were at the hub of what could only be Pretoria's staging post for military incursion into Angola. There were lines of Panhard armoured cars of the kind I had seen hundreds of kilometres inside Angola: there were whites sitting in the driving positions as though preparing to leave straight away. The Panhards' immediate destination was a parking area where they were beginning to be loaded aboard Hercules C-130 and Transall C-160 transport planes painted in black and green camouflage and with all registration and other identification marks obliterated. Next stop for the transport planes and their Panhard cargoes *had* to be Angola.

Soon we were flying back to Nova Lisboa. Savimbi's plane had landed, apparently routinely, at one of South Africa's most sensitive military bases: we had been given a glimpse into the heart of its unknown war in Angola. It felt surreal. The Lonrho pilots, for some reason best known to themselves and which I never asked about or subsequently discovered, had guided us direct to concrete evidence of South Africa's embroilment in the Angolan tragedy.

We joined up on return to Nova Lisboa with Mike's film crew and also with the *Newsweek* correspondent, seething because there had been no accreditation requirement and demanding, unsuccessfully, to know where we had been. We now flew by a Beechcraft light plane to the Angolan coastal city of Benguela and the neighbouring port of Lobito to do some eve-of-independence reporting. As we landed at Benguela we saw some 30 or so young fair-haired white men, stripped to their waists in khaki shorts, slide out of sight into a hangar just to the side of the airport's small terminal. Then, as we stepped into the terminal, a Hercules C-130, painted in exactly the same way as those we had seen a few hours earlier in South West Africa, came in to land. Before we could demand more information, UNITA soldiers hustled us into a minibus. But as we drove away we passed a Panhard armoured car guarding the narrow approach road to the airport. Its camouflage paint was identical to that which we had seen on other Panhards earlier in the day and the same also that I had seen on the Panhards at Silva Porto. The Benguela Panhard was surrounded by young whites in shorts relaxing in the sun.

Mike Nicholson's immediate problem was how to obtain film evidence of the obvious South African presence without the South Africans knowing they were being filmed. They would be certain to confiscate the film if they discovered it, otherwise the secrecy would be blown of their country's action – known to its political masterminds, in liaison with the CIA, as Operation Savannah.

After being shown around Lobito by UNITA soldiers, Nicholson's cameraman prepared for the return bus ride to Benguela. He sat next to the driver, his camera held casually on his shoulder and his eye turned away from the viewfinder. He had lined up the camera at an angle he thought would frame the Panhard and the teenage soldiers. As the bus passed the armoured car we all waved to the lounging troops while the cameraman casually depressed the record trigger.

We flew to Nova Lisboa for UNITA's celebration of Angolan Independence Day from Portugal on 11 November. While colleagues in distant Luanda, far to the north and controlled by the MPLA, filed independence celebration stories throughout the world, we were unable to communicate with our editorial headquarters. In UNITA's area there were no telephone or telex communications to the outside world, and the era of the mobile phone was as yet not even a dream. Water supplies and electricity in Nova Lisboa's once-comfortable hotels had collapsed.

We caught up with Savimbi on 13 November in Lobito, where he addressed a rally of 50,000 people. At a press conference afterwards in an abandoned hotel, Mike and I put to him our 'suspicion' that South African troops were maybe the secret behind UNITA's spectacular advances northwards over previous weeks. Of course, we did not tell him that we had gathered our own clinching evidence aboard his own plane or that Mike's cameraman had filmed South African soldiers in Benguela.

Savimbi's replies were revealing but ambiguous – reasonably so, because behind the story of the South African presence was a bigger cloak-and-dagger history of Savimbi pleading for open support from the Western democracies only to be guided by them to Pretoria for help on condition he denied knowledge of everything. The cynicism was immense, and my friend, the Lusaka-based journalist Trevor Grundy, eventually summed it up this way: the Western powers, knowing they could never publicly acknowledge support for apartheid South Africa, stood collectively on the South West Africa–Angola border, their left arms raised with open palms indicating stop, as they chanted, 'Get back you filthy South Africans' while their right arms waved and signalled the direction north towards Luanda as they added, 'The Cubans are that way.'

In Lobito, Savimbi assured us: 'There are no South African troops committed by the South African government here. I agree that we have some white troops – not soldiers, but technicians – working for us here, doing things that we don't know how to do. I need people to fight with armoured cars that we cannot operate ourselves. The MPLA had the Russians with them. We had to address ourselves to people who could match them.'

As the handful of other journalists, including the *Newsweek* man, picked up the thread of our questioning they too joined in. One asked whether the whites allegedly fighting alongside UNITA were mercenaries. It angered Savimbi, who said the MPLA was using mercenaries in the shape of the first contingent of 4,000 Cuban troops who had arrived by then to support the movement's cause. 'So, in my own mind, if I have to get support from anyone I will do it without any heavy conscience,' he said. 'It does not raise questions of morality. I am doing it to save the fate of my country.'

Later, as we left for Lobito airport, Savimbi, so recently a Maoist, stung by the pointed questions about South Africa, grabbed the *Newsweek* man's arm and said passionately: 'You journalists from Western countries, you say you want to oppose Communism, but you are the ones who just help Communism by the way you act. Why? You are weakening your democracy and giving a chance to the East to come up. We could not accept that the Communists will come here, but we knew that the MPLA was building up a strong army.

'Back in November 1974 I went to see every embassy of the Western countries in Lusaka. I told them, "The danger is this one, the danger is this one, the danger is this one" … but they did not act until the MPLA got us.'

The refusal of the West to respond adequately or openly to the Soviet-Cuban build-up in Angola was at the heart of Savimbi's dilemma. Faced with a choice between hapless submission to Moscow's and Havana's client MPLA or surviving to fight another day, he felt he had no choice other than to sup from the West's gift of a poisoned chalice and accept help from black Africa's sworn enemy, white-ruled South Africa. Dodging and swerving in that Lobito hotel in order to avoid admitting openly that he had received the West's South African bequest, he did relate a parable which effectively told the truth: 'If you are a drowning man in a crocodile-filled river and you've just gone under for the third time, you don't question who is pulling you to the bank until you are safely on it.'

I wrote my scoop about the South African military invasion of Angola aboard the Savimbi/Kaunda Lonrho jet as we returned to Zambia after the meeting with Savimbi. We landed after dark at Lusaka, where the twice-weekly British Airways flight to London was preparing to leave. Mike sprinted from the Hawker-Siddeley to the VC-10 airliner and tossed the bag containing his precious film through the open front door of the plane with shouted instructions to the stewards to phone his Independent Television News studios on arrival in London. The door closed, but as the plane began taxiing towards the runway, it reopened slightly and someone tossed the bag out, obviously for security reasons. Mike stood dumbfounded on the tarmac, and as the plane moved further away he shook his fist in impotent rage and shouted: 'I hope you crash, you bastards!'[3]

Mike's misfortune was a lucky break for me. It gave me more time to flesh out the narrative before I telexed a long story to Reuters just before midnight on 14 November 1975. My account was transmitted and became front-page news around the world long before Mike's film arrived in London aboard a flight the next day. My story was not published in South Africa, where it was censored.

Reuters was initially nervous about the fact that I wrote categorically that South Africa had invaded Angola. Because I had promised the Lonrho pilots that I would not reveal the main source of my knowledge, I could not tell my employer that I had been flown secretly into the heart of the South Africans' invasion base. So the story that the agency's international subscribers at first received began this way, after editors had worked on it: 'Columns of armoured vehicles manned by white personnel are slicing across great tracts of Angola through the defences of the Marxist-oriented MPLA, informed sources said. The major unanswered question is the origin of the white soldiers.' It was a question to which I knew the answer …

For days afterwards the story was reworked as I argued that the South Africans should be named. On 22 November my pleas bore fruit and the next day the story, now naming the South Africans, appeared in the *Washington Post*. The report changed the course of the war.

The Swiss Marxist philosopher Jean Ziegler said the *Post* report impelled the most powerful country in black Africa to change sides in the Angola War and support the MPLA: 'On 22 November 1975 Fred Bridgland published an unambiguous report about the presence of South African troops on Angolan territory. Nigeria, the leading political power of black Africa and supplier of petrol to the United States, changed camp, rejected UNITA and gave an immediate grant of US$ 20 million to the government of [MPLA leader] Agostinho Neto.'[4]

John Stockwell, a young career intelligence agent and Vietnam veteran who had been appointed head of the CIA's Angola Task Force, later wrote that my story undermined the South African effort in Angola and fatally weakened the CIA's covert support for Savimbi: 'The propaganda and political war was lost in that stroke,' said the CIA chief. 'There was nothing the Lusaka station (of the CIA) could invent that would be as damaging to the other side as our alliance with the hated South Africans was to our cause.'[5]

★ ★ ★

On 19 December 1975, three weeks after the *Washington Post* report, the US Congress cut off all covert aid to UNITA and the FNLA.

President Gerald Ford angrily denounced the decision as an 'abdication of responsibility' that invited 'more crisis tomorrow.' South Africa's leaders, outraged and embittered by what they saw as an American and more general Western betrayal, began a military withdrawal from Angola that was completed on 27 March 1976. Some countries – Britain, France and Zambia,[6] for example – got off the bandwagon so comprehensively that they switched sides and gave support to the MPLA and condemned Pretoria for the very SADF activities in Angola they had once slyly encouraged.

The then South African Prime Minister, John Vorster, wearily told *Newsweek* magazine that US Secretary of State Kissinger had urged the SADF incursion into Angola and then failed to provide the necessary back-up.[7]

Defence Minister P W Botha, who later became his country's executive president, explained to the whites-only Parliament in Cape Town the reason for the decision to pull out of the Angola conflict: 'I have on various occasions stated that South Africa is not prepared to fight on behalf of the free world alone. Furthermore, South Africa will defend with determination its own borders and those interests and borders we are responsible for.'[8]

As the South African forces retreated and Jonas Savimbi's UNITA guerrillas crept away into apparent oblivion, a top British journalist, Max Hastings, then a prominent BBC-TV documentary maker and later to become editor of London's *Daily Telegraph*, published a lament. 'In any internal power struggle in Africa the personal risks for those involved of execution or exile have always been high,' he wrote. 'So when entering a struggle the message of Angola is that it pays to be on the side the Russians are on. They win. Whatever amiable mutterings the American ambassador whispers into receptive ears, when it comes to the crunch he cannot deliver the cash, votes or guns from Washington to back them. And so now in Angola the Russians can confidently prepare to rake in their huge winnings, staked successfully upon the resounding apathy of the West.'[9]

Chester Crocker, who was the US Assistant Secretary of State for Africa, observed: 'The South Africans, who had become central players in a war they did not start, were left holding the can as Washington became reluctant even to acknowledge the obvious close links among all players in the Western-African coalition. Pretoria blasted what it saw to be Western flakiness, if not perfidy, and pulled out of Angola.'[10]

South Africa was in deep trouble. Its allies had deserted it in Angola, leaving the Republic more of a pariah state than ever. Many of its military limitations had been exposed, particularly in artillery. A big, modern, Soviet-equipped army, backed by Cubans, was camped on its northern South West Africa (described as Namibia from now onwards in this narrative) border and soon began training guerrilla fighters of SWAPO and the African National Congress (ANC) to penetrate Namibia and South Africa itself. Castro and Brezhnev, flushed with pride for their client's victory over a West in disarray, began speaking of revolution spreading all the way south to Cape Town and Cape Agulhas, the African continent's most southerly point.

Total victory for the MPLA and its allies in Moscow, Havana and East Berlin, followed by the fall of South African rule in Namibia and even the Republic itself, suddenly looked possible. In the green fertile valleys of Natal, next to the Indian Ocean, old white men in the Commando forces, the equivalent of Britain's World War II Home Guard, prepared ancient armoured cars and polished old rifles to be ready to give invading columns of cigar-chomping Cuban soldiers a hard time before they took the land and collectivised it.

Subsequent history, however, evolved very differently from what many at first foresaw in 1975–76.

The first miscalculation Brezhnev, Castro and the MPLA leadership made was to assume there would be no significant internal Angolan resistance to the Marxist-Leninist steamroller. US Senator Dick Clark (Democrat, Iowa), who had played a key role in securing the dismantling by Congress of the CIA Angola Task Force, told the MPLA, the Soviet Union and Cuba that 'the tide of history' was on their side[11] – and they were happy to believe this influential American with impeccable liberal credentials. They heeded also Clark's Congressional colleague, Senator John Tunney from California, who exulted: 'Savimbi has no illusions about how swiftly the end is coming. The war in Angola beyond guerrilla fighting is almost over.'[12]

In fact, the Angolan War had scarcely begun. It would turn out to be a long and big and increasingly famous war.

When Jonas Savimbi slipped away into the great forests of central and southeastern Angola with a band of several thousand loyal UNITA followers, Fidel Castro assumed that the small-scale resistance by the 'South African *fantoches* (bandits)' would either be quickly stamped out or would simply peter out. Savimbi's people endured phenomenal hardships initially. But Savimbi, drawing on the teachings of Castro's legendary comrade Che Guevara, with whom he formed a friendship in the mid-1960s, and more especially the guerrilla theories of Mao Zedong, at whose Nanking military academy Savimbi had learnt how to fight the Portuguese, taught his people first how to survive. 'If we survive, then things will begin to change around us,' he told his guerrillas as they began a Mao-style Long March deep into forest hideouts similar to those from which Castro the guerrilla had harried and then overthrown the regime of Cuba's rightwing dictator Fulgencio Batista back in 1959. (Six years after Savimbi began his Long March, I began researching a book on the civil war in Angola and the UNITA resistance, which involved my making several long trips into the war zone[13]).

When the world realised that UNITA had not passed into limbo but was beginning to worry the MPLA and its Havana and Moscow patrons, various countries began placing small side-bets on Savimbi in the forlorn hope that his guerrillas might perhaps reverse the tide of history – nothing substantial, nothing that was not plausibly deniable, but always enough to give enough encouragement to Savimbi that more might come if the UNITA resistance grew. China gave UNITA some arms, using Zaire as a conduit. France, Saudi Arabia, the Gulf Emirates and Egypt provided cash. Morocco offered training, including paratroop drops, for selected UNITA guerrilla specialists. Morocco also gave Savimbi arms which dropped off the back of trucks delivered by France and the United States for King Hassan's war against the Polisario Front in the former Spanish colony of Western Sahara.

Meanwhile, as the SADF modernised, its generals concluded that it made more sense to attack SWAPO in its bases deep inside Angola than to wait for its guerrillas to cross into Namibian territory.

The South Africa military re-entered Angola in May 1978, this time without Western encouragement and in the form of a massive raid by paratroopers, supported by fighter-bomber aircraft, on a SWAPO base at Cassinga, 250 kilometres north of the Namibia border. Some 600 Namibians were killed. Many of them were guerrillas, but there were also a number of women, children and Cuban soldiers among the dead. SWAPO depicted the raid as a massacre, but South Africa justified the attack on the grounds that SWAPO had stepped up its abductions and killings of civilians inside Namibia precisely at a time when delicate negotiations concerning potential independence for Namibia were being held.[14]

In August 1981 South Africa launched an even larger raid, with 4,000 to 5,000 men, deep into Angola, again targetting mainly SWAPO bases, but killing 13 Soviet military advisers as well as many MPLA soldiers. South Africa said ten of its soldiers were killed in the incursion and 64 wounded.[15]

In its strategic interest, South Africa decided to help keep UNITA alive and kicking, this time even more surreptitiously than before. South African help to Savimbi, which included weapons, diesel fuel for trucks and training for UNITA guerrillas, clearly had little to do with any commitment by Pretoria to multi-party democracy in Angola, for which Savimbi was arguing in order to impress his Western sympathisers. It was a matter of self-interest, pure realpolitik. The South African government resolved that SWAPO would never come to power in its Namibian colony by force, although it had already accepted that inevitably at some point Namibia would become independent. It saw support for UNITA's resistance as one way of making life more difficult for the Cuban-Soviet–MPLA–SWAPO–ANC axis.

★ ★ ★

By the mid-1980s the Angolan War was being fought on an enormous scale. UNITA's guerrilla army was rampaging many hundreds of kilometres across the country hitting MPLA and Cuban targets. The US Congress in July 1985 reversed its 1975 decision to ban the covert supply of arms to UNITA. American C-130 planes, painted light blue and with the logo 'Santa Lucia Airways' on their fuselages, began landing at Kamina airbase in southern Zaire four or five times a week. The base was controlled by CIA personnel carrying sidearms and more than a dozen UNITA soldiers who transferred planeloads of Stinger anti-aircraft missiles, anti-tank missiles, explosives, ammunition and other weaponry to smaller planes for delivery to dirt airstrips in UNITA-controlled areas of Angola.[16]

The White House described the help to UNITA as 'appropriate and effective assistance.' A US State Department spokesman said: 'We are trying to provide some balance to the vast amount of assistance coming from the Soviet Union to the other side.' Asked about the Kamina arms transfer operation, William Devine, a CIA spokesman, said: 'We neither confirm nor deny allegations of involvement.'[17]

The Angolan economy lay in ruins. Shops in the cities were empty and Angola's factories and great swathes of rich farmland were producing very little. Inflation reached 5,000 percent and the currency became almost worthless. What the MPLA government tried to build by day UNITA destroyed by night. The SADF was continuing its blitzkriegs across the border against SWAPO and was clashing also with Cubans, Russians and the MPLA. Each year the Soviets had to commit more arms and the Cubans more troops, not in pursuit of the original dream of revolution throughout southern Africa but in order to try to contain the growing UNITA insurgency and the devastating SADF cross-border raids.

By the end of 1985 the Cuban troop presence in Angola had reached 31,000 compared with 11,000 in 1975–76. The Cubans were supported by some 3,250 East German and Soviet personnel, mainly in operational planning, military training, radar, anti-aircraft, advanced engineering and intelligence roles.

At this time the eyes of the international community were much less firmly fixed on Angola than on South Africa, where a year of unprecedented unrest among the politically powerless black majority had resulted in a thousand or more deaths. While the world was transfixed by the continuing South African drama, so much more intriguing because of the stark black-white dimension of the conflict, Angola was moving inexorably towards a series of battles much bigger and more costly in lives than anything its people had yet known. The MPLA Army (Fapla, *Forces Armadas Popular de Angola*, or the People's Armed Forces of Angola), with Cuban and Soviet support, launched on 2 September 1985 its biggest offensive yet into vast areas of sparsely inhabited territory in southeastern Angola that UNITA had secured for itself since the mid-1970s. Eighteen Fapla brigades were assembled for the assault: they were backed by an Angolan Air Force that had been modernised and re-equipped over the previous two years by Moscow.

Western intelligence estimated Fapla's warplane strength at more than one hundred advanced Mig-23, advanced Sukhoi-22, Mig-21 and ageing Mig-17 fighter-bombers; 33 MI-24 'Hind' helicopter gunships; 27 French Alouette assault helicopters; and 69 MI-8 and MI-17 transport helicopters. Increasingly the aircraft were being flown by young Angolans trained in the Soviet Union, with back-up from Cuban and Soviet personnel. Eighty percent of the country's combat pilots were Angolan by 1985, compared with 40 percent in 1982. The air force had been restructured so that the attacking infantry columns could receive improved logistics support as Antonov-12 and Antonov-26 transport planes flew in supplies to remote bush airstrips that had been secured by the advancing ground troops.

The MPLA received more than one billion US dollars' worth of new Soviet weaponry between January 1984 and August 1985, according to Western intelligence estimates. Fapla's tank army was almost 500-strong by the time of the September offensive, consisting of some 350 T-55 main battle tanks, 150 old World War II T-35 tanks and 50 light amphibious PT-76 tanks.

By 7 September 1985 five of the Fapla brigades had advanced to a point just north of a river named the Lomba within reach of the outskirts of Mavinga, a vital UNITA stronghold in southeastern Angola some 300 kilometres north of the Namibia border. UNITA five years earlier had chased the MPLA from the little town, whose streets were lined with orange trees, and, although all its gracious Portuguese-era houses and other buildings had been wrecked and rendered uninhabitable in the fighting, it was a strategic and psychologically important landmark. Its most important feature was a long, red lateritic all-weather airstrip where all manner of strange planes from black Africa, South Africa and the United States (including the CIA's 'Santa Lucia Airways') landed supplies for UNITA. If the MPLA could take the airstrip they could bring in their own supplies to prepare for a major assault on Savimbi's headquarters, Jamba ('The Place of the Elephant'), a complex of thatched-roofed buildings spread over an area of some 3,000 square kilometres, rich in prides of lion and roaming herds of elephant, zebra, leopard, rhinos, wildebeest, roan antelope, ostriches and many other animals, about 200 kilometres to the south of Mavinga.

When the first Fapla brigades crossed the Lomba and probed to within 25 kilometres of Mavinga, Savimbi, who did not have sufficient weaponry to engage Fapla in conventional combat, considered withdrawing. At that stage the SADF came to his rescue on an unprecedented scale. It sent in a troop of three of its new radar-guided long-range G-5 guns which, together with Mirage F-1AZ fighter-bombers and ancient British Canberra bombers, pounded the advancing Fapla soldiers unmercifully. Fapla was stopped in its tracks and withdrew several hundred kilometres to avoid being trapped by the approaching rainy season.

On 7 October, Savimbi, denying any help whatsoever from South Africa, announced that UNITA had stood firm at Mavinga and repulsed the offensive. Soviet and Cuban officers had been helicoptered to safety while the defeated Fapla force was being attacked on its flanks as it retreated in disarray.

UNITA brought in foreign correspondents to visit the battlefields. 'We must have seen at least 50 smashed trucks and the blackened hulks of a dozen or more Soviet-made armoured personnel carriers,' wrote the London *Times'* Africa correspondent Michael Hornsby. 'In one small area some 20 Russian-made Zil trucks, one mounted with a multiple rocket launcher known as a Stalin Organ, had been destroyed. Near the Lomba River lay the twisted remains of an MI-24 helicopter.

'Many of the government units seemed to have been taken by surprise, suggesting the suddenness of an air strike. In one place a truck and an armoured personnel carrier had been hit. A soldier, his head half blown away, was still sitting in the back of the truck. Three other rotting corpses lay entwined beneath a haze of flies on the sand nearby and the bodies of two other soldiers lay further away, as if they had been cut down while running for cover.

'With or without direct South African intervention, it is fair to say that the further Luanda's ponderous armoured columns advanced through the clogging bush sand, the more exposed they became at the end of a tenuous supply line, whereas UNITA's more lightly armed infantry were fighting on home ground.'[18]

★ ★ ★

The MPLA disaster before Mavinga in September 1985 led Moscow to make another major reassessment of its involvement in southern Africa. Already in 1983 the Soviet leader Yury Andropov had told the Communist Party of the Soviet Union that the open-ended Russian commitment given by Leonid Brezhnev, who had died in 1982, to Third World devotees of Marxism-Leninism was at an end. Andropov said past largesse and mismanagement had dragged the Soviet economy down into deep crisis: the success of socialism outside the Soviet Union would henceforth turn largely on whether Russia could reverse its own economic misfortunes. By 1984 Andropov had virtually written off Mozambique, another former Portuguese colony, as the linchpin of the dream that scientific socialism would take root in southern Africa and institutionalise communist rule. Andropov told the then Mozambique President, the late Samora Machel: 'It is one thing to proclaim socialism. It is another to build it.'

Nevertheless, the Soviet commitment to the MPLA had been so colossal that, despite the accession to power in Moscow of the reformist Mikhail Gorbachev on the deaths of Andropov and Andropov's short-lived successor Konstantin Chernenko, it was decided that yet another prodigious effort must be made to eradicate the Savimbi blot and diminish South African scope for making mischief.

A top Soviet Army general arrived in Angola in December 1985 to take overall control of all forces operating in the country on behalf of the MPLA, including the Luanda government's own troops. The general was aided by several Soviet Army colonels and various counter-insurgency, artillery, missile and anti-aircraft specialists, including translators. Western intelligence agencies estimated that the general had about 950 fellow Soviets in command and training posts in Angola. Some 2,000 East German military men were deployed in the MPLA's intelligence and communications services.[19]

The scale of the Soviet re-supply operation for the planned offensive was formidable. Moscow even committed planes that were part of its strategic assets for any major conflict in Europe. These included several Ilyushin-76 transports and five of its total of 50 giant Antonov-22 long-range, heavy-lift turbo-prop transports. From the ports of Luanda, Lobito and Namibe these aircraft airlifted T-55 battle tanks, PT-76 amphibious tanks, and BTR-60 and BRDM-2 armoured personnel carriers to inland centres such as Menongue, Cuito Cuanavale and Luena. New Mig-23 fighter-bombers and MI-24 helicopters were delivered in quantities which more than replaced those lost in the 1985 offensive.

The Soviet military planners wanted to launch the new offensive in 1986, but it never really got underway – partly because the Fapla forces were divided into too many prongs instead of being concentrated in one mighty central punching thrust; partly because UNITA and the SADF launched a strong counter-assault against Cuito Cuanavale, the Soviet planners' main staging post for the offensive, and destroyed radars, artillery and bomb stocks; and partly because SADF Special Force frogmen slipped into Namibe port and sank one Soviet ship and badly damaged two others carrying weaponry needed for the offensive, while also blowing up three harbourside oil storage tanks.

The Soviets now had to delay the Fapla offensive until the ground was dry enough after the 1986–87 rains to allow heavily armoured and motorised forces to operate effectively. It did at least allow more time to plan effectively the 'make or break' onslaught against UNITA. Between mid-1986 and mid-1987, Western intelligence agencies estimated that Moscow sent another one billion US dollars' worth of arms to Angola, bringing to four billion dollars the total Soviet military aid to the MPLA since 1977.

The late William Claiborne, the gentle but keen-witted southern Africa correspondent of the *Washington Post*, visiting Angola on an MPLA-escorted trip, reported on 9 July 1987: 'During one four-hour period last week at Lubango's airport, a constant stream of Soviet Aeroflot transport planes landed and their cargoes, including air-to-air missiles, were quickly unloaded by Cuban and Angolan troops ... The scene at Luanda's airport was similar, with long lines of Aeroflot transports waiting on the taxiway for their turn to take off at intervals of only a few minutes.'

Earlier, at Cahama, near the Namibian border, Claiborne said he had been treated to a lecture by a young Fapla officer, Captain Carlos dos Santos, on how his troops had no need of Russian or Cuban help to drive the South Africans out of Angola, whenever or wherever they dared enter. Dos Santos demanded to know of the *Washington Post* man whether he could see any foreign faces around. Claiborne's report continued: 'As he (the captain) stepped outside an officer's mess in this bomb-scarred Angolan town a car skidded to a halt in the dust and a Soviet officer, his face red with anger, barked an order to Dos Santos to feed his troops at once. Then, warily eyeing several American journalists, the Russian roared away in a cloud of dust with a chastened Dos Santos at his side. The brief episode underscored the sensitive relationship between the struggling Angolan Army and the estimated 950 Soviet advisers and 37,000 Cuban troops in this country ...'

And the relationship was also delicate between Fidel Castro, his two top generals in Angola, Arnaldo Ochoa Sanchez and Rafael Del Pino Diaz, and the Russians.

Ochoa, then aged 46, was partly of Arab descent and had had such a dazzling career that he was seen as a contender to succeed Fidel Castro to the Cuban leadership. Ochoa was, by Cuban standards, an independent thinker who was well liked by his troops. As military men go in highly authoritarian societies, he was reputed to have a very sensitive personality and a tendency to bypass rules and regulations. His energy, flexibility and popularity had made him a natural choice down the years for a host of difficult missions. He had fought as a teenager with Fidel Castro and Che Guevara in the Sierra Maestra from 1956 to 1958 against Batista. From 1966 to 1968 he was seconded by Castro to command anti-government guerrillas in Venezuela. In 1973 he fought with a Cuban unit on the Golan Heights against Israel in the Yom Kippur War. Ochoa went on to command a Cuban infantry battalion against South African forces in Angola in 1975–76. In 1977 he was appointed head of his country's military mission in Addis Ababa and commanded the successful Cuban tank offensive against Somalia in the Ogaden in 1978. In June 1983 he was assigned to Nicaragua to reorganise the Sandanistas into a more mobile and efficient rapid-deployment force: under his direction the Sandanistas destroyed the southern US-backed *Contra* front from Costa Rica. By 1987 he was a deputy defence minister and a member of the Communist Party Central Committee. Castro thought so highly of Ochoa that in that same year he delegated him to head the Cuban military mission in Angola where, in cooperation with the Soviets, he was responsible for the massive 1987 transport of arms by air and sea into Angola in preparation for the offensive.

General Del Pino, aged 49 in 1987, was one of the most flamboyant products of the Cuban Revolution. As a teenager, he too had fought against Batista, and in 1961 he was acknowledged as the hero of the resistance to Washington's abortive invasion at the Bay of Pigs where, as a young pilot, he shot down two B-26 warplanes. He rose to become commander of the Cuban Air Force in Angola in 1975–76, carrying out the initial clandestine surveys for the arrival of Cuban troops and subsequently spending years trying to kill UNITA's Jonas Savimbi. By 1981 he was deputy chief of the Cuban Air Force with direct responsibility for the war in Angola, which he visited from Havana at least three or four times a year.

Ochoa, Del Pino and Castro thought the Soviet planners' attempts to launch a fresh offensive in 1986 against UNITA's strongholds were premature. They also opposed the 1987 offensive on the grounds that it was certain to run into big trouble with the South Africans and that too much of the planned effort was being put into a single thrust eastwards from Cuito Cuanavale which would enable the SADF and UNITA to concentrate their defence. Castro later complained: 'The Soviet advisers thought they were waging the Battle of Berlin, with Marshal Zhukov in command, thousands of tanks and 40,000 cannons. They did not understand, nor could they understand, the problems of the Third World, the setting of the struggle and the type of war that must be waged in that setting.'[20]

Nevertheless, the Soviets won the argument and Del Pino and Ochoa continued to help in planning the offensive. Castro, however, declined to commit whole Cuban brigades in support of Fapla to what he saw as a foolhardy campaign. But out of loyalty to his Soviet liege he agreed to attach up to 35 Cuban specialists to each Fapla battalion as military advisers and artillery and armour commanders.

General Del Pino flew to Moscow on 20 April 1987 to liaise with the Soviet Air Force on the annual draft of Cuban pilots for training in Russia. *Perestroïka* (reconstruction) and *glasnost* (openness) were newly in fashion at that time following the appointment in 1985 of a new Soviet leader, Mikhail Gorbachev. 'There was great confusion among young Cubans studying in Moscow,' said Del Pino, in conversation with the author of this book. 'They saw the Soviet government under Gorbachev reversing itself after 70 years of socialism and adopting a variety of reforms – there were the beginnings of private medicine, private restaurants, small private businesses. It was in stark contrast to what was happening back home where if some unfortunate cripple, for example, made milk shakes in his house so that his schoolchildren could have a snack he would have his mixer confiscated.

'Even in the midst of their confusion they (Cubans in Moscow) did not lose their sense of humour. They told one joke about the Cuban Communist Party entering important talks with the Soviet Communist Party for the transfer of Lenin's Tomb to Havana because Fidel Castro was the only man left who wanted to be the saviour of world Communism.

'I got back to Havana on 8 May and told Carlos Aldana, in charge of the Department of Revolutionary Orientation in the Central Committee, that I was surprised that none of what was changing in the Soviet Union was being published in Cuba. Aldana said it had to be censored or the Cuban people would turn anti-communist.'

Three weeks later, on 29 May 1987, Del Pino put his wife and three children aboard a Cessna light aircraft in Havana for an apparently routine leisure flight. He took off and touched down 90 miles away in Key Largo, Florida, to become the most senior defector ever from Fidel Castro's Cuba. Castro at first played down the escape, saying Del Pino was an emotionally unstable man of little importance. But later he admitted that Cuba's security had been endangered.

There was obviously more to General Del Pino's defection than unease about the absence of *glasnost* in Cuba. He described to me some of the issues which had influenced him when I met him in a 'safe house' in the small town of Tysons Corner, about 20 kilometres west of Washington DC. My purpose in meeting him, just a few weeks after his flight into exile, was to discuss the possibility of writing a book on his life and making a television documentary about his experiences in Angola. (Neither project came to fruition.)

Our conversations were long and wide-ranging and conducted through a silver-haired, impeccably besuited translator who seemed to be Del Pino's minder and who I presumed to be a CIA operative.

Del Pino said his unease with Cuba's 'internationalist mission' in Angola had grown increasingly from the time he first became involved in the project. 'Castro was drunk on the 1975–76 successes in Angola,' the general told me. 'There was great pride and excitement about the adventure among the Cuban people. They believed it was a just war because Castro is very intelligent and he presented it very skilfully.'

'He persuaded the people that we were going into Angola because of the South African invasion, a war of national independence as opposed to a civil war, and that we were there to help the people liberate themselves from the South Africans.'

All Cubans at the beginning wanted to go to Angola, Del Pino argued. Public morale was high, and it fitted with Castro's personal ambition to become a renowned international figure. 'He told the people that we defeated the South Africans because they were afraid of us,' said the general. 'The *povo* loved that rhetoric. He used the same method Hitler used with the Germans in his successes at the beginning with Czechoslovakia, Poland, Belgium and France. He whipped up national patriotic sentiments and convinced people that we had an invincible army. Before units left for Angola he would tell them: "Don't worry, we've already won the war." Our people were happy and proud, but then they did not know we would lose young men for many years as the commitment in Angola came to preoccupy all of our military personnel.'

Castro, said Del Pino, got most things right, but he made two mistakes: he thought time was on the Cubans' side and he never imagined that Savimbi was going to resist. He believed UNITA was dead and buried.

Del Pino shared Castro's belief in total victory for the first three or four years after the Cubans had helped put the MPLA in absolute power at the expense of multi-party elections promised for Angola under the Alvor Accord of 15 January 1975.[21] Del Pino and Castro believed surviving UNITA groups to be isolated from others and acting on their own. It was just a matter of mopping up, with armoured cars and helicopters, a few badly trained Africans possessing hardly any weapons.

Try as the Cubans might they just could not get Savimbi, who had been dubbed the Black Pimpernel by the international media, said the general. On two or three occasions Del Pino himself flew a Mig-21 and shot up ground troop groups with whom Savimbi was travelling. The UNITA leader kept escaping. His guerrillas at first had virtually no offensive capabilities, but the failure to capture or kill Savimbi was a source of increasing frustration to the Cubans who found by 1978 that they were devoting more and more time to pursuing a movement which moved into a new phase and began to launch hit-and-run raids.

'It was not until 1979 that it dawned on us that we could be facing a long war,' said Del Pino. 'It was then that UNITA guerrillas shot down for the first time one of our helicopters.' It happened at a place called Maria Delida, near Mussende, about 400 kilometres from Luanda. The MI-8 helicopter was firing rockets at a small group of guerrillas who stood their ground and returned rifle fire. One bullet penetrated a fuel tank, and when another rocket was fired the flame ignited leaking fuel and the helicopter exploded. All ten Cubans aboard – the pilot, co-pilot and eight soldiers – were killed.[22]

'My friend, Colonel Harry "Pombo" Villegas,[23] said it meant we now faced a very difficult situation and we would be bogged down in Angola for many, many years,' said Del Pino. Villegas' opinion was that the shooting down of the helicopter showed that some UNITA fighters had lost their fear of aircraft, which takes time and courage to master, and were clearly now prepared to answer air attacks with fire of their own: it demonstrated that they were getting used to the war and getting into shape. 'It would get more difficult for us because they were learning not to be afraid,' said Del Pino. 'Pombo knew about these things because he was one of the *Olivos* (literally 'Olive Drabs') who had fought with Fidel right through the Sierra Maestra campaign from 1956 to 1959, and he was one of only three guerrillas who survived the campaign with Che (Guevara) in Bolivia.'

The legendary Guevara, with his rakish beret and scraggy beard, became an international cult figure among youthful leftists in the 1960s and 1970s. Guevara, Del Pino and 'Pombo' Villegas fought alongside Castro in the Sierra Maestra and Guevara served as a minister in Cuba's first communist government until 1965. Guevara then resigned to test his theories of guerrilla revolutionary warfare first in the jungles of Belgium-ruled Congo and then US-aligned Bolivia. Guevara's quixotic attempt to inspire an uprising in the Congo failed ignominiously, but he believed he could rouse Bolivia's tin miners, who lived in appalling poverty, to insurrection with the support of radical underground movements in the towns. This attempt also was a disaster, fatally so. Few Bolivians rose in support of Guevara and his jungle band of guerrillas, and on 7 October 1967 Bolivian government Special Forces, armed and trained by the CIA for the military dictator General René Barrientos, trapped Guevara and his men in a forested ravine. There he was riddled with bullets and died soon afterwards either from his wounds or summary execution. 'Pombo' Villegas was in Bolivia with Guevara and was one of only three men to escape the government ambush.

Ironically, one of the last people with whom Guevara seems to have held talks in Africa about his revolutionary theories before disappearing into Bolivia was an aspiring young African who wanted to launch guerrilla warfare against the Portuguese rulers in his own country, Angola. Jonas Savimbi said he and Guevara had two long meetings in 1965 in Tanzania and Algeria, at which Che encouraged the then 33-year-old

Angolan Maoist to go back into his own country, set up guerrilla bases among the peasantry and eschew help from outside.[24] Guevara entered Bolivia in 1966, the same year as Savimbi and his first band of guerrillas entered Angola through the back door. Guevara died. Savimbi survived and eventually, in a great irony, his willpower and guerrilla techniques were put to their biggest tests against Che's close comrade, Fidel Castro.

But, in an even greater irony, Savimbi eventually died in the same way as Guevara – trapped in 2002 with a small band of his followers against the banks of a tributary of the Zambezi River by Angolan government soldiers. There Savimbi was riddled with bullets. His end was masterminded by one of UNITA's former top generals, Geraldo Nunda, with help from Israeli technicians and South African mercenaries who had once fought in the South African Defence Force alongside Savimbi against the Cubans.

The 'old guard' *Olivos* were not a success in Angola. Del Pino said Castro clung to them out of loyalty and his sense of romanticism about the Sierra Maestra years. There were 80–90 *Olivos* attached to each Cuban brigade, independent of the other troops and under their own guerrilla commanders. 'But they weren't young any more and their thinking did not change enough,' said Del Pino. 'They made a lot of mistakes, and when the MPLA realised the *Olivos* were no good they made a contract with Rosa Coutinho, and he hired former Portuguese counter-insurgency commandos who began replacing the *Olivos* from 1982 onwards and trained 500-strong MPLA commando Special Brigades.' (Retired Portuguese Admiral Rosa Coutinho, known as the 'Red Admiral' because of his leftist sympathies, was Portugal's last colonial Governor-General in Luanda who travelled secretly to Havana in 1974 to urge Castro to intervene with Cuban troops in Angola on behalf of the MPLA).

Cuban counter-intelligence reported increasing support for Savimbi from 1979 onwards as his guerrilla army grew and UNITA's operations spread. 'Counter-intelligence also reckoned that Savimbi had his agents in place within the MPLA government,' said Del Pino. 'To smear someone it became necessary just to call him pro-UNITA. It also provided an excuse when things went wrong: the government would say it was not its fault, but that of the subversives within it.

'For Fidel there could be no turning back at that time. As the years had gone on he needed success for the MPLA both for his own personal pride and as part of his quest to be an international figure. And, increasingly, he needed the internationalist mission in Angola to distract attention from all the internal economic problems and crises he continued to have in Cuba.'

Incidents began to pile up which more and more undermined Del Pino's faith in the Cuban Revolution he had fought to achieve. In 1983 some one hundred Cuban troops were unable to prevent a devastating defeat for Fapla forces besieged by UNITA, supported by SADF advisers and Special Forces, in the southeastern garrison of Cangamba. After an Alamo-style resistance by Fapla and the Cubans, UNITA fell back with heavy casualties, but 160 Fapla and 18 Cuban soldiers lay dead.

Cuban survivors were helicoptered to safety after a massive row broke out between Cuban and Soviet military planners: the latter wanted to pursue the retreating UNITA forces through the southeastern forests.

Castro cabled his other senior officers in Angola from Havana: 'You must insist with the Angolans that it would be a grave error to keep a Fapla unit in Cangamba ... that your orders are to withdraw the Cubans, all the Cubans, at once, even if they decide to keep a Fapla unit there ... We are shocked by the words of the head of the Soviet military mission. They reflect a complete lack of realism ... We cannot let more Cubans die, nor can we risk a grievous defeat because of absurd decisions.'

Castro's brother Raúl, head of the armed forces, followed up Fidel's cable with a 'categorical', 'irrevocable' order to withdraw from Cangamba. 'Do not waste one more minute,' said Raúl. Exhausted Fapla troops looked on in dismay as the Cubans pulled out.[25]

As fortunes began to be reversed, Del Pino alleged, Angola became less and less a proving ground for Cuban heroes and more and more a punishment posting for those whom Castro perceived to have failed him elsewhere. Del Pino gave as an example Colonel Redro Tortolo who was in charge of Cuban troops in Grenada when the Caribbean island was overrun by American forces in 1983. Tortolo was stripped of all rank and sent to serve as an army private in Angola along with 30 other similarly demoted officers. Meanwhile, Del Pino claimed, the sons of

Politburo members 'not only do not go to Angola, but they do not even do their military service.'[26]

Standards of command, discipline and technical maintenance in Angola also began to fall. In 1984, Del Pino, by now back in Havana as deputy chief of the Cuban Air Force, visited Angola to investigate a series of losses in crashes of fighter-bombers, transport planes and helicopters. Many had crashed through sheer carelessness, but the loss of one young flyer in particular infuriated Del Pino. Lieutenant Raul Quiala Castenada was a promising young pilot who had been sent to Angola for combat duty even though he had never done any night flying. One day his commander at Luena, in eastern Angola, ordered him to fly a night mission in a Mig-21 and bombard any area where he saw fires burning. 'It was absurd to assume that any fire would necessarily be a UNITA concentration, and it was irrational to suppose that any bombs tossed out at night at unspecified targets were anything other than wasted,' said Del Pino. 'But it was criminal to send out a kid on that mission who had never flown at night. He crashed and died. His family was told, according to the routine, that he had died heroically in combat.'

Del Pino fretted also that the Cuban dead were not sent back for burial at home and that the island's young men, far from home in Africa's HIV/AIDS belt among some of the most beautiful women on the continent, were beginning to pick up the killer virus. The first HIV/AIDS case was diagnosed in Cuba in 1985, and the conventional wisdom is that the virus arrived on the island as Cuban soldiers returned home from Angola and other parts of Africa in the 1980s.

The last straw for Del Pino came when one of his own sons, serving in the air force in Angola, disappeared on a mission in 1985. He was co-piloting an Antonov-26 light transport aircraft carrying Cuban soldiers from Luena to Luanda, a flight of some 800 kilometres. When no one was able to trace wreckage Del Pino flew to Angola to co-ordinate the search.

After a week he had found nothing and he reported that all the missing men must be presumed dead. 'That same night we heard, over the BBC from London, that they were alive and well in Zaire,' said Del Pino. 'Talks started with the government of Zaire, which was very hostile towards us, to secure their return. I launched an inquiry into what had happened and uncovered a can of worms.

'As soon as the plane had taken off it flew into heavy cumulus storm clouds. They found they were unable to make contact with the ground by radio, and, unknown to them at first, the plane's navigational system was malfunctioning. Although the instruments indicated they were heading at 310 degrees for Luanda, they were in fact flying almost due northwards on a heading of 350 degrees. By the time they realised their navigational system had gone wrong they had only five minutes' worth of fuel left and they were flying over mountains. They spotted a stretch of road on a small plateau and made an emergency landing. They believed they were on Angolan territory, but since UNITA controlled nearly all the countryside they burnt the aircraft and all their documents before beginning their march to safety. In fact, they were in Zaire and they were picked up by Zairean soldiers who didn't believe their story at all. They were eventually released after difficult negotiations and flown home to Cuba.

'Among the first things I discovered in my inquiries was that the commander of the Revolutionary Armed Forces in Angola, Colonel Tomas Benitez, had changed all radio frequencies for security reasons and failed to inform Luena. And then I discovered that the navigation systems of many aircraft had not been inspected or serviced for five years or more and that most of the entries in aircraft service logs were fraudulent. I sent the most damning report back to Havana. What was the outcome? Colonel Benitez was decorated shortly afterwards and returned to Cuba to command the Revolutionary Armed Forces in Oriente province. The men on the plane were investigated for two months, reprimanded for surrendering four rifles to the Zaireans and reduced to the ranks.'

Del Pino furthermore said he had grown weary of government corruption, particularly the practice in which Air Force pilots were deployed to flush up wildfowl from Cuban mangrove swamps when Castro went shooting at one of his weekend retreat homes. On one occasion, Del Pino alleged, a helicopter crashed and the pilot and co-pilot died when a flock of ducks flew into the rotor of the low-flying craft.

'It was common within our military for officers to characterise themselves as mercenaries propping up a corrupt group of politicians in power in Cuba accumulating fabulous riches for themselves in foreign banks and taking vacations in Europe while our young men died in Angola,' said Del Pino. 'I benefited from the system. I could buy Western goods of every kind at very low prices in special shops for military officers, and Fidel used to give his generals luxury houses. He offered me yet another new one just before I defected.

'I wanted to leave for many reasons, but Angola was one of the main ones. It had become a dead-end street, Cuba's Vietnam. Only Fidel and his brother Raúl had any faith in victory.'

★ ★ ★

Del Pino's final visit to Angola was made in February 1987 when he helped plan, with the Soviet high command, the offensive which later that year would erupt into warfare on an unprecedented scale. Back in Havana he continued to contribute to the planning. On 29 May Del Pino made his flight into a new life. Having helped plan it, he would now miss the War for Africa that was about to begin.

Notes

1   Milan Kundera, *The Unbearable Lightness of Being* (Faber and Faber, London, 1984).
2   Sadly, Mike Nicholson died on 11 December 2016. Many fond obituaries were written about him, including one by me in *The Herald* in Scotland.
3   Mike denied he shouted any such thing, but he did!
4   Jean Ziegler, *Les Rebelles – Contre L'Ordre du Monde* (Editions du Seuil, March 1983), p.259.
5   John Stockwell, *In Search of Enemies: A CIA Story* (Andre Deutsch, London), p.202.
6   Before switching support from UNITA to the MPLA, Zambian President Kenneth Kaunda had pleaded with Brand Fourie, the top civil servant in South Africa's foreign ministry, to ensure that the SADF continued pressing forward in Angola. Reuters, Lusaka (31 December 1975 and 28 January 1976); *Rapport*, (15 February 1976); Douglas Anglin and Timothy Shaw *Zambia's Foreign Policy: Studies in Diplomacy and Dependence* (Westview Press, Boulder, Colorado), pp.332–333.
7   *Newsweek* (17 May 1976).
8   Reuters, Cape Town (24 January 1976).
9   *Evening Standard*, London (10 February 1976).

10 Chester Crocker, *High Noon in Southern Africa: Making Peace in a Rough Neighbourhood* (W W Norton, New York, 1992).

11 Colin Legum and Tony Hodges, *After Angola: The War Over Southern Africa* (Rex Collings, London, 1976).

12 *Washington Post* (7 February 1976).

13 Fred Bridgland, *Jonas Savimbi: A Key to Africa* (Coronet Books, London, 1986).

14 Colin Legum, *The Western Crisis Over Southern Africa* (Africana Publishing Company, New York and London, 1979), pp.183–184; Irving Kaplan, *Angola: A Country Study* (Federal Research Division, Library of Congress, Washington DC, 1991), p.141.

15 *Leopold Scholtz, The SADF in the Border War 1966–1989 (Tafelberg, Cape Town, 2013).*

16 *New York Times* (1 February 1987, 27 July 1987, 14 December 1987).

17 *New York Times* (26 May 1988).

18 *The Times*, London (9 October 1985).

19 Controversy surrounds the name of the Soviet general. Most publications name him as Konstantin Shaganovitch, others as Pavel Gusev or Konstantin Kurochkin. Professor Vladimir Shubin, of the Soviet (now Russian) Academy of Sciences, denied in a 2001 article, ('War in Angola: a Soviet Dimension', *Review of African Political Economy*, Routledge, London) that the general concerned was Shaganovitch without naming who it might otherwise have been. Shubin, in the same article, says the mystery general had 2000 fellow Soviets under his command in Angola, not 950. I was among those who originally named Shaganovitch as the Soviets' top man. The general's true name will, for the time being, have to be left to some future Ph.D student to discern. Because the main narrative of this book from 1990 remains unchanged, so the title of Part 1 remains unchanged as 'General Shaganovitch's Offensive.' The fog, resulting from war, is a reminder of Oscar Wilde's splendid aphorism: 'The truth is rarely pure, and never simple.'

20 Speech by Fidel Castro in Mandela Park, Kingston, Jamaica, 30 July 1988, as reported in Havana by *Granma*, the official newspaper of the Central Committee of the Cuban Communist Party. Georgy Zhukov, an armour expert, was the most acclaimed Soviet general in World War II. Zhukov, raised to the rank of Marshal after the war, effectively led the attack on Berlin in April/May 1945 and throughout the whole Russian campaign was known as the 'man who did not lose a battle'.

21 The Alvor Agreement, signed in the small southern Portugal village of that name, granted Angola independence from 11 November 1975. It was signed by three liberation movements and the Portuguese government. It established a power-sharing coalition government which quickly fell apart as the country descended into civil war. Multi-party elections, promised under the Alvor Accord, did not take place for another 17 years.

22 Some accounts say the first Cuban helicopter was shot down in 1978.

23 Villegas, later a general, served in a top role with Del Pino in Angola.
24 Author interviews with Savimbi.
25 Jeremy Harding, 'Apartheid's Last Stand', *London Review of Books* (17 March 2016); Piero Gleijeses, *Visions of Freedom: Havana, Washington, Pretoria and the Struggle for Southern Africa* (University of North Caroline Press, 2013).
26 This particular sentence is a quote from *General del Pino speaks,* a 1987 publication by the Cuban–American National Foundation.

PART I

GENERAL SHAGANOVITCH'S OFFENSIVE

Marxism has placed its stake on force — which Marx called the midwife of history. And though the midwife perpetually delivers monsters, Marxists never tire of promising that the next child will be a splendid one.

Soviet dissident **Andrei Amalrik,**
in 1977.

You were there in a place where you didn't belong, where things were glimpsed for which you would have to pay and where things went unglimpsed for which you would also have to pay, a place where they didn't play with the mystery but killed you straight off for trespassing,

Vietnam veteran **Michael Herr,**
in his book *Dispatches.*

CHAPTER I

THE PRELUDE

In March 1987, South African Army reconnaissance teams deep in Angola detected big movements of Cuban and Angolan Marxist troops from the centre of that country towards the vast and empty region of the southeast.

The recce units, who spent almost as much of their working lives inside Angola as in their home bases, had located forces that the SADF (South African Defence Force) would soon engage in its biggest land battles since World War II.

Jan Hougaard, deputy commander of the SADF's 32 Battalion, guessed then that a major offensive was about to be launched against South Africa's ally in Angola, the UNITA (National Union for the Total Independence of Angola) resistance movement. He knew also, from past precedent, that his men would be the first to be thrown into the fray.

Commandant Hougaard's hunch was confirmed in May when 32 Battalion, also known as the Buffalo Battalion, was ordered to make a plan to destroy a major bridge across the Cuito River. The bridge, some 400 km inside Angola, was the only one across the river from the little town of Cuito Cuanavale, on the west bank, towards the east and the stronghold of UNITA.

'We sent out teams on close reconnaissance,' said Hougaard, regarded by many of his contemporaries as South Africa's best guerrilla-style fighter. 'There were two Angolan brigades, with Cuban support, defending the town. Its outskirts began just 500 m west of the bridge, a strong metal and concrete affair with a tarred surface that could take vehicles and tanks. So we presented our plan. We would have to accept heavy casualties, but we were prepared to do it.'

In the event, 32 Battalion's attack on the Cuito bridge never took place. The plan was vetoed after it reached the Chief of the SADF, General Jannie Geldenhuys, and the Chief of the Army, Lieutenant-General Kat Liebenberg.

The generals probably reckoned that not enough inconvenience would be caused to the gathering Angolan-Cuban forces to justify heavy SADF losses. The bridge's destruction would only slow the momentum of the enemy build-up. Its loss would be easily compensated for by the superb TMM mobile bridging equipment supplied by the Soviet Union in great quantities to its client in Angola, the Marxist MPLA (Popular Movement for the Liberation of Angola) government.

The generals' decision allowed the build-up by the Cubans and the MPLA army, known as Fapla (*Forces Armadas Popular de Angola* – People's Armed Forces for the Liberation of Angola), to go on undisturbed until August, by which time the SADF had begun moving small fighting units deep into Angola to counter the enemy thrust.

The two brigades detected by 32 Battalion's recces had by August grown to eight. Five Fapla brigades, the 16th, 21st, 25th, 47th and 59th, had pushed men and equipment across the Cuito River bridge whose destruction had been vetoed by the South African generals. A sixth brigade, the 66th, was deploying along the western bank of the Cuito, north and south of the river bridge, thus protecting the eastern perimeter of Cuito Cuanavale. A seventh brigade, the 13th, was in Cuito Cuanavale itself, giving direct protection to the town and its military airstrip. The eighth brigade, appropriately the 8th, was ferrying men, weapons and other equipment into Cuito Cuanavale from Menongue, 160 km to the west.

'There were still people in the higher echelons of the SADF who didn't believe there was an offensive imminent even when the Faplas had pushed two of their brigades across the river,' said Jan Hougaard, a thickset Afrikaner whose brown hair and beard had been bleached blond, his white skin cooked dark brown by constant exposure to the Angolan and Namibian sun. 'But 32 Battalion and a lot of intelligence organisations and other people had no doubt it was coming. UNITA had troops opposite Cuito Cuanavale monitoring those forces, and UNITA's Chief-of-Staff, Brigadier Demostenes Chilingutila, was busy bringing his guerrillas from other military regions of Angola to counter the offensive *he* expected.'

Captain Herman Mulder, 28, the senior intelligence officer of 32 Battalion, was also convinced of Fapla's serious intentions. With Colonel Jock Harris, 32 Battalion's commanding officer, he was flown by helicopter at night from Rundu (the SADF's forward base in South West Africa/Namibia) some 260 km into Angola in late June to meet SADF Colonel Fred Oelschig, who since early May had been liaising with and training UNITA's 5th Regular Battalion which was monitoring the Fapla build-up.

Harris and Mulder advised UNITA on stand-off mortar bombardments they were making against the Fapla concentrations. But Mulder was more concerned to know where the enemy brigades were each day and whether they showed signs of splitting up into battalion attack formations.

Mulder, Harris and Oelschig became the first South Africans to come under enemy fire in the Fapla offensive. Mig-21s of the Angola Air Force were already in the air regularly. And on 27 June 1987, as the three SADF men were working in a UNITA radio vehicle, parked at the source of the Cunzumbia River, Migs attacked the base.

'They came in to hit a diesel storage bladder,' said Mulder. 'The nearest missile to us landed 85 m away. We decided to get out of the area when Fapla began pounding the base with D-30 heavy artillery and 120 mm mortars.'

It was at this stage – late June, early July – that SADF operational commanders submitted proposals to Defence Headquarters, Pretoria, for countering the Fapla/Cuban build-up. The meeting, between Harris, Oelschig and the officer commanding the SADF's northwest Namibian sector, Colonel Piet Muller, at Harris' field HQ south of the Lomba River, became known as 'The Night of the Three Colonels'. It was a long and traumatic night with a lot of heavy arguing. The consensus finally was that the developing enemy offensive was too big for them to

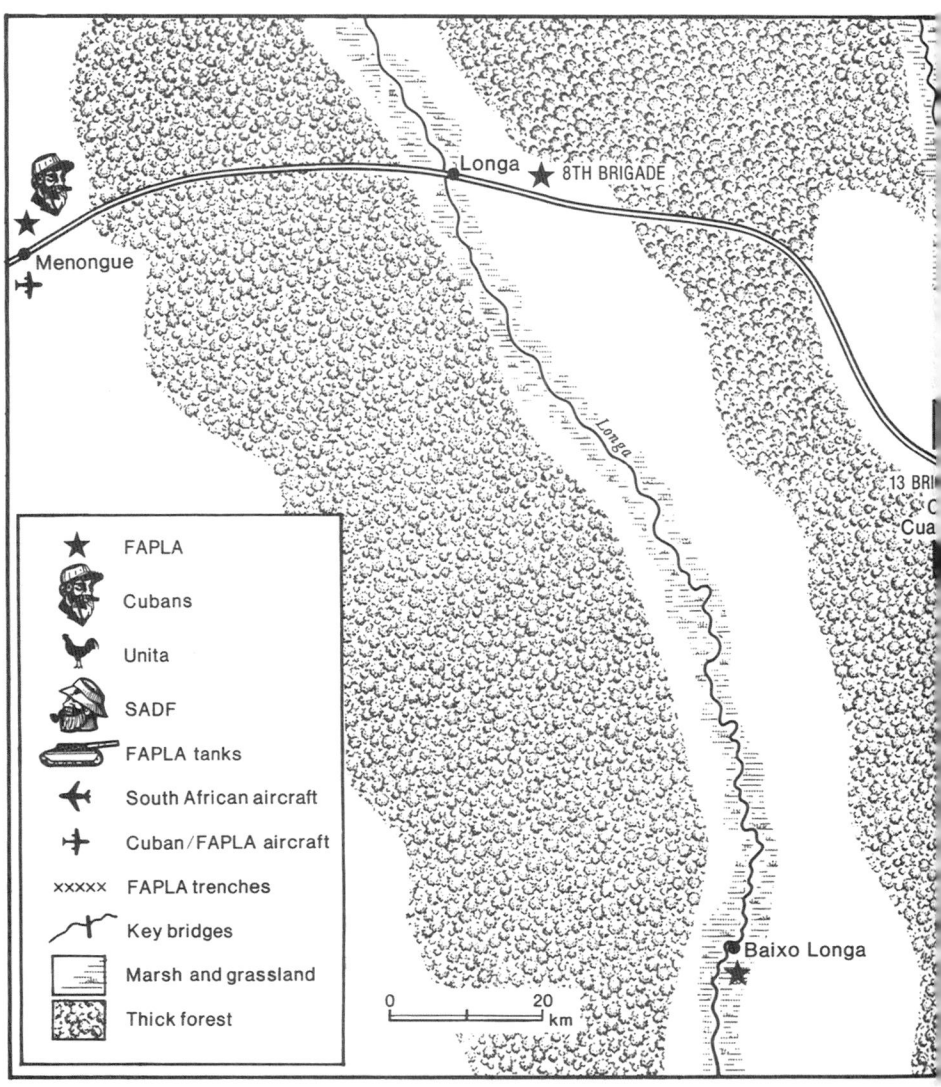

Legend:
- ★ FAPLA
- Cubans
- Unita
- SADF
- FAPLA tanks
- South African aircraft
- Cuban/FAPLA aircraft
- xxxxx FAPLA trenches
- Key bridges
- Marsh and grassland
- Thick forest

Menongue

Longa 8TH BRIGADE

13 BRI
C
Cua

Baixo Longa

0   20
        km

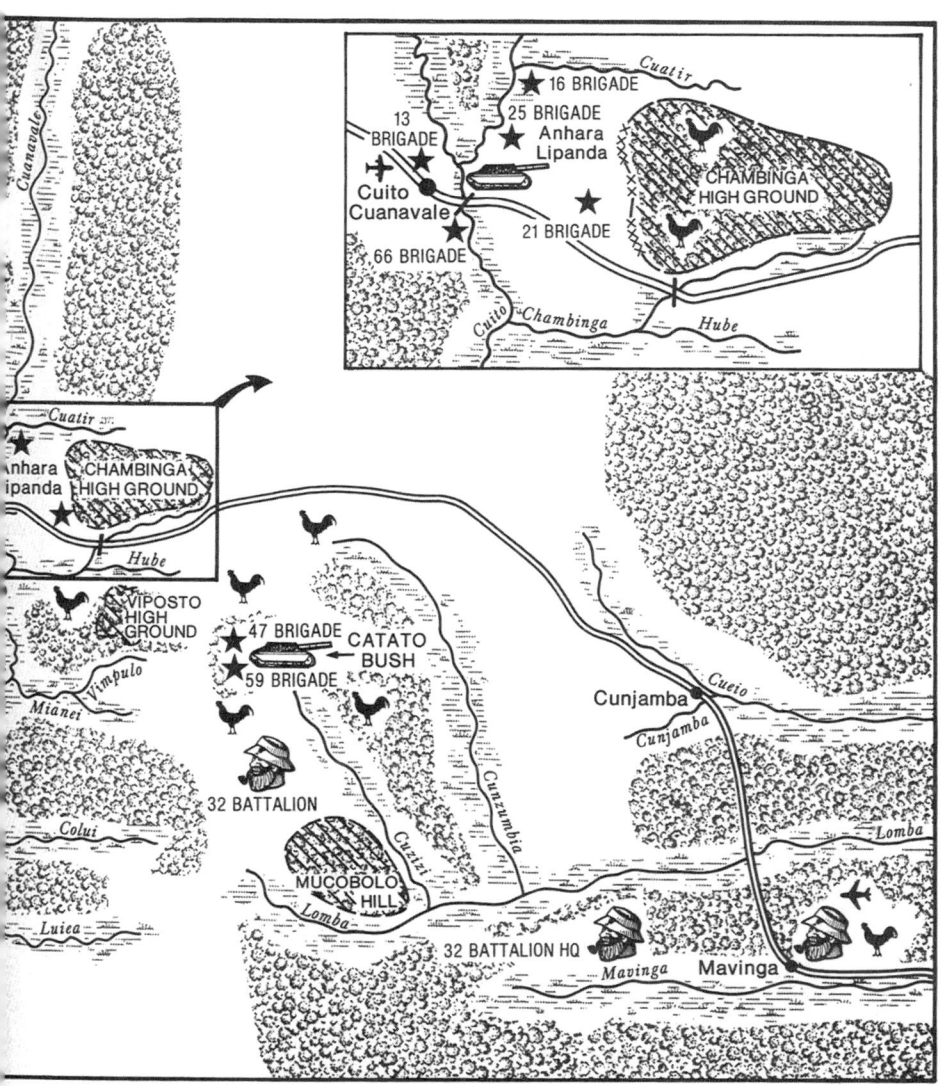

The military situation on the ground – 13 August 1987.

handle without the commitment of more South African forces and the creation of some sort of SADF brigade structure.

The favoured plan of the 'three colonels' involved sending a major battle group from Namibia northwards along the *western* bank of the Cuito River, attacking Cuito Cuanavale from behind, and controlling the narrow road from Menongue along which logistics were being ferried to the brigades.

By now the CIA was sending the SADF intelligence assessments on the Fapla/Cuban build-up from General Rafael Del Pino Diaz, whose extensive debriefing in Virginia, after his defection from Cuba, was almost at an end. Del Pino's advice also was that cutting the Menongue-Cuito Cuanavale supply road was the best and most logical way of stopping the offensive. It would be a tactical error for the South Africans and UNITA to concentrate their forces on Cuito Cuanavale.

'Strategically, it was on,' said one senior officer involved in planning the assault on the Menongue-Cuito road. 'But politically we didn't get permission.'

That decision was made at the highest level by the State President P W Botha. His fear, and that of his Cabinet, was of the international outcry that would follow if regular South African troops were perceived to be fighting several hundreds of kilometres inside Angola. For historical and strategic reasons it believed to be sound and just, Pretoria felt its involvement in the Angolan conflict was fully legitimate. But an attack towards Cuito Cuanavale from the west could not have been hidden and substantial casualties would have been inevitable. South Africa was already under heavy international pressure, in the form of sanctions, disinvestment and boycotts of various kinds, over its domestic race laws and the denial of the vote to the black majority. Few countries would be disposed to understand the presence of a major South African military force in the territory of a sovereign black African state: instead, it would be used as another stick to beat a country trying desperately to re-establish international respectability.

The South African Cabinet instead approved the commanders' secondary plan: a thrust into the area east of the Cuito River – a vast, sandy, tree-covered wilderness called the 'Land at the End of the Earth', an epithet applied by Angola's Portuguese colonial rulers who reserved the region for big game hunting – to prevent Fapla from capturing UNITA's strategic stronghold of Mavinga.

UNITA had held Mavinga since 1980. Once a town with barely a thousand inhabitants living along its two streets lined with orange trees, it had been deserted for 12 years and was now crumbling back into the red earth of Africa. But nearby was an important airstrip used by heavy transport planes bringing weapons and supplies to UNITA from Zaire, South Africa and other African points of origin. The airstrip and the surrounding UNITA bases stood on top of a plateau just south of the Lomba River: if UNITA were to lose Mavinga, the way would again be open, as had been the case in 1985, for Fapla and the Cubans to prepare a major drive towards Jamba, UNITA's 'capital' 250 km southeast of Mavinga. With the collapse of UNITA, there would follow the collapse of Pretoria's military and diplomatic game-plan for the southern African region.

South Africa had long been co-operating secretly with Jonas Savimbi, the UNITA leader, in the conviction that his movement enjoyed majority Angolan support against the Soviet-backed MPLA government. South Africa had also made its withdrawal from Namibia, administered by Pretoria in defiance of United Nations condemnation, contingent upon the return home of Cuban troops supporting the MPLA in Angola. It was UNITA which kept constant pressure on the Cubans and made it possible for Pretoria to insist on a 'double zero' pullout – South Africa from Namibia and Cuba from Angola – first proposed by P W Botha in 1978. If UNITA were to be eliminated there would no longer have been a clear 'moral equivalence' between the Angolan and Namibian situations; and South Africa would have faced a large Cuban force on the Namibia border demanding liberty for the territory with wide international support. The South African government had already concluded that Namibia's independence was inevitable, but that it would not come at the behest of Havana, whose military dictator Fidel Castro was demanding for Namibians and South Africans the kind of freedoms he denied his own fellow Cubans. Much as South Africans desired an end to their pariah status in the international community, they were not so soft-headed as even to consider succumbing to this kind of hypocrisy. They knew what the consequences would be of a militarily and ideologically confident Cuban force sitting on the Namibian border free of any challenge from within Angola: it would inevitably have meant a new kind of war for South Africa of major proportions and unpredictable consequences.

Approving the field commanders' secondary plan, South Africa's politicians told the fighters that the Fapla offensive must be halted and UNITA's power base strengthened. They further decreed that the SADF's involvement would be secret and sufficiently limited to be 'plausibly deniable'. Any successes would be attributed to UNITA. The role of the SADF force would be purely defensive, not offensive. There was a further set of instructions which caused wry and sometimes bitter amusement among the combat officers: no men must be lost; no equipment must be lost; and you must achieve all your objectives.

'Those are very difficult and heavy restrictions to put on anyone who is supposed to be fighting a war,' said Jan Hougaard. 'But that's the way we work in the SADF. We can't afford to lose one guy.'

CHAPTER 2

THE SOUTH AFRICANS MOVE IN

Commandant Robert Hartslief of 32 Battalion got orders in mid-July to move a 'limited and clandestine' force into Angola to prepare to stop the 10,000-strong Fapla/Cuban force before it reached Mavinga. Effectively, the South Africans would be pseudo-UNITAs.

Hartslief, a hefty 32-year-old armour expert who had been posted to the Buffalo Battalion in 1987 after it was upgraded to a full conventional battalion of the SADF, set about organising his force at Fort Buffalo, 32 Battalion's main base in a spectacularly beautiful game reserve on the banks of the Kavango River in Namibia's Caprivi Strip. The battalion took its alternative name from the great herds of wild buffalo that roamed the forests of their base, and the battalion emblem was a particularly ferocious-looking buffalo.

By early August about 100 combat group and forward headquarters vehicles were ready to move.

The first South African military convoy left Fort Buffalo and crossed the Angolan border opposite Rundu on 5 August 1987. It consisted of Hartslief and his HQ vehicles, plus 120 infantrymen (Delta Company) of 32 Battalion. Hartslief reached Savimbi's tactical headquarters at Mavinga on 8 August after three days and three nights of driving over some of the toughest terrain in Africa – deep-rutted, sandy tracks in which vehicles were sucked to a halt and through which they could move at a top speed of scarcely 30 km per hour.

Another 120 infantrymen (Charlie Company) of 32 Battalion moved across the Angolan border on 6 August with eight multiple rocket launchers ('Papa' battery) and their support vehicles. And on 8 August a 120 mm mortar battery left Fort Buffalo with 32 Battalion's reconnaissance teams.

Mac da Trinidada, the sergeant of one of 32 Battalion's four (five-man) recce groups, accompanied the mortar team to Mavinga because the mortarmen did not know the route. Da Trinidada, on the other hand, knew it well. He had spent months every year inside Angola living by his wits, his athleticism and on special ration packs (ratpacs) ever since he joined the battalion in 1978 as a 17-year-old black African refugee from Angola. He had experienced many adventures, sitting for days and nights within 50 m of bases of Fapla, the Cubans and the Namibian liberation movement, SWAPO, throughout southern and central Angola. Da Trinidada, tall and slim with big white Louis Armstrong eyes that rotate busily and intelligently, operated with the same four men all the time: 'In our kind of work you've got to know and like and trust one another without question. You've got to be friends and buddies. And you've all got to know that each of the others is willing to die for you when the going gets tough.'

In Mavinga, Da Trinidada joined Hartslief who had been briefed by Special Forces of 1 Reconnaissance Commando, one of five elite and highly secretive reconnaissance regiments specialising in covert intelligence gathering and undercover attacks behind enemy lines. The recce units are South Africa's equivalent of, and a match for, Britain's SAS or West Germany's *Fernspaher*. (The small recce units of 32 Battalion are independent of the Special Forces Reconnaissance Regiments.)

The Special Forces told Hartslief that the forward companies of Fapla's 47, 59, 21 and 16 Brigades were between the sources of the Cuatir and Chambinga Rivers, 20 km east of the wide and deep south-flowing Cuito and Cuanavale Rivers of which they are tributaries. The Cuatir and the Chambinga rise on the Chambinga High Ground, a physical feature which was to be important strategically during the looming military campaign.

Forward Fapla infantrymen and support vehicles had dug in on the western flanks of the Chambinga High Ground, which is the watershed between the Cuando River system, to the east, and the Cuito and Cuanavale system to the west. From the Chambinga High Ground seven small rivers, which were to be landmarks in the campaign, flow directly westwards into the Cuito and Cuanavale. From north to south the tributaries are the Cuatir, Dala, Tumpo, Chambinga, Hube, Vimpulo and Mianei.

The Cuzizi and Cunzumbia Rivers rise to the east of the Chambinga High Ground and then flow south-eastwards to join the Lomba. The Lomba flows directly eastwards, passing just north of the Mavinga Plateau before reaching its confluence with the Cuando. (See map, ch. 1.)

The tributary rivers, clear, swift-flowing and deeply cut into the sandy terrain, are scarcely four or five metres wide. But they are lined by broad swamps. Between the tall grasses of the marshes and the barely elevated treelines, narrow strips of firm ground make the edges of the flattened river valleys ideal advance routes.

The Lomba and its swamps in the river's lower reaches are sufficiently wider than the other tributary rivers to present a difficult physical barrier to an army advancing from the north.

The Chambinga High Ground is thickly forested dune-like terrain, some 100 m higher than the Cuito floodplain. Its height attracts unusually heavy rainfall on the western slopes, where vegetation in the gullies is reminiscent of rain forest, with ferns trailing from branches of moss-covered trees. The area is rich in tropical birds, buck, warthog, lion, leopard and troops of baboons.

On 10 August Commandant Hartslief was ordered to move his headquarters, with one multiple rocket launcher (MRL) battery, from Mavinga to a UNITA logistics base south of the confluence of the Cunzumbia River with the Lomba. He moved out that same night, and at his new HQ liaised with Special Forces who said forward elements of the enemy brigades had moved south from the Chambinga High Ground towards the source of the Hube River. From there they seemed to be preparing either to move due south to the source of the Mianei or cross some 15 km eastwards to the Cuzizi source. Either move would indicate that the full push towards Mavinga was beginning.

★ ★ ★

Jan Hougaard, who had been brought back in late July from an operation in southwest Angola against SWAPO to be second-in-command of the whole campaign in the east, was working from brigade headquarters in Rundu. Confronted by a big enemy force, with limited forces of his own and subject to strict guidelines from SADF headquarters in Pretoria, his tactical options were limited.

'We were really only monitoring the situation,' he said. 'I think at certain times we were confused by the orders we got – *not* to get into a fight; only to use artillery when we were really in trouble or UNITA was in big trouble.

'Our orders were *not* to stop the advance but to prevent the enemy from taking Mavinga.

'I think at that time there were still people higher up who were sure that UNITA could stop the advance. But we were telling them: "Forget it, they can't stop it. And if you want us to stop it, you must expect casualties – if the *minimum casualties* restriction is more important than the success of the operation, it's not on." At that time we had already started asking for tanks and more artillery in the form of G-5 guns.'

Fapla Mig and Sukhoi warplanes had near total control of the skies over south-east Angola in the absence of any presence by the South African Air Force (SAAF). The only air support South Africa's soldiers were given was Puma helicopters, to evacuate casualties and to fly in senior officers at night from Rundu HQ for liaison purposes.

Hougaard was amused when he met his old friend, Colonel Fred Oelschig, during one of his night-time helicopter forays into Angola. Oelschig, the SADF's senior intelligence liaison officer with UNITA, had been observing the Angolan Air Force's performance. He was not too impressed. The planes had failed to locate any of the small South African units, which operated only at night and laid up during the day under heavy camouflage. The attacks on UNITA positions had been light as well: the Fapla pilots, fearing Stinger ground-to-air missiles supplied to UNITA by the United States, stayed high on bombing runs and consequently their bombing attacks were very inaccurate.

'Oelschig was having a leak when he experienced his first low-level Mig attack,' said Hougaard. 'He ran so fast to drop into his hole that he only realised when he got to the bottom of it that his pants were soaking wet.'

From that incident was born the '100 Metres Club' – anyone who was within 100 m of bombs dropped in an air attack and who lived to tell the tale qualified as a member.

The hole Oelschig dropped into was a refinement the SADF had learned from UNITA, who in turn had picked it up from Vietcong guerrilla manuals.

'The conventional way we had been taught was to dig long, zigzag trenches,' said Hougaard. 'It was part of our doctrine. But UNITA taught us to dig deep round holes, deeper than yourself. They were very successful: the only way you could come to any harm was if a shell or bomb landed directly in the hole with you. Under the UNITA system, every guy had his own hole, with as narrow a circumference as possible. Some of those holes were so deep that you had to get another guy to pull you out.'

Among the Fapla planes was an Antonov-26 transport which flew constant reconnaissance missions taking photos as far south as Mavinga. The Antonov was packed with sophisticated monitoring equipment and had facilities to enable the crew to develop and analyse the photos while still in the air. South African intelligence monitored the Antonov's flight paths to see if there was a pattern which might indicate the planned line of advance of the Fapla ground forces.

But UNITA and the SADF ground forces were more concerned about the intelligence the Antonov was gathering about *them*. UNITA tried unsuccessfully to destroy the plane with Stingers, but it flew too high.

Hougaard and other senior SADF commanders asked Pretoria to allow the South African Air Force (SAAF) to shoot down the Antonov. 'The Air Force made an operational plan, but permission for them to go for the plane was never given,' said Hougaard. 'Later, when our fighter-bombers became involved in combat, the Antonov didn't appear any more because it was too vulnerable.'

CHAPTER 3

SNIFFING OUT THE ENEMY

Commandant Robert Hartslief moved 36 km northwest from the UNITA logistics base to the tactical HQ of 1 Recce Commando at the source of the Mianei River. Hartslief's own command vehicle at this time was a makeshift affair – a Buffel anti-mine personnel carrier, packed with communications equipment. Hartslief moved through the thick bush and across the grasslands at night, to avoid detection by enemy planes, and he left his MRL battery at the source of the Lomba about 20 km south of his position.

From the Mianei, Hartslief sent out Sergeant Mac Da Trinidada to gather more intelligence about enemy movements.

Da Trinidada set out with his 32 Battalion recce team to locate the brigades precisely: 'We went north of them so that we could follow in their tracks. Before we left we'd been told there were four tanks with each brigade. But the first time we crossed the tracks of 47 we got a big shock: there were 22 tanks with the brigade, plus a lot of other armoured assault vehicles. I radioed Commandant Hartslief and he didn't believe it. He said it was not possible.'

Da Trinidada turned to Pierre Franken, a tall, blond, excruciatingly shy Afrikaner artillery major attached to the recce group as a forward observer, and insisted that *he* speak to the Commandant. Hartslief got the message and prepared to fire the first South African shots in anger.

'The intelligence appreciation I received was that it was now obvious that a major thrust would be made down the Cuzizi to cross the Lomba well to the west where the river headwaters were not a major obstacle,' said Hartslief.

On 19 August, 47 Brigade and elements of 59 Brigade assembled in an area of particularly thick bush on slightly raised ground known as Catato about seven kilometres northwest of Hartslief's forward HQ. That evening Hartslief moved up his MRL battery from the source of the Lomba to open ground 14 km south of Catato to prepare for a night bombardment.

'We brought a first ripple of MRLs in on the enemy, and then another, but neither was very accurate,' said Mac da Trinidada. 'We must have put down about 200 shells on them, but we probably missed them by about 100 m.'

After that opening failure, Hartslief moved his headquarters and his artillery rapidly south of the Lomba. He knew that the sheer weight of his bombardment would have alerted Fapla to a South African presence and that his tiny force could not confront an enemy armoured brigade. Meanwhile, Mac da Trinidada, his recces and Pierre Franken got on the tail of 47 Brigade. Also with the five men was an Angolan with whom Franken worked closely – Lieutenant Ventura, UNITA's liaison officer attached to the South African artilleryman.

'Some of the time, on the first day as they pushed out of the Catato bush, we were as near as 30 m to their troops and vehicles,' said Da Trinidada. 'Major Franken was amazed. It was the first time he had seen enemy forces as close as that. There were 1,600 men in the brigade.'

Franken's memories are of Da Trinidada insisting that they keep not only within visual range of the brigade but that they stay close enough to pick up voices and snatches of enemy conversation and even the barking of dogs, brought by Fapla to warn them of UNITA infiltration units. Da Trinidada moved parallel with 47 Brigade, keeping the enemy force between himself and the river. A big worry was that a mechanised infantry company moving far behind the main convoy as a protection element might move suddenly to engulf the recce group. Franken was grateful for the scattered platoons of UNITA soldiers who were deployed to give early warning to Da Trinidada of any movement of enemy forces from the rear.

The next day 47 Brigade moved due south so exceptionally fast that Da Trinidada and his men were unable to keep up with them.

Sergeant Da Trinidada ordered his team to move southwestwards because he was certain 47 Brigade would eventually turn in that direction to go round the source of the Lomba. But 47 Brigade continued heading south along the west bank of the Cuzizi, and Da Trinidada had to double back to pick up the Brigade: 'One of the reasons we wanted to beat 47 to the source of the Lomba was to get water. By the time I realised we would need to turn back towards the Cuzizi, we had already marched 28 kilometres that day. We had no water left, and we were very thirsty. We were carrying big and heavy packs – several days of rations, all the ammunition, weapons, everything.'

After its rapid drive south, 47 Brigade assembled on a wide area of higher ground about six kilometres to the northwest of where the Cuzizi flowed into the Lomba.

Unbeknown to the 47th, they had come within range again of 32 Battalion's MRL battery at its new position south of the Lomba. Franken, worried at one stage that the 47th would assemble so far south that it would be too close for the MRLs which have a minimum firing range of eight kilometres, was determined this time that the SADF artillery barrage would be accurate and inflict damage. He and Da Trinidada worked their way on to the western edge of 47 Brigade's higher ground by about 6.30 pm, just as the sun was going down.

'We could see them clearly in their night base, even without binoculars,' said Da Trinidada. 'But you need binoculars to pinpoint what is on top of the trucks and where they are keeping their food.'

Using the eight metre rope he always carried, Da Trinidada tried to climb into the crown of a tree for a better view of all the trucks so that he could pass on a precision RV (grid reference bombing target, and sometimes a rendezvous point) to Hartslief's artillery. As he climbed, with his Soviet-made AK-47 rifle over his shoulder, a branch snapped loudly and attracted the attention of a small Angolan patrol which moved towards the noise. Da Trinidada slithered down the tree and rapidly organised an ambush. Just as the recce group was about to open fire, Lieutenant Ventura recognised the Angolans as a UNITA reconnaissance group. Da Trinidada shouted at them in Portuguese, and they identified themselves as UNITA.

It was a bad moment. Not only had they nearly shot each other, but if the firing had begun 47 Brigade would have been alerted and the planned artillery barrage would have had to be aborted.

Franken was furious. UNITA groups were not meant to be in the same vicinity without prior notification by radio or other means. He radioed Hartslief urging a tightening up of SADF–UNITA liaison.

That night Franken and Da Trinidada brought down two MRL ripples, each ripple consisting of 192 60-kg fragmentation shells fired from the eight rocket launchers in precisely computerised but apparently random sequence.

The first ripple came in at about midnight on 23–24 August. 'We got back from our EW (electronic warfare) people, listening in to the enemy radio communications, that the western side of the brigade had been hit, and we made a small correction eastwards in mid-ripple,' said Franken.

'There was a bit of chaos there because we could see vehicles burning and two tanks went up. Commandant Hartslief told me that radio intercepts indicated that some of their artillery had been hit.'

The whole of 47 Brigade began dispersing northwards in a broad fan. Its BM-21 'Stalin Organs', of which the SADF's Valkirie 127 mm MRLs were a much improved development, moved northwest to a small *shona* – an area of open grassland – and began firing on the SADF artillery position. 'It was not an accurate attack,' said Franken. 'I think their technical and forward OP (observer post) skills were not up to standard. Knowing that, we could take risks even within their artillery range throughout all the months of the campaign.'

Franken brought in another ripple at 5 am on 24 August, and then moved out rapidly with Da Trinidada's recce team as 47 Brigade sent out big tactical search groups. 'Moving around in that bush was very difficult because there are very few clear landmarks,' said Franken. 'For two days we were completely lost as we moved or hid, and sometimes went between enemy ambushes.'

The recce group, now out of rations, had to make up its mind whether to call in a helicopter to pull it out or to make its own way back to Hartslief's tactical HQ. Da Trinidada decided the helicopter option presented too many risks. So he led his team across the headwaters of the Lomba, where the swamps were reasonably narrow, and found a UNITA unit which gave his exhausted men a lift 25 km along the south bank of the Lomba to Hartslief's HQ. There food, clean clothes, rest and encouraging news was waiting for them: according to the EW radio intercepts, Fapla was reporting several damaged vehicles and tanks as a result of the second MRL bombardment.

Now the 32 Battalion recce baton was passed to one of Mac da Trinidada's fellow sergeants, a former French Army marine commando known inevitably as 'Frenchie', who has since left the SADF to work as a game ranger.

'Frenchie', a diminutive, cheerful man who had fought many battles inside Angola with 32 Battalion, soon got lost as he took his group of Angolan recce 'buddies' across the Lomba. First they were stuck in exceptionally heavy swamps at their chosen crossing point, and then for five days Frenchie was unable to trace 47 Brigade which, unknown to him, was heading determinedly west to go round the Lomba source as he manoeuvred eastwards towards the Cuzizi.

47 Brigade's persistence in advancing, even after Hartslief's damaging artillery attack, necessitated a major reassessment of the battlefield situation by SADF commanders in the field.

Various tactics, other than the artillery bombardments, had been tried to unnerve and dissuade 47 Brigade. Hougaard formed a special anti-tank group of about twenty Reconnaissance Commando men who tried to get into the brigade's defences with jeep-mounted and hand-held weapons to knock out a few tanks. 'But we couldn't get close enough because they had infantry moving well in advance of the tanks,' said Hougaard. 'At night they dug in well in front of the armour, forming a whole defence laager around it.'

Try as it might, the anti-tank group was unable to manoeuvre into positions where it could fire its 106 mm recoilless guns, RPG-7 anti-tank rockets and Milan anti-tank missiles effectively. SADF officers always turn coy or enigmatic when asked how they managed to acquire the Milans, NATO's standard advanced anti-tank missile, which is theoretically denied to South Africa under the international arms embargo. The SADF seems to have received virtually unlimited supplies of the weapon.

UNITA was retreating tactically in front of 47 Brigade, hitting the Fapla troops with mortar fire at night and planting mines ahead of them. Hougaard was impressed by UNITA's grit and optimism: 'They told us we mustn't worry. They were going to pull in the 47th far from its logistical support and at the farthest range of Fapla's warplanes, and then destroy it. It made sense tactically, and we listened to UNITA because there were people in our SADF group who said we must start attacking Fapla seriously north of the Lomba. Colonel Oelschig, working with UNITA, was one of our guys who strongly opposed that idea.

'But we knew UNITA's actions were all small stuff. We knew UNITA could never stop those brigades. They didn't have the weapons capability.'

CHAPTER 4

FAPLA'S ADVANCE CONTINUES

By late August SADF intelligence had formed a coherent picture of the Fapla/Soviet strategy and how well it had been planned. It reeled back in shock after gleaning information about the scale of the Soviet weaponry committed.

On 1 September 1987, 47 Brigade began moving around the source of the Lomba and prepared to move along the south bank of the river towards Mavinga, 80 km to the east. Probing elements of Fapla's 21 Brigade were arriving on the north bank of the Lomba, some 55 km east of the Lomba source and within about 25 km of Mavinga. Fapla's 59 Brigade was heading towards the Lomba between the Cuzizi and Cunzumbia tributaries. North of 21 Brigade was 16 Brigade, ferrying logistics over difficult countryside and apparently preparing to join 21 Brigade when the assault began on Mavinga. (See map, ch. 9).

Officers flown in from Chief of Staff Intelligence (CSI), the supreme SADF division overseeing all military intelligence units from Pretoria, were working round the clock with Captain Herman Mulder and other intelligence experts assessing Fapla/Cuban intentions. At this stage, information from intercepts of enemy radio communications and the SADF's own reconnaissance teams' ground observations provided the most solid material. Mulder was also receiving information from UNITA reconnaissance teams, but he had problems in assessing its objectivity: Savimbi's intelligence officers tended to embroider information in attempts to cajole the SADF into more aggressive action.

The intelligence conclusion was that 47 Brigade would forge along the south bank of the Lomba to help 59 Brigade and 21 Brigade cross the river from the north for the main attack on Mavinga. The SADF and UNITA would need therefore to prevent the establishment of 59 Brigade and 21 Brigade bridgeheads and they would need also to stop 47 Brigade joining up with them. Mavinga would come under particularly serious threat if 21 Brigade got across to the south of the Lomba.

★ ★ ★

Senior officers like Jan Hougaard were perplexed as to how the big and aggressive enemy brigades were to be stopped by a small SADF force with one arm tied behind its back by the generals and politicians: 'We were pleading for more forces and we were complaining quite strongly about the restrictions imposed upon us – don't lose any equipment, don't take any casualties, and so on and so on.'

Not only were the SADF up against a big force, but they were facing an army which had learned many lessons from its defeat during its disastrous 1985–86 offensive towards Mavinga. Artillery co-ordination had improved, tactics on the ground were more aggressive, a wide range of radar and missile systems accompanied the brigades, the logistics were infinitely better and Fapla had tanks. Every day some eight to ten giant Ilyushin-76s flew into Menongue with weapons, ammunition, spares, fuel, food and other supplies. Every six days a logistics convoy of 400 vehicles, escorted by two brigades, moved from Menongue to Cuito Cuanavale.

'We were already reckoning that it was costing the Russians millions and millions of dollars,' said Hougaard. 'The logistics they pumped in there were colossal. It took us by surprise. For example, we had been working on the assumption that they would again have lousy food supplies. But later we found the support vehicles we shot out were stacked with big tins of the best Japanese tuna. I dined on it, and, hell, it was very good tuna!'

PART 2

THE DEFENCE

I don't think the Boers will have a chance, although I expect there will be one or two stiff little shows here and there... I think they are awful idiots to fight, although we are of course very keen that they should.

Lieutenant Reggie Kentish,
of the Royal Irish Fusiliers, in a letter
from South Africa to his parents, 1899.

Perhaps they hadn't even told him (a 19-year-old Cuban soldier shot dead through the chest) where he was going or whose war he was going to fight. Just as they never told us. All we knew was that the Angolans were fucking one another up and we had to move in before the Commies took over. But hell, it wasn't our war either. Like that young Cuban, we were fighting someone else's war for them.

SADF Troopie Louis Myngardt,
in Andre Brink's novel *Rumours of Rain.*

CHAPTER 5

SOUTH AFRICA STEPS THINGS UP

By the time 47 Brigade was approaching the source of the Lomba the officers on the ground had persuaded the generals of the seriousness of the situation, and they in turn worked on the politicians. Permission was given for a battery of G-5 guns to move into Angola in support of 32 Battalion. The G-5s, which the SADF claim as the finest artillery in the world, have a computer-controlled fire system. They can deliver a variety of 43,5 kilogram shells up to 42 km or as short a distance as three kilometres.

A battle-hardened SADF fighting force, 61 Mechanised Battalion, which had its main headquarters and training base at Oshivelo and Bittersoet in northern Namibia, was alerted to prepare to join in the action.

The SAAF was also given permission to step up its involvement beyond the Puma helicopters. C-130 transport planes began flying logistics into Mavinga at night. It was a very demanding form of flying. The old Portuguese airstrip at Mavinga is of uneven compressed red laterite. The night lighting system consisted of beer cans half filled with paraffin-soaked sand which UNITA soldiers lit at the sound of a whistle from the radio tent during the last minutes of a transport plane's approach. The moment the plane touched the ground the lights were doused.

A technical improvement UNITA made to the beer can landing lights caused problems at first for the C-130 pilots. Instead of placing the cans on the ground at the edges of the runway, the UNITA men mounted them on hand-held sticks. Often the SADF pilots on their approach would swerve from side to side as they tried to line up for the landing. Unfortunately, as the plane veered, so the UNITA men swerved too, moving with their hand-held landing lights from side to side to line up with the plane. A couple of pilots had to abort their landings in the last few seconds when they realised the landing lights were off centre. After a corrosive exchange of words on the ground between allies, the advanced UNITA system was stabilised to everybody's satisfaction and the pilots' nerves were soothed.

Mirage-3 jets were also brought in to fly photo reconnaissance missions, each one escorted by two Mirage F-1CZ all-weather fighters for protection. The Mirage-3s, armed only with high-definition cameras, took off from Grootfontein in Namibia and once over Angola hugged the ground at about 50 m to avoid Fapla Mig-23 fighters and ground-to-air missiles and artillery. As they approached the photographic target area, they pitched up steeply spending as short a time on enemy radar as was necessary to take their photos, and then dived rapidly to the ground again to make their exit. The aerial photos of the brigades helped confirm the immensity of the Fapla thrust.

In an important South African escalation in early September, Pretoria committed to the war Canberra bombers of 12 Squadron, based at Waterkloof, near Pretoria, and Mirage F-1AZ fighter-bombers of 1 Squadron, based at Hoedspruit in the Eastern Transvaal.

The squadrons flew high across Botswana to base themselves at Grootfontein, the SAAF's biggest airfield in Namibia, 220 km south of the Angolan border.

From Grootfontein the Mirage F-lAZs and the Canberras pounded Fapla's 47 Brigade almost daily as it came round the source of the Lomba River and began heading east for Mavinga.

Captain Reg van Eeden, a dashing, dark-haired airman in his twenties with a black military moustache and the brisk politeness of air force men everywhere, flew one of the 12 Mirage F-lAZs which came to Grootfontein from Hoedspruit. Like all young pilots early in a war, he was pushing for sorties and was eager to apply against the enemy the special bombing techniques he had learned back home.

Early on, the SAAF high command decided it made no sense to use orthodox bombing methods against an enemy whose modern Soviet aircraft were technologically more advanced than South Africa's warplanes, or against a wider range of Soviet ground-to-air missiles than even the Israeli Air Force had faced in its sorties into Lebanon's Bekaa Valley and beyond the Golan Heights into Syria.

Instead of flying into enemy territory at great height and then diving precipitously beyond the speed of sound to drill bombs into the target, the SAAF did everything the opposite way round.

'Our motto was: "Low level is survivability," said Reg van Eeden. 'Once the Army had given us a target grid reference, we would fly in towards it at 540 knots at no more than 30 to 80 m above the ground.

'Everything was pre-briefed. As soon as we taxied out on to the Grootfontein tarmac we entered complete radio silence. It caused problems. Once there was an SAAF Dakota over Grootfontein running out of fuel at 2,200 metres as we prepared to take off on a sortie.

'The pilot was frantic with fear because the controllers in the tower were forbidden to break radio silence, so they weren't replying to him. Eventually one controller could bear it no longer and he sent a straightforward message: "For Christ's sake, bugger off." The pilot must have sighted the first of our Mirages streaking at ground level towards Angola, because he held on and eventually got down safely.

'We had routes planned from all directions towards the target area, although the final run-in, over less than 30 nautical miles (55 km), was very specific. In our pre-flight briefings we would study the navigation features in great depth. The tracks through the bush were totally unreliable: new ones were springing up all the time, and most of the terrain was completely flat. There were no crossroads, towns or railway lines to use in lining up for attack. But the rivers were beautiful navigation features. There was one bend in the Lomba that made the outline of an exquisite woman's breast – that was a honey and it became known as "David's tit" after the pilot who first saw its possibilities. The *shonas* also stood out. After a while we knew the features so well that southeast Angola was like a general flying area.

'We had recently updated computerised navigation systems aboard the Mirages, but we flew with 1:100,000 hand maps. Every time we were over an identifiable natural feature we fed corrections, usually of the order of about 0.1 to 0.2 kilometres, into the computer.

'The Army provided us with an IP (initial point) grid reference from where to begin our bombing run. The shorter the distance between the IP and the target, the more accurate our attack would be: the less the distance was than 30 nautical miles, the more effective were our bombs on the ground.

'In those last minutes in the approach to bomb release, everything started. Almost invariably you'd enter enemy radar range, and as soon as their radar illuminated you the systems in the Mirage would warn you. I used to wet myself with fear. But at the same time it made the adrenalin flow, and on the final run-in to the target I was concentrating so hard on all the different technical procedures and instrument and computer checks that there was no time to be frightened.'

The moment of truth had approached after hundreds of hours spent training day in, day out over the Transvaal in special 'toss-bombing' practice attack profiles.

The essence of the toss-bombing technique is to rise up steep and fast from ground level and release the bomb at a specific height during the climb so that it is lobbed on to the target. Given an accurate grid reference for the ground target, the right speed and angle of climb in relation to distance from target can be calculated in order for the bomb to be 'tossed' accurately from a distance of seven to eight kilometres.

'All the data were fed into the computer and updated right up until the last moments,' said Captain van Eeden. 'The release cue was given by the systems of the aircraft. There was a moment of relief when you felt the bombs go – it kind of tickled your bum, and you knew immediately if the release mechanisms had worked or not.

'Then the aim was to get out of the climb quicker than quick and get back to less than 30 m from the ground. Again, there was no time to be scared, but I was always very conscious of what was going on. All the time you had to be looking high for aircraft and low for ground-to-air missiles.

'The manoeuvre was three-dimensional – rolling, pitching down and accelerating so that if an enemy aircraft got locked on to you during those 45 seconds of vulnerability at height you were moving away from him as fast as possible to the carpet.'

According to Colonel Dick Lord, the SAAF regional commander in Namibia in 1987–88, the F-1AZ pilots often began their return journeys home at speeds of more than 600 knots at less than 15 m above the ground.

CHAPTER 6

SOUTH AFRICA'S FIRST DISASTER

The SAAF also began flying light Bosbok spotter planes at night from Rundu to Mavinga. The Bosboks were to help 32 Battalion carry out visual reconnaissance of the advancing enemy brigades and help bring in artillery fire as accurately as possible.

Hougaard particularly needed help in locating the precise positions of 21 Brigade, massing north of the Lomba alongside a small stream called the Gombe, 26 km east of the Cunzumbia-Lomba confluence. The terrain was very flat, which made 'eyes on the ground' observation by recce teams and artillery observers very difficult.

The first Bosbok took off into Angola from Rundu at dusk on Wednesday 2 September, landing at Mavinga in darkness about an hour later. It arrived as the first G-5 battery from the Artillery Regiment moved into firing positions about 21 km south of the Lomba River. With the SAAF pilot of the Bosbok was the commander of the Artillery Regiment, Commandant Johan Du Randt, as the observation officer.

SADF intelligence appreciation at the time was that 21 Brigade had anti-aircraft protection only with 23 mm guns, Sam-7 missiles and a few somewhat more sophisticated Sam-9 missiles mounted on BRDM armoured cars. 'We knew the capabilities of those weapons, so they didn't worry us,' said Hougaard. 'Flying east-west along the Lomba, the pilot kept out of their range. Du Randt, using binoculars by moonlight, brought in the first G-5 battery shots of the war. On our radio intercepts we heard both the Cubans and the Russians saying that we had hit 21's HQ.'

That night the Bosbok returned to Rundu. It could not stay at Mavinga because enemy Migs were now in the air every day from first light.

Whatever damage the G-5 fire had caused, it did not halt 21 Brigade's advance. More units continued to move up behind the advance group near the Lomba's north bank, so Hougaard asked the Bosbok to return the following night for another artillery reconnaissance mission.

The pilot reached Mavinga, refuelled, and took off again towards the Lomba, receiving radio messages from Hougaard about the positions of SADF and UNITA forces.

Then the Bosbok pilot, Lieutenant Glynn, reported that Fapla had fired an RPG-7 at the plane which had missed. Hougaard checked Glynn's position and instantly became alarmed: the plane was too far south of the Lomba to be within the maximum 500 m range of an RPG-7.

Hougaard's immediate thought was that SADF-UNITA forces south of the Lomba had fired on their own aircraft. He radioed angry messages to his own commanders, but all denied that they had fired at the tiny single-engined Bosbok weighing barely more than a tonne.

On the ground, north of the Lomba, Piet Fourie, a pocket-sized, chunky little Afrikaner, the son of a High Court judge, was sitting in a tree within 800 m of three big advance units of 21 Brigade. 'They made fires and then dampened them down. But with night sight binoculars I could pick up the glow and clearly see the circles of fires,' said Fourie, a recce sergeant with 32 Battalion.

From his tree perch Fourie was calling in SADF artillery on 21 Brigade. Then he saw a streak of fire, glowing white-hot like an oxy-acetylene blowtorch, heading skywards and southwards from a position about 25 km to his north. He recognised it immediately as a very power-ful long-distance ground-to-air missile. The SADF had assumed the Angolans would not be able to move heavy missiles, and their lumbering launch and control platforms, hundreds of kilometres across the punish-ing sands of the south-east.

Fourie sent radio messages to the Bosbok that it must get out of the area.

Independently, Hougaard was also sending messages to the Bosbok to break off and head south for Rundu and not even bother to stop at Mavinga. 'At first, I couldn't get the Bosbok, but then the pilot came on to say a second RPG-7 had exploded very near to the plane and it had shaken them. I told them to move out and then they went radio-quiet. We feared something had gone wrong ...'

Sergeant Fourie had watched two missiles flash overhead and he saw the Bosbok in the glow of the explosion from the second. Then a third missile covered 30 km and exploded near the little plane. For a split second, Fourie saw the Bosbok diving vertically towards the earth.

He was witnessing the first two South African deaths in the 1987–88 War for Africa.

★ ★ ★

The Bosbok had been flying at about 1,000 m just south of the Lomba as Fourie watched it begin its death dive. Like Fourie, Commandant Du Randt had been pinpointing 21 Brigade's positions and directing G-5 fire on to them until seconds before his death.

'I reported the Bosbok's disappearance back to Rundu with deep foreboding,' said Hougaard. 'Both Sergeant Fourie and UNITA had reported the plane had been hit by missiles. There was no real possibility that Du Randt and the pilot had survived, but we didn't know, and so we hoped they were alive. At the time our government was incredibly sensitive about anyone getting captured – they warned us: "If you let anyone get caught, you've got problems. It must never happen".'

Hougaard ordered SADF forces to begin an urgent search for the plane before the enemy could get to it. He also requested help from UNITA.

'UNITA proved then that in that type of situation you can really rely on them to do their utter best,' said Hougaard. 'Our own guys said they couldn't recover the plane because it had crashed among the enemy. But UNITA got to it. It had dived nose-first up to its wings into the marshes to the south of the Lomba.'

UNITA's tactical headquarters ordered the guerrillas to remove the plane and the bodies before Fapla could get to it. 'They cut it up and pulled it out bit by bit,' said Hougaard. By daybreak the Bosbok had been removed entirely, along with the bodies, which were sent back to Rundu by Puma the following night.

Captain Herman Mulder, busily monitoring and deciphering enemy radio communications from his intelligence headquarters, beneath camouflage netting under a tree south of the Lomba, heard the delight of the enemy as messages told of the shooting down of the SADF plane. But Fapla's use of the code word 'Cosasa' gave away the weapon they had used. From previous intelligence, Mulder realised they had fired powerful Sam-8 missiles: against a Bosbok, it was rather like crushing an ant with a steamroller. But the discovery of the steamroller – coupled with the deaths of Du Randt and Glynn, and the loss of the Bosbok – led to an immediate strategic reappraisal by SADF chiefs.

CHAPTER 7

ENTER THE FALCON

The presence of Sam-8s was unexpected and unwelcome. 'It was a very good plus point for the quality of Russian equipment,' said Durban-born Colonel Dick Lord, a graduate of the American Air Force 'Top Gun' school in Florida and a former British Royal Navy fighter-pilot. 'We had worked on the assumption that it would be used as a strategic weapon for the protection of big installations. We couldn't believe that a sophisticated weapon like that could stand up to hundreds of kilometres of *bundu*-bashing. It gave everybody a hell of a big fright.'

Herman Mulder reported that it was likely there were eight Sam-8 missile systems with the advancing Fapla brigades. The Angolans were closely following Soviet doctrine of two brigades working closely together: 47 and 59 Brigades formed one team, and 21 and 16 Brigades another. Soviet doctrine also called for one battery of Sam-8s to be attached to every pair of brigades, with each brigade receiving a troop of two Sam-8 systems.

Having failed initially to detect the Sam-8s, Hougaard decided it was likely there were yet other missile and weapons systems in the enemy brigades that threatened instant death. He sent out recce commandos on intensive patrols to look even more closely at 47, 59, 21 and 16 Brigades.

Meanwhile, there was a short halt in the SAAF bombing attacks on 47 Brigade, still edging its way bit by bit along the south bank of the Lomba. Hougaard protested, pointing out that whatever missiles or anti-aircraft guns Fapla were using, the toss-bombing technique so consistently caught them by surprise that the SAAF planes were usually five minutes into their return journey before the enemy opened fire: the enemy fire usually went on for about ten minutes in wasteful shock without any obvious kind of control and without any targets.

The SAAF withdrew the big, lumbering Canberras from the fight, but resumed hitting 47 Brigade with four or more Mirage F-1AZ toss-bombing attacks at sunrise each day.

★ ★ ★

General Jannie Geldenhuys, head of the SADF, together with his Army, Air Force and Navy chiefs, decided that the new situation called for a special man to take charge on the battlefield.

Colonel Deon Ferreira, a former commander of 32 Battalion, was kicking his heels on a joint staff course at Hoedspruit, near the Kruger Park, some 2,500 km away from the action in Angola.

Ferreira, in his early forties, knew the battle zone well. Tall, swarthy and portly, verging on tubby, he was a big man in every sense. During his time with 32 Battalion, he had been in and out of Angola regularly with his men on raids against SWAPO and in support of UNITA. In a two-day operation in May 1980, 32 Battalion attacked the southern Angolan town of Savate with three companies of infantry and a mortar platoon. Fifteen 32 Battalion soldiers died in the attack and about 40 were wounded. But the 'Buffalos' killed more than 400 Fapla soldiers defending the town. 32 Battalion then handed Savate to UNITA, who used it as a rear base for its guerrilla thrusts far north into Angola through the subsequent years.

Ferreira, the son of a farmer in the desolate Great Karoo of the Cape Province, was one of a succession of commanders who transformed 32 Battalion from a confused, bungling, ill-disciplined bunch of Angolan brigands into one of Africa's most formidable fighting forces. Ferreira was also one of a number of reformers who integrated 32 Battalion fully into the SADF, raised pay levels to those of other regular battalions, extended the number of its specialist units, and opened the way for its black recruits to become full commissioned officers and send their sons and daughters to universities in the Republic.

On Friday, 4 September 1987, Ferreira, known as 'The Falcon', was ordered by General Jannie Geldenhuys to be in Rundu that same night. He was to form, organise and take command of an understrength SADF brigade, to be known as 20 SA Brigade. It would act in Angola and make sure that the Fapla/Cuban advance was stopped. The Ferreira-led operation was codenamed 'Moduler'.

Ferreira managed to get from Hoedspruit to Windhoek on 4 September, and took charge at 20 SA Brigade's Rundu headquarters on 5 September. His arrival was greeted with enthusiasm by the men in the field. Those who had served under his command knew that the SADF would soon begin to take the initiative. Ferreira was renowned as a daring battle planner who, during his years with 32 Battalion, had first taken action in the field and only afterwards sought permission from higher authority to carry it out. He was the sort of man who constantly outraged stuffier souls among senior officers at SADF Headquarters in Pretoria.

Before one major operation, codenamed Protea, in 1981, the then Commandant Deon Ferreira, sent a letter to Major Afonse Maria, commander of the Fapla brigade based at Ongiva, in southern Angola, suggesting that the Angolan troops lie very low because 32 Battalion was about to make a major attack on their ally SWAPO. Ferreira signed the letter and titled himself 'Commander of SADF forces in Angola'. The attack was a major success, and no Fapla troops came to SWAPO's defence.

His career continued to progress because, for the most part, his daring freelance skill achieved success. However, his occasional failures were also remembered, particularly 'Operation Perfect Lemon', which he planned with his air force friend Colonel Dick Lord against a SWAPO base north of Mupa inside Angola in 1982. After weeks of meticulous planning by commanders and staff, who plotted every SWAPO position inside the Mupa camp, 16 Mirages swept in on a dawn attack and landed every bomb on target. It proved to be an expensive operation both in time and bombs wasted. In the final days before the attack, every SWAPO guerrilla moved out and not one was killed. To this day Ferreira is teased by his brother officers as the 'Managing Director' of Perfect Lemon while Lord is remembered as his 'Export Manager'.

Within hours of his arrival at Rundu, Ferreira flew in at night by Puma to establish his tactical headquarters about ten kilometres south of the Lomba so that he would not be too isolated physically from the fighting. He soon received bad news. Pierre Franken, scouting with Reconnaissance Commando Special Forces north of the Lomba, radioed in on 6 September that one South African had been killed and several others wounded in a clash with reconnaissance troops of Fapla's 59 Brigade. The good news was that one of the enemy had been captured: he was brought in for questioning and gave more precise details on the composition of 59 Brigade's units and their positions between the Cuzizi and the Cunzumbia than had yet been obtained.

Ferreira, as a precaution, quickly withdrew his tactical HQ to the position of the G-5 battery, seconded from Fourth South African Infantry (4 SAI) Battalion, some 25 km south of the Lomba. He reorganised the disparate forces in his command into two artillery-supported combat groups. Combat Group Bravo, composed mainly of companies from 32 Battalion and the Ovamboland-based 101 Battalion, with support from UNITA's 3rd semi-regular Battalion, was placed under Commandant Hartslief's control. Hartslief's area of responsibility was the southern bank of the Lomba eastwards from its confluence with the Cunzumbia. His task was to prevent 21 and 59 Brigades, and possibly 16 Brigade, from crossing the Lomba and bringing Mavinga under direct threat. Combat Group Alpha was to consist mainly of 61 Mechanised Battalion, by then on its way into Angola from its training base at Oshivelo in northern Namibia, with support from units of 32 Battalion and UNITA's semi-regular 5th Battalion: Alpha was charged with stopping Fapla's 47 Brigade, heading eastwards along the south bank of the Lomba, from forming bridgeheads and linking up with 59 and 21 Brigades.

Ferreira was adamant that Fapla's 21 Brigade, the nearest enemy force to Mavinga, must not be allowed to cross the Lomba. Like 47 Brigade, it was a very strong and experienced brigade and it was accompanied by a tactical armoured group with tanks. But, most disturbingly, South African intelligence had established that 21 Brigade had chemical weapons in its armoury. This was not a total surprise, since General Konstantin Shaganovitch was a known chemical warfare specialist.

The SADF had technical experts working on the problems of chemical warfare, but the fighting men had received only very rudimentary training in anti-gas tactics and with the kind of equipment that involved.

'Our guys got their training there and then, on the ground and in the bush at the Lomba,' said Jan Hougaard. 'Chemical detection teams were sent in from the Republic. The SADF purchased several thousand gas masks pretty quickly from somewhere or other, and we were all issued with them.'

The Chief of the Army, General Liebenberg, spent many days at Ferreira's tactical HQ trying to assess the extent of the threat. He was deeply worried because of the minimal means his forces had of countering gas and because of their total lack of experience with it.

The intelligence Liebenberg received came mainly from radio intercepts. Herman Mulder discovered that the D-30 artillery and BM-21 'Stalin Organs' with 21 Brigade had already tried unsuccessfully to fire gas shells against UNITA and the South Africans. From a series of intercepts he concluded that a round of chemical shells had been fired towards an area from where, 21 Brigade's artillery commander calculated, the gases slowly released from the shells would drift with the prevailing wind into the South African and UNITA lines.

'But the wind changed about 45 degrees, and the gas missed our positions and wafted back across the Lomba and over 21 Brigade's own trenches,' said Mulder. 'The commander of 21 Brigade told his infantry that UNITA was using chemical weapons, and Luanda in one of its war communiques made the same allegation.

'Later, a Fapla POW from 21 Brigade told me that for two days their infantry was not able to get out of their trenches because they were totally paralysed. When they recovered their commanders asked them to describe the experience in detailed debriefings. Other POWs I interrogated described yellow liquid in the chemical shells which smelt like onions or garlic.'

Mulder picked up radio intercepts in which Fapla commanders said the chemical weapons should only be committed if a withdrawal became necessary.

Hougaard also recalled radio intercepts from 47 Brigade, making painful progress of about one kilometre a day under constant night bombardment from the SADF's G-5s and MRLs and early morning bombing attacks by the Mirage F-lAZs. 'We got radio intercepts of the commander at Fapla's 6th military region headquarters at Cuito Cuanavale giving orders to 47 Brigade: "Bury your toxic bombs".' said Hougaard.

'From this we realised that Cuito Cuanavale was already anticipating 47 Brigade running into major problems.' said Hougaard. 'Later on, Cuito Cuanavale HQ was still hammering away at 47: "Did you bury those bombs, or did you destroy them?"'

CHAPTER 8

THE FIRST LAND BATTLE

Commandant Robert Hartslief set up his unit HQ for his new Combat Group Bravo command a few kilometres into the treeline southwest of the confluence of the Gombe with the Lomba. According to the intelligence he was being given, the most likely point at which 21 Brigade would try to cross the Lomba was just to the west of the Gombe confluence. There was no bridge, but UNITA had identified a good fording point: a successful crossing there would put 21 Brigade within 35 km of Mavinga with scarcely a natural obstacle in their path.

However, no immediate crossing was expected. The intelligence forecast was that 21 Brigade would wait for 47 Brigade to forge eastwards, and only then would a bridgehead be established to allow the two brigades to link up for a joint thrust on Mavinga.

Under the SADF's heavy artillery bombardments, 21 Brigade had ceased to move *en masse*. Against standard Soviet tactics, it had dispersed into units of battalion strength. Its commander was also sending out small probing teams; these tended to clutter the general intelligence picture, and specialists like Herman Mulder concentrated their attention on the main formations.

21 Brigade, by now some 125 km from its Cuito Cuanavale starting point, was also having logistics problems. 16 Brigade had abandoned all pretensions of acting as an offensive force and was concentrating on assisting 25 Brigade in ferrying logistics to its badly stretched comrades in 21 Brigade.

★ ★ ★

Everything suggested the optimal time was some way off for 21 Brigade to attempt to cross the Lomba. So it came as a great surprise to Commandant Hartslief when, late in the afternoon of Wednesday 9 September, UNITA's 3rd Battalion reported that two 450-men infantry battalions of Fapla's 21 Brigade had crossed the Lomba on foot to establish a bridgehead.

Hartslief sent a small reconnaissance force to the crossing point at Cariata, a small abandoned African village 16 km to the west of where the SADF was waiting for the Angolan force. The 21 Brigade battalions had set up a foothold base just in the treeline about three kilometres to the south of the Lomba. The UNITA 3rd Battalion had forward foxholes about 500 m from Fapla's outer trenches.

The reconnaissance force consisted of a troop of four Ratel-90 anti-tank armoured cars and two 120-strong companies of 101 Battalion riflemen in 30 Casspir infantry combat vehicles. Hartslief was still waiting for the arrival of his own Ratel-90 command vehicle fitted with four radios, tape recorders, a map table and air conditioning to cool an interior super-heated by the equipment packed into it.

On the morning of Thursday 10 September, with the 21 Brigade bridgehead still in place, Ferreira ordered Hartslief: 'Sort them out.'

Hartslief launched his attack with the two companies of 101 Battalion and the four Ratel-90s. Further back, in reserve were eight Ratels under the command of Major Hannes Nortmann of 32 Battalion. Nortmann, a tall, wiry, dreamy-looking man in his late twenties, was a career officer on the verge of establishing a reputation as one of the most formidable armour fighters in the SADF.

At first light on 10 September, shortly after Hartslief had commenced his attack, Nortmann was astonished to spot a TMM mobile bridge across the river about one kilometre to the east of the 21 Brigade positions. As the sun rose higher, Nortmann saw Fapla engineers putting finishing touches to the mobile bridge while infantrymen stood around very casually hands in pockets watching the work.

From his position in the treeline, Nortmann watched the enemy activity at the bridge across a three kilometre-wide stretch of flat, marshy grassland. All the time he was providing a running commentary to Ferreira in the Brigade HQ.

Ferreira ordered Nortmann to hold back. 'Wait, wait, wait,' said Ferreira. 'Let's see what's going to happen here. If they come over that open space they will commit suicide.'

Then a BRDM armoured scout car rolled towards the bridge. The moment Nortmann reported the armoured car was on the bridge, Ferreira ordered: 'Shoot it.'

A South African ZT3 anti-tank missile, making its debut in warfare and fresh off the first production line, sped across the grassland. It destroyed the BRDM, and all the soldiers standing around it were killed. A second ZT3 destroyed the giant Soviet GAZ truck which had been adapted for laying the bridge.

The ZT3s, untested in battle until that day in September 1987 and still on the official secret list to this day, was developed by Armscor in the teeth of the international arms embargo. It has a range of 3,5 km which is claimed by the SADF to be longer than any other modern anti-tank weapon. It has possibly been developed from NATO's Milan missile with the help of some of the many West European weapons engineers hired to develop the Republic's fast-growing arms industry.

Nortmann commanded the only four Ratel-90s which at that time had been adapted to fire ZT3 missiles. A special turret had to be built for those Ratel-90s which were converted to Ratel-ZT3s.

After shooting out the BRDM and the GAZ truck, Nortmann was shocked to notice five T-54 tanks already on the south bank of the Lomba and heading westwards to ambush Hartslief's force which was embattled with the two 21 Brigade battalions a kilometre away. With his Ratel-ZT3s and four conventional Ratel-90s, Nortmann immediately attacked the tanks, knocking out three of the tanks within minutes while the other two retreated back across the river.

Meanwhile, Hartslief's fight with 21 Brigade went on throughout 10 September, with G-5, MRL and 120 mm mortar teams providing artillery support. The ground battle continued into 11 September; one Fapla battalion had virtually been destroyed while the other retreated in disarray to the north of the Lomba River to regroup.

For many days afterwards vehicles and tanks from 21 Brigade kept forming up in the northern treeline and probing to find crossing points across the Lomba. The SADF deterred them with Ratel-90, Ratel-ZT3 and artillery fire.

While this cat and mouse game went on, Ferreira deduced from intelligence reports that one of the main objectives of 21 Brigade's efforts was to locate and destroy the SADF's G-5s.

'The G-5s were giving them a lot of problems, so day-in, day-out they had been trying to locate them with their Migs and Sukhois,' said Jan Hougaard. 'But they flew too high and our daytime camouflage was too good.'

The G-5 teams had plenty of warning of the approach of enemy aircraft. Recce commandos hugging the African earth near the runways at Cuito Cuanavale and Menongue immediately reported by radio every time Fapla warplanes took to the sky.

Hougaard said the recces' early warnings were vital: 'The G-5s had started shooting during the day. It had become necessary to take the risk as 21, 59 and 47 Brigades continued pushing forward. But it's not easy to camouflage a whole G-5 battery. It takes a lot of activity because there are a lot of support vehicles, so the alerts in good time by the recces were well appreciated.'

A piece of intelligence that worried Ferreira heavily, however, was that Soviet military advisers had suddenly become very active on Fapla's artillery fire control radio networks. One Russian voice in particular was clearly directing the whole artillery support plan for 21 Brigade. 'Even though the bridge and the vehicles had been destroyed, they were still preparing for a big attack,' said Hougaard. 'We could hear the Russians talking about how they were going to use a lot of artillery and bring in a lot of airstrikes.'

Deon Ferreira was particularly worried that the Soviets might give Fapla permission to use gas, especially in view of his own forces' limited ability to combat it.

Then on 22 September, SADF radio engineers picked up a message that Fapla had decided to use gas against the South Africans. 'I checked the wind direction, and immediately ordered the movement of all SADF forces 15 km eastwards,' said Ferreira. Hartslief and Nortmann were very upset at what they saw as an unnecessary retreat when they held the advantage over 21 Brigade.

However, soon after the tactical withdrawal had been completed, Fapla launched a massive artillery bombardment on the vacated South African positions. 'It was the biggest and best co-ordinated attack they carried out in the entire war,' said Jan Hougaard. 'Their planes and artillery came in for four hours.'

The SADF picked up radio messages indicating that 21 Brigade believed the South Africans had suffered heavy losses and that the survivors had withdrawn. 'The Boers have gone,' reported one Fapla commander. The radio intercepts indicated that 21 Brigade was preparing to move its remaining forces back across the river to the south bank of the Lomba.

Ferreira wanted to move Hartslief's Combat Group Bravo back quickly to 21 Brigade's crossing point to staunch a potential deadly wound in the body of the SADF-UNITA defences. But he was still worried that gas had been used, and, when he sought the locations of the specialised chemical detection teams, he learned that they were too far back to arrive and do their work in time to permit Hartslief to move in quickly enough to stop 21 Brigade consolidating a position on the southern Lomba.

The SADF soldiers who now drew the short straw were 32 Battalion's own reconnaissance commandos, introduced as a new arm of the unit by Ferreira when he was the Buffalo commander. He chose them to probe the bombed positions and report whether gas had been used.

Two men were taken in a Ratel and then dropped to walk forward into the abandoned SADF trenches, strung out through the treeline for some three kilometres.

Much to their surprise and relief the recces found a small group of UNITA soldiers sitting in the trenches smoking, having survived the whole enemy bombardment. When the astounded commandos asked the UNITA men whether they felt sick or something similar, Jan Hougaard said they replied: 'No, we're fine, but that bombing was a big, big, heavy story.'

The UNITA troops said they had watched a Fapla reconnaissance team cross the river and explore the distant western end of the trenches before returning to 21 Brigade.

Word that all was well was sent back quickly by the 32 Battalion recces to Colonel Ferreira, who ordered Combat Group Bravo to return to the crossing without delay.

Hartslief's forces were moving back among the abandoned trenches as 21 Brigade formed up on the north bank and started to advance across the Lomba by yet another unsighted mobile bridge.

Hougaard recalled: 'We couldn't believe it at HQ as we got the reports from Commandant Hartslief at the front. He said he could see at least two battalions of infantry stretched out single file, with tanks among them, coming across the river.'

Hartslief waited until the infantry were strung out across the *anhara* flood plain, some three to four kilometres wide, to the south of the river. Then he ordered a bombardment by the G-5s, MRLs and 120 mm mortars, while the ZT3s aimed for the tanks. As the Fapla troops began retreating in fear and panic across the plain, with its alternating patches of firm and marshy ground, Hartslief released the 30 Casspirs of 101 Battalion and the Ratels of 32 Battalion. The 101 Battalion troops poured rifle fire through the portholes of the Casspirs while the 32 Battalion troops sprayed the retreating enemy with 7,6 mm machine-gun and 20 mm high explosive cannon fire.

'They were running into the marshy areas and trying to hide among the reeds,' said Jan Hougaard. 'But our guys were riding behind them and killing them in the water. They were crying and shouting and pleading not to be killed. Most of them were just youngsters and they couldn't believe what was happening to them.'

Robbie Hartslief went on: 'They presented fine targets for our machine-guns, mortars and artillery. The G-5s destroyed the mobile bridge. Our machine-guns mowed down their infantry as they fled into the mud and struggled.'

At the end of the short encounter, the South Africans quickly counted more than 300 dead on the battlefield from 21 Brigade, but estimated the enemy's total losses in all the September encounters at 400 to 600 dead. The SADF had suffered only one man slightly wounded from shrapnel.

21 Brigade, although partly emasculated, continued to make desultory efforts to cross at the same point, but were easily repulsed by Battle Group Bravo. Ferreira, well-acquainted with the inflexibility of Soviet military doctrine, nevertheless marvelled at the futility of the exercise: 'It is unbelievable that a tenet can be so rigid that it can force people to commit suicide all the time.'

It was only when the battle was over that Hartslief at last took delivery of his command vehicle.

CHAPTER 9

THE SECOND 'RUMBLE ON THE LOMBA'

No sooner was the initial 10 September 'rumble on the Lomba' with 21 Brigade over than the SADF-UNITA force faced a new threat *(before the 22 September gas warfare alert)*. During the evening of Friday 11 September UNITA's General Chilingutila, liaising directly with Ferreira at the South African's tactical HQ, had reported that another Fapla detachment about two battalions in strength had appeared on the south bank of the Lomba: the force was about six kilometres to the east of the Lomba-Cuzizi source.

The first intelligence assessment was that 59 Brigade, moving aggressively and cohesively from the north, had managed to bridge the Lomba and push men and machines across the river. This would not have been entirely unexpected, for Sergeant Piet Fourie, shadowing the movements of the main 59 Brigade formation, had reported on the enemy brigade with considerable regard. One of its battalions was made up of *Luta Contra Banditos* (War Against Bandits) troops, who had been particularly well trained by former anti-guerrilla commandos of the Portuguese colonial army in Angola. The Portuguese, who had once earned their living killing MPLA guerrillas, had been recruited to help their old adversaries by the pro-MPLA 'Red Admiral,' Rosa Coutinho, of the Portuguese Navy.

Fourie and his men positioned themselves at nights within 300 m of 59 Brigade's positions and then guided in artillery fire. 'We could hear them talking, and after each bombardment they would swear and

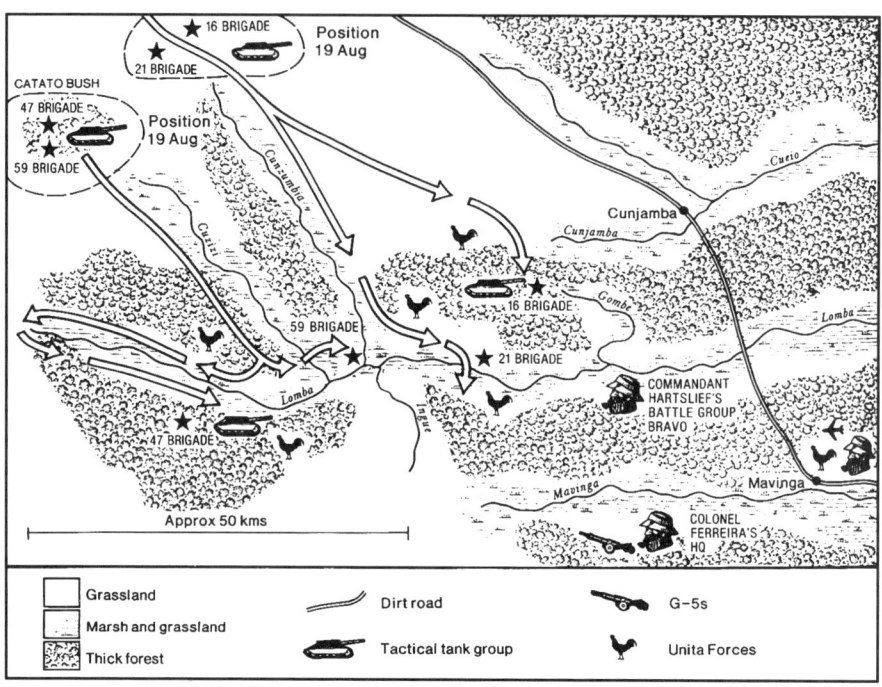

Positions of Fapla, SADF and UNITA Troops immediately prior to the battle between Fapla's 21 Brigade and the SADF's Battle group BRAVO 13 September 1987.

laugh and shout out something like "This is our land, and we're not scared of you South Africans. Come on, try again!" I felt like shouting back "OK, we're going to!" But I just kept quiet. At one stage they were doing their shouting and then a really solid bombardment came in, and the next moment you heard young men crying and screaming in agony for help.'

The belief subsequently developed that it was 47 Brigade's tactical armour group, the Brigade's highly mobile and autonomous 'extra fist', rather than 59 Brigade, that had moved eastwards with lightning speed to establish the position.

But whoever it was, they had to be attacked because it was clear that 47 and 59 Brigades were trying to link up on the Lomba. It was among Ferreira's highest priorities to keep the enemy brigades spread over the widest possible front and prevent them joining up to give each other mutual physical support.

Hartslief was ordered to move his Combat Group Bravo back into the fray to prevent 59 Brigade from crossing the Lomba and linking up with 47 Brigade's tactical group.

'I studied the map and all the intelligence immediately available, and it seemed clear that Fapla was taking up positions in an old UNITA logistics base,' said Hartslief. 'I knew the base well because I had been there a few times. It was spread out over a huge area and honeycombed with foxholes and zig-zag trenches, some of them three metres deep, enough to swallow our Ratels.'

The base, in the treeline, extended about three kilometres from east to west and two kilometres from south to north. At the eastern end of the base the bush was light and allowed good visibility. It gradually thickened towards the west where the trees and undergrowth were very dense. Huts were scattered throughout the base. One rough sand track ran through it from east to west; another track branched off it to the northern edge of the base. Between the northern edge of the base, running along the treeline, and the Lomba there was a two kilometre-wide stretch of open *anhara*.

Captain Herman Mulder and his intelligence team were hard at work interpreting interceptions of enemy radio communications and reports from SADF recce teams and forward artillery observers to give Hartslief a more sophisticated picture of the force he would confront. 'I also listened to reports by UNITA commandos,' said Mulder. 'These were passed on by UNITA's own intelligence officers. But I had battles with those guys every day. There was a tendency to give disinformation to try and get more action from the SADF side. So all the time their intelligence material had to be treated with utmost caution.'

Mulder concluded that the Fapla force was probably composed of two battalions of the main 47 Brigade, although he also believed some companies or platoons of 59 may have crossed the river to join it. However, the most dangerous threat to Hartslief's combat group lay not within the old logistics base, but three kilometres further west. It was there that 47 Brigade's tactical armour group seemed to be assembling, although earlier intelligence had suggested the tank force was some ten kilometres away.

Hartslief wanted to attack at first light on Saturday 12 September. But there were problems with logistics and vehicle repairs after the first battle with 21 Brigade, and so he was forced to delay by 24 hours: 'If 47 Brigade's tactical group intervened I calculated the battle could be prolonged for up to two days. So I had to make sure all the vehicles were stacked with the full amount of ammunition.'

Hartslief declined an offer of direct UNITA infantry help for the attack. But a UNITA liaison officer, Major Mickey, joined Hartslief's Ratel-90 to guide the combat group into the logistics base. 'He took us in so many wrong directions that the attack, which I had planned for 6 am, didn't begin until 11 am,' said Hartslief.

★ ★ ★

Mac da Trinidada and his 32 Battalion recce team slept in bush on the south side of the Lomba on the Saturday night as they prepared to cross the river on a reconnaissance mission behind 59 Brigade's lines. He watched the Ratel-90s of 32 Battalion and Casspirs of 101 Battalion move west early on Sunday along the old Portuguese 'road', a barely discernible sand track.

On top of one of the Ratels was Captain 'Mac' Macallum, the commander of 32 Battalion's Foxtrot infantry company. One Foxtrot platoon, composed of black Angolan refugees, had been ordered to go forward in the Ratels to provide close infantry support during the attack. The young white national servicemen crewing the Ratels were very frightened, and so Macallum, a battle-hardened veteran, decided to accompany them to give them mettle.

Macallum, a close friend of Mac da Trinidada, spotted the black Angolan and his recce team and shouted down to them: 'We're going into a big punch-up against lots of enemy and maybe some tanks. Don't be selfish buggers. Save some of that whisky in your flasks for me.'

Da Trinidada laughed and gave Macallum a thumbs-up sign. About an hour after one Mac had waved farewell to the other, Da Trinidada received orders to forget his mission among 59 Brigade and to march his men westwards to make themselves available for the battle as well.

★ ★ ★

Hartslief reached the eastern entrance of the base with his force and, having become confused by UNITA's intelligence, quickly encountered problems.

A UNITA radio report said the enemy were no longer deployed in the logistics base itself, but in new positions two kilometres to the west of it. Hartslief refused to accept that, and he called in 120 mm mortar fire before pushing deeper into the base, moving his vehicles on the straight and narrow 'road' axis to avoid running into the deep trench systems.

'In fact, there were no enemy at all on the eastern side of the base,' said Hartslief. 'So I thought, OK, this time UNITA are right. We can drive right on through the base past all the trenches and just do a straight-forward mechanised attack on them. In the base, where Fapla had the advantage of the trenches, our infantry would have had to deploy from the Casspirs and Ratels to carry the brunt of the fighting.'

Then, as the column reached the centre of the base, Major Mickey tapped Hartslief on the shoulder and told him he must not go any further: the enemy was now very close, *inside* the logistics base, said Mickey. 'I was white-hot with fury,' said Hartslief. 'I realised immediately that UNITA had decided not to tell me the truth beforehand for some strange reason of their own. They actually *knew* at that time that the enemy was in the base. The only thing I understand about that behaviour was that it threatened to get my men killed.'

Hartslief had no time there and then for a blazing row with UNITA. He quickly called in artillery fire from the G-5s and 120 mm mortars, which put down shells within 200 m of his units. He had no forward observers, so he had to guess where the enemy might be. This drew an ineffectual Fapla mortar response, with the bombs landing between the SADF vehicles.

Hartslief's little force – eight Ratel-90s, four Ratel-ZT3s, and some 200 infantrymen aboard the Casspirs – continued probing east to west across the base, but after about 500 m the leading company commander spotted large numbers of enemy infantry to his right and reported that they were withdrawing to the north.

Hartslief ordered his column to swing north and pursue the retreating enemy across a landscape pitted with deep trenches. As the SADF vehicles threaded their way between the earthworks, their crews readied the guns for the heavy firing that would soon begin. In the Ratel-90s the gunners selected special shells which spread anti-personnel shot in a wide and murderous arc. The 200-round disintegrating steel-link ammunition belts feeding into the three 7.6 mm machine-guns atop each Ratel were checked; back-up ammunition was made ready, for each belt would spit out its 200 steel darts of death in less than a minute. Smoke grenades were prepared for the mortar launchers at the sides of the turrets. Aboard the Casspirs infantrymen manned the 7.6 mm machine-guns and 20 mm cannons on top of the armoured infantry combat vehicles, while inside riflemen prepared to pour out R-4 assault rifle fire from a dozen tiny firing slits.

Combat Group Bravo passed through two lines of residual Fapla infantry and caught up with the main body of fleeing soldiers where the treeline met the *anhara*. The Angolans, realising they could not escape across the grassland and marsh, started running northwestwards along the treeline. But there was no escape. The Ratels and Casspirs spewed cannon, machine-gun and rifle fire among them, and soon some 200 Fapla soldiers lay dead on the tree-lined fringes of the Lomba marshes. Jackals and hyenas would pick their bones, and relations back home would probably never know where or how their sons, brothers and husbands died.

Now the combat group concentrated on mopping up small pockets of straggling Fapla infantry who fought on with great bravery. Pierre Franken, for once not behind enemy lines bringing in artillery fire, had accompanied the combat group as an observer in a Buffel, a lightly armoured troop transporter not designed for prolonged cross-country travel. The Buffel, along with two of the Ratels, got wedged into one of the giant trenches.

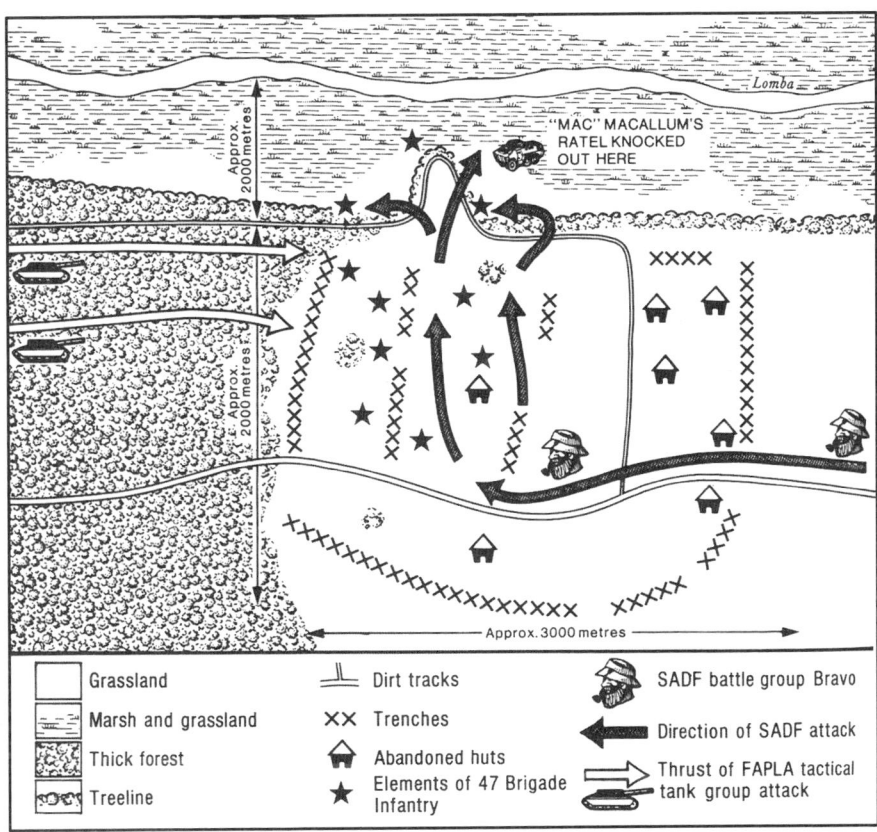

SADF Battle group Bravo's 13 September 1987 battle on the Lomba with elements of Fapla's 47 Brigade.

Major Theo Wilken, commander of a 120 mm mortar battery, was travelling in Hartslief's Ratel as fire support co-ordinator between the G-5 battery, the mortar batteries, and two young officers who had gone forward with the infantry in Franken's normal artillery forward observation role. As bullets pinged against the Ratel's armour, Wilken saw a Fapla soldier with an RPG-7 anti-tank rocket launcher creeping up on Franken's Buffel. Wilken grabbed his R-4 rifle, developed from the Israeli Galil assault rifle, pushed open one of the hatches above the troop compartment, and shot the Fapla man.

Then Hartslief spotted Fapla infantry close by on his left. 'I only had time to scream "shoot them" at everyone,' said Hartslief. 'There were at

least four Fapla soldiers within three metres of the Ratel.' Popping out
of the hatch again, Wilken was in time to see Major Mickey – who had
clung to the outside of the Ratel throughout the battle and miraculously
survived – open fire on the Fapla men with his AK-47 rifle. Wilken joined
in with his R-4 and soon the little knot of enemy soldiers all lay dead.

Hartslief was told that to his right a third Ratel was pulling out one
of the two Ratels entrapped in the trenches. In every direction he could
see Casspirs mopping up little groups of infantrymen with cannon and
machine-gun fire.

All seemed to be going well when Major Nortmann, Hartslief's second-in-command for this battle, received a radio message from Lieutenant
Alves, leader of a Ratel troop (four Ratels per troop). Alves, some 500 m
ahead of Nortmann, said there were enemy tanks to his left. Alves then
went off the air: a few moments later a sergeant came on the radio and
said Alves had been shot through the neck and was dead. Alves's white
national serviceman driver, shocked by the lieutenant's death, drove wildly
into the open *anhara* and became bogged down in deep mud.

'The sergeant called for help,' recalled Hartslief. 'I told him to fire a smoke
grenade so that we could locate them and send a recovery vehicle to get
them out. But then a T-55 tank exploded out of the bush from nowhere,
ignored two of our mobile Ratels and went straight between them for
Alves's vehicle. It stopped just 25 m from the Ratel and fired one shell into it,
killing everybody on board. Then it withdrew as suddenly as it had arrived.'

Combat Group Bravo's position had deteriorated seriously. Enemy
tanks were causing chaos; and Hartslief's communications with some of
his troop and company commanders had broken down. The thin-shelled
Casspirs were in particular trouble with the tanks. Everywhere they were
fleeing as fast as they could before determined tank thrusts, surviving
only because the bush was so thick that the enemy tank commanders
and gunners did not have clear lines of fire.

One T-54 tank burst from thick bush, like some rampaging rhinoceros
stung by a swarm of angry hornets, in pursuit of a Casspir fleeing like the
wind. The Casspir was throwing smoke grenades of every colour – orange,
white, green, yellow – at the T-54 on its tail. 'It was like a combined scene
from *Apocalypse Now* and the *Keystone Cops,*' said Hartslief. The tank's gun

turret was pointing to the rear because it was unable to swivel in the dense vegetation: instead, it was trying to ram the Casspir.

The Casspir disappeared into another clump of thick bush. The tank cut sideways, stopped, swivelled its gun and opened fire from 150 m on armoured ambulances and recovery vehicles grouped under Nortmann's command. The first tank shell went under one of the armoured ambulances, which have about 40 cm of clearance: a second just missed the rear of the same ambulance which had slithered forwards in the choking sand after the first shell missed.

The tank opened fire on another Casspir which appeared in the clearing. The shell detonated in the branches of a tree just above the open top of the Casspir, severely wounding Commandant Bert Sachse, a Parachute Brigade officer who had been sent to Angola to liaise with UNITA.

The tank traversed again and fired a shell which missed Hartslief's Ratel-90 only narrowly. Hartslief's gunner was unable to get a sighting on the tank, but Hartslief ordered him to fire to raise a dust screen between the tank and the Ratel. As the dust began to settle the gunner acquired the tank in his sights. It had swivelled and now presented a bigger, side-onwards target. Nine high explosive anti-tank (HEAT) shells were fired rapidly at the tank. Two shells penetrated the vulnerable turret base, setting the tank ablaze and forcing the crewmen to evacuate.

With his first enemy tank under his belt, Hartslief ordered the Casspirs to withdraw while the Ratels continued to engage the T-54/55s and rescue mired vehicles.

'The tanks had surprised us,' said Hartslief. 'UNITA's intelligence had failed again. They had told us we would be up against PT-76s [thin skinned armoured vehicles which are similar to the Ratel inasmuch as they have no stabilising system for the main gun, which makes it impossible for them to fire while on the move]. We were confident of taking PT-76s on and knocking them out.

'But there is no military manual which advises you to take on a T-54 with a Ratel. The T-54 can shoot much further than a Ratel. It fires more effective anti-tank ammunition, because its gun is more robust and of a bigger calibre. It has very much thicker armour protection. With the stabilising system for their guns, the T-54s and T-55s can shoot on the move.

'All in all, it isn't advisable for a Ratel to pick a fight with a T-54. But in that dense kind of bush the Ratel had a chance. The T-54 lost the advantage given it by the range of its gun, and its manoeuvrability compared unfavourably in those circumstances.

'A couple of Ratels which hadn't got stuck in the trenches actually flaunted themselves in front of the T-54s, and then they withdrew into the bush as the tanks chased them. The Ratels then turned in ever smaller circles with the tanks chasing them until the Ratels, being more manoeuvrable, came up on the tanks from behind and shot them out. That was good old Boer guerrilla tactics, invented on the spot. It wasn't a trick we'd thought about beforehand.'

Meanwhile, Major Hannes Nortmann had embarked on one of those single-handed bouts of manic courage which mark many battles but which cannot be pre-planned.

Driven by the generals' imperative that no men and no equipment must be lost, Nortmann leapt out of his Ratel into a trench and ran along it to ask Hartslief where the combat group's crippled vehicles were stuck. Hartslief, who had been concentrating fully on his encounter with the tank, had no idea. Nortmann ran back again to his line of armoured ambulances and recovery vehicles. Moving off again on foot to find the stranded Ratels and other vehicles, Nortmann ordered a sergeant, Rian Rupping, to follow him in a recovery truck. Nortmann met the crew of one of the trapped Ratels, who said they thought men might still be alive in Alves's Ratel which had been shot out by the tank on the *anhara*. With artillery shells and mortar bombs exploding all around him as small fights continued everywhere, Nortmann sprinted out of the treeline over the open grassland to check the crippled Ratel. He quickly saw that Alves and the driver were dead, and then ammunition aboard the smoking vehicle exploded. Nortmann narrowly avoided death when a metal door blown off in the blast flew just over his head and landed 40 m away. Realising that no one could survive the inferno, Nortmann sprinted back again to the treeline through a hail of Fapla small-arms fire.

Nortmann climbed into the recovery vehicle with Rupping and joined up with two Ratels. They moved off together, but when Nortmann spotted one of the trapped Ratels he again jumped down and ran towards it. As he ran round the vehicle he came across a Fapla infantryman who was levelling his AK-47. Nortmann fired first from the hip with his R-4, killing the Angolan. Then another Fapla soldier who had been looting the Ratel burst out of the main troop compartment and started running. Nortmann fired round after round at the fleeing infantryman and could not understand why it took so long before he at last fell dead. Closer inspection showed that looted ration tins in the soldier's back pack had stopped many of the R-4 bullets.

Nortmann entered the Ratel's main troop compartment. The food, weapons and ammunition had been looted by Fapla. All that was left was the black sack containing the Ratel's camouflage net. Nortmann was about to leave when he saw the sack move slightly. He kicked it and heard a small, strangled cry. Ripping open the sack, he found the Ratel's young driver in a state of catatonic fear. He had hidden in the sack as the Fapla men approached the armoured car and almost incredibly they had failed to spot him. After his ordeal, the young man could barely speak and he later suffered a nervous breakdown. Nortmann waved in the recovery vehicle to pull the Ratel free. As they worked they saw more Fapla tanks in the far distance coming towards them. As the tanks came nearer, the Ratel was at last tugged free and Nortmann drove it to safety behind the recovery vehicle. Nortmann and Rupping then returned and recovered another two Ratels and Franken's Buffel. Both men were subsequently awarded the Honoris Crux decoration, one of South Africa's highest awards for bravery in battle.

Hartslief finally told Combat Group Bravo to break off the fight when he received information that six more tanks were on their way from 47 Brigade to join in the battle.

He informed Colonel Ferreira, who ordered his reserve combat group, Charlie, to move forward and recover or destroy vehicles abandoned on the terrain. It was now dark, and the group had not received any illumination shells. Major Dawid Lotter, the commander of Combat Group Charlie, ordered several huts in the vicinity to be set ablaze, and by the light of the fires two Casspirs were taken back and two which were irrecoverable were blown to bits.

All seemed to be going well when just before midnight Lotter's combat group was ambushed by eight T-55 tanks at a distance of about 100 m. Confusion reigned among Lotter's force, which also came under fire from Fapla artillery on the northern side of the Lomba. Worse still, Lotter could not call in all SADF artillery because some elements of it had begun redeploying after Hartslief's battle, not anticipating that Lotter would encounter major enemy forces. That Lotter was able to reorganise his force and begin a withdrawal in 100 m bounds was largely due to the bravery of Lieutenant Johannes Kooij of 61 Mechanised Battalion who organised a troop of four Ratel-90s to join battle with the tanks and to cover the main withdrawal. Using similar Boer guerrilla tactics to Combat Group Bravo's, and taking advantage of the Ratel's superior mobility, Kooij himself shot out two tanks and was later also awarded the Honoris Crux.

Thanks largely to Kooij, Combat Group Charlie emerged from the encounter with only two wounded. A soldier in one of the Ratels' crew was seriously injured by the recoil of the anti-tank gun. Another was badly shocked when a bullet penetrated his battle helmet and became partly embedded in his skull. The bullet was simply plucked out and he was soon back in battle. UNITA, however, suffered major losses when its infantrymen got caught between the Ratels and T-54/55s.

Hartslief returned to the battlefield with Bravo on Monday 14 September for mopping-up operations. His count showed that Fapla had lost between 250 and 300 men. Five enemy tanks and a truck had been destroyed and a TMM bridging vehicle captured. His own losses were eight dead and four wounded. One Ratel and two Casspirs had been destroyed.

For Hartslief it had been a very intense personal experience: 'It's a terrible shock to be confronted by a T-54 tank when you're not up against it in a tank of your own. The first thing that strikes you is that a T-54 is big and that its gun is very long. That and the dreadful noise of battle and the unbelievable dust all contributed to the terrible shock effect.' Hartslief was also nursing a badly burned hand. In his Ratel's fight with the tank, he acted as gun loader, but in the intensity of combat forgot to pull on the special gloves which give protection against the great heat which builds up under constant firing in the steel of the anti-tank gun's breech.

★ ★ ★

Mac da Trinidada arrived on the battlefield on 13 September in time to join in some of the skirmishes. He saw the Ratel-90 exploding and burning on the *anhara* after Nortmann had made his dramatic rescue attempt. What Da Trinidada learned later was that the Ratel was the last resting place of his friend 'Mac' Macallum and the untested young national servicemen.

In 32 Battalion they say that Macallum's ghost lives on. He was a popular man, with no enemies, and a strong soldier. Whenever there are minor problems at 32 Battalion, such as cars going missing for illicit trips into town by the ranks, the black troops say: 'Ah, it was not us. It must be Captain Mac who is back among us.'

★ ★ ★

With 21 Brigade's attempted crossing of the Lomba foiled and 47 and 59 Brigades' planned link-up thwarted, Jonas Savimbi rested easier at his tactical HQ near Mavinga. Colonel Ferreira had been told by Savimbi that UNITA intelligence showed that Fapla intended taking Mavinga by Thursday 17 September. On 18 September Savimbi told Ferreira: 'If it hadn't been for the SADF forces, Fapla would have been here yesterday.'

But the pressure was still on. Both 59 and 21 Brigades were still near the north bank of the Lomba trying to find ways of pushing across, and the main body of 47 Brigade was still probing eastwards along the south bank of the Lomba in its attempt to establish bridgeheads for 59 and 21 Brigades.

Ferreira instructed Hartslief's Combat Group Bravo to concentrate on stopping further crossings by 59 and 21 Brigades, while Combat Group Alpha concentrated on the priority objective of knocking 47 Brigade out of the war.

PART 3

THE STING

When Boer Commandant-General Piet Joubert argued against pursuing the defeated English at Nicholson's Nek, he quoted the Dutch aphorism: 'When God holds out a finger don't take the whole hand.' Corporal Isaac Malherbe thought that might be sound theology, but it was no good in making war.

Colonel Deneys Reitz,
in *Commando − A Boer Journal of the Boer War.*

In war there is no second prize for the runner-up.

US World War II **General Omar Bradley.**

CHAPTER 10

WAITING AND WATCHING

Captain Piet van Zyl arrived from his mountain farm in northern Natal to join Battle Group Bravo on 13 September. A former national serviceman who was now an officer with a Natal Commando of the part-time Citizen Force, the tall, blond Afrikaner adventurer had volunteered for regular spells of duty with 32 Battalion in times of need. Ferreira cabled him to say this was one of those times. So, leaving his cattle and sheep herds in the care of his chief Zulu stockman and having instructed his brother on procedures during the coming potato harvest, Van Zyl reached the Lomba on 13 September, the day Captain 'Mac' Macallum was killed on the river's floodplain.

He was ordered to take command of Macallum's Foxtrot company, now consisting of one platoon of 30 black Angolan infantrymen with four Ratels and another platoon of infantrymen protecting Bravo's MRL battery. On 14 September he joined Foxtrot at their position to the south of the Lomba, opposite 21 Brigade's main position on the north bank of the river, 12 km to the east of the Lomba-Cunzumbia confluence. Enemy tanks shot out in the battle of 10 September were still out on the *anhara*.

When Van Zyl arrived he was asked by Major Nortmann – in temporary command of Bravo while Hartslief visited Mavinga to receive new orders – to take charge also of 32 Battalion's 81 mm mortar platoon. Nearby were the MRLs, another 32 Battalion company, a 101 Battalion company and the 32 Battalion recces' rest and recuperation camp.

As Van Zyl settled in, he felt almost as if the war was unreal. Barely three kilometres away across the river he could see the Fapla trenches. Every day enemy soldiers strolled down casually from the treeline to fetch water. 'When Mac da Trinidada arrived for a period of R and R, he couldn't believe how near the Fapla were and how much noise they made at night,' said Van Zyl. 'There were lights blazing, little generators humming, doors slamming, fires being lit for coffee.'

Combat Group Bravo was ordered *not* to cross the Lomba. It was to block 21 Brigade's path southwards while SADF artillery and the South African Air Force, guided in by the recce teams and forward observers, pounded 21 and 59 Brigades relentlessly, taking out more and more of their anti-aircraft capabilities and wearing down their will to persist.

On the night of 15–16 September Van Zyl was unable to sleep as Pierre Franken, having infiltrated right inside 59 Brigade's lines with recces of 5 Reconnaissance Commando the previous night, brought down some hundred or so 43.5 kg shells from the G-5s on key targets. The giant artillery pieces were so overstrained that tragedy struck.

One gun suffered a 'cook-off', an explosion of a shell in the breech. One of the six-man crew was killed instantly and the rest badly wounded. There was nothing left of the nine metre-long gun except a blackened steel stump. The wounded were in such bad condition that the Puma helicopters broke their normal rule of night operations only and came in by day to take the stricken gunners back to Rundu.

An inquiry into the accident concluded that the 'cook-off' occurred in the gun barrel when it became extremely hot after firing many rounds of ammunition. At this stage of the war each G-5 was firing up to 80 shells per day. The inquiry team concluded that a shell, lying in the overheated barrel, had exploded after a forward observer had ordered: 'Stop firing.' The barrel heat had transferred to the stationary projectile and an explosion had followed. This led to an adjustment of fire order procedures. 'Stop firing' was replaced by a 'cease loading' order from the forward observers – that is, the loaded round would be fired, but no more shells would be put into the breech until fresh orders were given to resume firing.

Though the SADF recces were regularly pinpointing key 59 and 21 Brigade positions and bringing in heavy bombardments, Combat Group Bravo had to dig in deep against very intense Fapla bombardments. Every day the B-10, D-30 and BM-21 shells would come down while from far overhead the Migs were dropping bombs, albeit inaccurately.

Piet van Zyl remembers sitting on the pit latrine when a shell from a D-30,122 mm gun broke the sound barrier as it hurtled over his head. A second came. Van Zyl ran and jumped down a three metre-deep foxhole. Shells were raining in, joined by 82 mm mortar bombs. 'The noise was appalling,' said Van Zyl, 'and there was sand and earth pouring down on us in barrow-loads. When the firing stopped three of my men were completely buried and we had to dig them out.' There were constant bombardments like these which took out a number of the SADF's softer skinned vehicles.

The deep foxholes saved many lives, but they could also be traps for the unwary.

Admiral Dries Putter, the CSI chief, was among the many VIPs who visited the front from time to time. On one occasion, General Jannie Geldenhuys, Chief of the SADF, and Lieutenant-General Kat Liebenberg, Chief of the Army, were there at the same time as the Admiral. As usual, the generals wore the same combat drabs as the troopies and shared their bully beef and boiled rice from tiffin tins. The Navy, however, has a reputation for sartorial elegance and doing everything in style, and Geldenhuys and Liebenberg entered Admiral Putter's tent to find him in immaculate white uniform sitting down at a neatly laid table and being served by his batman with a succulent steak and good red wine.

Geldenhuys and Liebenberg, their mouths watering, politely refused the wine they were offered and went their more prosaic ways. Towards midnight, taking a walk outside before retiring to bed, they were taken aback to see the SADF's intelligence supremo approaching soaked in sweat and his once trim white uniform crumpled and covered in red dirt. Admiral Putter saluted ceremoniously, wished the generals good night, and re-entered his tent, offering no explanation for his appearance.

Only after the war did he admit to Geldenhuys and Liebenberg that, strolling after his meal, he had fallen into one of the foxholes. Reluctant to suffer the chaffing that would inevitably come from the generals if he called for rescue from his ignominious position, he spent more than two hours digging away the sides of the foxhole with his hands to form a loose sand ramp which he used to scramble up unaided back to ground level.

★ ★ ★

21 Brigade persevered in massing supplies on the north side of the Lomba with the intention of crossing the river, but was hammered unsparingly by the South African artillery.

'From my position it was almost unreal, like watching a movie,' said Piet van Zyl. 'A G-5 would pick off an ammunition dump well back from the river, and up would go a plume of smoke and fire.

'When their water gatherers came out of the treeline each day my company would hit them with 81 mm mortars as they started filling their bowsers and cans. One of my Angolan mortarmen, Sergeant Bambi, was a particularly accurate shot. He first pinned them down with high explosive bombs, and when they flattened themselves on the ground to avoid the blast of follow-up bombs he changed to devices with white phosphorus which spread on impact and burned. Sometimes Commandant Les Rudman, a CSI liaison officer with UNITA, turned up to supplement Bambi's barrages with fire from World War II-vintage Vickers machine-guns mounted on top of his two Blesboks [mine-protected trucks].

'One time we located one of their nearer D-30s and I got Bambi to fire his white phosphorus mortar bombs. Afterwards we could see Fapla gunners running around trying to put out the flames.

'Sometimes the MRLs would fire on 21 Brigade's positions in the treeline. Afterwards you could see them carrying bodies away and beginning to dig their trenches even deeper.

'As well as the recce patrols behind their lines, we had to send out patrols to the east and west to check whether they were preparing crossings. As the patrols moved on, they left trip-wire flares to act as warnings.

'I sometimes went out on patrol myself. Once, when one of the 5 Reconnaissance commando majors was ill, I went with Piet Fourie behind 21 Brigade's lines to locate their B-10 cannons and Stalin Organs. It was easy to pick them up from the green glow of their infra-red night sights.

'On another occasion I went with Commandant Hougaard to General Ben-Ben's UNITA base just south of the Lomba-Cunzumbia confluence. There was a 32 Battalion OP post there watching 59 Brigade. I climbed up into a high tree to see what I could and got the shock of my life when two Mig-23s came in low on a recce run. I could see the pilots' faces. I nearly fell out of the branches.

'Sergeant Mac [da Trinidada] reported back one day that 21 Brigade seemed to be making a particularly big build-up for an attempted crossing some five kilometres to the east of my company's position. Mac said there was a line of tanks deep inside the treeline.

'I moved east with my Ratels, infantrymen and a 101 company with Casspirs, while the G-5s and the MRLs prepared for the signal to open fire. We slowed down before we approached the position and listened in to their communications in our EW vehicle. They were saying that the area was clear and that they were ready to start. Then the tanks and vehicles and infantry came right out on to the *anhara* on their side of the river. That's when we told the MRLs and the G-5s to open up. The G-5s caused terrible devastation.'

[The computer-controlled G-5s deliver fragmentation shells, which detonate some ten to 20 m above the enemy and blast downwards nearly 5,000 steel shards and slivers which kill or maim any man in their path and penetrate soft-skinned vehicles. Military analysts have assessed the South African shells as being twice as effective as any similar projectile in use by the world's armies. A system known as base-bleed, adapted from technology supplied from Sweden, gives the G-5 shells ten per cent extra range, meaning that away from sea level the range is up to 42 km. When a normal shell is fired it creates a vacuum in its wake which causes drag, acting like a brake. A base-bleed shell has a special chemical pellet in its tail which burns and injects gases into the vacuum, thus reducing drag.]

As the campaign progressed the G-5 gunners became more and more impressed with the accuracy of the weapon. With the guidance of forward observers, the gunners could make corrections of 25 m per shot until they hit an individual target vehicle.

Piet Fourie recalled sitting in the shade of a tree on the east bank of the Gombe River bringing in G-5 fire on 21 Brigade's artillery positions beyond the opposite bank: 'We were going for their Sam-8s. I gave the G-5 commander all the coordinates, and after one or two corrections he landed a shell right on top of a Sam-8 launcher. Some of the Sam missiles just zoomed off in haphazard directions. Then we hit another Sam-8. We really hit them hard.'

CHAPTER 11

RECCE HARDSHIPS

Being a recce, as Fourie describes, sounds easy − a matter of lying shaded from the sun on a river bank and watching the artillery men do their work.

In fact, it is one of the toughest and most thankless of tasks. A recce spends lots of time alone, dirty, hungry, thirsty and very, very frightened.

'Any man who says he has never been scared on our type of operations is a liar,' said Fourie. 'Sometimes we would be sitting within visual distance of the enemy for two whole days. It takes a lot out of a man to be so close to the enemy during daytime. You can't describe it to anyone who has not been scared in those circumstances. It's genuinely bad. You feel totally wrecked because of the pressure on your nerves: you want to shit yourself. You keep seeing things and the whole time you're telling yourself: they've picked me up.'

Then there were the flies.

'Worse than the heat when you're hiding near the enemy are the flies. Swarms of little black mopane flies drive you almost mad. And when you pull down the fly net in front of your face they start packing on to it until you can see nothing and you can hear nothing. It's a terrible noise. And they go into your eyes if you lift the net and they go into your hair. And if you squash some of them they give off a smell which pulls in thousands of others. They're worse than the enemy. You feel like suicide, you want to shoot yourself.'

And then there were the SADF's allies.

'I had to work closely with UNITA recces. Those guys really frightened me. They scared me more than the enemy did. They were reckless. When the sun went down it was party time. It was fires and noise and conversation around the mealie-pap pot. They thought that when night fell the war was over for the day; but that's when the SADF's type of war actually begins.

'There were some very good UNITA guys, but a lot of their recce officers I worked with would tell you they were going to do one thing and then would do another. If you'd ask them what time we were leaving towards an objective they'd say 8 pm, and eight hours later you had still not moved.

'And they scared me by walking on clear trails all the time, trails that were sure to be known to the enemy. If you're in an area a long time there's an obvious temptation to get slack and stick to the trails. But it's necessary to get off them, because anyone in our kind of work on the enemy side goes for a trail and ambushes it.

'I used to keep my sanity by walking right at the back of a column. That's the safest place to be because in most ambushes the attackers shoot at the biggest group in the middle. I figured that if I was at the back I could turn round and run from any ambush. I used to repeat a motto to myself: Make war today and run away tomorrow, and then you'll be back again. But if you want to try and be a hero today, you won't be back tomorrow.'

Sergeant 'Frenchie's' frustrations were sometimes more with the SADF than with UNITA.

'My recce team would come back from a dangerous mission, having walked up to 40 km a day for five days following an enemy brigade, and there would be no food at the logistics base. Often there had been a delivery of fresh meat but the resident guys had eaten it all. We had nothing and we had to beg for ratpacs. It was really demoralising.'

Mac da Trinidada found the main problem with his five-man recce team, all black Angolans like himself, was the sudden collapse of morale in early October after nearly three months of ceaseless work in the war zone.

'There had been constant contacts with the enemy, lots of hitting and running,' he said. 'Then we ran into a big ambush by 21 Brigade, and my guys were so exhausted and their nerves so shot to pieces that they performed very badly and we were lucky to come out alive. I contacted HQ by radio and said my team had to be given a rest outside the war zone. Senior commanders take it very seriously when a recce sergeant reports that his men are shattered.

'We were told that we would be given seven days leave back at Buffalo base in Namibia, but first we had to go to the Cuito River to investigate whether there was any possible place to bridge it south of Cuito Cuanavale. On our way to the Cuito we met men from 1 Reconnaissance Commando who were on their way back for home leave even though they had arrived in Angola later than us. My guys were really stirred up by that and I had to contact HQ again to warn them that spirits were dangerously low.

'Afterwards we were sent to Mavinga and flown to Rundu, where the bar was waiting open for us at midnight. The next morning we went by truck to Buffalo and stayed at home there for seven days. My mum, three sisters and two brothers didn't see much of me. I spent a lot of time drinking with my friends before we did the return journey to the front.'

CHAPTER 12

THE AIR FORCE GEARS UP

21 Brigade became more and more weakened by the constant South African artillery bombardments, and there came a time when Ferreira concluded its anti-aircraft defences had been sufficiently destroyed to risk the first SAAF bombing raid against that brigade.

On 25 September the Mirage F-1AZ ground crews at Grootfontein were told to ready the aircraft for a series of major raids the following day. Loaders prepared 450 kg cluster bombs which eject 40 spherical bomblets that bounce on impact up to six metres and then detonate, hurling metal fragments groundwards. They also loaded 250 kg high explosive fragmentation bombs.

Captain Reg van Eeden was keen to get the straps over his shoulders again, though life at Grootfontein between missions was very acceptable:

'We spent a lot of time on the golf course, which had no grass on the fairways. And we used to eat often at a little restaurant called Dan Louis's which served the most tender garlic calamari. There was splendid draught beer at one hotel where we also played a bit of pool.'

The first Mirage wave went in against 21 Brigade at first light on Saturday 26 September. The Mirages 'tossed' their 450 kg and 250 kg bombs, and as soon as they cleared the area the G-5s opened up with a 15-minute barrage. The pattern was repeated another three times that morning, and, as usual, the pilots had been briefed on the positions of SADF forces so that they could overfly them at ground-hugging level on their way back home.

'The idea was to lift the ground forces' morale,' said Van Eeden. 'Although we knew where the troops were, they were impossible to see. The camouflage was fantastic. I used to make a distinct point of trying to pinpoint our guys on the ground, and only once did I see someone waving from a vehicle which was not properly camouflaged.'

Van Eeden 'tossed' all his bombs successfully that day, but as he began his pitch-upwards after one bombing run he saw three Sam-7 anti-aircraft missiles streaking up from the ground towards the Mirage formation, which broke up to clear the 'cone of vulnerability'.

Applying the 'low level is survivability' dictum, Van Eeden came out of his pitch as early as possible and entered a vertical dive back to ground level.

'But I overdid it. I left it longer than usual to pull out of the dive, and I was sure that I'd left it too late. I thought this life was over. There comes a moment in that kind of situation when you've done everything possible with the machine to get it to level up, and from then onwards you can only pray. I was diving down right into the Cunzumbia River pulling the stick back until it was almost wrenched free. I began to feel the Mirage level out, but I was still sure it was too late. And then the next thing I knew I was flashing along above the Cunzumbia at about ten metres and 540 knots.

'I began shaking and trembling, and after I landed I didn't want to talk to anyone or join in any of the traditional chaffing that goes on. I was sitting in the mess avoiding the others, thinking about so many things. Then one of my friends, Major Ed Every, started chaffing me very heavily and wouldn't let up. It was something I really didn't need at that moment. Finally, I told him to shut his fucking mouth and I walked out of the mess. My squadron leader carpeted me and ordered me to apologise to Ed, but I told him I couldn't and I never did.'

★ ★ ★

Piet van Zyl had watched the Mirages going in and the G-5 bombardments coming over his head from his company's position on the south bank of the Lomba. 'Otherwise, it was a quiet day for us,' said

Van Zyl. 'We were just sitting under our camouflage looking through binoculars at 21 Brigade troopies less than five kilometres away walking through the treeline across the river. In the afternoon I tuned in one of the Casspir radios to the Currie Cup Final [between the Transvaal and Northern Transvaal rugby union teams]: no South African wanted to fight that day because everyone wanted to listen to the rugby. The last wave of Mirages came in just after 4.30 in the afternoon, and they were followed by a 15-minute G-5 and MRL bombardment. The enemy artillery responded and then everything fell quiet just in time for us to hear the final minutes of the rugby.'

The Mirage attacks of 26 September were among the most decisive SAAF actions of the war. Seven Soviet military advisers attached to the command HQ of 21 Brigade were wounded in the attacks. Back in Cuito Cuanavale senior Soviet officers ordered MI-24 Hind helicopter gunships to go in and bring out the Soviet wounded and about 30 other Soviet military men attached to the commands of 59 and 21 Brigades. SADF EW teams picked up the information that the helicopters were coming to evacuate the Soviets. Pierre Franken, back from his mission north of the Lomba, identified two *shonas* where he thought the choppers might land. When two helicopters were heard clattering in on the afternoon of 27 September, Franken ordered the G-5s, 120 mm mortars, and MRLs to prepare to put down heavy barrages on the co-ordinates of the two open spaces. As the helicopters landed at 21 Brigade, the SADF artillery pounded the landing zones, and Piet Fourie, still pretending to be a thorn bush within a short distance of the enemy, reported back that one of the MI-24s had been hit and destroyed in a huge blast. Fapla HQ at Cuito Cuanavale ordered 21 Brigade to pull back, and on the night of Sunday 27 September the brigade, now down to about one-third of its original strength, retreated several kilometres to the northwest.

The SADF had won the first stage of the War for Africa.

CHAPTER 13

WAR IN THE AIR

Throughout September air fighter superiority established by top-cover Cuban and Angolan Air Force Mig-23 fighter-bombers severely limited the South African Army's scope for action during daylight. The Mig-23s, incorporating latest state-of-the-art technology, outmatched for speed the SAAF's Mirage F-1CZs, delivered from France in the mid-1970s before the international arms embargo bit really hard.

'Angolan and Cuban air strikes were spectacularly inaccurate and unsuccessful throughout the war,' said Commandant Hougaard. 'But their constant presence in the air placed a major restriction on us. We couldn't move with our vehicles during the day. And our infantry could only move in more than company strength at night. So we did our movements at night and laid low during the day. At about five o'clock in the morning we would just dig in and camouflage.

'They missed us because their target acquisition was lousy, with poor ground-to-air co-ordination; they released their bombs from too great a height; and our camouflage was good. Every time their fighters took off from Cuito Cuanavale our recces there on the ground gave us early warning so that we could perfect our cover.'

Brigadier Jan Steyn, director of SAAF operations throughout the Lomba River fighting, said the Air Force senior command had accepted from the beginning that it would not be possible for South Africa to dominate the air space. 'We realised the technical lag was there, and it would be useless to confront the enemy in air-to-air combat and reveal one of our weaknesses. We therefore set ourselves clear limits, and one of these was to avoid direct combat with enemy fighter planes as far as possible.'

Major Reg van Eeden put it another way: 'It's one of the biggest myths of the war that our Air Force was beaten. They certainly had air-to-air superiority in their own backyard. But we adapted our tactics to fit the situation. If you had to fight Mike Tyson you wouldn't stand up and slug it out. You'd lose if you fought him by the Queensberry rules.'

Nevertheless, the Mig-23s, though they stayed high for fear of UNITA's American-supplied ground-to-air Stinger missiles, were what Colonel Dick Lord described as a 'buggerance factor' because of the limitations they imposed on SADF ground troops' daylight movements. The Mig-23s tried particularly hard to knock out the G-5s, and there was intense fear that one of their bombs might by chance destroy some of the giant guns, South Africa's most formidable weapon in the War for Africa.

The 'buggerance factor' and the threat to the G-5s led to a high-level decision that the SAAF fighters must at least *try* to take on the Mig-23s in aerial battle and deter them from constant presence over the battlefields.

★ ★ ★

On Thursday 3 September the pilots and ground crew of the SAAF's Mirage F-1CZ fighter 3 Squadron at Waterkloof, near Pretoria, had one main collective thought in mind – the scheduled wedding on Saturday 5 September of one of the pilots, Captain John Sinclair.

'Every pilot in the squadron was to be part of the guard of honour,' recalled Sinclair's fellow pilot, Captain Arthur Piercey. 'And we were looking forward to one hell of a party after the nuptials.'

But later that Thursday six of the squadron's 13 planes were ordered to fly to Rundu to enter the war. The other plane crews were put on a round-the-clock standby at Waterkloof. Captain Sinclair's wedding was postponed.

Piercey, a tall, gangly 30-year-old, had been a plane-crazy youngster since his schooldays. On leaving Pretoria's Clapham High School he joined the SAAF and began his pilot training in 50-year-old piston-engined Harvards before moving on to Italian-designed Impala light attack jet aircraft.

Piercey graduated to Mirages in 1984, but he had never been in combat. Now he was deeply excited as he prepared to fly towards the war zone.

'It was a frantic rush to get everything ready,' said Piercey. 'We were ordered to be in the bush [at Rundu] by Friday afternoon. There were no approach aids at Rundu, so we were told we must leave by 3 pm in order to land before dark.

'We finally got away at 3.05 pm, and half way there, high over Botswana, the sun began setting. Luckily, Rundu is the only town for hundreds of kilometres in that part of Namibia, so we picked out its lights and then the lights of the airfield. We made a very hairy landing in the dark because the runway is only 2,000 metres long. When we got down, the controllers said they hadn't been expecting us and it wouldn't be possible to begin getting us combat-ready before Monday. So John could have got married after all and we could all have gone to the thrash.'

At Rundu there were none of the comforts for 3 Squadron enjoyed by 1 Squadron further south at Grootfontein. Rundu is a true frontier town with one dismal motel restaurant. 1 Squadron's accommodation was in army-issue tents next to the runway. 'We called our quarters Little Siberia because they were as hot and as uncomfortable as hell,' said Piercey.

Now began a period of utmost frustration for the fighter pilots. Several times they were scrambled for action, but on each occasion they were called back when the emergency passed. As time dragged on most of the squadron members got gyppo tummies in Rundu's tropical heat. They went on to a diet of flat, warm Coca-Cola and dried bread, so they were unable to take advantage of the one luxury available to them – 32 Battalion's mess bar at the perimeter of the air base.

Then, on 17 September, Arthur Piercey was one of four pilots on standby duty. Two F-1CZs, Piercey's one of them, were scrambled for action somewhere over Mavinga to intercept a pair of threatening-looking Mig-23s.

'We took off in such a smooth and well oiled way that it seemed like a routine training mission out of Waterkloof,' Piercey recalled. 'But when we climbed to height and were ordered to jettison our spare fuel tanks, we knew this time it was for real. The adrenalin was really flowing.

'We were flying at more than 10,000 m (beyond the reach of enemy ground-to-air missiles) just north of Mavinga when we got the sighting of our first two Mig-23s. All four planes flashed past each other, and we turned as a pair behind the Migs. Each Mirage fired a Matra 500 [a French heat-seeking air-to-air missile], but they missed. There was no time to get off other missiles because the Migs plunged towards the ground and we couldn't follow them down into the enemy missile layer. It was a big disappointment. We think the missiles exploded on the heat plumes behind the Migs instead of going right through the plumes and knocking out the planes.

'Once they dived we had to go home, but there was a lot of excitement and drinking in the bar that evening and not much talk about stomach troubles.'

Another ten days of sheer boredom followed the action over Mavinga, relieved only by the occasional scramble and the inevitable abort of the mission shortly afterwards. 'Every time the scramble phone rang we answered it half-heartedly,' said Piercey. 'We'd get into the cockpit and begin all the checks, knowing that very soon we'd be clambering out again.'

But on 27 September all hell broke loose when radio operators picked up Cuban pilots speaking Spanish to each other as their flight of Mig-23s headed towards the Lomba River to provide cover for the Hind helicopters rescuing the Soviet advisers from 21 Brigade's HQ.

'My letter home went flying as we scrambled,' said Piercey. 'It was three in the afternoon and it was very hot. After take-off we hugged the ground. With all the air rising from the baking ground, it was a bumpy ride with great whirls of dust being kicked up at the back from the after-burn and jet blast.

'Fighter control HQ was passing a stream of information to us about the enemy force. We wanted to know how many enemy there were and in what formation they were flying. I was second man in our formation of four.

'Then the order came to pitch up, and we soared like homesick angels. Next came the order to jettison the spare fuel tanks, and when I saw a 1,200 litre tank falling away from the lead aircraft I knew it was serious. The adrenalin was flowing again.

'Soon we realised that at least two Migs had come to rumble with us and were flying only 300 m below us. I must have been flying at something like Mach 1.3 (about 1,600 km per hour) when one Mig passed right through us. My mind is now blank as to what happened in the next fraction of a second, but then I saw the second Mig coming straight towards me. I flicked the trigger release on the missile-firing stick and prepared to squeeze the trigger the moment the Mig flew through the sight.

'Again there was a minute fraction of a second when I was in a dream thinking what a beautiful aeroplane the Mig-23 was and then remembering that I wasn't there to admire the scenery. Next I saw a bright orange flash and saw this telephone pole screaming towards me with a white tail of smoke.

'In training they say: "Fly directly towards the missile. The bigger the angle between its infra-red heat-seeking head and your hot backside, the better. The missile has then got less chance of turning because of its great speed and small fins." So by heading towards it you try to force it to overshoot because it can't maintain the necessary degree of turn.

'But faced with reality I found it took a lot of willpower to fly straight at something I knew was hunting me and trying to kill me. However, I kept breaking towards it and I watched it shoot over my shoulder. Then I heard a thud, but there was no indication from the gauges that the aircraft had been damaged. At the same time the Mig which fired the missile was flashing past me, and when I looked back it had gone.

'I told the leader I thought I might have been hit, and he said: "OK, let's go home." In the SAAF we believe in live cowards rather than dead heroes.'

With hindsight, Piercey worked out that the whole fight lasted no more than 20 to 40 seconds from the time he got the 'pitch-up' order to the 'go home' command. His fighting manoeuvre in that short period of time had consisted of one 360-degree turn.

'The next moment I was pointing the Mirage straight at the ground,' he said. 'The nearer you get to the ground and the faster you go, the less chance there is of a second missile picking you up. I left the throttle stuck and I was screaming downwards thinking "I'll not get out of this in one piece." But I bottomed out.

'By now I was separated from my leader and I was getting an audio warning in my helmet that someone at 6 o'clock [from behind] was looking at me on radar. I radioed to the boss that I thought someone was behind me. I was petrified. In a situation like that you don't look back. You just keep going as straight and as fast as you can. If you turn you allow your pursuer to cut the corner and close the gap.

'I told the leader I was so low that I was raising a dust cloud. Those crazy American Road Runner cartoons flashed through my mind. I assured the leader that I couldn't get any lower, or fly any faster than the 750 knots I was doing.

'At this stage I was beginning to think that I'd over-reacted, that I might not have been hit and had got out of the fight too early. Despite the cockpit radar warning, the plane was not handling too badly and there was no vibration.

'Five minutes later, half-way home, the first orange warning light flashed on, telling me that the electro-pump which maintained constant fuel pressure to the engine had failed. I recalled all the checks I'd gone through a hundred times in the flight simulator, and finally told the boss I'd got a failure. He pulled out his emergency check list, and started reading it to me. I affirmed that I'd followed all the correct procedures.

'He hadn't finished reading when a second failure showed on the panel, this time the right-side fuel pump. The boss began reading me a new set of procedures, but he hadn't gone halfway when my panel showed a failure in the hydraulic H-2 system. [The main hydraulic system is known as H-1, and the standby system is H-2].

'This worried me because so many of the controls are hydraulically operated, including the flaps, undercarriage and brakes. However, the controls were still working off the main hydraulic system, and the only important thing I knew I'd lost completely was the nose-wheel steering.

'By now I was beyond the area covered by the Angolans' radar, so I started climbing to a height where flying was safer and fuel consumption lower.

'Next I began getting audio warnings, but no panel warnings, which I didn't understand at first. Then I remembered from the simulator that this particular warning pattern meant there was an oil failure caused by oil dripping out. That really alarmed me because the throttle works through a mechanical system which requires oil.

'I had to go on to emergency throttle. I threw a toggle to switch on an electric motor which replaces the normal throttle functions. But it was very unresponsive, so I realised there had also been some loss of electric power.

'By now the boss had come alongside me again, and he reported fuel streaming from the right hand side, lots of shrapnel damage on the tail, and the drag-chute gone.

'Flying a perfectly healthy F-1CZ into a 2,000 m runway without a drag parachute is hard work. It is very difficult indeed in emergency conditions when the chute is gone and the engine's response is unpredictable.'

Piercey, approaching Rundu, got streams of advice from his flight leader and ground control on how best to get the crippled Mirage down. The techniques of landing are very complicated. But basically what Piercey decided to do was to come in very steeply so that the moment he touched down as much as possible of his forward momentum would be absorbed downwards. He also aimed to land as near the end of the tarmac as possible to give himself the maximum length of runway to try to halt the aircraft. It was a dangerous action: if he miscalculated and came in too steeply the plane would simply be smashed to bits on the runway.

Piercey pounded his Mirage safely on the end of the runway. 'But when I slammed on the brakes the only thing that changed was the expression on my face,' he recalled. 'I was travelling along that tarmac at 170 knots and my main thought was: "This plane will not stop."

'With only 500 m of runway left, I pulled on the emergency handbrake. At the end of the runway there's a big sandpit to break the momentum of any aircraft which overshoots. It was now my main hope, but the plane went through it like a hot knife through butter.

'There was a dip beyond the sandpit going down towards a perimeter fence with a river beyond. The question flashed through my mind: "What will stop me, the fence or the river?"

'As I went through the fence the nose wheel hit a boulder and instinctively I put my hands up in front of my face. The force of the plane hitting the boulder must have fired the ejector seat because it went off with a loud bang and I felt the chute hit me in the face as it began to unravel. I obviously blacked out because the next thing I knew I was lying on my right side in the sand with the fire brigade rushing towards me.

'I told them not to touch me until the doctor arrived. The seat had not separated as it should have done: it was still strapped to my back.

'The fact that I couldn't move my legs didn't bother me so much as the pain in my left arm which was badly broken. I asked for painkillers and must have passed out again. When I woke up my boss was standing there with doctors: I learned later that he had been so shaken by the incident that he had had to make three landing attempts before he was able to get down successfully.

'The doctors gave me an injection, and I was out even before they put me in the ambulance. I woke up ten days later in the intensive care ward of 1 Military Hospital, Pretoria, and didn't leave it for another seven months.'

Captain Arthur Piercey had fought his first and last aerial battle. In the accident his sixth and seventh vertebrae had been badly fractured and his spinal cord partly severed. He is now confined to a wheelchair as a quadriplegic, but his sparkling humour and lively mind are undimmed. Still a member of 3 Squadron, he is working on the unit's computerisation programme at Waterkloof.

That Piercey survived at all staggered those of his colleagues who reached the scene of the crash. 'When I saw him lying there, my first thought was: He's in such a mess that it will be best if he dies,' said Colonel Dick Lord. The doctors told Piercey's father that his son had only a one in 20 chance of living. He had hurtled through the air at great speed for 100 m with the heavy ejector seat strapped to him: the ejector parachute failed to open properly.

An inquiry into the accident found that an elastic safety net at the end of the Rundu runway was not raised as Piercey made his emergency landing. It would probably have saved Piercey from his extreme injuries. The results of the inquiry have never been published, but rumours persist that SAAF men responsible for raising the net had been drinking before the Mirage landed.

★ ★ ★

Captain Piercey's tragic accident also meant the abandonment, after only two dogfights, of any further attempts by the SAAF's principal fighter-interceptor aircraft to challenge the Cuban and Angolan Mig-23s in air-to-air combat. 3 Squadron's F-1CZs were taken out of the war and redeployed to Waterkloof.

From October onwards the SAAF limited its fighting activities to low-level bombing attacks, with the Mirage F-1AZs playing the central role backed up by British-manufactured Buccaneer strike aircraft.

However, there was a third dogfight involving one of the F-1AZs, which have a secondary air-to-air role.

Commandant Johan Rankin, the officer commanding 1 Squadron, is the SAAF's fighter pilot ace of today, achieving the only two SAAF 'kills' of enemy aircraft since the Korean War. In Korea South African Sabre jets flew more than 2,000 missions as part of the United Nations force fighting the Chinese and North Koreans.

Twice when Angolan Mig-21s tried in the early 1980s to interfere with SADF operations against SWAPO bases in southern Angola, Rankin, then flying F-ICZs with 3 Squadron, had taken them on and shot them down.

Now, in October 1987, flying the lead F-1AZ in a ground attack bombing mission just north of the Lomba River, Rankin saw Mig-23s at altitude over the target area. The Mig-23s were always reluctant to descend from the heights into the range of UNITA's Stingers, but on this occasion one Mig pilot came down to low level to try to mix it with the South Africans. Rankin took him on and succeeded in getting inside his foe's turning circle and then behind the Mig. To Rankin's frustration, he found he could not close on the enemy plane because of the Mig-23's greater speed. The nearest Rankin got to the Mig's tail was 700 m, and despite firing two missiles and 139 rounds from his 30 mm cannons he was unable to bring down his opponent although he outmanoeuvred him in the air.

CHAPTER 14

LAYING THE TRAP

After Fapla's 21 Brigade began retiring from the fight, Deon Ferreira concentrated his energies on the destruction of 47 Brigade, which had been the spearhead of the Angolan thrust towards Mavinga. If 47 Brigade could be slain, the threat to Mavinga and UNITA's headquarters at Jamba would be over.

From the moment 47 Brigade came round the source of the Lomba in early September Ferreira's strategy was to slow the force and wear it down with constant air and artillery bombardments. His hope was that 47 Brigade would eventually bog down and that by then General Jannie Geldenhuys would have persuaded the Cabinet to give Ferreira a sufficiently sophisticated force to destroy the enemy brigade completely.

Sergeant Mac da Trinidada and Major Pierre Franken were closely involved in the early harassing attacks on 47 Brigade as it straightened up eastwards along the southern bank of the Lomba.

On 1 September, as 47 Brigade started coming around the Lomba source, Mac da Trinidada, accompanied by three recce commandos of 32 Battalion and about 40 UNITA soldiers, prepared an ambush.

'We had a very good ambush position,' said Da Trinidada. 'We saw the enemy coming, and then we saw the first T-55 tank. We fired a 75 mm recoilless anti-tank cannon from the top of one of UNITA's little jeeps, and the tank burnt out. It was noon, but it went dark all around us from the smoke of enemy shells and mortar bombs which began falling on our position.

'I thought "Man, we must run." So we started pulling back eastwards along the Lomba: we desperately needed water as well. But the enemy started to head in the same direction, so we had to try to outrun them in our UNITA jeeps. The Faplas were moving pretty quickly with their assault vehicles and tanks. Some of our jeeps got stuck in mud near the river and we had to leave them because the enemy was so close.

'It sounds bad, but I laughed aloud from sheer tension when one of the jeeps carrying the UNITA boys got hopelessly sucked into the mud. As each person jumped out they got sucked in too, and most of them were taken prisoner.'

Da Trinidada and his group found water and then pulled back into deep bush about six kilometres east of the Lomba source. 47 Brigade stopped and reformed inside the treeline about three kilometres from the source. For five days Da Trinidada's group monitored 47 Brigade as it advanced at the rate of about two kilometres a day, sending very aggressive patrols out ahead of the main force. Whenever Da Trinidada could locate 47 Brigade, he brought in ripples from the MRLs.

At the end of the five days, on Sunday 6 September, Da Trinidada's team had to turn back to base to replenish their rations. On the way they linked up with another four-man 32 Battalion recce team, under Sergeant Frenchie, which was also returning to base after completing a mission north of the Lomba.

As Frenchie and Da Trinidada moved eastwards they received orders to link up with Commandant Les Rudman, a CSI liaison team leader, whose three Casspirs mounted with old Brownings and Vickers and captured 12.7 mm machine-guns had been sent by Robert Hartslief to investigate a rumoured crossing of the Lomba near the Cuzizi confluence by an unidentified Fapla battalion.

Rudman's team, and two other CSI liaison teams operating in Angola, had dual tasks. First, they liaised in an intelligence and training role with UNITA's commanders. Second, they had a high degree of operational autonomy, fighting in liaison with, but independent of, the standard South African Army battalions. Rudman and others were answerable directly to CSI boss Admiral Dries Putter. A typical 18-man liaison team included a protection unit of 11 members of 1 Parachute Battalion's Pathfinder

Platoon, tough men trained in survival, clandestine work, the handling of a wide range of weapons, first aid, driving and radio operation.

With Rudman was Pierre Franken, who had been directed to bring in artillery fire on the enemy battalion if it was located. Rudman set up a temporary base about eight kilometres southeast of the Lomba-Cuzizi confluence. It was in woodland just to the north of an open *shona* some three kilometres long and one kilometre wide. (See map.)

At eight o'clock in the morning of 6 September, Rudman ordered Da Trinidada to prepare his men to accompany Franken and his two Buffels on a scouting mission to find the mystery battalion. Da Trinidada protested that his black recces were too exhausted from their previous mission to be sent out immediately on yet another tough assignment; they needed at least a week's rest. Rudman therefore designated four of his seven white Afrikaner CSI Pathfinders to go with Franken. Da Trinidada's and Frenchie's men were ordered by Rudman to guard the CSI vehicles which, as well as the Casspirs, included three Blesbok supply trucks and a Gemsbok recovery vehicle.

'Around nine o'clock I told my guys that we were going to guard the vehicles and that they must all take quick instruction on how to fire the weapons brought by Commandant Rudman's CSI team – the Vickers, Brownings, 12.7 mm gun and an 81 mm mortar, all mounted on top of the Casspirs,' said Da Trinidada.

'By about ten o'clock we'd got the hang of the weapons and we'd all finished breakfast. Major Pierre was getting ready to move out with the CSI guys.

'Then one of my guys came running in and said there were a lot of people coming towards us through the trees from the west. As recces we always *walk*, and walk *cool* even in an emergency. We only run if danger is absolutely imminent. So I *walked* forward to see what was going on. When I saw 300 or so infantrymen in line abreast walking towards me, I *ran*! And when the recces saw me running they rose as one man, put on their combat jackets and ran towards me with the CSI men to form a line. We weren't expecting so many enemy, so we thought it must be UNITA. They kept approaching, and when they were just 60 m away one of my corporals shouted in Portuguese: "Are you UNITA or Fapla?"

'They replied with a volley of shots and killed one of the CSI men, Lance-Corporal Beneke. A company from 32 Battalion was just at that moment bringing in food and supplies for us, and five of them got wounded. So within seconds of beginning a fight in which we were hopelessly outnumbered, we had one dead and five casevacs.

'They tried to outflank us in the bush to the north to push us into the open *shona*. But we killed 12 of them in those opening seconds, using mainly our 40 mm grenade launchers. They spread a lot of shrapnel and must have given the enemy the impression there were more of us than was actually the case.' [The South African-developed grenade launcher punches out six grenades in a 15-second burst rather like a six-shooter pistol, and is highly effective within a range of 30 to 150 m.]

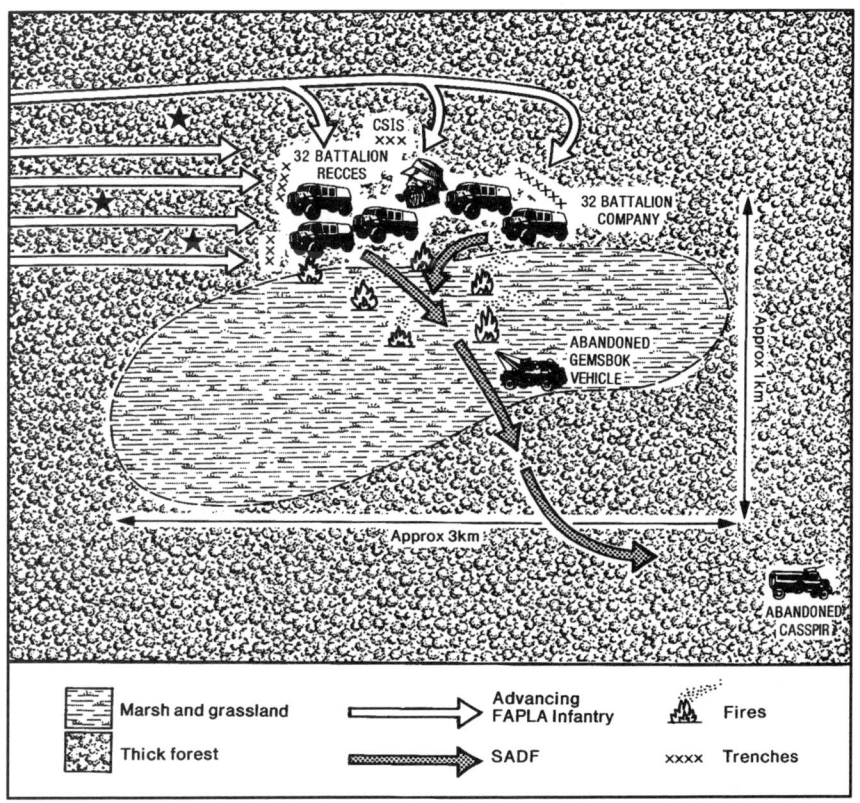

Mac Da Trinidada's 6 September 1987 encounter with Fapla's 47 Brigade.

The intense firing in the opening exchanges set the tinder-dry grass in the *shona* ablaze. Rudman ordered the Casspir, Buffel, Blesbok and Gemsbok drivers to take their vehicles through the wall of flames and black smoke. Rudman was the last to leave in his command Casspir, giving covering fire from a 12.7 mm machine-gun to the recces as they too turned and sprinted through the burning grass of the *shona*.

'It had been a really heavy contact,' said Da Trinidada. 'We fought with everything we had. As well as the grenade launchers, we were firing 7.6 mm Soviet PKM light machine-guns, Soviet Kalashnikov rifles and Soviet RPG-7 rocket launchers. Just before we broke off contact we were exchanging fire with Fapla troops at only 30 m.

'Until Rudman ordered it out, the 81 mm team on one of the Casspirs was firing almost vertically in the air so that its bombs would land among the enemy. We covered the vehicles until the last one, Rudman's, had pulled out through the flames which were rising more than three metres.

'Then Frenchie and I ordered our men to run. It was the only choice left to us. We were hopelessly outnumbered and about 40 Fapla soldiers had outflanked us to the north. As we ran through the flames into unburnt grassland on the open *shona*, Rudman came back to give us covering fire. His gunner was hit and fell out of the Casspir. Rudman fired like a madman while the driver leapt out to pick up the wounded gunner. Another Casspir came back as well, and one of the CSI men, Sergeant Strydom, was hit three times while he operated the Vickers. But that guy was very brave: he didn't stop firing, and he lived.

'From then on it was just running across the open grassland, trying to catch up with a vehicle and jump on to it. The vehicles and the thick smoke from the burning grass together saved us. There were mortar bombs and RPG-7 shells fired by the Faplas exploding all around us. When the Casspirs slowed down we threw our weapons into them and the other guys just pulled us up on the move. We didn't feel the gashes and bruises until later.

'The vehicles thrashed through the long grass to the cover of the trees on the other side of the *shona*. It wasn't easy. All their tyres were flat because they had been shot out in the fighting. The Gemsbok overheated badly and we left it behind after firing an RPG-7 shell into the engine compartment. One of the Casspirs managed to go on for two kilometres after a wheel was shot off, but we eventually had to abandon it as well.

'When we got to the trees on the other side Pierre Franken shinned up one of them to get a good view of the approaching enemy. Then he brought in fire from two of the guns in the G-5 battery about ten kilometres to the southwest of us, and after that the Faplas broke off their pursuit.

'We regrouped and I discovered that one of my guys was missing. Commandant Rudman agreed we would have to go back and find him. We got orders from HQ that the priority must be to get the seven casevacs and the dead man, Lance-Corporal Beneke, back to HQ before we went out on the search.

'But I insisted on going back to get my man. In the recces we don't leave anyone, and it's essential for morale in tough conditions for men to *know* they won't be left. As we were preparing to go, we got a radio message from HQ that enemy helicopters were active in the area, so we must camouflage the vehicles very quickly. Then soon afterwards we got another message to say the missing man had turned up at HQ. He had been so frightened that he ran faster than the Casspirs and covered something like 12 km in less than an hour!'

Meanwhile, one of the 1 Parachute Battalion pathfinders, 19-year-old national serviceman Lance-Corporal Johan Venter from Pretoria, had made three dashes under heavy fire back into the temporary base in an attempt to rescue wounded men. Venter recovered Beneke's body and pulled one of his pathfinder comrades, Lance-Corporal Coetzee, 40 m to safety. Venter, now an insurance broker, was subsequently decorated with the Honoris Crux.

SADF forces who returned to the scene of the battle the next day picked up a prisoner who said the 40 SADF men – the recces of 32 Battalion, the CSI Pathfinders, and the 25-man 32 Battalion supply company – had faced a 300-strong 59 Brigade force consisting of one infantry battalion and a mortar support company. The enemy troops had come across the Lomba to try to link up with 47 Brigade and find and destroy the G-5 guns. The prisoner said 59 Brigade had suffered many casualties in the clash and its officers thought they had confronted a big SADF force.

★ ★ ★

Da Trinidada, Frenchie and their men had left lots of equipment at the battle site – field radios, backpacks, crates of ammunition, light machine-guns, etc. The SADF follow-up team found only the remains of the equipment, which had been burnt out in the fury of the grassland fires.

CHAPTER 15

FANCY TRICKS AND DIRTY TRICKS

While preparing for the final showdown with 47 Brigade, Deon Ferreira employed the fullest range of special tactics at his disposal. At his request, General Geldenhuys sent to the front HQ two psychologists from Defence HQ in Pretoria who had made a special study of the African psyche in warfare. Heaven alone knows how scientifically legitimate their analyses were: but they had several wheezes they thought would help break down the morale of ordinary soldiers in the isolated 47 Brigade and Fapla's other troubled units.

The 'ground-shout' vehicle was one idea they came up with. These were Casspirs mounted with powerful loudspeakers which ventured out at night to within three kilometres of the enemy brigades and poured out torrents of propaganda designed as much to keep enemy soldiers awake as to persuade them of the error of their ways.

'We worked on their nerves and morale,' said Jan Hougaard. 'God knows, we were very, very tired ourselves because we had limited numbers and the war just seemed to be going on and on. But those guys got very little sleep at all, least of all come nightfall. The psychologists' theory was that if we could keep them awake all the time they would inevitably take casualties at an increased rate because of exhaustion. That would undermine their morale to a point where it would be opportune for us to go in for the final kill.

'The psychologists consulted UNITA closely to learn exactly how the Faplas' minds worked and what we could best say to them. We took Fapla prisoners forward with us in the ground-shout Casspirs. Typically one of them might be told to say: "Good evening. I'm Rifleman Jose Antonio, 47 Brigade, 3rd battalion, second platoon. Do you still remember me? I was with you yesterday. Now I'm with UNITA. You're all going to get killed. They are very strong."

'Every night we played music to them and shouted at them that tomorrow night they would burn and die. Then we'd make sure they got an air raid or an artillery attack just at the time they reckoned the threat had passed. Then the next night we would tell them the bombardment was proof that we hadn't been lying. We would ask: "How many of you died yesterday?" And later on, when the Cubans and Russians began to be pulled back from the battle zones, we shouted: "Where are the Cubans and Russians now?"'

Helium-filled balloons with radar reflector devices suspended beneath them were floated towards Fapla positions. 'They picked up the balloons on their radar, and they let go at them with their missiles,' said Hougaard. 'They wasted a lot of very expensive missiles in that way. But our main aim was to get on their nerves and keep them awake. On a couple of occasions their radar observers reported back that there were South African warplanes in the air and the pilots scrambled, only to find that their foe was a bloody balloon.'

Other balloons programmed to deflate over the enemy brigades were filled with propaganda pamphlets and books, about the collapse of the Angolan economy, the corruption of the MPLA's leaders, and UNITA's strength, designed by Jannie Geldenhuys's psychologists. In truth, their production did not need a psychologist's skills, just a certain Machiavellian commonsense.

The SAAF played a critical role in the psychological warfare game. Among their deadly payloads of fragmentation bombs were seeded 450 kg high explosive bombs with time fuses set to detonate them between one hour and 48 hours after they had ploughed into the sandy soils of southeast Angola.

'Those brigades used to move in a square of about five by five kilometres,' said Hougaard. 'It was no problem for our air force to pitch their bombs widely over a target of that size, and the enemy couldn't possibly tell where they had all penetrated. If they did find them they were very difficult to defuse, stuck in the ground up to their tail-fins.

'Those bombs really got on their nerves and wore them down: they couldn't tell just when the next might explode. And the psychologists instructed the air force to time a certain percentage of them to explode between four o'clock and five in the morning when most of the Fapla soldiers were in their deepest sleep: the psychologists said that particular hour had been widely recognised as the "suicide hour" for anyone pulled out of slumber.'

Pilotless planes, or remote piloted vehicles (RPV), developed by Armscor and operated by the SAAF, were among the most important cards Ferreira had to play in his special tactical game. Critically, the radio-controlled RPVs carried video cameras which gave 'real time' information: as the plane cruised over the enemy brigades along the Lomba valley, its cameras beamed back live pictures to monitor screens at the RPV base at Mavinga.

'The joke started that RPV pilots were fearless,' said Hougaard. 'Fighter-bomber pilots would get pulled off their squadron for a year to work in a special unit [10 Squadron] with RPVs, and there they were operating these things and sitting far away from the action.'

Like many of the weapons developed by Armscor since the implementation of the international arms embargo against South Africa, most information about the SAAF's RPVs is classified. But they are almost certainly based on Israeli technology, which finds its way to Armscor despite denials by Pretoria and Tel Aviv of close co-operation with each other in the field of military technology.

The Israelis' first notable success with radio-controlled RPVs was during their 1982 military invasion of Lebanon. The Israeli Scout RPV carried transponders which emitted signals identical to those of the Israeli Air Force's US-made warplanes. Syrian Soviet-made anti-aircraft radars were turned on to track what they thought were Israeli fighter-bombers coming in to attack. Israeli electronic warfare aircraft circling over the Mediterranean then obtained fixes on the radar systems and accompanying missile batteries and called in real fighters with air-to-ground missiles and ground attack planes to hammer the Syrian positions.

According to the US defence technology magazine, *International Combat Arms* (May 1989), the Israeli RPV-led attacks knocked out 80 per cent of Syria's anti-aircraft defence capability in the opening hours of the battle. The US Navy and Marines subsequently bought an improved version of the Scout which was used for unmanned reconnaissance in the Persian Gulf.

The South African RPV, known as the 'Gharra', costs about US$ 350,000 to produce. It is slightly bigger than the kind of model plane you might see small boys (or, more likely, their fathers) flying in a public park. The small petrol-powered engine drives a rear propeller. South African forces always knew one of their RPVs was going into 'action' by the approaching whirring sound of the engine.

The main role of the RPVs was to identify enemy positions which were subsequently quickly bombarded by South African artillery and fighter-bombers. But they also produced other results. As with the Syrians and the Israeli Scouts in the Lebanon, the Angolans and Cubans picked up the Gharras with their radar systems, thought they were warplanes, and let fly with all their anti-aircraft capabilities.

'They lost their cool and panicked, and even put their Migs after the RPVs,' said Jan Hougaard. 'The pilots used to come in thinking, at first, that they were attacking a real plane. We watched them chase the Gharras, but they would overshoot all the time because the RPVs travelled too slowly. On one occasion a Mig chased a Gharra all the way back to Mavinga, overshooting all the time, before it gave up and turned back.

'Fapla used to open up on them with their missiles and anti-aircraft guns, and we lost a couple of RPVs as a result. One was shot down on 21 September. It had flown over 16 and 21 Brigades, and was shot down by a Sam-8 over 47 Brigade. But they paid a big price for it. They fired more than a dozen missiles worth several million dollars, and when they fired, our artillery forward observers identified their positions. The G-5s battered their artillery emplacements, and there were a couple of explosions followed by enemy missiles streaking off all over the place. On 26 September a Sam-8 from 21 Brigade got another Gharra. But those little planes more than earned their keep.'

CHAPTER 16

THE CAVALRY – 61 MECH – RIDES TO THE RESCUE

61 Mechanised Battalion was the only conventional SADF unit based permanently in northern Namibia. Operating out of its base at Oshivelo, about 200 km south of the Angolan border, 61 Mech was the main destructive fist readily available on the ground to senior SA Army officers in the border region. Manned mainly by conscript national servicemen and a few regulars of the Permanent Force, 61 Mech had been deeply engaged in the cross-border war over a period of ten years. It had acquired a formidable reputation, and anyone posted to it was virtually guaranteed fighting action. It had no tanks permanently attached, but its soldiers operated the whole range of half-a-dozen or so different-function Ratel armoured cars and the family of exceptionally tough logistics vehicles which can keep pace with the Ratels over the roughest country.

32 Battalion, which bore the early brunt of the fighting in Operation Moduler, was by contrast a semi-conventional force, operating mainly in company or platoon strength without heavy weapons and on foot, although sometimes in mine-protected vehicles. It combined guerrilla, commando, and counter-insurgency capabilities, striking deep into Angola time and again on countless small to medium operations.

However, during major operations 32 Battalion acted mainly as a screening and mopping-up force for the main mechanised infantry thrust. Specialist units had gradually been attached to it on an *ad hoc* basis, but in southeastern Angola through August 1987 officers like Jan Hougaard and Robert Hartslief were constantly urging that, although

32 Battalion had performed many miracles, it could not continue to hold off 10,000 enemy troops backed by tanks and a range of the most modern missiles and fighter-bombers in the history of warfare.

It was inevitable that at some point the generals would see the need to involve 61 Mech. However, when the call first came it was for the proud unit to act merely in a deception role, rather as the charismatic and talented US General George Patton had been assigned by Eisenhower at the beginning of the 1944 Battle of Normandy to command 45 phantom divisions in southeast England to fool Adolf Hitler into thinking the Allied invasion would come from opposite the *Pas de Calais.*

'At the end of June we were ordered to move up to the Bittersoet training area (about 30 km) southwest of Rundu, and from there we moved into Angola along the western bank of the Kavango River,' said Major Laurence Maree, the deputy commander of 61 Mech whose natty, British military-style blond bristle-moustache failed to make him look older than his 28 years. 'We moved around there for eight days, only in daylight, as a show of force so that Fapla would see us and be dissuaded from assembling its brigades at Cuito Cuanavale. However, the plan didn't work because the enemy had such second-rate reconnaissance.'

Later 61 Mechanised Battalion reassembled at Bittersoet in full battle readiness. But the generals and politicians forbade the Ratels to cross the border to support 32 Battalion. Only a few Buffels were permitted to cross together with an MRL battery. At the tactical HQ near Mavinga Commandant Bok Smit, 61 Mech's commander, joined in the planning conferences on countering the advancing Fapla brigades. It was agreed that *if* 61 Mech was eventually committed, its main task would be as the spearhead against 47 Brigade. But at this stage the plan was still only to deploy 61 Mech if a final defensive battle became necessary.

The restriction on 61 Mech was lifted at the end of August, at about the same time as the SAAF was given the go-ahead for cross-border attacks. On 2 September Bok Smit was flown by helicopter into Angola to join the planning team again at forward headquarters, and just before he left Bittersoet 61 Mech's main force started to move towards Angola.

The convoy consisted of 55 Ratels of various configurations, five Rinkhals armour-protected ambulances, 62 logistics trucks and four recovery vehicles. A fleet of diesel tankers and trucks carrying tyres and other spares had gone on ahead.

It took the convoy a week to cover the 400 km to Mavinga over some of the most hostile, back-breaking and unforgiving ground in the world. 'The sand was very loose,' said Maree. 'The vehicles overheated as they churned through it. Pipes burst and oil spurted out and was spread by the fans and compacted with whirling sand, leaves and twigs. We eventually learnt to lower our tyre pressures to make it easier to plough through the sand.

'Until Luengue (100 km south of Mavinga) we moved by day. But then we came within range of the enemy Migs and we had to start moving at night only. It caused lots of problems.'

One of the main difficulties was navigation. The journey from Luengue to Mavinga is across a true wilderness where the leopard, the lion and the martial eagle are kings. There are no roads, no people, not a trace of development. The voyager must snake and twist northwards over low forest ridges and through valley grasslands, and find fording places across deep rivers.

The sandy soils are particularly fine and deep, and no sooner has one trail been opened up than the ruts become hopelessly deep and clogging and another trail has to be pioneered. This meant that the lead vehicles had to smash down trees and bounce over them. Headlights got smashed, engines became fiery hot and their grilles became blocked with dust and forest debris. Soldiers all the time had to watch for crashing timber; many South African casualties in the War for Africa came from trees falling across struggling trucks and armour. Later one 61 Mech troopie was killed when his Ratel dashed into tree cover after an air raid warning and he was crushed between the armoured car's hatch and a hefty tree branch. Tiffies (mechanics) had to perform miracles and work 24-hour days to service and repair the machines and keep the columns moving.

'We stopped at sunrise, spread the convoy, camouflaged everything under the trees, and then rested all day,' said Maree. 'At sunset we started again, but only one of our Ratels had night navigation electronics. It would set a course for Mavinga and then weave its way through the forest towards the destination. We had to move very slowly and stop constantly to check by radio that all 126 vehicles were within sight of each other.'

When one Ratel broke down, the driver and gunner were ordered to wait with the vehicle for tiffies coming up with the rearguard. The rearguard chose the wrong one of a number of trails, and the two 61 Mech men waited in the wilderness for a fortnight, working their way through all the food and water, before a search party found them.

By 7 September most of 61 Mech had arrived at its assembly point 25 km southeast of Mavinga. Colonel Ferreira had arrived in the battle zone just 48 hours earlier and had assigned Commandant Bok Smit and the bulk of 61 Mech to Combat Group Alpha to take on 47 Brigade when the moment was right.

The wait began.

CHAPTER 17

SOFTENING UP 47 BRIGADE

47 Brigade had been subjected to a constant artillery barrage since it came around the Lomba source at the beginning of September. Its early speedy progress eastwards had been slowed to barely a kilometre a day as the SADF G-5s, MRLs and 120 mm mortars pounded it all night and later began to hit it for short periods during the day. Once the most dangerous and aggressive of the enemy brigades, it was now the most vulnerable. It had planned to link up quickly with 59 and 21 Brigades to receive new ammunition and fuel supplies, reserves of which were beginning to run low.

Ferreira's strategy was to exhaust the brigade and draw it into a 'killing ground' where the advantage would be with his small force which, like the Boer armies of old, aimed to keep the enemy off balance with fast-moving, unorthodox and aggressive manoeuvres until Fapla began to make major mistakes.

One of Ferreira's first decisions was that the SAAF had to begin supporting the artillery with ground bombing attacks. The first strike by Mirage F-1AZs, Buccaneers and Canberras was planned to take place at first light on Friday 11 September.

Major Pierre Franken was sent out with Special Forces of 5 Reconnaissance Regiment and a UNITA unit to place phosphorescent flares to identify the position where 47 Brigade, exhausted by the constant artillery fire, had dug in four kilometres south of the Lomba-Cuzizi confluence. As well as identifying the target, Franken's team marked the path of the bombing run after being given the necessary co-ordinates by the SAAF. In darkness this was a dangerous and difficult but vital mission.

'We got all the flares in place, and then they said they were cancelling the raid,' said Franken. 'Then they changed their minds and said they were coming, only to cancel the raid once more. Everybody in the team was furious, and it didn't help when I had to send some of the recces and UNITA soldiers back again to bring the flares out because I was under orders not to let them fall into Fapla's hands. UNITA was meant to carry out a harassing raid that day on 47 Brigade, but they refused after the SAAF failed to arrive.'

What Franken did not know at the time was that the SAAF's attack plan had been overridden by President P W Botha at the last moment. Diplomatic negotiations had reached a critical stage on a prisoner exchange involving SADF reconnaissance commando Captain Wynand du Toit, captured by Fapla in 1985 while preparing to lead an attack on a US-owned oil refinery in the northern Angola province of Cabinda. The President did not want anything to foul up the release of Du Toit, whose capture some 2,000 km beyond South African-administered territory had caused great embarrassment to Pretoria.

Du Toit was swapped for some 170 Fapla soldiers captured by UNITA and the SADF. According to sources close to Amnesty International, all the Fapla soldiers were executed for failure in battle after they had been returned by the International Committee of the Red Cross to Luanda, Angola's capital.

47 Brigade, unable to retreat and increasingly desperate to link up with 59 and 21 Brigades, was now in danger of getting bogged down in the position south of the Lomba-Cuzizi source. Its commander made a desperate attempt to join hands with 59 Brigade which led to the 13 September battle with Hartslief's Battle Group Bravo. Ferreira drew up new plans for another assault to try to finish off 47 Brigade. He received assurances from Pretoria that political considerations would not cause another last-minute cancellation of a major airstrike he planned for Wednesday 16 September. The strike would soften up 47 Brigade and then Commandant Bok Smit's Combat Group Alpha would enter the war for the first time in an attempt to wipe out the beleaguered Angolan force.

Again 5 Reconnaissance recces were sent in on the thankless task of marking the east-west bombing run and targets for the air strike planned for the early morning of 16 September. Pierre Franken was not with them this time. He had set up an observation post on a hill to the north of the Lomba to bring in artillery fire throughout the night before the air raid and Combat Group Alpha's attack.

Commandant Smit planned to hit 47 Brigade from behind, and so his force of assorted Ratels moved out at 4 am on 16 September, passing south of 47 Brigade and then swinging north to attack from the west. Against a force of more than 1,000, Smit was attacking with only 250 men. 'It was 4 to 1 against us, compared with textbook recommendations of 3 to 1 in the attackers' favour,' said Ferreira. 'But we had no choice.'

Sitting on his hillside, Franken watched four Mirages strike just before 6.30 am and drop clusters of fragmentation bombs among 47 Brigade positions. A follow-up bombing run by three Buccaneers was cancelled when they were picked up on the Angolan radar. Franken instead called in a devastating G-5 bombardment which led 47 Brigade's commander to report to Cuito Cuanavale that the brigade was in serious trouble.

But 61 Mech was also in trouble.

Laurence Maree said: 'We manoeuvred for more than four hours until we got around behind them on their tracks. But then we found the bush was much denser than we had expected. We could see hardly further than ten metres. We could only move very, very slowly and had to stop often to confirm that the vehicles were keeping within sight of others. It was nearly midday before we began to make contact with elements of 47 Brigade.'

Pierre Franken realised too late that 61 Mech had misjudged also its line of attack. Through his binoculars he watched as the Ratels advanced west-east along a line too much to the north of the brigade. When contact was made it was not directly with the main body of 47 Brigade but with a flanking element, giving the enemy officers time to organise a response to the SADF intrusion.

'Their flanking force opened up with small-arms fire and RPG-7 rockets, and then we came under heavy artillery attack from BM-21s, D-30s and 82 mm and 120 mm mortars,' said Major Maree. 'We were looking for the enemy but we just couldn't see them because they were so well dug in among the thick bush. At the same time Commandant Smit had a fearful job keeping all the Ratels together.

'Because there were so many trees a lot of enemy shells and bombs detonated among the heavier branches, causing more shrapnel problems than we had anticipated. Whole trees fell on to the Ratels and the infantrymen who had debussed spent most of their energy sheltering from flying debris. By late afternoon we had lost one infantryman killed and three wounded and, as far as we could tell, all we had knocked out was one of their mortar pits.'

Commandant Smit decided the attack had become a kamikaze mission, and just before sundown he asked Colonel Ferreira for permission to withdraw and attack again the next day.

61 Mech withdrew under a screen of white phosphorus laid down by the mortar teams. Ferreira weighed up the chances of success and ordered Smit to break off altogether. He decided to wait a bit longer for 47 Brigade to make a fatal error. In the meanwhile he would concentrate on demoralising the Fapla troops with Mirage F-1AZ fragmentation and delayed detonation bomb raids and artillery attacks. It became possible to inflict more damage than before because 47 Brigade, which had been moving forward in a five by five kilometre square, now dug in more permanently in an ellipse roughly two kilometres long and 1.5 km deep at its thickest point.

'By then we had realised we would have to destroy 47 Brigade by confronting it with a mechanised force,' said Franken. 'They were digging in deep, and we knew from our own experience that it would take many heavy barrages to break them. I decided to economise with our G-5 ammunition, bringing in single shots only on vehicles that we could see. Between 17 September and 3 October we shot out two tanks and eleven trucks and armoured cars in this way'.

The earlier fiery encounter between Robert Hartslief's Combat Group Bravo and the armoured tactical group and forward elements of 47 Brigade had caused major fears back in Pretoria that 59 and 21 Brigades were about to push across the Lomba in force.

On the same day as Combat Group Alpha's abortive 16 September attack on 47 Brigade, a whole planeload of top brass led by General Jannie Geldenhuys flew in to Mavinga to assess the 'crisis situation'. It was not until late in the evening that Deon Ferreira joined Geldenhuys,

Major-General Willie Meyer (the commander of the South West African Territory Force), Admiral Putter, Colonel Dick Lord, Jonas Savimbi and two of UNITA's top generals, Demostenes Chilingutila and Ben-Ben Arlindo Pena.

They were surprised to find Ferreira in a jaunty mood, confident that the end was near not for the SADF-UNITA forces but for Fapla.

★ ★ ★

When Fapla's 21 Brigade abandoned its attempt to cross the Lomba it was ordered by HQ in Cuito Cuanavale to hand over the supplies it had for the beleaguered 47 Brigade to 59 Brigade to complete the delivery.

21 Brigade put a TMM mobile bridge across the Cunzumbia River and gave the materials to 59 Brigade, whose commander then sent a supply convoy with two battalions of infantry to a point just a few kilometres northeast of the Lomba-Cuzizi confluence to await the arrival of 47 Brigade on the south bank of the Lomba.

Pierre Franken, meanwhile, had established a more permanent observation post on the southeastern slope of the 1,260 metre-high Mucobolo Hill, just 800 m northwest of the Lomba-Cuzizi confluence. His team consisted of another artillery observer, Lieutenant Hans May, a young national serviceman; several UNITA guerrillas; and, when they had rested after their unexpected set-to of 6 September with 47 Brigade, Sergeant Mac da Trinidada and his recce team.

'We had to monitor all three of the enemy brigades,' said Franken. 'From about 21 or 22 September we saw units from 47 Brigade bringing out logs from the treeline and laying them across the marsh to build a kind of road towards the Lomba. 59 Brigade started doing the same from the north and moving a TMM bridge southwards along it towards the river. Once we'd reported that activity, we were told our priority was to prevent 59 and 47 Brigades from joining up. We brought such constant artillery fire down on them that they were forced to work at night only.'

Franken and his men worked shifts in their lookout post at the top of a ten metre tree. 'I wore a Fapla uniform,' said Franken, 'and I coated myself so thickly with blacking that I was more beautiful than Sidney

Poitier. I'd forgotten everything my mother ever taught me about personal hygiene. I don't think I'd washed for eight weeks. My trousers became so dirty and thick with grease that I wrote my calculations on them to work out target co-ordinates for our guns.'

Franken worked occasional 13-hour shifts in the tree, burdened with a 10 kg radio, map, compass, binoculars, night sight equipment, torch, protractor, rifle and ammunition. Every hour or so he would haul up a flask of water and a packet of protein biscuits at the end of a rope.

CHAPTER 18

THE TRAP CLOSES

Meanwhile, Colonel Ferreira had decided the time had come to destroy 47 Brigade. Of the 1,400 men who had left Cuito Cuanavale two months earlier with the crack Fapla outfit, SADF intelligence estimated that some 300 were now dead and 200 wounded. The brigade was growing short of food, ammunition and fuel. Its morale was getting very thin, too. If a *coup de grâce* was not attempted soon by the SADF, 47 Brigade might escape across the river to regroup and re-equip itself to fight another day.

The first inkling Captain Herman Mulder got that something big was in the offing came on Sunday 27 September when he was ordered by Ferreira to transfer from 32 Battalion and perform his intelligence duties with 61 Mechanised Battalion, which had yet to see action on the scale for which it was trained and equipped.

Ferreira told Mulder, a 28-year-old, broad-shouldered career officer who had completed six years of intelligence work with 32 Battalion, he needed the best possible intelligence map he could draw up of the base area of 47 Brigade and its accompanying armoured tactical group. Mulder, abandoning his latest course of study, in the Zulu language, went to work with his full range of intelligence tools – enemy radio intercepts; reports from recce teams and artillery observation posts; air reconnaissance photography; interrogation of prisoners; assessment of UNITA intelligence reports; and interpretations of Radio Angola.

Mulder's final report and charts told Ferreira that 47 Brigade's main trench positions were in deep bush about four kilometres due south of the Lomba-Cuzizi confluence. But some elements had moved north into a hook-shaped area of forest protruding into the *anhara;* at their nearest point they were only two kilometres south of the Lomba River.

Ferreira weighed everything up and decided to launch his attack on Monday 5 October. Commandant Bok Smit's Combat Group Alpha, composed mainly of a full range of Ratel squadrons and platoons from 61 Mech, would be the spearhead. But the combat group would be strongly reinforced by an infantry company from 32 Battalion and by four UNITA battalions, one of which would help in the attack on 47 Brigade while the others made diversionary assaults on 59 Brigade. In reserve was Combat Group Charlie, composed almost entirely of 61 Mech troops plus a few small 32 Battalion elements, under the command of Major Dawid Lotter.

On Monday 28 September Ferreira's planning sessions with Hougaard, Smit, Lotter and Hartslief at forward HQ were interrupted by a summons to travel 70 km to Mavinga to talk to some 'top brass' who had pitched up in a C-130. They consisted of the State President P W Botha; Defence Minister Magnus Malan and his deputy Wynand Breytenbach; General Geldenhuys; General Liebenberg; Admiral Putter; and General Willie Meyer. Recurring visits by swarms of VIPs from the President downwards in Gucci safari suits and with bulging food hampers became the butt of bitter humour among ordinary fighting soldiers, whose sentiment was: 'If they provided us with as many fighting reinforcements as fucking right-hand men and advisers, we would wrap this up in no time and all be home for Christmas.'

For some reason, a wave of panic had spread in Pretoria that Fapla's 59 Brigade was about to bridge the Lomba and cross to the south bank, and that the SADF's thin blue, orange and white line was about to break. Botha and Malan were surprised when the grime-covered Ferreira breezed in full of confidence and apparently unaware of the crisis they were sure had developed. When Meyer asked Ferreira whether he was worried about the consequences of an attempted crossing by 59 Brigade, one of those present at the conference, in a big earthen command bunker, recalled Ferreira's eyes flashing as he replied: 'Hell, that will be a pleasure.'

Ferreira's upbeat mood and report impressed Botha and Malan. Geldenhuys was soon promised additional forces and funds to wage the War for Africa.

★ ★ ★

Sitting on Mucobolo Hill on Wednesday 30 September, Pierre Franken received reports from recces that a small party from 47 Brigade had made contact with 59 Brigade at the Lomba during the previous night. They passed over some seriously wounded troops and received a small consignment of food and ammunition which they carried back on their shoulders.

Franken radioed the information to Herman Mulder, who had already established from other sources that 59 Brigade had found a drift [fording place] about a kilometre to the east of the Lomba-Cuzizi confluence and had moved a TMM bridge to within three kilometres of it in the treeline to the north. Franken could also see ribbons of felled tree trunks and branches poking far out on to the *anhara* like lizards' tongues from Fapla positions in the treeline on both sides of the drift.

47 and 59 Brigades were clearly building corrugated wooden highways across the marshes for their vehicles and armour. But the question Ferreira wanted answered by Mulder was: is 59 Brigade intending to push southwards, or is this road being built to permit 47 Brigade to retreat north?

Either way, the time had come to attack 47 Brigade without further delay – either before it escaped across the Lomba, or before it was reinforced on the south bank by 59 Brigade.

Ferreira ordered Commandant Smit and Major Lotter, who were getting their troops and equipment ready for the planned 5 October attack at an assembly point near a lagoon some 22 km to the southeast of the drift, to bring their preparations forward as much as possible. They would be striking at the enemy earlier than anticipated.

By 1 October Mulder was able to give Ferreira a detailed military assessment of which enemy brigade the wooden log road was being prepared for. His EW experts had intercepted and deciphered enemy communications between Cuito Cuanavale and the officer commanding 47 Brigade, Commander Silva, in which the brigade was ordered to withdraw north of the Lomba. Silva resisted, saying the brigade was still viable and would be able to push east towards Mavinga if reinforced.

On 1 October Silva was ordered to begin the withdrawal or face a court martial. One message said: 'No excuses will be accepted, especially if the Russians are caught.' It was the first concrete evidence Mulder had obtained of a Soviet presence with 47 Brigade, though he had assumed from past precedent that there would be seven or more Soviet military advisers at the brigade HQ.

On Friday 2 October Franken reported that work parties from 47 Brigade had fully extended the wooden road out two kilometres across the marshes to the drift. Vehicles were assembling in the treeline, while to the south of this marshalling area, well inside the bush, the rest of the brigade had dug into new trenches within striking distance of the wooden road. Franken also spotted three T-55 tanks from 59 Brigade just inside the treeline on the northern side which obviously intended to give 47 Brigade support in its retreat across the Lomba.

Then he saw several score of trucks, missile carriers and armoured cars moving into an assembly area right on the treeline to the southeast of the drift across the open *anhara*. They were obviously preparing to begin an orderly retreat back to the north, covered by the guns of 47 Brigade's own infantry, a little further back in the treeline, and the heavy artillery of Fapla's 59 and 21 Brigades.

Franken, Lieutenant May, Sergeant Da Trinidada and their men and the supporting UNITA scouts on Mucobolo Hill now played an absolutely vital role in holding up 47 Brigade's retreat while Smit and Lotter continued working around the clock to get their combat groups ready for the big attack.

'Through our binoculars, we estimated that there were more than 100 vehicles spread out in the assembly area,' said Franken. 'We brought down more or less constant G-5 and MRL bombardments on the vehicle groups and over the infantry concentrations. Herman Mulder radioed me to say that Colonel Ferreira was very happy because he was now convinced that 47 Brigade was feeling very lonely.

'Then a couple of hours before dusk (on 2 October) some small groups of vehicles made a break across the *anhara* towards the drift. Unnoticed by us, 59 Brigade had got the TMM bridge into place, reinforced by lots of logs.

'The first vehicles to arrive at the bridge included two Sam-9s. They were the first to attempt to cross, which was logical because they needed a good air defence system on the northern bank to protect the full crossing when it got underway'.

[The Soviet Sam-9 is a tactical short-range air defence system, firing 'Gaskin' surface-to-air missiles with ranges of eight kilometres from four launcher tubes mounted on top of the chassis and body of a BRDM-2 amphibious armoured car.]

Franken redirected the G-5 fire to the bridgehead and the little knots of vehicles gathering near it.

'In the process of adjusting you bring in fire from just one gun before all eight in the battery begin to shoot,' he said. 'It was interesting. The orientation gunner fired his first round and the shell fell well off line. I gave him a correction to make to the right. His next round fell precisely on top of a BTR-60 armoured personnel carrier, destroying it completely. I doubt whether anyone aboard it survived. A shot like that requires a lot of skill and training, but it needs a bit of luck as well!

'That caused a lot of fright among the Fapla forces. The vehicles moved away in two directions from the burning BTR, and there I think I made a mistake by trying to divide the G-5 fire between both groups. One managed to regroup and retreat back across the *anhara* to the bush, and one of the Sam-9s managed to cross the bridge to safety on the north bank.

'Then I saw the second Sam-9 approaching the bridge, so I brought down concentrated fire on and around the TMM. We hit the Sam-9 as it rolled heavily across. That blocked the bridge to other vehicles. One of the T-55 tanks of 59 Brigade came down to try to recover the Sam-9, but they couldn't pull it out because they were hampered by our shelling.'

★ ★ ★

An odd incident occurred up on Mucobolo Hill. As Franken brought down the heavy bombardment on the bridgehead, Da Trinidada suggested that he take out a reconnaissance patrol for some five kilometres because Fapla was bound to realise there was an SADF OP (observation post) directing the shelling and send out a team of their own to try to locate and destroy it.

'I went out with two of my team,' said Da Trinidada. 'We'd gone about four kilometres when we saw men moving in the bush ahead. The bush was quite thick there so we kept moving forward until we were about 100 metres from them, and then we suddenly realised they were Fapla. They stopped dead in their tracks at almost the same moment: they'd obviously sensed we were SADF. It was a surprise for us, and it was a surprise for them. But, strangely, neither of us opened fire. We both just turned around and walked away. We reported to Major Franken and told him that we would have to be very careful.'

But there was little time left to think about being careful.

One of the most important land battles in South Africa's history was about to begin.

★ ★ ★

Through the night of 2 to 3 October Franken, using passive night vision equipment, could still see the outlines of vehicles and people working at the bridgehead. 'Every time we saw movement we brought down fire on them to stop them recovering anything or getting across,' he said. 'During the night we shot out a few vehicles and there were big fireballs lighting up the darkness. And then a couple of hours before dawn the 47 Brigade vehicles finally tired of trying to establish the bridgehead and retreated back across the *anhara* to the treeline. I went to sleep for the first time in 48 hours, and asked to be woken again the moment there was any sign of movement.'

An hour later Franken was rudely shaken from a deep sleep. The man on watch had heard the distant rumble of scores of armoured cars, and the noise was getting nearer.

61 Mechanised Battalion was on its way to attack 47 Brigade.

CHAPTER 19

THE DESTRUCTION OF
47 BRIGADE

War is confusion. You often don't know what happened until you've read the book.
General Jannie Geldenhuys.[1]

The battle between the SADF's 61 Mechanised Battalion and Fapla's 47 Brigade of 3 October 1987 was a swirling, fast-moving, bloody and prodigiously noisy affair over rough, undeveloped terrain in one of the remotest areas on earth.

To help the reader peer through the clutter and jumble of that day's warfare, Captain Herman Mulder, the 32 Battalion intelligence officer attached to 61 Mechanised Battalion, Major Laurence Maree, second-in-command of 61 Mech, and Artillery Regiment Major Pierre Franken, who watched the whole battle from his OP on Mucobolo Hill, tell how the battle looked from each of their vantage points on Saturday 3 October 1987.

Herman Mulder's Story

At the assembly area it had been like organised bedlam trying to make sure that everything was fully prepared for the attack. It was only at 3 am [on 3 October] that all the ammunition was ready and loaded; that the logistics had been fully planned and prepared; and that we felt we had gathered all the intelligence possible about the enemy.

'I was drained before we even set out. My assistant, an Air Force intelligence lieutenant, and I had not slept for two nights. For 48 hours nonstop we had been collecting and processing every available bit of information to try and think through all the possibilities that lay ahead that day.

'I reconstructed in map form, as best I could with the information available, the base area of 47 Brigade for Commandant Bok Smit. I also drew a sketch for him of how I thought the enemy would take up battle positions.

'The movement of our attack force was to be first from south to north towards the Lomba. Then we were to begin swinging westwards so that we would attack directly from the east along the line of the *anhara* and the trees until we were right in among 47 Brigade's positions. I expected Fapla's armoured tactical group to place its tanks in defensive positions well inside the treeline, so we put a platoon of four Ratels carrying ZT3 anti-tank missiles on our western flank.

'Then I got into a Ratel for the first time in my life. My Ratel-90 was to move in a beeline behind Bok Smit's command Ratel, which itself was to move 80 m behind our leading Ratels moving in extended line abreast. My radio team was in an EW Ratel directly behind me.

'We moved off at 5.20 am in darkness, with more than 50 Ratels (which included the full range from Ratel-20 infantry carriers, whose main gun is a 20 mm cannon, to the Ratel-90, whose main roles are anti-tank and "bunker-busting" with its turret-mounted 90 mm gun) in three lines abreast, interspersed with other vehicles like armoured ambulances and recovery trucks, and the Ratel-ZTBs to the side.

'All that movement kicked up so much dust that we had to have our headlights full on. We taped them so that there was just a minimum beam, in the hope that that would reduce the warning to 47 Brigade that we were on our way.

'As chief intelligence officer, I was also responsible for navigation. So it was a hell of a relief to me when we succeeded in hitting our first RP (rendezvous point) just after first light to the east of 47 Brigade's positions. Lieutenant-Colonel Setti of UNITA's 3rd Regular Battalion met us there. Two hundred of his men were to move 800 m ahead of our front rank to pick up the enemy positions and lead us on to them, draw the opening fire, and then break away to the flanks to leave the way clear for 61 Mech's attack. [UNITA's 5th Regular Battalion and its 275th Special Force Commandos, SAS-style fighters trained by the SADF, were positioned to the southwest of 47 Brigade in case the Fapla forces staged a retreat in that direction.]

'We continued to push forward, but they obviously began to hear our engine noise because suddenly we were bombarded by ZIS-3s [Soviet 76 mm field guns with a range of 13 km] and D-30s [Soviet 122 mm Howitzers with a range of up to 21 km]. Bok Smit ordered everyone to cut their engines and maintain radio silence, and they stopped firing after a while because they were no longer able to work out where we were. But that was only a temporary reprieve. When we entered the battle those guns, fired by 59 and 21 Brigades and to some extent also by 47 Brigade, opened up again and never let up all day until it was all over at 6.20 pm. We were also bombarded by teams of Mig-21s.

'UNITA intelligence officers met up and liaised with us and gave their latest assessment of 47 Brigade's locations. They said the vehicle force was strung out in the edge of the treeline for several hundred metres westwards and eastwards of the southern end of the wooden road.

'Bok Smit ordered a probing attack, and from then on I hardly remember the precise order of events. All I know is that after we spotted their positions we called in an artillery bombardment. We attacked and after two hours we withdrew to load up with fresh ammunition and to make minor repairs.

'Five times we attacked that day to try to break them, and each time we had to withdraw for repairs and new supplies, to reform and to give our men short respites from the non-stop bombardments of the guns of three enemy brigades and Fapla's Migs.

'Every time we withdrew they thought we were retreating, so they gathered tanks and infantry for a counter-attack, and it was only after they had concentrated their forces for that purpose that Bok Smit would order us to attack again.

'All the time my Ratel was with Bok Smit's within 100 m of the front line. I have never experienced anything like it. I said goodbye to my life at least six times that day. All the time there was bombing and bombing and bombing. The noise was beyond belief. It was driving me mad. All the time I was thinking: "I just want to get out of this fucking vehicle." Even when 61 Mech was ordered to stay static, my vehicle and Bok Smit's continued to draw enemy artillery because we couldn't go radio silent like the other Ratels.

'I was afraid in the biggest sense you can think of it. You know all the time that the next shell might be for you.

'When we engaged 47 Brigade in the first morning attack we couldn't see through the bush anywhere for more than 15 m. At the end of the day we could see for 800 m, which gives an idea of the intensity of the fire. Shells and shrapnel slashed down the trees and shrubs and constant explosions started raging fires. In a few hours a great area of tropical forest was reduced to a waste resembling a World War I no-man's land.

'In the first few hours of the fighting our Ratels, with 90 mm guns, were taking on T-54 and T-55 tanks, with much more powerful 100 mm guns and thicker armour, at ranges sometimes of only 10 to 15 m. We were outgunned, and so we had to rely on the Ratel's greater manoeuvrability and our men's better training and greater skills.

'In those conditions the only moment you saw an enemy tank was when it fired. It was the same for them with the Ratels. So gunners were firing at each other's flashes. We used four Ratels at a time to eliminate one tank. We would manoeuvre the Ratels into a half moon around the tank and then rake its estimated position with searching fire. It then had to veer around looking for the different sources of the gunfire: it was like a rhino trying to butt off and stamp on a molesting pride of young lions. We would dodge back into cover and then pop out again for another bite. It usually took at least four to five rounds of 90 mm fire from each Ratel before a shell found the vulnerable area of the tank at the front just below the turret. Shells which hit other parts of the tank just clanged off the armour.

'Each time I was overcome by fear I felt like it was my turn to die. It was a physical feeling spreading up from your feet as though someone has grabbed you and squeezed you. Then you realise: "I'm not gone." In the end you just learn to accept this hairy feeling. You recover, and then it comes again. For the first time, I realised the devastating feelings that must grip a Ratel gunner sitting behind his 90 mm gun.

'But during that spasm of terror you completely lose five or six pieces of information coming in. I had to receive, process and analyse four different types of new intelligence every minute. My radio team in the EW vehicle was listening to and transcoding all the enemy frequencies and passing on the information to me. All the time I was having to evaluate rapidly these little fragments of enemy chatter.

'Heat of battle conversations are muddled and ambiguous. You couldn't be sure whether it was a tank or a piece of heavy artillery that a commander was ordering to switch its fire towards a target on its right. As I analysed all this stuff I had to pass on vital information quickly over our radio nets to Bok Smit and to my Ratel commander, driver and gunner. At the same time I had to monitor conversations going on between scores of Ratels. Then there was Pierre Franken sitting on his hill and giving a constant supply of information on his radio net.

'You sit in the vehicle concentrating on all the information, with all the enemy tactics and doctrine in mind learnt from the past, processing new information in seconds to decide whether it's true and evaluate what it means. All the time I was playing with my pre-battle sketches, amending them, drawing in a new position and building up new pictures.

'At one time I had such vital but complex information for Bok Smit that I had to leap out of my Ratel and run through our infantry, with metal flying around all over the place, to his vehicle. Looking back, I don't know how I did it. I'm not so courageous that I could make a cool, detached decision to do something like that.

'Every time we withdrew I went to Bok Smit to give him a more considered, in-depth briefing. I was his battlefield brain. I had to think like the enemy commander and play his role, telling the Commandant what I would be considering doing next if I was his opposite number. On my analysis, he made his new battle decisions. If I gave him nonsense, it could kill a lot of our men.

'Later I couldn't believe how much work I'd done. I had scribbled 20 folio pages of tight-packed notes during the whole battle. Even though we'd had no sleep for all those hours, my adrenalin was still pumping long after we'd withdrawn from the battle area. However, my Air Force assistant was so shattered from lack of sleep that he nodded off at the height of the fighting with an inferno raging all round. I had to hit him hard across his chest to wake him up; I couldn't rouse him any other way.

'The critical moment in the day came at about 2 pm. 47 Brigade's tactical group had tried, not too confidently, to envelop us from the flank with a tank attack. But as they made their effort the brigade's northern-most battalion [47 Brigade comprised three battalions] suddenly broke across the *anhara* towards the river in a totally undisciplined way after our Mirage F-1AZs had bombarded 59 Brigade, to reduce its artillery pressure on us, and UNITA's 3rd Regular Battalion had made a flanking attack on 47 Brigade from the southwest. Pierre Franken brought down MRL fire on the enemy infantry now exposed on the open grassland and wiped out nearly all of them. Soon afterwards another battalion broke and ran. Some of our Ratels moved among them, and I reckon that by the end of the day about 600 soldiers from 47 Brigade had been killed out on that grassland.

'At one stage there were more than 100 enemy vehicles strung out across the *anhara* on the wooden road trying to get to the river. Pierre Franken was picking them off one by one with the G-5s. I was liaising with him. I'd process raw material picked up by my EW men, and after a while I was able to work out which type of vehicles were out on the *anhara* and in what sort of order. So we could select priority targets. By the end of the day Pierre was able to hit a single tank which was on the move with only two or three G-5 bombs. If the gunners fired to the left of the target, he would report back to them and they would make a correction to the right. If that fell slightly too far to the right, the next correction ensured that the third one did not miss. It fell right on top of the tank.

'The third enemy battalion stayed with Commander Silva at his HQ inside the southern bushline together with the tactical group. They fought with much more grit and tenacity than we had expected. They had more tanks and BMP-1s with them than we had picked up from our intelligence work. [The Soviet BMP-1 is an armoured infantry combat vehicle mounted with a 73 mm gun and Sagger wire-guided anti-tank missiles.] We hadn't expected the three T-55s of 59 Brigade either which came to the north side of the Lomba to join the battle.

'Just after 4 pm the tanks from 47 Brigade's tactical group moved out on to the *anhara* to try to recover some of the vehicles abandoned by the 47 infantrymen who had tried to flee. They got hit heavily then. Commander Silva went off the air and we tried to drive the remnants of the third battalion onto the grassland where the MRLs could take them out.

'By just after 5 pm all of the tanks on the south side had been shot out, except for one last one which managed to carry on firing till 6 pm when we finally destroyed it. There were 127 enemy vehicles left between the treeline and the river – either bombed or abandoned. Their artillery stopped and it was quiet for the first time that day. They brought up another platoon of three T-55 tanks from 59 Brigade which started firing again from the north bank. But by then we had withdrawn out of range. At 6.20 pm they too fell silent, and it was all over for that day.

'I felt very proud. The sheer volume of the sophisticated Soviet weaponry committed to the push from Cuito Cuanavale had shocked us South Africans as it dawned on us what we would have to confront. It was by far the biggest offensive by any side in 12 years of Angolan warfare. But we had taken them on, and we had won ... and I had come out of it alive!'

Laurence Maree's Story

'We moved up that morning and by first light we were in the position from which we planned to launch the attack. Commandant Smit ordered the Ratel commanders to take up the pre-arranged combat formation. The advance fighting force was a squadron of 12 Ratel-90s, and in support just behind was a mixed squadron of Ratel-90s and Ratel-20s carrying a company [120 men] of infantrymen. Just to the north of our main force was a platoon of three Ratel-20s carrying infantrymen and the Ratel-ZT3 anti-tank platoon.

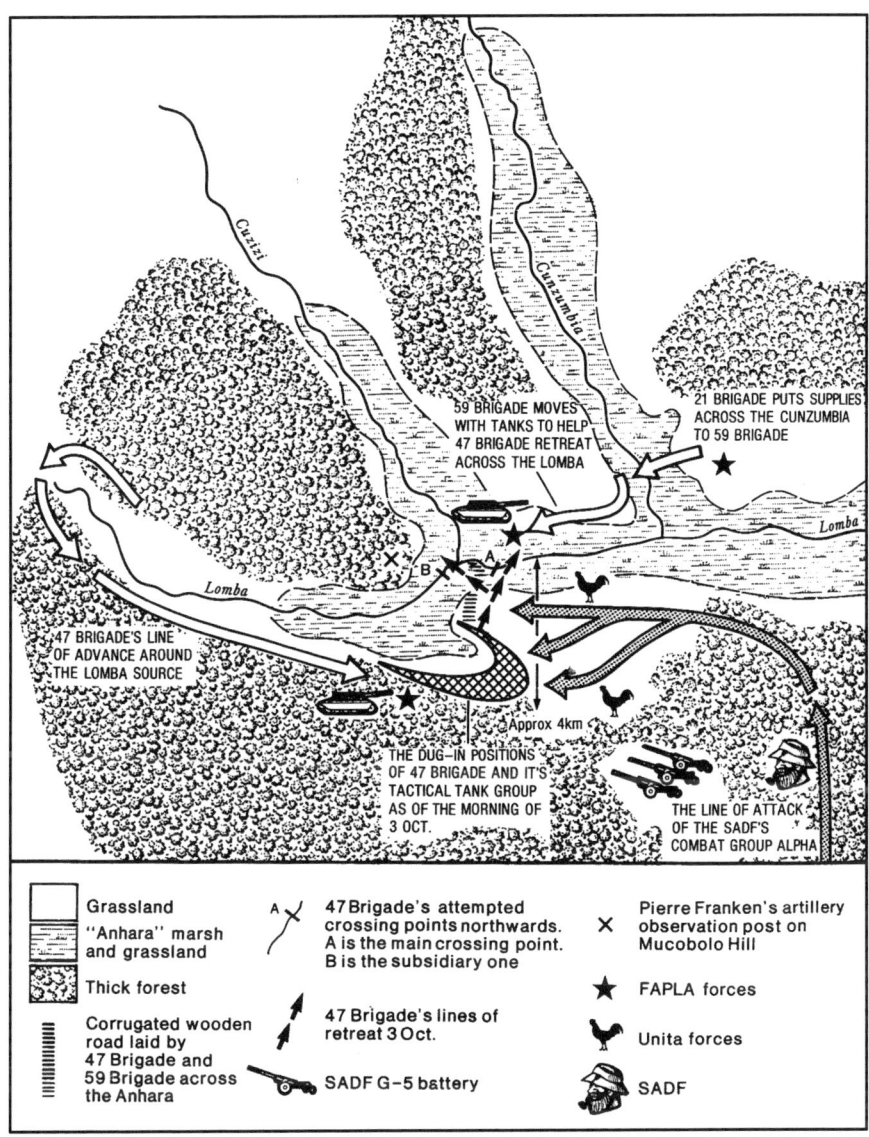

Lomba battle 3 October 1987.

A Ratel-81 mortar platoon was deployed inside the formation to keep leap-frogging forward to provide close artillery support. In reserve were another 20 or so Ratels [of Combat Group Charlie] under Major Dawid Lotter.

'We moved forward in combat formation behind UNITA's 3rd Battalion, which made contact with the enemy at about 10 am. They broke off and Pierre Franken brought down the full range of our artillery – G-5s, 120 mm mortars and MRLs – on their positions.

'We were pushing cautiously through what seemed like virgin bush that had never known the intrusion of man when, suddenly and with total surprise, the fight just erupted with great violence. Within minutes of engaging 47 Brigade we got the first report of one of the enemy tanks being knocked out.

'That and what followed was the most awesome and exhausting ordeal I've ever experienced. Indirect fire was raining in all around from the enemy artillery. Bushes were burning, trees were falling, and there was a constant pinging and resonating ringing as bullets and bits of shrapnel ricocheted from the Ratels.

'The luck was with us that day. I remember one Ratel had its tyres shot out, and a Withings recovery truck [an armoured vehicle with winching equipment] came up from the rear to tow it back to be refitted. The guys in the Withings drew up near the Ratel and jumped out to adjust the towing chains. They'd just got back into the Withings when an enemy mortar bomb exploded between the two vehicles. If they'd still been on the outside they'd all have been killed.

'I don't know how many times the enemy Migs attacked us that day, but the number of raids seemed to be enormous and went on right through the day. Colonel Ferreira told us later that there had been between 40 and 60 enemy aircraft sorties.

'They were coming in at 60 m, so low that you could see the pilot in the cockpit. We couldn't fire at them because we were so busy with the firefight on the ground. We had hoped they wouldn't try airstrikes against us since we were in close contact with their troops and they could just as easily hit their own forces as us. But even though they were dropping bombs and firing cannon from such low heights they didn't do any serious damage. Our lives were extraordinarily charmed. I personally think it was the Hand of the Lord that was over us there. It can't have been anything else because I can't think that the Fapla and Cuban pilots were so bad that they couldn't hit us accurately.

'We first broke combat after about two hours. We needed to put more gas in the recoil systems of the guns of the Ratel-90s and to replenish ready-to-use ammunition. Pierre Franken brought G-5 fire on the enemy and the Faplas didn't disturb us while we were catching our breath. We withdrew no more than 300 m, but I was able to get out of my Ratel and squat down and make a cup of coffee right next to it. Soldiers were walking around between the Ratels; guys were standing on top of them hauling up freshly unpacked ammunition and repacking it in the bomb carriers.

'By 1.15 pm everybody had reported "combat ready" to Commandant Smit, and back we went. We made contact again with the enemy after only 150 m.

'By the time of our midday withdrawal we had already knocked out four to six tanks. They were confirmed hits. We could see them burning. There were others which were hit and burning out which continued moving until they were out of sight in the bush.

'Now we made contact with the tanks again. They manoeuvred on to the Ratels and again there was direct and indirect fire bursting all over the place all the time. I don't think they often knew where we were even though the field of vision had been opened up by the destruction of the morning's fighting. The Ratels would stand and fire and then scuttle off into some clump of bush before reappearing elsewhere for another shot. They changed positions all the time, emerging again and again to fire another round.

'Right through the day the guys in the EW vehicle gave us a stream of very good tactical information from what they were picking up from the enemy radios. It enabled us to move in on them and neutralise them before they began a new manoeuvre. It was incredible how cool, calm and collected the EW guys were. No matter how heavy the bombing and shelling or how many shards of metal clattered against the Ratels, they monitored every situation and summed it up for us.

'At one very critical stage, when the enemy were starting to manoeuvre very aggressively, Commandant Smit asked the EW engineers to use our latest electronic equipment to jam the radio systems of the tanks. It was amazingly effective. They were driving around on the battleground, up and down, backwards and forwards. They didn't really know where they were.

'I remember hearing their tank commander – his call sign was "Cobra" and he was trying to call "Cobra Two", "Lion", "Python" and so on – failing to get anyone because of our jamming. His temper was exploding like a rocket because no one was answering him on the radio nets.

'We took advantage of that to press home our attack very belligerently. The fighting ground had been cleared of so much vegetation that we were now firing at each other from ranges of 40 to 75 m. The Ratel-90 gunners really did a tremendous job. With luck they could KO a tank with one 90 mm round, but usually it took more like seven rounds before a tank started to burn.

'I can't tell you how much courage it takes in a Ratel driver and gunner when a tank is charging towards them to summon up the will to stop still for long enough to stabilise their firing platform and get their round off. [Unlike a T-54/55 tank, which has in-built stabilisers and can fire on the move, a Ratel, like other armoured cars, can only fire from a static position.] Of course, as soon as they'd fired, off they sprinted like turbo-charged hares.

'One of our guys died that afternoon facing down a T-55 in his Ratel. A 100 mm shell from the tank skipped up from the sandy ground and went right through the turret. The Ratel commander, Lieutenant Hind, was terribly wounded and he died later. We had two others very seriously wounded that day, and another three with light wounds. The medics just pulled the shrapnel out of those who were slightly hurt, cleaned up the wounds, and they went straight back into combat.

'All day 47 Brigade had been reporting on its radios to Cuito Cuanavale that their situation was bad. After our second attack they said the situation was critical and that the Boers had come in enormous strength. In fact, they outnumbered us in manpower by four to one.

'We intercepted replies from Cuito Cuanavale of the Fapla HQ telling them that no matter what happened they must stay in their positions and confront the Boers. Intercepting messages like that gave us a lot of positive feelings and fighting ability to keep on going forward again and again.

'We broke contact again at about 2.45 pm. The firing had been so intense that the Ratel-90s were at rock bottom on ammunition. The main attack force was beginning to develop a few mechanical problems also, especially with the recoil systems of the guns. Bok Smit wanted to reorganise, put the Ratel-ZT3s and some mechanised infantry into the front line and bring Dawid Lotter's reserve force into combat.

'No sooner had we moved back than we got a radio message from Pierre Franken that something strange was happening. As soon as we broke combat small groups of Fapla infantry began to cut and run from their positions in the treeline and sprint across the *anhara* in unorganised retreat to try to get to the river. Bok Smit ordered all Ratels which were combat fit and ready straight back into action.

'When we reached the *anhara* they were really running wildly for the river. Many were without their equipment. Bok Smit ordered the Ratel-81 mortars into immediate action. The Ratel-81s sat in the southern treeline, giving the fire group commanders a clear view across the grassland and marsh of the enemy running. In those circumstances it wasn't difficult to bring down highly effective high explosive and white phosphorus mortar bombs on them.

'The high explosive shells scattered an arc of shrapnel on impact. Those soldiers who weren't scythed down that way were burned by the phosphorus. They were fleeing full pelt in large numbers and all the time the mortars were slaying them.

'Then more enemy vehicles and tanks moved out on to the *anhara* to try to get away. Our Ratels went in amongst them and there were fights all over the place. There were tanks scattered across the grassland burning. There were all kinds of vehicles. Some of them were abandoned. We were ordered not to get gun happy and shoot everything out because some of them would be wanted back in the Republic for our own research and development. Only if a vehicle was a threat did we neutralise it.

'Dawid Lotter was rescuing Lieutenant Hind's crippled Ratel inside the treeline when a tank sprang on him. It was shot out by Lieutenant Kooij [the same Kooij who had distinguished himself in the 13 September battle by destroying two tanks.] And, while we were mopping up in the last hour and a half before sunset, Kooij also shot out 47 Brigade's last active vehicle.

'It was sad. A ZSU-23 self-propelled anti-aircraft gun was rampaging around everywhere, taking many hits and fighting like a tiger until Kooij finally got it.

'It was only when we examined it later that we realised the driver had been abandoned by the rest of the crew; he hadn't been able to get out because the gun turret had been left swung round in such a position that it had jammed over his escape hatch. In all that frenzied driving he'd been trying to find a route to safety. He died under Kooij's fire.

'All across the *anhara* there were tanks and other vehicles burning. Some of the tanks got to the Lomba and tried to cross it. But as they approached the river they got stuck in the mud and deeper water. We could see the crews abandoning them before swimming and wading across. Then they wedged one tank on an armoured car in the river, and another tried to use it as a bridge to get across but fell off to the side when it was on top. We couldn't approach too near the bridgehead because we were drawing fire from 59 Brigade's T-55 tanks on the northern bank. Our Ratels' 90 mm guns had an effective range of only 1,200 m, whereas we were confronted with guns on the T-55s with ranges of 2,000 to 2,500 m.

'When there was no longer any effective enemy left to fight, we followed through for a quick inspection of the battlefield. There were tanks abandoned undamaged: their crews had just jumped out and run. There were mobile anti-aircraft missile systems standing there, BTR-60 armoured personnel carriers, BRDM-2 amphibious armoured cars, all kinds of Soviet trucks, including Gaz, Zil and Ural models, and Brazilian-manufactured Engesa trucks. Some in the treeline were just parked there undamaged under camouflage. Their crews, too, had just abandoned them and run.

'We didn't get a long look, because 61 Mech was ordered to move right out of the area that evening back to rear HQ in case big retaliatory air raids were launched the next day.'

★ ★ ★

Pierre Franken's Story

'On 3 October I was woken at about 6 am. 47 Brigade's vehicles were just standing there in the *anhara* after their efforts of the previous day to get across the Lomba. At 7 am their motors started up and they moved back southwards to take up positions inside the treeline. I could see them clearly, and so I was in an excellent position to pinpoint enemy concentrations and guide 61 Mech towards them with good directions.

'61 Mech made its first contact with the enemy, and the artillery observers moving at the front of the battalion asked me to take over direction of the fight. The observers were basically in line with the combat group itself so they could see little detail of where the enemy forces were. From our position on Mucobolo Hill I could see the whole battlefield spread out like a panorama; the action unfolded before me as though I was watching theatre-in-the-round from a seat at the top of the stalls.

'I told 61 Mech's observers that it was no problem. I would bring down the artillery fire but keep a path safe for 61 Mech if it marked the positions of its advancing lines with white or yellow smoke.

'There was some confusion to begin with. Because Colonel Ferreira had brought forward the time of the attack by 48 hours, short cuts were taken as preparations were accelerated. Critically, for me, I hadn't received details of 61 Mech's fireplan, the targets they intended engaging. I needed to know so that I could plot the targets accurately for our artillery boys and help them adjust their fire, as well as bring bombardments down on the bridgehead to prevent an enemy escape across the Lomba.

'As 61 Mech came in we had some misunderstandings. I was bringing down G-5 and MRL fire on the Fapla concentrations. But there were a few "in-flight prematures" as our MRL shells flew high over the heads of 61 Mech. Commandant Bok Smit told me in very colourful language that I was bringing down South African artillery fire on the SADF itself, not the enemy, and that he didn't appreciate it.' [An 'in-flight premature' is when a rocket explodes too early before it impacts on or near the target; with the MRLs about one in every 30 shells bursts prematurely, making a heavy noise and causing a lot of confusion.]

'We eventually settled that problem, and then at last one of my assistants manning the radio got 61 Mech's fireplan,' said Franken. 'He plotted it on my map, a huge thing which we'd prepared well. It was covered with fluorescent colour pen markings indicating all manner of positions and paths. It was the size of a double bed sheet, which made it a bit difficult to work with when you were perched at the top of a tree.

'Fifteen of 61 Mech's infantrymen, walking across the *anhara* as an advance contact group, came in on their radio net and told me it looked as though the enemy was preparing to move again out of the trees to the river. On that evidence, I suggested to Bok Smit that he should adjust his line of advance because 47 Brigade seemed to be preparing to abandon its positions. Then I saw one enemy truck move out of the treeline towards the river. As the fight went on, enemy soldiers in ones and twos started running out across the *anhara* towards the Lomba crossing. More and more of them began running until at one stage we counted some 350 Fapla infantrymen spread out across the open grassland in little knots trying to get to safety. Then a group of vehicles started coming out from their defensive positions among the trees. I began bringing artillery fire down on them, and the next moment they broke in all directions like confused ants.

'A strange thing happened next. A big part of the Fapla force started moving towards our position, which was really puzzling because we hadn't located any bridges west of the Lomba-Cuzizi confluence. The first two T-54 tanks leaving the chaos came right up to the river bank in front of us. The first tank drove into the river, which was narrow but deep and steep-sided, and jammed itself in it. The second tank then drove across the first. But the same thing happened as at the main bridgehead: the tank slipped off its brother and fell on its side to the left. The next vehicle was a PT-76 [light amphibious tank], and that also slipped off to the right side. After that they didn't attempt more crossings there with vehicles.

'At that stage the whole *anhara* was full of Fapla troops. I felt sorry for them. The MRL ripples were inflicting devastating casualties among them. While the MRLs hit the infantry, I was bringing down the G-5s on the vehicles.

'Trucks began to reach the river. Some got to the "tank crossing" in front of us and the crews just left their vehicles and ran across the tank top or swam across the river. When they began crossing we sent out about ten UNITA people under Mac da Trinidada to mount early warning patrols for us. We were scared with so many of them coming towards us. We seemed to be directly in the line of their escape route, and we had no idea how many were fleeing to the west of the Lomba-Cuzizi confluence and how many to the east of it.

'Mac and the UNITA guys brought back 15 Fapla prisoners. They were easy to capture, and Mac had to let others go because he couldn't handle any more. Mac said they were exhausted. Some had no weapons with them or just one magazine of ammunition. As they came close, Mac and his men just stood up from the undergrowth and ordered them to surrender. None fought back. We gave them food and water. They begged for water: they said they had been too scared to stop long enough at the Lomba to drink.

'Many of them were barefooted and some were very young. One sergeant was 16 years old! We gave him a tough interrogation; we asked him whether he wanted to go back to 47 Brigade or whether he would prefer that we shot him. He said the situation in 47 Brigade was very bad. He told us the Russians in the brigade had been getting on badly with Fapla and he complained that the Russians got special food. UNITA took eight of the prisoners away and I don't know what happened to them. We tied up the other seven; Mac and his recces took them back across the river to our HQ the following day.

'By now there were two main fire centres protecting 47 Brigade's withdrawal. Three tanks from 59 Brigade established a kind of direct fire support base to help their people get across the Lomba. A few tanks and armoured cars from 47 Brigade hung back towards the southern treeline to cover the retreat of their buddies; 61 Mech concentrated its attacks towards the end of the day on destroying those vehicles, but Fapla fought with more tenacity and courage than anyone in the SADF had expected.

'When there were very few Fapla troops left alive on the southern side of the river, three Angolan Mig-23s passed low over our position and bombed the abandoned vehicles to prevent them falling into SADF hands. Fortunately, we later found they had missed some of the juicier targets, including tanks abandoned near the river towards the end of the battle.

'As the sun began to sink, there was only mopping up going on. So we concentrated on counting the different types of vehicles dispersed across the *anhara*. There were some big, strange machines out there which we couldn't identify because by this time visibility was not so good in the setting sun...'

Note

1   In an interview with the author, Pretoria, 30 July 1989.

CHAPTER 20

BOOTY FROM THE BATTLEFIELD

Night fell, but Franken and his men kept constant watch on the shadowy silhouettes of the vehicles out on the *anhara*. Every time figures were detected flitting between the bits of equipment Franken brought down a short MRL ripple to scare off suspected Fapla demolition teams. Come the morning of Sunday 4 October, the SADF intended retrieving as many intact Soviet weapon prizes as possible.

Armscor was hungry for advanced Soviet weapons to see if there were ideas that could be incorporated into its own South African military designs and technology. Other captured weapons, particularly anti-aircraft guns, AK-47 rifles, RPG-7 rockets and Sam-7 missiles, became part of the SADF's own standard battle inventory and were supplied to UNITA.

With the dawn Franken's team saw clearly that the 'strange' machines out on the *anhara* were three or more vehicles belonging to Sam-8 anti-aircraft missile systems.

Franken immediately sent a message to HQ and Jan Hougaard, standing by to send in recovery teams to claim prizes, was ordered into immediate action by Colonel Deon Ferreira who realised that with the Sam-8s the SADF had hit a real jackpot. No Western country had managed to capture one of the systems which were first seen in public in Moscow in the mid-1970s.

Each Sam-8 missile system is mobile and consists of three separate vehicles. The launcher is built on the chassis of a six-wheeled amphibious vehicle. Six launcher tubes carry missiles ready to fire. Travelling at twice the speed of sound, a Sam-8 missile is deadly against warplanes up to a height of 12,000 m and at a distance of more than 13 km. They frightened SAAF pilots greatly. At least another eight missiles are carried inside the launch vehicle's hull, while a logistics vehicle follows with 36 additional missiles.

At the rear of the launch vehicle surveillance radar is mounted, while in front of it there is an array of radars and transmitters for guiding the missiles on to their targets. The third element of one single Sam-8 system is the fire control vehicle. It is a specially modified BTR-60 armoured personnel carrier stacked with all kinds of radio and other electronic technology.

'I briefed my team all through the night,' said Hougaard. 'They were all from 32 Battalion since 61 Mech had moved right out of the area. When Franken told Deon Ferreira that there were Sam-8s standing there, as new, among all the burning, exploding and wrecked machines, the Colonel's order to me was very succinct: "Get the thing".

'That was a hell of a night, because I was trying to deal with the needs of two different army commanders at once. I was the SADF liaison officer at that time with General Ben-Ben Arlindo Pena, a fine chap and one of UNITA's best field commanders. Colonel Ferreira came in with his orders just as Ben-Ben was telling me that his forces had located the tattered remains of Fapla's 21 Brigade crossing the Cunzumbia 30 km north of where it flowed into the Lomba.

'21 Brigade was joining up with elements of 59 Brigade which had fallen back, and together they were trying to form a new brigade structure. Ben-Ben wanted SADF artillery to pound this enemy concentration before it could begin to function effectively: he said his ground forces had pinpointed the location 100 per cent, but when we examined the map together I had to tell him that those forces had pulled back out of the range of our guns.

'Ben-Ben asked instead for an SAAF air bombardment as soon as it got light. It was a tricky situation. I couldn't tell him I was busy thinking of how to rescue booty from the field of battle with 47 Brigade. We knew that one of our problems out there would be with UNITA who had sent out three companies of their people during the night to prepare to clear up the battlefield. Those UNITA guys are nobody's lackeys. They're deeply into black pride and can teach white South Africans a thing or two about racism. Even though 61 Mech had fought 99 per cent of the battle, Savimbi regarded them as guest warriors on "his" territory. Abandoned enemy weaponry was therefore "his" also.

'I had to keep Ben-Ben cheerful. The problem was that an air raid took a lot of organising. When the SAAF hit a target they really went for it, but before Air Force commanders would commit their planes they required a lot of information and intelligence. I worked hard on the air attack, but since I couldn't also delay the Sam-8 rescue I designated Captain Piet van Zyl (of 32 Battalion) and Major Johann Lehman of CSI to get moving with six 32 Battalion guys to rescue the Sam-8s.

'It was obviously going to be difficult for Piet and Johann. Not only were there swarms of UNITA guys ready to get the enemy machinery, but pockets of Fapla infantry were still stuck, and continuing to resist, from their trench positions inside the southern treeline. Also small Fapla sabotage parties were coming back from north of the river with hand grenades and RPG-7 rockets to destroy the abandoned equipment.'

Van Zyl and Lehman took their small 'Sam-8 Salvage' force towards the battlefield in a Casspir. Their mission began in Fred Karno style. Halfway towards the objective the Casspir broke down and they had to thumb a lift in a truck in which the very UNITA soldiers they were trying to avoid were packed like sardines.

The truck stopped where General Chilingutila had established a forward base. He told Van Zyl and Lehmann that they could continue through the area, but since it was under UNITA control they would be subject to the commands of UNITA officers. Before pushing onwards the SADF men radioed back for a Withings recovery truck to be sent forward to join them.

'We quickly located the fire control vehicle for one of the Sam-8 systems in the treeline', said Van Zyl. 'It had been abandoned without any attempt to smash the gadgetry. We told the Withings crew to take it straight back to 32 Battalion's forward HQ.

'Major Lehman and I were still with UNITA forces, and at that stage we were playing by the rules. We wanted to get on to the *anhara* and find the Sam-8 launcher. A guerrilla colonel said OK, but his soldiers must accompany us and lead the way among the abandoned vehicles.

'We were just about to start when shooting broke out from one of the dug-in Fapla pockets of resistance. I started to "black up" with camouflage cream. The UNITA colonel held his troops back because of the shooting and he told me he was refusing me permission to go forward without them. I told him there was no way he was going to stop me and I ordered my men out on to the *anhara*.

'We located the Sam-8 launcher. It was stuck in the mud and we could see that Fapla had tried to pull it out. Then we spotted the logistics vehicle carrying the spare missiles just inside the treeline.'

In the Sam-8 launcher Van Zyl found a complete manual on how to operate the whole system, from starting the vehicle engine to firing the missiles. This caused some groans back at CSI because they had paid a great price for just such a manual through one of its clandestine operatives in the Middle East earlier in the year.

The manual was of no immediate use to Van Zyl because it was in Russian, and while he pondered how to get the Sam-8 out of the mud and into the hands of the SADF he came under fresh Fapla fire. He and his men retreated to a stretch of abandoned enemy trenchline, from where they saw a group of Fapla soldiers working under the bonnet of a Ural truck loaded with yellow drums of diesel fuel. Eventually the Faplas got the truck going and moved down to the river. Van Zyl's party laughed at the irony at having to let such a perfect target get away undamaged because they could not afford to disrupt their own retrieval mission.

'Lying out on the *anhara* were lots of tanks and other machines such as Stalin Organs,' said Van Zyl. 'Some of the vehicles had been abandoned with such suddenness that their engines were still idling in neutral. I went to a T-55 tank. I'd never been in a tank in my life, though I had driven bulldozers. But I managed to start it, hooked it up to the Sam-8 launcher (weighing more than 30 tons), pulled the launcher out of the mud and towed it back into the bushline. My mastery of the T-55 was minimal. I kept pulling and pushing the wrong knobs and levers. It was like a bucking bronco out of control and we shot right through the UNITA lines before we tamed it. Thank God no one was killed or hurt or there would have been hell to pay.

'We had to move fast because a unit from 59 Brigade, which proved to be tanks, was coming down again to the north bank of the Lomba. We could see its dust cloud getting nearer and nearer and every so often a Mig would sweep over the battlefield bombing the discarded vehicles.'

Hougaard, having eventually got Ben-Ben's air raid organised and launched, hiked towards the battle area with a platoon of 32 Battalion infantrymen over difficult terrain and around several continuing firefights between Fapla and 32 Battalion's G Company, which had been given the task of mopping up. He arrived in time to find Captain Van Zyl charging through UNITA lines in the Soviet tank with the giant and unique Sam-8 missile launcher bouncing along behind.

There was a lot of equipment to retrieve, so Van Zyl began teaching UNITA soldiers how to drive the T-54 and T-55 tanks and adapt them as recovery vehicles. It was a problem at first. Tanks in the hands of UNITA would veer off in totally unpredictable directions, disappearing out of control deep into the bush for five minutes at a time before re-appearing. But eventually the great towing operation was underway and all day long until about 4 pm serviceable bits of equipment were dragged back into the treeline.

'It was an astounding scene,' said Hougaard. '59 Brigade on the other side began firing its guns again after midday, and then in the late afternoon groups of Fapla were coming across the river and burning vehicles and shooting them up near to us and in amongst us. I walked around on the battlefield to try to assess how much Soviet weaponry was worth trying to recover. There was a stack of equipment there – tanks, artillery, trucks, including lots of brand new Brazilian Engesas whose seats were still covered with plastic from the factory. There was absolutely nothing wrong with many of the pieces. The milometer of one T-55 tank showed that the only distance it had travelled was from the Angolan port of Lobito to the war front. There were other Sam-8s, but they were completely burnt out.'

Sappers first inspected the abandoned equipment for booby traps before the recovery team removed worthwhile equipment from the *anhara*. One BTR-60 armoured personnel carrier puzzled the engineers because all its hatches and firing ports were shut tight from the inside and there was no way to get in. Then one of the portholes opened and an empty corned beef tin looped out. The iron shutter immediately slammed fast again. The engineers hammered on the side, but the only response was the ejection of another empty meat tin. Eventually a door opened and out stepped a Fapla officer who had made sure he was well fed before surrendering and becoming a prisoner of war.

Commandant Jan van der Westhuizen, who took command of the Artillery Regiment after the death of Johan Du Randt, was also drafted into the battlefield salvage force. He flashed his torch into another BTR-60 to see whether it could be recovered. He climbed in, and seeing only some abandoned clothes on the driver's seat he sat down to see whether he could get the machine started. Suddenly the pile of clothes began to writhe. Van der Westhuizen, scared silly, climbed out of the Soviet machine much faster than he had entered. The pile of clothes turned out to be an Angolan soldier who had been wounded and left behind by his comrades. He had fallen asleep as the battle raged around him only to be woken up when 20 SA Brigade's artillery boss sat on him.

Once Hougaard was satisfied that Van Zyl's virgin UNITA tankmen had minimally mastered their new T-54s and T-55s, he told them he was going to let them get on by themselves with the mass rescue of metal and machinery.

It proved difficult. With Migs occasionally sweeping the battlefield, the UNITA men were reluctant to venture onto the *anhara*. 'They were just sitting there laughing at the sight of Fapla demolition teams blowing up their own vehicles,' said Hougaard. 'I was swearing at them to do something about recovering the equipment. Eventually I got to Colonel Tarzan, their local commander, and persuaded him that he must get his men into action to get as much stuff as possible. I had to be careful how I spoke to him because I knew they were deeply suspicious about our intentions with the Sam-8s.'

Once UNITA had been badgered to busy itself on the *anhara,* its officers were mainly interested in bringing out trucks to supplement the convoys on which Savimbi sent weapons and other supplies to his guerrilla forces operating many hundreds of kilometres inside Angola.

Hougaard now concentrated on getting the three pieces of the intact Sam-8 system away to safety. He requisitioned the Sam-8 fire control BTR-60, in perfect working order, as his command vehicle and assigned Major Lehman to secure the logistics vehicle. Lehman, worrying all the time about enemy artillery and small-arms fire, encountered a lot of difficulties in working out how to get his machine started. But he mastered the ignition after about an hour and headed deep into the bush.

Hougaard helped Van Zyl move the vital launcher away from the conflict area. The towing tank, in which Van Zyl had overrun the UNITA lines, developed engine and air filter problems. All the tyres of the launcher vehicle had been shot out and the oil circulation system had been punctured in the blast from one of the SADF's MRL fragmentation bombs; the skin of the vehicle was peppered by a lot of neat little holes made by spitting ball bearings. But nothing vital had been damaged other than the oil system and the tyres.

Hougaard radioed HQ in Mavinga for advice on how, following the breakdown of the tank, he might get the launcher vehicle moving. He was instructed on how to pour oil through the system by hand. That way he could move the vehicle under its own power, though it would be slow progress stopping constantly to decant more oil.

'We got the launcher vehicle's engine going and moved little by little all through the night, stopping every few minutes to flush oil through the works and then starting again,' said Van Zyl, who did the driving. 'It was pitch dark as we moved through the trees and across stream beds. We had to be extraordinarily careful because, with all the launcher tubes and radar paraphernalia on top, the machine was very high and it could easily have been damaged by overhanging branches.

'We stopped moving at first light [on Monday 5 October]. In 12 hours we had moved just eight kilometres south from the battlefield. I was exhausted. I hadn't had a proper sleep for two weeks. I helped put camouflage netting over the launcher and to layer it with leafy branches, and then just collapsed from where I stood onto the ground and fell into a deep sleep.'

Hougaard at last had a chance to take a really good look at the prizes his men had plucked from the chaos. He was elated at his full realisation of the value of the booty. 'They were magnificent machines, fantastic,' he said. 'The launcher vehicle was massive, much bigger than I'd anticipated.

'We parked the three machines in the bush with 200 m between each and camouflaged them. As soon as we'd dug ourselves in I contacted Colonel Ferreira to tell him what we had got. He said he couldn't maintain radio contact for very long for fear of giving away our position. He said our EW people had intercepted messages from the Russians giving orders for a big effort to destroy abandoned equipment so that nothing valuable got into SADF hands. The Colonel said we had to intensify our effort to get the Sam-8 system out.'

Then a wave of Migs arrived, sweeping low over the forest and dropping parachute-retarded bombs right among the positions occupied by Hougaard, his men and the Sam-8s.

Van Zyl was shaken awake from his deep but short hibernation as the bombs detonated: 'I didn't dare get up because there was shrapnel flying all over the place. When the noise stopped I just had time to run to a bunker and leap into it before the planes made another bombing run. They obviously knew what they were after and roughly where we were. I watched their bomb bays open and the parachute bombs descend. The next moment the whole fucking earth was shaking.'

Men and magnificent machines survived that attack and another, final, one 20 minutes later. But it was imperative to get moving again. Spare tyres had been found to replace the shredded rubber ribbons on the wheels of the launcher, but there was no jack among the vehicle's tool kit to lift the machine. It was impossible to push on for any significant distance with the improvised oil feed system. Hougaard radioed Mavinga urgently for recovery vehicles, and three were sent forward with a team of engineers.

When darkness fell the Sam-8 convoy moved northeastwards to its next halting place, General Ben-Ben's UNITA attack HQ, where the three pieces of equipment were again hidden in the bush – some three kilometres away from the base, because Ben-Ben's HQ was receiving heavy attention from Fapla's artillery and Migs. Fapla had got bearings on the HQ from the heavy radio traffic coming into and out of the base.

'It wasn't safe there, and we were desperate to find the right time to get those things out from under UNITA's nose,' said Hougaard. 'While we waited we had a good look inside the logistics carrier, and there were 25 intact missiles. They were worth a lot to us.'

General Chilingutila then arrived and told Hougaard he had received a message from Savimbi saying all the Sam-8 equipment must be handed to UNITA because the movement had pledged it to its 'friends'. Down the years UNITA's 'friends' have come and gone and sometimes come back again: but on this occasion the term was a euphemism for the United States, which had abandoned UNITA in 1975 and only resumed arms supplies to its client more than a decade later in 1986.

Hougaard was furious, not least because South Africa had stood by Savimbi during his darkest times, precisely those years when Washington had chosen the soft option. And, unlike the US, South Africa had given the lives of its young soldiers for Savimbi.

'I told Chilingutila I couldn't help him,' said Hougaard. 'I didn't set out to upset him, but I was firm. If the Sam-8 system was to be handed to UNITA the decision would need to be taken at the top level in South Africa. Meanwhile, it would stay under my command.

'I sent a message to Colonel Ferreira saying he'd better do something fast to help me because UNITA was cutting up rough. When I came off the radio net Chilingutila said Savimbi was insistent that the fire control vehicle and five of the missiles were to be surrendered to UNITA immediately. I had to play it by ear. So I said OK, they could take the five missiles: their "friends" would learn a lot from them. But the fire control BTR-60 was now my command vehicle and it would stay with the SADF because it was South Africans who had done most of the fighting against 47 Brigade.

'Chilingutila, whom I liked, said he wanted to put a company of UNITA troops under the command of Colonel Tarzan with the Sam-8s. Stalling for time, I said OK, fine. Then a team of our top Air Force scientists, engineers and technicians, summoned at top priority from Pretoria by Colonel Ferreira, arrived. They aimed to examine the missile system as comprehensively as possible and learn as much as they could in a short time, because there was clearly a chance that we might lose it to Savimbi and the Americans.

'Tarzan and his lieutenants said they couldn't allow our Air Force guys into the launcher. Permission would be needed directly from Savimbi. I said "Listen, it's not your vehicle. It's actually my vehicle, and I'm in charge of it. You're only here to guard it".

'They stepped back, but that company followed us all the way back to Mavinga. They stayed with the vehicles until one night the Air Force simply drove them away towards the south. The Air Force made a hell of an effort. They drove those things all the way to Rundu, moving only at night.

'It was very slow work, and they had to put guys on top of the machines with pangas to chop down overhanging branches.'

So it was that South Africa became the only western country to acquire a complete Soviet Sam-8 missile system. It was of immense intelligence value and Armscor quickly went to work to incorporate any of the worthwhile technology into its next generation of indigenous weapons products. It is possible by now that a powerful Kruger-8 mobile anti-aircraft missile system is ready to roll off the production line!

Some kind of negotiation did take place over the Sam-8s between Savimbi and the top brass of the SADF. But more than a year later the UNITA leader, always touchy about perceived affronts to his dignity, was still complaining to any visitor who would listen that the South Africans had tricked him over the Sam-8s and treated him like some ignorant village chief.

CHAPTER 21

FAPLA'S OFFENSIVE ENDS

Pierre Franken and his team stayed on Mucobolo Hill until the late afternoon of Sunday 4 October, helping Van Zyl, Lotter and UNITA to identify serviceable enemy vehicles worth removing from the *anhara*. When the rescuers had removed the last of the loot, tactical HQ ordered the Mucobolo men to return to base with their seven Fapla POWs.

When Franken came down his tree for the last time, he immediately passed out with exhaustion until he was woken by one of 32 Battalion's black recces with a mug of hot tea. Besides the fatiguing tree watches, Franken had walked more than 300 km in the previous 30 days carrying food, 12 litres of water, radio, batteries and weapons as he returned to base every six days to replenish supplies. Much of the walking had been through the thick, sucking mud of the Lomba marshes.

Mac da Trinidada ushered the Fapla soldiers, hands tied behind their backs, across the T-54 tank jammed in the Lomba River. He reflected on what he had witnessed: 'I had never seen so many enemy troops as on that day, 3 October. There were hundreds of them running. You could see that some of them were wounded. I felt really sorry for those guys. They had no real chance. We bombed the shit out of them. They were mown down like swathes of grass.'

Once across the river, Franken's party passed near part of the huge network of 47 Brigade trenches and bunkers. 'There were still enemy logistical and infantry people dug in there, and we were shot at,' said Franken. 'We went through some of the trenches. They were dug really deep and had thick roofs of logs layered with sand as overhead protection. We picked up a few weapons left in the trenches and as many tins of tuna as we could carry. Then we had to wait there for several hours through the night for a UNITA VW Unimog which took us to Commandant Hougaard.'

Franken, Mac da Trinidada, Hans May and their handful of men from Mucobolo Hill were warmly welcomed back at HQ. Their critical role in the destruction of 47 Brigade was well recognised.

★ ★ ★

October 3 was a particularly big day for Deon Ferreira. It had been exactly a month since he was placed in charge of the South African brigade under the standard SADF instructions: Lose no men. Lose no equipment. Achieve all your objectives.

Conflicting emotions had surged through him as he ordered 61 Mech to move up through the night for the attack. One sentiment was similar to the thoughts of US General Omar Bradley before the final 1944 battle for Normandy: 'This is an opportunity that comes to a commander not more than once in a century. We are about to destroy an entire German army.'

In Ferreira's case it was the chance to destroy an entire enemy brigade – an opportunity that had never before fallen to an SADF commander and probably will never do so again.

Ferreira nevertheless was beset by spasms of doubt about the outcome even when Franken reported, later that day, that 47 Brigade was beginning to break as its infantrymen ran across the *anhara*.

'Fapla's 47 Brigade contained four times as many men as were available to me. Not only were we having to absorb artillery fire from 47 Brigade itself, but 59 and 21 Brigades were joining in as well. Throughout the battle, enemy Migs were overhead almost permanently. We had no close air support – only intermittent ground attack bombardments by the SAAF on Fapla's 59 Brigade.

'It was an abnormal situation. We counteracted Fapla's control of the air by heavy emphasis on night movement, camouflage and concealment. We never concentrated our forces.

'Our heaviest calibre anti-aircraft weapons were 20 mm guns, but the fact that UNITA had Stinger missiles and captured Soviet-made 23 mm anti-aircraft guns forced the enemy to fly at 6,000 to 7,500 m for much of the time. Dropping or firing weapons from that height is a very hit-or-miss business, and when the Angolan Air Force did make low level attacks its planes were highly vulnerable to UNITA firepower.

'We also used UNITA infantry and guerrillas intelligently to draw Fapla fire and to keep 59 Brigade busy with counter-bombardments.'

[According to UNITA's own figures, some 1,000 of its men were killed in action between June 1987 and 4 October that year in combating the Fapla offensive.]

Fapla's failure to lay mines on the southern side of the Lomba also worked in the SADF's favour, said Ferreira. Fapla attempted few of the kind of recce penetrations of its enemy's lines which were such an important part of the SADF strategy. All this meant that the SADF could move relatively freely in its zone and needed to divert only a handful of men and weapons to protecting its logistics convoys.

'No other forces were immediately available to me other than 61 Mech, 32 Battalion and a couple of companies of 101 Battalion,' said Ferreira. 'When Pierre Franken reported that 47 Brigade were on the move and in the open, it was a question of either letting them go or taking a chance. I decided that Bok Smit should take them on. I took the decision on my own without referral to higher level. If we had failed, my army career would have been finished.

'In the end the tally was one SADF man killed and one Ratel shot out against 600 or so of their men killed, wounded and captured and many millions of dollars worth of equipment destroyed or captured.[1] Only one Sam-9 and two Sam-13 launcher vehicles got away.

'61 Mech's attack was the most successful of our entire operation in southeast Angola, bearing in mind that we had no tanks at that time and they had 22. It turned the Fapla/Cuban offensive into a retreat. As far as I am concerned, it was the best conventional military operation in Angola in 13 years. It changed the war completely. Much of the credit was due to people like Bok Smit and Pierre Franken and, of course, to our superior artillery equipment and firepower.

'When I went forward towards the end of that afternoon, 47 Brigade soldiers were trying to destroy vehicles left on the south bank of the Lomba so that they would not fall into our hands. I could also see Fapla wounded being shot by their own people because they couldn't evacuate them. That sort of thing is terrible for an army's morale. Many of the infantrymen were lads of 16 and 17, not knowing what the hell they were doing there.'

Ferreira, in his discussions with the author, said nothing of one of his decisions – of how he intervened to stop the slaughter of 47 Brigade's soldiers when it was clear that the enemy was comprehensively beaten. I subsequently met, by chance, a young officer who had been a member of Ferreira's HQ staff on the Lomba, and he told me: 'Deon Ferreira is not only a very fine soldier, but he is also a devout Christian. He was thrilled by the victory but was appalled when the killing out on the *anhara* turned into a turkey shoot. He sent out the order that the survivors should be allowed to flee. Ferreira's HQ *dominee* [chaplain] flew into an uncontrolled rage when the Colonel ordered the killing to stop. The *dominee* was a Dutch Reformed Calvinist of the old-fashioned kind from some little *dorp* in the Orange Free State. He was so beside himself with fury that he was using the most obscene language as he threw at Ferreira references from the Old Testament about the justification for smiting your enemies and wiping them out entirely. The Colonel stayed very calm and just let the one-man storm pass over him.'[2]

Ferreira waited for the Sam-8 system to be recovered on 4 October before sending a message to General Meyer. 'As soon as I knew the missile vehicles had been moved well away from the battlefield, I reported to my General: "My mission has been accomplished. We have stopped the advance to Mavinga. They are redeploying north and then west." It took some time to convince HQ that we had stopped the offensive, but the message eventually sank in. We were then instructed to pursue the enemy brigades and inflict maximum casualties on the enemy forces still east of the Cuito River while waiting for reinforcements so we could go over to the offensive.'

★ ★ ★

The War for Africa had effectively been won. But nevertheless, the most difficult and heaviest fighting still lay ahead.

Notes

1   According to official SADF figures, the following 47 Brigade equipment was either destroyed or captured up to and including the 3 October battle:
    21 T-54 and T-55 tanks (four T-54s captured and handed to UNITA for incorporation into the rebels' own tank squadron);
    4 SA-8 missile launcher vehicles (one 3-vehicle unit captured intact);
    1 BTR-60 Sam-8 logistics vehicle (captured);
    1 BTR-60PU Sam-8 command vehicle (captured);
    22 BTR-60 armoured personnel carriers (11 captured);
    4 truck-mounted 122 mm BM-21 Multiple Rocket Systems, or 'Stalin Organs' (2 captured);
    3 BMP-1 Mechanised Infantry Combat Vehicles (2 captured);
    83 logistics trucks (45 captured);
    2 BTS-4 armoured recovery vehicles (1 captured);
    26 BRDM-2 amphibious scout cars;
    2 TMM mobile bridges;
    1 Flat Face air defence radar (captured);
    6 23 mm ZU-23 anti-aircraft guns (4 captured);
    3,122 mm D-30 Howitzer long-range guns (2 captured).
2   The story, it should be said, is one that is denied by Ferreira himself.

PART 4

THE STALEMATE

Hasten slowly.

Suetonius

With bombs and guns and shovels and battle-gear,
Men jostle and climb to meet the bristling fire.
Lines of grey, muttering faces, masked with fear.
They leave their trenches, going over the top,
While time ticks blank and busy on their wrists,
And hope, with furtive eyes, and grappling fists,
Flounders in mud. O Jesus, make it stop!

Siegfried Sassoon (1886–1967)

CHAPTER 22

FORWARD BEYOND THE LOMBA

Colonel Deon Ferreira's new orders were to clear all enemy forces from the eastern side of the Cuito River – 'Savimbi-land' – before 15 December 1987 as well as to inflict maximum casualties so that no fresh Fapla offensive could be launched in 1987 or 1988. 15 December was an important date because all those national servicemen nearing the end of their two-year call-up had been promised by General Liebenberg that they would be home in time for Christmas.

But there were major problems to be overcome if the wishes of the political bigwigs and top military brass in Pretoria were to be granted, according to Jan Hougaard. 'We were a small force of 1,500 and we still had a hell of a big force against us. There were 15,000 Fapla troops between us and Cuito Cuanavale. The Ratel-90s had performed beyond all expectations in their "guerrilla" role against tanks during the Fapla offensive. But with their light armour and the limitations of the 90 mm gun, they were inadequate by themselves for the task of pursuit and annihilation. For that we needed tanks.

'All our planning had been for a defensive operation. Overnight we were meant to switch onto the offensive and begin a long-distance chase of a big conventional army. Colonel Ferreira foresaw that as we moved north our logistics problems would increase and the volume of supplies we needed would multiply. We already had very, very long logistical lines. It was incredible: you're not actually meant to wage war in that way, army academies tell you. The further north we pushed the more critical we knew the logistics would be for our artillery batteries. They were our key weapons, but they use a hell of a lot of ammunition, and if you think you're going to run out of it you just can't shoot freely.'

There was another problem to consider in the shape of the SADF's UNITA ally. Although probably the finest guerrilla army in Africa, UNITA had very limited experience or expertise in the more conventional role that would now be expected of it.

There was one worry, however, that Ferreira did not share with Pretoria, said Hougaard. 'It was clear to those of us on the ground that the Fapla offensive was over for 1987. On 5 October our EW people intercepted messages from Cuito Cuanavale ordering all the Fapla brigades to withdraw north to an area at the source of the Cunzumbia River and to dig in. There were people in the higher echelons in Pretoria who believed those brigades still had the *capacity* and the willpower to come south again. But *we* knew they could never do it.'

The withdrawals of 59, 21 and 16 Brigades and the tattered remnants of 47 Brigade to the Cunzumbia source were accomplished relatively easily and methodically, despite harassment from SADF artillery and SAAF bombardments. 'Our troops on the ground were totally buggered,' said Hougaard. 'They couldn't give chase. They needed sleep and replenishment. A big effort was made to bring in fresh meat and vegetables to them together with cold drinks and beer.'

Ferreira had been promised an additional force of mechanised infantry, the 4th South African Infantry Battalion (4 SAI), as soon as the young national servicemen in its ranks had been fully organised by their regular officers; a squadron of 13 Olifant tanks; an additional battery of eight G-5 guns; and a troop of three G-6 guns, the new self-propelled version of the G-5. But it would be several weeks before these heavyweights arrived. Meanwhile, Ferreira could not afford to twiddle his thumbs and allow the Fapla brigades to regroup and bring in new supplies at their leisure. He needed to act.

His first major decision, taken on 8 October, was to move the SADF combat groups and artillery 45 km rapidly northwestwards from south of the Lomba to positions just south of the Mianei River, a tributary flowing due westwards into the Cuito. With typical temerity, Ferreira had the first units moving towards the new front even before formal approval was given by Pretoria.

Ferreira's aim was threefold – to get the G-5s into position to be able to bomb the military airfield at Cuito Cuanavale, well within the big guns' range just 35 km from hilly ground south of the Mianei; to provide a solid protection force for the G-5s, which on no account whatsoever could be allowed to fall into enemy hands; and to infiltrate units behind Fapla lines to harass the brigades, raid in rear areas and disrupt logistics.

Ferreira also despatched recce groups with artillery observers to take up positions northeast of Cuito Cuanavale on high ground between the Dala and Cuatir Rivers with an uninterrupted view over the enemy-held town. These groups were trooped in by Puma helicopters by night to within walking distance of their positions some 350 km inside Angola.

It was critical to bring Cuito Cuanavale under bombardment. Sixteen Mig-21 and Mig-23 fighter-bombers were permanently based there together with six MI-24 Hind helicopter gunships. From take-off at Cuito Cuanavale it was just three minutes flying time before the Migs were over the Lomba or Mianei. If Cuito Cuanavale could be closed down, the nearest Fapla air base would be at Menongue, 175 km to the west. Flying time from Menongue would be 17 minutes and the Angolan Air Force planes would have a shorter holding time over the SADF for fuel reasons. The South Africans would also have advanced early warning of impending air assaults from recces infiltrated around Menongue.

On 8 October Combat Groups Alpha and Charlie moved off early in the morning under Commandant Bok Smit. They headed westwards along the south bank of the Lomba before swinging northwestwards around its source across the watershed towards the source of the Mianei. Commandant Robbie Hartslief's Combat Group Bravo followed about 10 km behind.

That day the SADF ignored its golden rule about thwarting the air superiority of Fapla's Migs and Sukhoi-22s by sticking to night movements – and it paid the price. Two Mig-21s swept in low under top cover provided by two Mig-23s and destroyed a Ratel-90 of Combat Group Alpha, killing one crewman and seriously wounding four others. It was scant compensation that UNITA brought down one of the Mig-21s with a Stinger and that the pilot's body was found in the debris.

Captain Piet van Zyl had been assigned with his Foxtrot company of 32 Battalion infantrymen to a newly formed unit christened Task Force Delta to act for the Mianei combat groups as a reconnaissance-cum-raider unit laying ambushes behind enemy lines.

Task Force Delta, under the command of 32 Battalion's Major Lourens du Plessis, comprised Foxtrot company of 32 Battalion infantrymen in Buffels; two jeep-mounted 106 mm recoilless anti-tank guns with crews; three Unimog light trucks; four 81 mm mortars with crews; and two Milan anti-tank missile teams.

Task Force Delta reached the source of the Lomba on the night of Thursday 8 October, at the same time as Bok Smit's 100 or so vehicles of Combat Group Alpha.

'There were vehicles moving through the bush like it was rush hour in Johannesburg,' said Van Zyl. 'There were military police bringing the machines through in single file. They moved slowly and close together so as to maintain contact. Bok Smit, not in the best of moods after the bombing of the Ratel, told us we would have to wait until all his vehicles had passed. That was going to take hours, so we slept at the source of the Lomba and then moved 20 km northwards to join up with General Ben-Ben and UNITA's 3rd Regular Battalion four kilometres west of the source of the Cuzizi.'

Four weeks followed of inconclusive manoeuvring and skirmishing for the SADF combat forces while they waited for the tanks and 4SAI to arrive from South Africa.

Ferreira took the opportunity to reorganise his small brigade. Combat Group Charlie, 'the eternal reserve,' was dissolved and merged into Combat Group Alpha, so that now there were just two combat groups – Alpha, under Bok Smit, and Bravo, under Robbie Hartslief, plus the Task Force Delta marauders.

Ferreira also persuaded Savimbi to move five UNITA units, in addition to the 3rd Regular Battalion attached to Delta, into the watershed area between the Hube and Chambinga headwaters and those of the Cuzizi and Cunzumbia to harass Fapla and attempt to interrupt its logistics.

Fapla HQ at Cuito Cuanavale sent 25 Brigade across the Cuito River with new supplies for 59, 21 and 16 Brigades. The convoy, accompanied by Soviet advisers, included ten replacement T-54 tanks and half-a-dozen BM-21 Stalin Organs. Another Fapla brigade, 66, was sent across the Cuito to guard the vital Chambinga River bridge. Ferreira was anxious to destroy this low, wooden span, since it provided the enemy with its most direct retreat route northwards. He hoped Task Force Delta with some of the UNITA battalions might be able to devise a way to demolish it.

On the evening of Wednesday 14 October the G-5s bombarded Cuito Cuanavale, the opening shots of a long-range artillery barrage on the key Fapla-held town which would go on for months. EW teams picked up Angolan messages saying that at least 25 Fapla soldiers perished in the first blitz from south of the Mianei.

The G-5s subsequently moved and redeployed constantly so that Fapla planes could not pinpoint their positions. The perpetual movement through the heavy forests south of the Mianei meant that only limited stockpiles of the G-5's big shells and charge packs, weighing 43.5 kg and 23 kg respectively, could be built up. This contributed to the SADF's growing logistical headaches, because trucks gasping into the Mianei area after more than 100 km of *bundu*-bashing from Mavinga were requisitioned as mobile stockpiles and could not unload immediately to make the return journey for more supplies. To save scarce ammunition, the G-5 battery was at times limiting itself to fire from one gun at a time.

The opening G-5 salvo on Cuito Cuanavale galvanised Fapla. That same day, 14 October, 59 Brigade received new supplies from 25 Brigade and on 15 October was ordered to move westwards to the Mianei to find the G-5s and destroy them. The commitment of an entire brigade to attempt to wipe out just eight guns was clear indication to SADF military intelligence of just how seriously Fapla's morale was being dented by the G-5s. Elements of 21 Brigade followed 59 Brigade westwards as a reserve force while 16 Brigade, still largely intact, withdrew northwestwards to defensive positions at the source of the Chambinga River.

59 Brigade moved fast and aggressively. Its tank squadron, boosted to near full strength by the transfer of 21 Brigade's remaining T-54s, smashed through thick bush, creating a path for other vehicles.

Lourens Du Plessis's Task Force Delta was right on the tail of 59 Brigade. But, as Piet van Zyl explained, the men of Delta were frustrated in their desire to inflict damage by the enemy commander's skilful use of the dense forest: 'UNITA kept us informed all the time of how 59 Brigade was moving with the tanks in three lines forward, some 700 infantry following in vehicles and on foot, and with Fapla recces all around.

'To inflict damage with the limited kind of weapons we had we needed to catch them in open *shonas*. The moment we moved against a big force with tanks like that in forest where we could not bob and weave we were bound to take big casualties. But all the time we were getting orders from HQ: "You must do something."

'We got very frustrated because they never moved into a *shona* and we weren't able to make a single attack.'

Ferreira decided that Combat Group Alpha should attack 59 Brigade while the enemy was still deploying north of the Mianei source. If he waited, the G-5s would come under great danger; they would be engulfed if 59 Brigade made a rapid breakthrough.

Ferreira planned the attack for first light on Saturday 17 October. During the night Bok Smit's Combat Group Alpha moved up to positions four kilometres south of the Mianei source. Robbie Hartslief's Combat Group Bravo deployed further south in reserve and ready to intercept 21 Brigade should it come storming down from the northeast to intervene in the battle. Lourens Du Plessis's Task Force Delta was ordered onto the Viposto High Ground, just north of the Vimpulo River, with orders to intercept any force from 16 or 66 Brigades that might come down directly from the north.

'War is to some extent like a card game,' said Major Laurence Maree, leading 350 infantrymen of 61 Mech in Ratels as well as three Ratel anti-tank teams attached to Combat Group Alpha. 'We had carried out careful reconnaissance just north of the Mianei source partly in the hope and partly in the conviction that 59 Brigade would choose to deploy there. And when they did just as we anticipated, Colonel Ferreira told us to give them a good knock.'

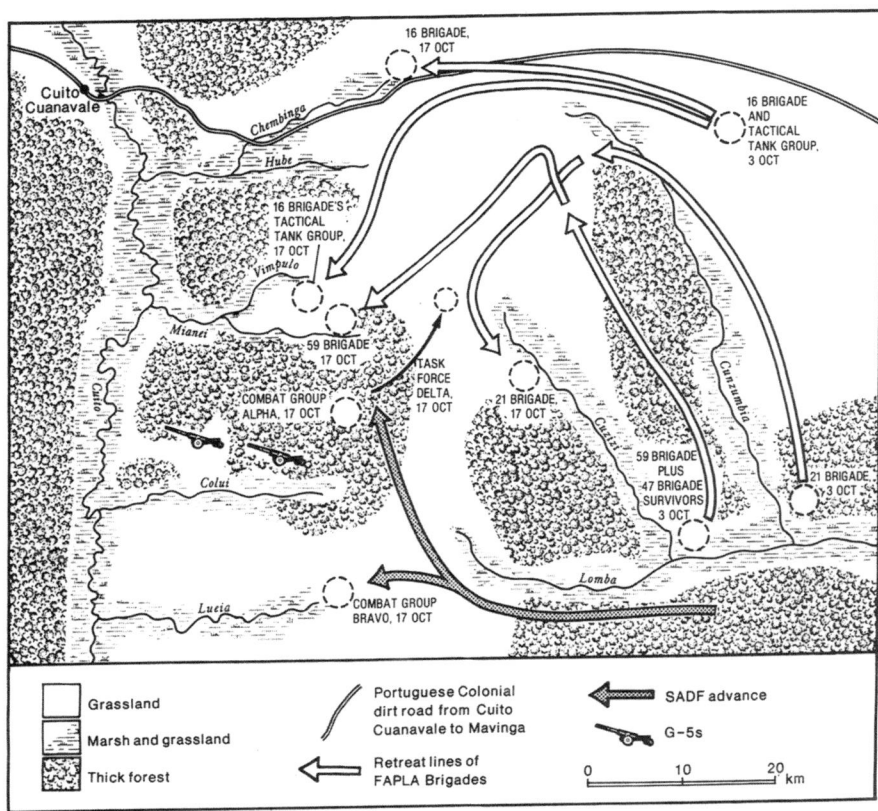

The first stage of the Fapla retreat, 3 October–17 October 1987

Bok Smit swung Combat Group Alpha east of the Mianei source where he picked up 59 Brigade's tank tracks. The tanks had left the deployment area and were heading due west just to the south of the river. Unable to break its own path through the tangled trees, the SADF force pursued 59 Brigade behind a shield of UNITA infantry on the enemy's tracks.

'There was no other choice,' said Laurence Maree. 'The bush was incredibly dense and we had no tanks of our own to bulldoze an independent path. We made contact with the enemy just after 8 am. But, literally, we couldn't see them and we never did see them. We only knew we were in a fight because shells began to bring down trees and branches around us. They had laid a simple ambush across their own tracks with three tanks, RPG-7s and B-10s (recoilless anti-tank guns). We ran full into it. They fired straight back down the tracks at us. We were in a very big confusion because the bush was so dense that the Ratels lost all their advantage of manoeuvre. Mig-21s were dropping bombs on us, but fortunately from the usual high level. UNITA hit one with a Stinger and later the SAAF Buccaneers and Mirages came in to help pin 59 Brigade down, hitting a couple of their Sam-13s and causing quite a few casualties.

'Commandant Smit told us to get the hell out because we were in a killing ground. We only made it to safety because the G-5s and our other artillery reacted quickly and put down an intense and accurate bombardment on 59 as we retreated in a lot of disarray.'

Meanwhile, further north, Lourens du Plessis's marauders arrived on the Viposto High Ground to find Sergeant 'Frenchie' of 32 Battalion and his recce team in position but minus a lot of equipment. Two days earlier 'Frenchie' had been told that the tactical armoured group attached to 16 Brigade was heading south with nine tanks to try to link up with 59 Brigade. He was ordered to investigate intelligence reports that an advance unit of the tactical group had already reached the Vimpulo River and built a bridge for the tanks.

'I took my radio man, two UNITAs and an air force forward air controller with me,' said Frenchie. 'We picked up the tracks of the enemy and we stopped every 50 m to check that we weren't walking into an ambush. The tracks eventually took us to the river. There was no bridge, but it wasn't necessary because the water was so shallow that it was easy to ford.

'We sweated heavily on that trip because we weren't sure about what we might run into. We moved back a bit from the river, but the next morning the enemy's advance motorised infantry team came back northwards across the ford and passed very close to us. We would have been dead if they had seen us. After they had passed my radio man started to freak with the strain of it all. His big eyes started to roll and then he just got up and ran off with the radio. He disappeared and one of the UNITAs followed him. So he left us alone without the radio. All we had was its long antenna!'

Frenchie and the remaining UNITA soldier now went down to the river to fetch water. What they did not know was that a platoon of Fapla soldiers from the tactical group was still on the southern side of the river. Frenchie and the guerrilla had started filling their flasks when heavy fire opened on them from inside the treeline across the river. They fled across the stretch of open grassland into the cover of the northern trees, leaving their rifles, compasses and water bottles behind in the rush.

As he ran, Frenchie was shocked to see the air force man sitting in a tree, so clearly visible that it was obviously him who had alerted the Fapla troops. The tree was completely isolated and it had no branches left on it,' said Frenchie. 'It was like a telephone pole in an asparagus field. I thought: he's gone mad. So I had to go and pull him down so that we could all move away. We were lucky to escape with our lives.'

Lourens du Plessis gave Frenchie new supplies and sent him on his way back to HQ before planning an ambush of the tactical group by Task Force Delta. When all the members of the tactical group's advance unit had moved back northwards Du Plessis ordered Piet van Zyl and a sergeant to lay mines both to the north and the south of the Vimpulo ford. They had laid more than 50 anti-tank mines by the time they began to hear the tactical group's tanks changing gear as they came southwards.

'We'd hardly finished when Major du Plessis told us we'd been ordered by Colonel Ferreira *not* to attack the tactical group but to stalk it and establish targets for the G-5s,' said Van Zyl. 'So we had to go back and defuse and lift all those mines. We were working against time. We were all totally frustrated because we wanted to fight. Du Plessis is a man who really loves to fight, so Colonel Ferreira repeated his orders to him several times *not* to shoot. We could see the tanks as they came down to the ford, but we had to stay hidden. Then the G-5 shells started landing and a few vehicles with the tanks were shot out. The column stopped moving.'

Battle Groups Alpha and Bravo and Task Force Delta now had 59 Brigade, 16 Brigade's tactical group and advance units of 21 Brigade pinpointed. The major objective became to keep 59 Brigade isolated; prevent it being reinforced; and continue softening it up with artillery and SAAF bombardments until a major ground attack became possible. The tactical group was shelled so heavily that on 21 October it gave up its attempt to join 59 Brigade and withdrew its tanks northwards.

The SADF artillery was greatly helped in the task of pinning down the enemy by recces and forward observers who penetrated the perimeters of 59 and 21 Brigades and sat inside them in immense discomfort and fear for their lives as they guided in shells on precise targets. Piet Fourie, for example, was inside 21 Brigade's lines for four days, sometimes within 25 metres of Fapla soldiers. Fourie gave invaluable information to Pierre Franken – at this time directing the MRL 'Papa' battery – about the pattern of 59 Brigade behaviour after SAAF Mirage attacks. Fourie said everyone began emerging from their foxholes and relaxing about ten minutes after the last South African plane had gone. Franken timed an MRL ripple on 59 Brigade eleven minutes after an SAAF raid with devastating results. Franken's growing reputation for craftiness had by now won him the nickname 'The Jackal'.

By 23 October Colonel Ferreira was sufficiently confident that he had 'fixed' 59 and 21 Brigades to begin another major reorganisation of his force. He wanted to detach a substantial number of troops to move back to the Mavinga area to prepare for an SADF tank attack on 16 Brigade from the northeast. He also sent Commandant Jan Hougaard back to Rundu with a few specialist forces to prepare for a top-secret mission deep inside another part of Angola altogether.

★ ★ ★

Ferreira disbanded Task Force Delta and incorporated it into Robbie Hartslief's Combat Group Bravo, which consisted largely of 32 Battalion and 101 Battalion troops with support from UNITA units. However, a couple of 32 Battalion companies, including Piet van Zyl's, were sent to Mavinga to be briefed for their new role in combination with the tanks.

Bok Smit's Combat Group Alpha, consisting almost wholly of companies from 61 Mechanised Battalion, was also ordered to withdraw from the Mianei to Mavinga to be part of the big force being prepared for the attack on 16 Brigade. Combat Group Bravo would remain behind on the Mianei to protect the G-5s from 59 Brigade.

The coming phase of much heavier warfare required a new top-level command structure. Ferreira remained the officer commanding the 20

SA Brigade which, for some esoteric military reason, was renamed 10 Task Force, but which this book will continue to refer to as 20 Brigade. To allow Ferreira to concentrate on the job of warfare on the ground, a divisional structure was created with a senior brigadier, Fido Smit, coming in from Pretoria to liaise between the fighting forces at the sharp end and the brass and ribbons brigade sitting behind desks hundreds of kilometres away. Fido Smit, recognising Ferreira's key role, established only an extremely modest divisional HQ on the Lomba River around a command Buffel stuffed with communications equipment.

As Bok Smit, Piet van Zyl and company prepared to pull out, the G-5s began redirecting their fire more towards Cuito Cuanavale after concentrating for many days on pounding 59 and 21 Brigades and the tactical group.

Adapting traditional Boer guerrilla deception tactics to air warfare, four Mirage F-1AZs sortied low and fast towards Cuito Cuanavale on the afternoon of Saturday 24 October. They had no intention whatsoever of braving Cuito Cuanavale's formidable anti-aircraft defences to bomb the town. However, their simulated approach, deliberately 'leaked' by the SADF over its radio nets, brought Migs out of their reinforced concrete slit hangars at Cuito Cuanavale. As they taxied towards the end of the runway the G-5s at the Mianei began a full-force barrage and destroyed one Mig on the ground. Meanwhile, the F-1AZs had swung round and were racing back to Grootfontein and the pleasures of the golf course, cold draught beer, the pool tables and garlic calamari at Dan Louis's restaurant.

Captain van Zyl admired how the artillerymen also used guerrilla tricks to fool Fapla Migs, searching for the G-5s, as to the big guns' true positions. 'There were 81 mm mortar groups operating with the G-5s,' he said. 'When word came that Migs were on the prowl, the mortars would fire from positions some distance from the G-5s with special shells which were aimed to land several hundred metres from the big guns. They exploded on impact with a flame and puff of smoke which closely resembled the recoil flash and fumes from the firing chamber of a G-5 after it had launched a shell. The G-5 teams sat drinking mugs of tea while they watched the Migs attack "their" positions. When possible, they used to warn the UNITA Stinger teams to get into position to fire at the Migs as the planes attacked the exploding mortar shells.'

One Stinger shot netted two valuable propaganda prizes on 24 October. Two Cubans baled out of a Mig-21 hit by a UNITA missile and were taken prisoner by Savimbi's men. They were Lieutenant-Colonel Manuel Rocas Garcias and his co-pilot Captain Ramos Cacadas. The captain was newly arrived in Angola and was making his first sortie over enemy territory. Both men remained POWs for many months before being released in a big exchange of prisoners.

Within 72 hours of the G-5 team hitting the Migs on the ground at Cuito Cuanavale, the guns also destroyed two Hind-24 helicopter gunships as they prepared to take off from there. These bullseye shots were thanks to accurate information radioed back by 5 Reconnaissance Regiment commandos who had crossed the Cuito River and were ensconced in camouflaged ratholes within a short distance of the Cuito Cuanavale runway.

By Wednesday 28 October the Cuito Cuanavale airbase had been so comprehensively battered by the G-5s that it was no longer in use by Fapla jets or heavy transport planes.

The outstanding performance of the G-5s was a source of enormous pride to Colonel Jean Lausberg, the officer commanding the SADF artillery regiment in Angola.

Lausberg, based normally at the SADF School of Artillery in Potchefstroom, was celebrating his youngest daughter's birthday in the first week of October at a wildlife lodge in the Kruger National Park when he received a wireless message to take over command of the artillery in Angola from Commandant Jan van der Westhuizen. The expanding scale of the SADF involvement required the presence in the field of a more senior officer. 'I already had my kit packed,' said Lausberg. All the top artillery officers were hoping they would be the ones ordered to see some real action.'

Having returned his family to Potchefstroom from their truncated holiday, Lausberg was in Rundu by 10 October. He took off in a Puma helicopter for the SADF brigade tactical HQ near Mavinga at 9 pm the same night. 'We touched down at Mavinga at 11 pm. I had no idea where we were. I was completely disorientated.' said Lausberg. 'We had flown in total darkness at treetop height, and at Mavinga there was a complete blackout. I found somewhere to sleep under a bush and was woken in the morning by thousands of mopane flies buzzing around my head.

'At that time 4 SAI was moving in from the Republic with the additional G-5 battery and the G-6 troop. It was a huge logistical task. In addition, there was a lot of reorganisation that needed to be done of all our artillery batteries. But the flies were driving me so mad that I couldn't solve even comparatively simple problems, like how to get 4 SAI and 61 Mech gunners to their respective rearranged batteries. And my colleagues laughed when I complained that the mopane flies were even floating thick on the coffee I was served.' Lausberg soon learned how to tolerate the mopane flies, stay sane and wage war at the same time.

'By the end of October I had OPs (forward observers) all over the show,' said Lausberg. 'My gunners were receiving such a stream of information that they practically never slept. They were firing by day and by night. If something moved we would fire at it.'

The close relationship which had formed between UNITA and the CSI liaison teams also helped the gunners. 'Commandant Les Rudman (of CSI) knew all the SADF radio frequencies, and on 19 October he contacted me on the regular artillery net,' Lausberg recalled. 'He said a UNITA recce at the Chambinga crossing could see lights approaching the bridge from the west. It was night. When I asked Les how he got the information he said he had a good radio man who had picked it up after it had been passed on through nine UNITA relay stations. So Les was the 10th and I was the 11th!

'So I told Les, OK, but how do we direct fire onto the Chambinga bridge from the G-5s 30 km away south of the Mianei? He suggested that the UNITA man communicate through the 11 radio relay points how far the G-5 shells were landing north, south, east or west from the bridge. I didn't have much faith in the idea, but I decided to give it a try.

'I gave the fire orders and the crews reported: Ready. The UNITA recce reported that the first round had landed approximately 400 m northwest of the bridge. I gave the gunners a correction and the second round hit the bridge directly. Rudman said the recce was ecstatic but said the vehicles were still coming. It takes a G-5 shell between 60 and 90 seconds to travel 30 km, so through Rudman's link-up we asked the UNITA man to tell us when vehicles were about 90 seconds from the bridge so we could hit it as one of them arrived. We caused a lot of problems that night, thanks to the UNITA recce and Rudman's radio man. Later I gave Savimbi a special memento, a G-5 shell detonator fuse encased in perspex, to give to the guerrilla.'

CHAPTER 23

THE REINFORCEMENTS ARRIVE

The national servicemen of 4 SAI moved from their permanent base at Middelburg in the eastern Transvaal to Army Battle School at Lohatla, in the dry expanses of northern Cape Province, where they underwent special training before moving off in mid-October towards the Angolan border.

4 SAI was joined by a squadron of 13 Olifant tanks from the SADF's School of Armour at Bloemfontein, a second battery of eight G-5 guns, and a troop of three G-6 guns.

The G-6s, self-propelled versions of the G-5, were only toolroom prototypes because the production line for the huge mobile guns was not yet operational. The three 37-tonne monsters, the most powerful self-propelled guns on wheeled chassis in the world, were undergoing testing at the Artillery School in Potchefstroom when the surprise call to battle came. The G-6 has a top speed of 90 km per hour, and in Angola it was able to smash through the bush like the tropical equivalent of an icebreaker at speeds of up to 40 km per hour. From 1988 onwards the G-6, the envy of many of the world's armies, began to enter service with all the SADF's mechanised units after production line work began.

The powerful new attack force crossed the Kavango River from Namibia into a holding area some 50 km inside Angola on 20 October. Here there were intensive conferences between the different commanders to finalise logistics and co-ordination. Meanwhile, the troops endured more training in tropical warfare while the big-barrelled guns of the new G-5 battery, the G-6s and Olifants were 'shot in' so that they were battle-ready for the heavy fighting to come.

The tank crews were particularly eager to get moving towards the battle-front with 16 Brigade. South African tanks had not been to war for more than 40 years since Shermans of the 6th South African Armoured Division participated in the final northern Italian battles of World War II which led to the surrender of German forces on the Po Valley plains in May 1945.

The test would be important for the Olifants, based on 1950s-era British Centurion tanks bought in various states of repair from India and Jordan – despite the international arms embargo against South Africa – and transported across the Indian Ocean on giant barges to Durban for remodelling by Armscor. Their mobility was increased by ripping out the original petrol engine and fitting a more powerful West German diesel engine and transmission. The old 84 mm gun was replaced by a much heavier South African 105 mm gun based on the British Vickers company's highly acclaimed L-7 tank gun whose specifications had somehow found their way to Armscor. Improved suspension, a new fire control system and Israeli laser range finder, and lots of other electronics from West Germany, Israel and the United States, together with equipment copied from Soviet T-54/55 tanks captured in Angola in 1981–82, brought the Olifant up to the same modern standards of Centurions that had been refitted in Israel and Switzerland.

After crossing the Angolan border the Olifants came off the transporters which had brought them northwards from Bloemfontein and Lohatla. With the G-6s they smashed a way for the convoy of 250 vehicles all the way to Mavinga, moving only at night so that Fapla did not know they were coming. The worst hazard on this journey was snakes that got shaken out of the trees into the confined tank compartments through open hatches. The Olifant squadron took its first casualty when an unfortunate young lieutenant found himself sharing his cramped space with a deadly black mamba highly upset at being dislodged from its tree home by a Boer tank. The mamba bit the soldier who lived to tell the tale thanks to quick work by SADF medical orderlies. After this, soldiers learned to thwart snakes which fell through hatches with fire extinguishers. A tank crew sergeant was the next loss, knocked out of the war before even reaching Mavinga when one of the many trees which came crashing down on the Olifants and their support vehicles hit him and broke several ribs. A helicopter was called in to remove him to hospital in Rundu.

The big convoy began to arrive on 30 October at Mavinga, where Combat Group Alpha was waiting. Commandant Leon Marais of 4 SAI, who had taken the new force up from South Africa, was told by Colonel Ferreira that he would lead it into battle under the name of Combat Group Charlie. With its tanks, Charlie was the strongest fighting unit to be put into battle in more than a decade of war in Angola. Charlie fielded two infantry companies totalling 300 men in Ratel-20s. Marais also had at his disposal Ratel-90s, Ratel-81s, Casspirs and 20 mm self-propelled anti-aircraft guns mounted on a 'Ystervark' mine-protected chassis powered by a West German-designed engine. The precious G-6 prototypes, G-5s and MRLs were placed under the direct command of Colonel Lausberg.

Despite the arrival of the strong new force, the SADF still had only about 3,000 men in Angola at this time against more than 15,000 Fapla soldiers in and around Cuito Cuanavale and to the east of the town.

★ ★ ★

Piet van Zyl had arrived at and passed through Mavinga before Combat Group Charlie got there. However, the likely intensity of the coming push was obvious to him from the scale of SAAF activity at Mavinga's dirt runway where half a dozen transport planes were landing each night plus several helicopters with military supplies.

This represented an increase in the normal level of busy air activity at Mavinga. For the whole eight months of the Cuito Cuanavale campaign Hercules C-130s and Transall C-160s of the SAAF's 28 Squadron, supported by ancient Dakotas from other transport squadrons, made an average of three sorties a night into the Mavinga strip, guided only by UNITA's improvised and unpredictable paraffin landing lamps.

'Every night it was hellish hairy for the transport crews,' said Colonel Dick Lord. 'The war went on a lot longer than anyone expected. On the ground the logistics were tedious and very hard for the men and very expensive in vehicles. The Army couldn't maintain the necessary rate of supply and the burden fell more and more on the SAAF.

'It was a very demanding form of flying to keep landing those big C-130s and C-160s on the dirt strip in darkness. But getting the plane down safely was only the beginning of the work. There was no mechanised equipment at Mavinga for unloading supplies, and there was some very heavy equipment being brought in. It was really tough coolie work for SADF and UNITA men together. Everything had to be off and hidden by daylight and the plane had to be back home.

'Also our Puma and Super-Frelon helicopters went into Angola every night of the war. They would leave just before sunset and find their way with their Doppler navigational radar. They flew at low level. There were no features to guide the pilots and during the rainy season, when the moon and stars were blotted out, it was pitch dark. To find a landing zone in the middle of nowhere when the night is black in the heart of Africa is a highly skilled job, believe me.

'The daring of the helicopter pilots was one of the main reasons why our fatality rate was so low. We had good medics right in there with the fighting men. They treated wounded soldiers at the front line and then took them in mine-proof ambulances to helicopter landing zones. They knew that when darkness fell the helicopters would arrive unfailingly if called and get men back to the intensive care unit at Rundu. The very serious cases were flown on by C-130 to 1 Military Hospital in Pretoria.'

★ ★ ★

Having re-equipped his company in Mavinga, Piet van Zyl moved north 75 km to the source of the Maquelengue River to prepare for the arrival of Combat Groups Alpha and Charlie. It marked the beginning of a short period of phoney war for Van Zyl and his men from which every inconsequential pleasure was remembered better and more lovingly than the details of battles. Van Zyl was joined by two

32 Battalion platoon commanders, Lieutenants Jurg Human and Thai Theron, both old friends.

They found a lagoon about 200 metres wide similar to many others which dot the floodplains of southeast Angolan rivers. Since neither Van Zyl nor Human nor Theron had washed themselves or their clothes for two months or more, they decided a session of prolonged self-purification was called for. 'We bathed ourselves and washed our clothes and then sunbathed on a little beach,' said van Zyl. 'Then we made hooks and caught fish and *braaied* (barbecued) them. We swam and the water was beautifully clear. Our men tried to torment us by shouting "crocodile" every now and then. But nothing could have ruined those days. There are periods when you just get perfect peace. I'll remember that time in an untouched place in the middle of the Angolan wilderness for the rest of my life.'

Friday 6 November marked the last day of Piet van Zyl's 'Club Mediterraneé' holiday. That evening he sat with Thai Theron next to the lagoon musing about life, death and the hereafter, and he remembers part of the conversation with his friend: 'Thai said the time had been very relaxing because water brings peace. Then for some reason Thai told me he would shoot himself if he lost a leg in the coming fighting rather than go on living.'

The idyll ended just after midnight when radio messages said the leading screen units of Combat Groups Alpha and Charlie were approaching and they would appreciate being met by scouts to guide them into Van Zyl's vacation resort.

Colonel Ferreira began intense briefings, using sand models built on the forest floor by intelligence officers, on his plans for attacking 16 Brigade. The SADF's EW teams had discovered that the Fapla brigades had been ordered to attempt fresh thrusts southwards and eastwards to re-activate the offensive against Mavinga. This scarcely worried the SADF high command at all. On 4 November the MPLA had issued a statement in Luanda admitting for the first time that Fapla had suffered 'substantial' losses in fighting in Savimbi-land. (The SADF estimated that 2,500 Fapla soldiers had been killed or wounded by early November 1987 out of some 18,000 deployed from Cuito Cuanavale from July onwards.) On the same day SADF military intelligence learned that General Pedro Benga Lima, the Fapla Chief of Staff, had been summoned to Luanda from Cuito Cuanavale and dismissed for his conduct of the campaign.

The new Fapla 'offensive' therefore looked more the result of a decision taken in desperation rather than one that had been coolly considered. The intelligence reports showed that 21 Brigade and 16 Brigade's tactical armoured group were to join up with 59 Brigade and move south of the Mianei to a point where it would be possible once again to loop around the source of the Lomba towards Mavinga. The main 16 Brigade force was to pick up the old Portuguese dirt road which ran due east from the Chambinga bridge and forge east towards the Cueio River before turning south to Mavinga. This would put 16 Brigade on a direct course for the area where Combat Groups Alpha and Charlie were gathering at Van Zyl's holiday camp at the Maquelengue River, a tributary of the Cueio. Radio intercepts showed that Fapla had no idea that the SADF had injected its biggest fighting force yet into the area and was preparing to attack 16 Brigade.

Ferreira wanted to strike as soon as possible, catching 16 Brigade off guard before it launched its own planned attack. 16 Brigade was in a relatively isolated position near the Chambinga River source. If it could be defeated as comprehensively as 47 Brigade had been on the Lomba River, 59 and 21 Brigades to the south could be cut off by SADF forces from their withdrawal route to safety – westwards between the Hube and Chambinga River sources, onwards across the Chambinga River bridge, and thence to Cuito Cuanavale.

★ ★ ★

Ferreira sought assurances from his senior commanders that all units were battle-ready. Colonel Lausberg reported that he had received a disturbing report from the Artillery Regiment chaplain about the condition of the 150 men of the G-5 Quebec battery on the Mianei. 'The gunners are so weary that they are ceasing to care,' Lausberg told Ferreira. 'They have been on active service, night and day, for more than three months. They are caked in dirt and their clothes are coming apart at the seams. They are no longer following the prescribed drills. They are not dropping the barrels of the guns and camouflaging them when there are warnings of enemy aircraft.'

Ferreira listened sympathetically to Lausberg. Both men knew how gruelling a gunner's lot was physically and psychologically. Manhandling 43.5 kilogram shells and 23 kilogram charge, or propellant, packs into the breech was an exhausting task, made more arduous by the gunners' equivalent of Boer *machismo*. They refused to use European-supplied shell carrying cradles (four men to a cradle) and instead favoured brute strength, hoisting each shell in their arms. When the gunners were not firing night and day – snatching only catnaps – they were chopping down whole areas of forest with axes each time the 50 vehicles of the battery made one of their frequent shifts to a new position.

Ferreira asked whether Lausberg had any answer to the problem. The artillery colonel said he had already put a plan into practice. He had consulted the Artillery Regiment doctor who had told Lausberg to get the Quebec battery men into a safe area for just one day and give them all the beer they could drink, all the meat they could eat, new overalls and enough water for each man to have a proper bath.

Lausberg had not been able to find the necessary several thousand rand in his budget to give 150 men a good Angolan Saturday night out. But, as luck would have it, Defence Minister Magnus Malan and several other cabinet ministers arrived at Mavinga for a fact-finding stopover. The ministers were accompanied by the chairman of Armscor, Commandant Piet Marais, and Armscor export director Mr Thielman de Waal, who were seeking to make a foreign exchange killing for South Africa from overseas orders for the country's new generation of indigenous weapons on the back of their performance in the War for Africa. Also in the party was one of the best-loved generals in the South African Army, General Frans van den Bergh, a master gunner who in his supremo role as Director of Artillery had played a major role in the development of the G-5 from its Canadian prototype. Lausberg approached Van den Bergh, an avuncular, modest soldier known to artillery men as the 'Gunners' Godfather,' and told him his problem.

'General Van den Bergh summoned the Armscor men, and then Mr de Waal summoned me and told me to get the party organised for my G-5 men,' said Lausberg. 'Armscor would guarantee the bill.'

Lausberg immediately radioed his shopping list to Rundu and told the Quebec battery men on the Mianei to withdraw to Mavinga. At the same time he ordered new gunners and their teams from 4 SAI to move to the Mianei to take over the G-5s and incorporate themselves as a new unit, Sierra battery. Within 24 hours of becoming operational Sierra battery scored a direct hit on Fapla's forward front HQ next to the Cuito Cuanavale runway. EW picked up a message from Major Ngueto, the Fapla front commander, to Luanda which said: 'Enemy artillery making my position impossible.'

On the night of Thursday 5 November a Puma helicopter flew in loaded only with chilled Castle beer, frozen steaks, potatoes, fresh tomatoes, new overalls, soap, toothbrushes and toothpaste for Quebec battery. The 150 dog-tired men partied, ate, drank, washed and slept throughout Friday before moving north to take over, in the name of a reinvigorated Quebec battery, the new G-5 guns brought in by 4 SAI.

PART 5

THE COUNTER-OFFENSIVE

With the Boers, appearances are often deceptive – what might seem to be a mob of fugitives one day might well prove to be a formidable fighting force on the next.

Colonel Deneys Reitz,
in *Commando – A Boer Journal of the Boer War.*

CHAPTER 24

THE ATTACK ON 16 BRIGADE

Ferreira scheduled his attack for Monday 9 November. 'Army chaplains came in to talk to the men before they went into battle,' said Van Zyl. 'Many of the guys were very apprehensive. They were national servicemen in their teens and most of them had never fought before, unlike Jurg, Thai and myself who had years of experience with 32 Battalion on and over the border.'

The combat groups began moving out on the evening of 8 November to be in position to strike the next morning. Combat Group Alpha, now led by 61 Mech's new Commander Mike Muller instead of Bok Smit, who was totally exhausted from his efforts against 47 Brigade and had returned to the Republic to a new posting at Army College in Pretoria, was to make a feint attack from the southeast, the direction in which 16 Brigade's defences were aligned. Then Combat Group Charlie was to launch the main attack from the north as soon as Mike Muller had broken contact. The Olifants were to lead Charlie's attack, and after going right through 16 Brigade's positions they were to push onwards to the source of the Hube and begin establishing a barrier across 59 and 21 Brigades' lines of retreat.

Piet van Zyl's company of 32 Battalion infantrymen – all black Angolans except for Van Zyl and four other white officers – was assigned to Combat Group Charlie. This time Van Zyl had less reason to fear that he would fail to see action. His company was assigned to walk in front of the combat group's Ratels, locate 16 Brigade's base area correctly, start the battle, and then let the armoured elements and mechanised infantry take over.

'We moved 30 km west from the lagoon, riding in Ratels,' said Van Zyl. 'We passed the tank squadron and its support Ratels under the command of Major André Retief of 4 SAI. That man really knew how to look after his troops. He had brought a refrigerated canteen truck all the way from South Africa. We hadn't seen a cold drink for months, so we organised a 32 Battalion guerrilla raid when the truck was unguarded and liberated the last two cases of chilled lager. Man, that was nectar from Heaven.'

Combat Group Charlie deployed about 15 km due north of the Chambinga source while the three G-6 guns (Juliet troop) moved into a position 15 km to the northeast of 16 Brigade, and was joined by the rejuvenated gunners of Quebec battery. Several artillery observers, recces and UNITA Special Forces had been sitting on high ground to the north and northwest of 16 Brigade for several days. Charlie's commander, Commandant Leon Marais, was therefore confident that he knew 16 Brigade's exact dispositions.

More than a hundred 'Charlie' vehicles then moved southwards towards the enemy before halting at 3 am on 9 November. 'Sitting waiting inside the Ratels, everybody got tense, including myself,' said Van Zyl. 'I felt as though I was in a coffin and I kept remembering how many bits Captain "Mac" (Macallum) was in when they put him in a sugar bag after his Ratel-90 was knocked out by the T-55 on the Lomba.'

Combat Group Alpha moved up for six hours from its deployment area at the source of the Cuzizi before launching its feint attack at 7 am.

Combat Group Charlie crossed its start line at 4 am, eight kilometres north of 16 Brigade. At 5.30 am the G-5s, G-6s and 120 mm mortars launched a ten-minute 'softening up' barrage on 16 Brigade.

'At about 6 am, when we were four km from the target, my company debussed from the Ratels to form a screen at the front with the two mechanised infantry companies behind, one to the left and the other to the right,' said Van Zyl. 'Next came the Ratel-90s and then the tanks with Ratel-20s and Ratel-ZT3s spread out between them.

'In the kind of warfare I'd been used to, you stayed as quiet as leopards on the prowl. Here it was so noisy with all the vehicles behind that we felt like sitting ducks. Usually I felt in control of things: here I didn't.'

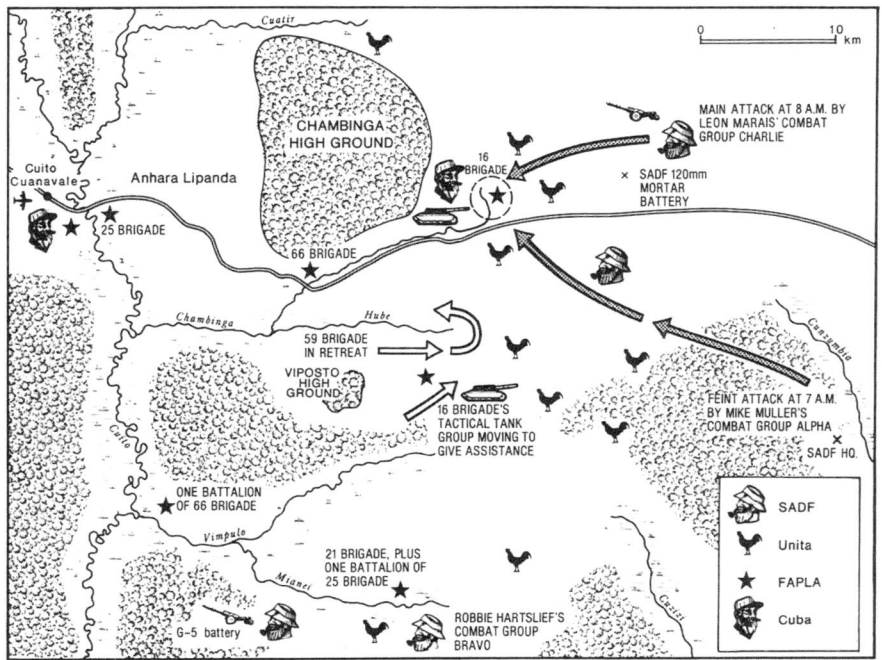

The Attack on 16 Brigade, 9 November 1987.

At 6.30 am SAAF Mirage F-1AZs bombed 16 Brigade before Combat Group Alpha's diversionary attack began. Mike Muller pounded 16 Brigade from a safe distance with mortars and the guns of the Ratel-90s. He also ordered his drivers to make as much vehicle noise as possible, revving up and changing gears, to divert attention from the approaching Combat Group Charlie. Then Muller broke off without any losses and moved rapidly four kilometres eastwards to lay up as a reserve force.

'Our battle orders were straightforward – fight and win,' said Van Zyl. 'Some UNITA Special Forces had gone ahead of us, but we had lousy communications with them. My company was busy moving in on the left flank in a general south-southwest direction when a UNITA messenger came and said there were enemy tanks ahead on the left. I couldn't believe it because Commandant Marais was so certain that all the enemy's positions had been charted. I sent Vos (Lieutenant Tobias de Villiers Vos, one of Van Zyl's platoon commanders) ahead to check out the UNITA intelligence and he came back and confirmed there were five tanks deployed to the left in an ambush position. We sent a message back to the Commandant and twice he responded: "Tanks? Are you sure?" He couldn't believe it at first, but then he redirected a company of 4 SAI infantry in Ratel-20s and a squadron of Ratel-90s to take on the enemy tanks.'

Once the emergency attack force had redeployed the Olifants also swung out of line and moved up through the Ratels and infantry to lead the combined force. Within nine minutes of Marais ordering the action against the tank ambush, an Olifant had shot out the first enemy tank to fall to a South African tank since 1945 on the north Italian plains. The official 4 SAI log records that the T-55 was shot out by Lieutenant Hein Fourie, known to his friends as 'Mieliepap' (Maize Porridge), at 8.09 am on Monday 9 November 1987. Eight minutes later another T-55 had fallen to the Olifant of Lieutenant Abrie 'Sirkusleeu' (Circus Lion) Strauss.

The SADF tanks overran infantry positions at the ambush site, destroyed a BM-21 Stalin Organ and captured another intact. A Fapla soldier taken prisoner from one of the BM-21s confirmed that the main 16 Brigade base was still much further forward. A valuable map of Fapla minefields and defensive gun emplacements was captured. By the end of the engagement a third tank had been destroyed and two others captured intact; several trucks and a fuel tanker had been set ablaze; at least 20 Fapla lay dead and two had been taken prisoner. The South Africans lost no men or equipment, but by the time the last resistance had been mopped up and the ambush position cleared nearly two hours had been lost and several 16 Brigade units had escaped from the main position.

'It took a long time for the Olifants to manoeuvre back into line from the flank,' said Van Zyl. 'My infantrymen were deployed 600 m ahead of the main force with a dozen Ratel-90s and Ratel-20s. They rode forward in the Ratel-20s before dismounting and fanning out on foot. Before the Olifants had got back into line properly we had walked into the perimeter of 16 Brigade's base and they opened fire on us some time after 10 am with everything they had got – small arms, mortars, tanks. One of my black troops was killed instantly when a mortar shell burst among us and scattered heavy shrapnel. We pressed forward. The Ratels were behind us and we got really mad at them when they kept stopping because they thought we were stuck.

'We crossed the first trenches and the Fapla infantrymen withdrew under our rifle fire and as we slung grenades. There was 23 mm fire coming in from somewhere which forced us to run all the time at a crouch.'

Meanwhile, the two companies of 4 SAI's mechanised infantry which were meant to take over the fighting from Van Zyl's men had run into difficulties. The 4 SAI company on the right (B Company) had problems in linking up with the forward Ratels because the thick bush restricted visibility more than had been anticipated. Smoke markers had to be used to indicate the boundaries of the company formation and this enabled Fapla artillery observers in the treetops to pin down the infantrymen by directing heavy mortar and 23 mm fire on them while they were still deploying. A Ratel-90 was badly damaged by 23 mm fire and the tailgunner was cut to pieces. An infantryman was killed by small-arms fire soon after he had dismounted from a Ratel-20. Another Ratel-20 was surprised by a T-55 which exploded unexpectedly from a particularly dense patch of bush. The Ratel gunner managed to slot a score of armour-piercing shells beneath the Soviet tank's turret and it blew up. But a second T-55 appeared and slammed a 100 mm round into the Ratel, killing the gunner and the driver.

The 4 SAI company on the left (A Company) was quickly confronted by Fapla tanks. Immediately after the infantry dismounted from the Ratels a 120 mm mortar bomb fell among them, killing two men and wounding four.

Major André Retief moved his reserve troop of three Olifants across to the right to deal with the serious position in which B Company found itself. The Olifants came into contact almost immediately with the Fapla tanks and in the exchange of terrifying and tumultuous close fire a wheel and the track were shot off from one of the South African tanks. The tiffies went to work, shortening the track and linking it around the bogey and remaining wheels to enable the Olifant to limp back to safety under its own power.

The Olifant squadron found it difficult to manoeuvre according to plan in the dense bush. But, nevertheless, the action in support of A and B Companies ended with five T-54/55s destroyed and one T-55 captured in mint condition with only a few kilometres on the clock.

Piet van Zyl listened to the noise of battle behind him with increasing frustration. His men had overrun the first set of enemy trenches, but they could not advance without further support. They were pinned down in the trench system by small arms, mortar and 23 mm fire. Gradually, the weight of the firepower directed against them began to diminish as the SADF artillery observer travelling with the tanks began to direct fire from the distant G-6s on outlying 23 mm gun positions; as the Ratel-20 gunners began to dislodge Fapla snipers from the trees; and after Combat Group Charlie's 120 mm mortar battery knocked out one of 16 Brigade's own 120 mm mortar nests.

'I wept with relief when André Retief arrived in his command Ratel accompanied by the first Olifant,' said Van Zyl. 'The rest of the tanks came through between our Ratel-90s and we regained momentum. Elements of 4 SAI's two infantry companies began arriving and we all ran between the tanks tossing hand grenades into the trenches and bunkers to clear them.

'Thai was running near me when he realised his platoon was no longer with him. He went back to find out what had happened. One of our ammunition vehicles was exploding and his men thought it was enemy infantry pinning them down. He got them moving again and soon we were passing burning enemy tanks. By early afternoon most of the Fapla infantry had pulled out. While our tanks pushed onwards we concentrated on clearing the battlefield. There wasn't much fighting. There were only a few pockets of Fapla to deal with, but there was a lot of abandoned equipment that we had to collect together so that it could be removed. That wasn't straightforward because Fapla Migs began coming in, occasionally quite low, and dropping bombs to cover 16 Brigade's retreat. By late afternoon we were very tired and thirsty. We couldn't get our wounded out in daylight, so the doctors were working hard keeping them alive until the casevac helicopters could fly in after sunset. I sent off Corporal Wessels to find our dead guy, because in my battalion we take every one of our men back home, dead or alive. Wessie couldn't find the body, but he discovered that a UNITA group which had come in behind 4 SAI had buried him. I ordered the grave to be located. We dug him out, put him in a rubber body bag and moved him to the helicopter pad to be buried at home.

'We needed to rest and regroup. But we couldn't believe it when we got orders to pull all the way back to our original deployment area. I couldn't understand it because I'd always been taught that in conventional warfare you continue to occupy ground you've taken.'

The Olifants meanwhile had moved on beyond the SADF infantry and by 2.30 pm were right through the 16 Brigade positions. But then, instead of pressing on to the Hube source, according to original plans, the tanks were ordered to pause and were later pulled right back to a laager area a few kilometres north of the battlefield.

Replenishment and repairs went on right through the night as military intelligence assessed the outcome of the battle. 16 Brigade had taken a heavy hammering. In the first encounter with the ambush group and the second inside the main enemy positions, Combat Group Charlie destroyed ten T-54/55s and captured three intact; captured one BM-21 and destroyed another; captured one 76 mm field gun and destroyed another; destroyed two 23 mm ZU-23 guns and captured a further two; and captured fourteen SA-7 and SA-14 anti-aircraft missiles, a 14.5 mm anti-aircraft gun and an 82 mm mortar. Three of the tanks were credited to the eight G-5s of the Sierra battery and the three G-6s of Juliet troop whose gunners fired 760 big 155 mm shells between them on 9 November. 'The accuracy of our guns really surprised me,' said Colonel Jean Lausberg. 'The whole turret was thrown off one T-54. But what really helped us were the thin external fuel drums carried on the Soviet tanks because of logistics problems. If they were hit, the whole tank became a blazing inferno.'

In addition some 30 or so trucks were either destroyed or captured. These included 18 Brazilian Engesa trucks which fell into UNITA hands in one of the war's many bizarre incidents. At the height of the day's battle several trucks loaded with infantry drew up scarcely 100 m in front of Combat Group Charlie's 120 mm battery. From the casual way in which the soldiers began dismounting and relaxing, the battery commander assumed they were UNITA soldiers who knew about his position. Headquarters then gave the commander a distant target on which to direct fire. The infantrymen, Fapla to a man, fled in panic as the first bombs hurtled high over their heads from the SADF mortar tubes. They left behind all their Brazilian vehicles. Several of the Fapla soldiers, who had been trying to manoeuvre northeastwards to launch a flank attack against Charlie, were killed or captured by UNITA troops protecting the mortar battery.

UNITA inherited the Engesas and much of the other equipment captured in the day's fighting. Teams of guerrillas spent the night moving the spoils away to swell Savimbi's big military inventory. The SADF hung on to some of the more sophisticated equipment, including the good-as-new T-55s, for delivery to Armscor. However, as an SADF driver moved one of the T-55s to the rear, he frightened the life out of a UNITA platoon who thought they were being attacked by the MPLA. The guerrillas raked the tank with machine gun fire, trapping the driver inside until an SADF liaison officer was able to persuade them that it was a *South African* Soviet-built T-55.

Seventy-five Fapla dead were counted on the two battlefields and six were taken prisoner. Given the SADF's loss of only seven men killed and two wounded, one Ratel destroyed, one Ratel badly damaged and one Olifant damaged, the inventory indicated a clear South African victory. But the fact is that the attack was a failure in terms of the objectives Colonel Deon Ferreira had set – the elimination of 16 Brigade and the cutting off of 59 and 21 Brigades so that they could be destroyed virtually at the SADF's leisure.

16 Brigade, despite its heavy losses, escaped with the bulk of its men and equipment intact to fight again another day. Several Cubans escaped with two Cuban Army tanks which had not been committed to battle. The failure of Leon Marais's Combat Group Charlie to close the Chambinga-Hube gap left open the getaway route to the Chambinga bridge for the Fapla brigades.

The decision to halt Combat Group Charlie's advance proved to be one of the major mistakes and turning points in the war. It gave Fapla's forces a reprieve which enabled them to reorganise and make life infinitely more difficult for the SADF than it would otherwise have been. It caused a huge row at Brigade level, with Colonel Ferreira particularly incensed by Commandant Marais's decision not to press on to the source of the Hube. Subsequent political as well as military history might have been very different if 16, 59 and 21 Brigades, as well as 47 Brigade, had all been destroyed before the end of 1987.

Mitigating factors contributing to the unexplained decision not to press on with Combat Group Charlie to the Hube were: (a) the long hold-up caused by the unexpected tank ambush; (b) the fear of further losses of equipment and men by officers operating under the shadow of the impossible 'lose no men, lose no equipment, achieve all your objectives' philosophy; (c) the realisation on 9 November just how tardy the high command in Pretoria had been in releasing only 13 Olifants to take on several scores of Fapla tanks; (d) the unexpected aggressiveness of the T-54/55s and the unanticipated denseness of the bush; (e) the dented morale of many of the young national servicemen who, seeing battle for the first time that day, watched their comrades die terribly and grew up faster than they had dreamed.

★ ★ ★

'That night Commandant Marais told us we would go straight back into the attack the next day (Tuesday 10 November),' said Piet van Zyl. 'To give us time to rest he scheduled the attack for mid-afternoon. But shortly after we moved off one of the 4 SAI guys shot himself in the stomach accidentally as he jumped from a Ratel during an air raid alert. He had to be operated upon on the spot, and by the time he was evacuated we had lost so much momentum that the attack was called off in case we ran into the same kind of problems as on the previous day.'

The attack was rescheduled for the morning of Wednesday 11 November. Meanwhile, throughout 10 November, the burden of keeping 16 Brigade busy fell on Juliet troop, Sierra battery and the neo-hedonists of Quebec battery, with their bloated stomachs, starched overalls and clean teeth and armpits. The 16 guns of Sierra and Quebec batteries between them fired 1,134 155 mm rounds on 10 November. With enemy Migs on constant prowl trying to seek out the big guns, the physical and emotional stress on the gun teams was especially great. And morale took a particularly grave knock that night when one of the gunners, sleeping next to a bush, was run over and killed by a truck bringing in food supplies.

This tragedy was a symptom of the growing strains on the SADF logistics system. Each G-5 battery had ten 10-tonne ammunition trucks attached to it; but between them the trucks could only carry 960 shells and propulsion packs. The batteries also needed copious supplies of fuel, water and food, especially during major battles. It was not only the G-5 batteries which needed resupplying. The Papa battery of MRLs, for example, fired more than 1,000 127 mm rockets on 10 November from south of the Mianei. 'Every night before and during the battle with 16 Brigade transport aircraft were landing at Mavinga with G-5 and MRL projectiles,' said Jean Lausberg. 'The record was four ammunition landings in one night. A C-130 could bring in 100 projectiles at a time, but when our guns were firing rapidly it was never enough should the pressure stay heavy for a prolonged period. It was a very difficult logistics situation. We also ran high security risks because at the height of battle we had to give all our latest logistics demands to Rundu by high-frequency radio.'

The SADF intensive use of forward observers inside enemy lines again proved invaluable to the artillery in acquiring targets on 10 November. 'We had one observer, Major Cassie van der Merwe, protected by recces from 5 Reconnaissance Commando, at Candonga, part of the Chambinga High Ground rising to nearly 1,300 m immediately north of the source of the Chambinga River,' said Lausberg. 'Cassie said he had spotted a BM-21 Stalin Organ, two T-54 tanks and a logistics vehicle all camouflaged within a triangle some 600 by 600 by 600 m,' said Lausberg. 'Troops were spread out and resting throughout the triangle. I went to our military intelligence people for their appreciation. They said they were sure there was a lot more equipment inside the triangle than Cassie had been able to spot. We requested an Air Force attack.

When it was turned down, Cassie started bringing down G-5 fire from Quebec battery which was positioned at the source of the Cuzizi. We did a lot of damage there.'

★ ★ ★

By the time the SADF was ready to resume its attack on the morning of 11 November, 16 Brigade had redeployed in two groups – the strongest immediately south of the Chambinga source, and the other directly east of the Hube source with tanks of 16 Brigade's tactical group moving rapidly north from the Mianei area to join up again. Intelligence reported that 16 Brigade was expecting the next SADF attack to come from a northeast direction. Marais therefore decided to re-deploy Combat Group Charlie southwards, scissoring behind Combat Group Alpha as Mike Muller launched yet another feint attack from due east. Charlie would then swing through a sharp fish-hook curve to strike at 16 Brigade from the south.

The tactics were good and they might have had excellent results if, at last, everything had begun to go according to the plans outlined on the scale models made in sand on the Angolan forest floor. But from the start there were delays and the day's timetable kept getting put back. The early hold-ups were caused again by the unexpected thickness of the bush, with the armour officers unable to see ahead much more than 20 metres. It took longer than expected for Charlie to cross behind Alpha, whose commander ordered as much engine-roar as possible from his drivers to drown out the noise of Charlie's subterfuge. Muller's feint attack was delayed several times waiting for Charlie to cross behind him, but finally his force went in and came out smoothly without loss. Charlie meanwhile had run into even thicker bush, and an attack by two Mig-23s in which a 4 SAI soldier received shrapnel wounds meant that all element of surprise had been lost. Small Fapla infantry teams then located Charlie which came under intermittent small-arms fire.

The bush became yet thicker with visibility down to five metres and the Mig-23s returned again to bomb the force. Combat Group Charlie finally arrived at its first target, at the source of the Hube, more than two hours behind schedule only to find that the Fapla force there had already withdrawn westwards. Edgy SADF infantrymen, seeing movement on top of a vehicle knocked out in an early morning bombardment by the G-5s, began shooting only to realise they were attacking a troop of resident baboons who gave a first-class demonstration of how to retreat under fire at top speed.

'It was a very difficult day for the infantry commanders,' said Piet van Zyl. 'It was long, tense and tiring for the men. Early on I conserved my men's energy by putting them in the Ratels while Vos and I took others up on top of the tanks for the ride. After we passed the first objective we still had a long way to go northwards to the second. Nevertheless, we ordered more of the men to walk so that they were fully alert. The 32 Battalion boys began to take it in turns with the 4 SAI guys to fan out on foot in front. By now there were Mig-21s and Mig-23s circling above almost constantly and our anti-aircraft people were shooting with everything they had to keep the planes high. The bombs came zooming down but were inaccurate.'

As the long day dragged on the foot soldiers got more and more careless. 'When we approached one particularly thick piece of bush someone started firing into it unprovoked,' said Van Zyl. 'The next moment nearly everybody was letting loose. We had a hell of a job to get them to stop.

'Major Retief told Commandant Marais it was essential for the infantry to have a short rest. By then it was about 2 pm and they had been on the move for nearly ten hours since Charlie moved out of the overnight laager at 4 am. Marais agreed. The Ratel crews got out of their vehicles and lounged in the grass with the infantry. I was stretched out on the back of an Olifant.

'What we didn't know was that we had stopped right in the centre of 16 Brigade's arc of defensive fire. Suddenly they opened up with everything they had – mortars, field guns, anti-aircraft weapons, sniper rifles, rockets. Bullets and shells were shredding the trees and making sawdust of them as I leapt from the tank. Two of my guys were killed when a mortar shell fell on the turret of the Olifant on which they were resting. Another was seriously wounded when he was hit by a 14.5 mm shell.

'When I got my feet on the ground I worked with Vos to get our guys to link up with the 4 SAI infantrymen. Major Retief, commanding from a Ratel-20, got his Olifants organised with amazing speed. They started a fire belt action (a firing pattern in which every tank fires simultaneously). That gave us a slight breathing space but I could see some of our Ratel-20s burning which had been shot out by Fapla tanks.'

Seven infantrymen were hit by treetop snipers in those early minutes before the threat could be eliminated. A tank commander was also wounded and evacuated. Meanwhile, the EW teams began to pick up more bad news. Military Intelligence had estimated that Fapla had gathered 22 tanks with 16 Brigade at the Chambinga source. Now it seemed, according to the EW men, there were three separate groups of tanks together totalling more than 30. Charlie could no longer predict from what direction a tank charge might suddenly erupt.

Commandant Marais, Major Retief, Captain van Zyl and other officers reorganised the force and got it moving forward again in reasonable order. The lead Ratels soon ran into Fapla's infantry fire and then the first of the enemy tanks emerged into the open. 'As we moved forward we could see the T-55 moving towards us,' said Van Zyl. 'The next moment it was spewing smoke and it came to a standstill. As the crew jumped out the men in my platoon shot every one of them dead.'

Van Zyl thought the T-55 had been shot out by an Olifant. In fact, it was a Ratel-20. 4 SAI Rifleman M J Mitton, the Ratel gunner, found himself facing the T-55. He fed a belt of armour-piercing shells into his 20 mm cannon and began spitting the projectiles towards the T-55 at a rate of 12 per second until the tank began to smoke. Mitton had just enough time to send the message 'T-55 visual. Eliminated' to Major Retief's radio operator before a second T-55 loomed behind the first and sent a 100 mm shell ripping through the Ratel's small observation window, killing the driver instantly and seriously wounding Mitton and another crew member. Mitton elevated his cannon to allow the driver to escape through his hatch, not knowing that his comrade was in several pieces. Mitton then scrambled out of his own hatch and fell exhausted from the vehicle. His buddies pulled him clear of the burning Ratel but he died later from his injuries.

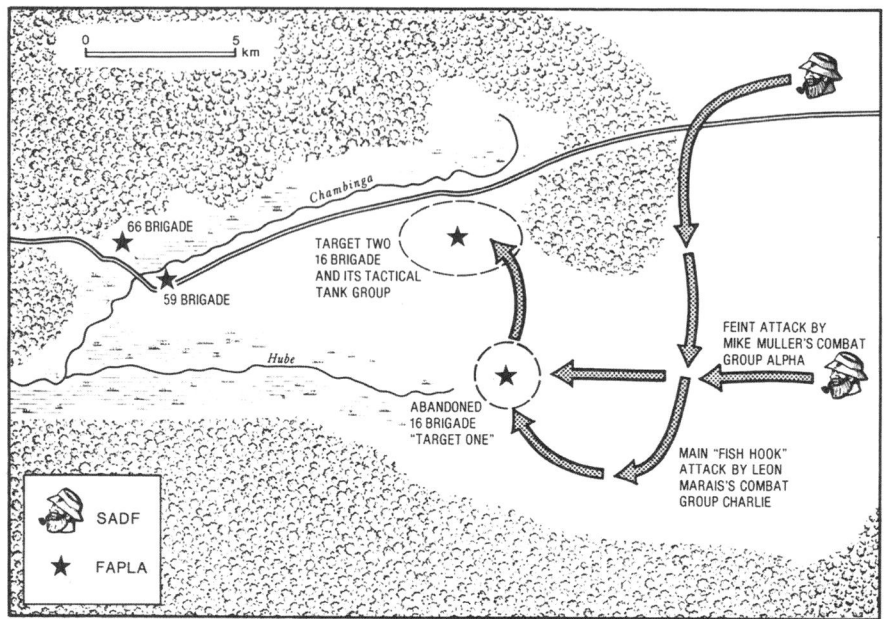

Follow-up Attack on 16 Brigade, 11 November 1987.

Despite its losses, Combat Group Charlie now had 16 Brigade on the run, with the 4 SAI and 32 Battalion infantry advancing steadily and occupying abandoned Fapla trenches. The Olifants moved through to take the initiative but instead ran into a minefield. It was marked on SADF maps, but as the adrenalin pumped in the heat of battle some of the tank drivers moved forgetfully into the minefield and Abrie Strauss's Olifant detonated a mine which blew off one of the steel tracks and severely damaged the suspension. A Ratel also detonated a mine and the driver was killed when an enemy tank shot out his stranded vehicle.

'All the infantry people were psyched up and were prepared to go through the minefield,' said Van Zyl. 'So we called for the *plofadders* and fired two of them, but neither detonated. Next we tried to send some Ratel-90s on a flank attack with a group of 32 Battalion infantry led by Jeug Human. But they ran into Claymore and anti-personnel mines. It was bloody frustrating.'

[A *plofadder* is a long sausage-like string of explosive weighing 500 kgs which is fired by rocket over the minefield from a specially adapted

Right: General Jannie Geldenhuys.

Below: General 'Kat' Liebenberg (centre).

Jonas Savimbi, the Swiss-educated rebel leader of UNITA. Savimbi, trained at China's Nanking Military Academy, was once recognised by international observers and many governments as one of Africa's finest guerrilla commanders. © Fred Bridgland.

A SADF liaison officer with Savimbi at UNITA headquarters, at Jamba, in southeast Angola.

SADF Valkyrie Multiple Rocket Launcher (MRL) deployed near Cuito Cuanavale during the war.

Demostenes Chilungutila, senior UNITA general. © Fred Bridgland.

Ben-Ben Arlindo Pena, senior UNITA general. © Fred Bridgland.

Commander of 20 SA Brigade. Colonel P. S. Fouché with two M-46 Russian artillery pieces taken by the SADF during the Operation Hooper attack on 21 Brigade.

South African 155-mm G-5 artillery on the outskirts of Cuito Cuanavale pounding Cuban and Angolan positions. The guns were carefully camouflaged against enemy air attacks.

Captain John Mortimer in a Casspir attached to an SADF/UNITA liaison team; he stood in for Les Rudman's team during their home leave.

Above: UNITA troops inspect Fapla Soviet-made T-55 tank knocked out by a wire-guided ZT-3 missile, a top secret South African weapon.

Below: Cuban infantry in Angola hitch a ride on a BRDM armoured car.

This Mirage F-1AZ of 2 Squadron SAAF made repeated sorties over southern Angola in spite of the presence of superior, faster and more sophisticated Mig–23 aircraft flown largely by Angolan pilots, but also by Cubans.

Puma helicopters rendered sterling service throughout the campaign. Because of the presence of enemy jets, they tended to work at night. This one is shown over Ovamboland, northern Namibia, with members of an SADF Reaction Force unit ready to deploy.

Right: A ZU-23 anti-aircraft gun captured from Fapla and deployed by the SADF.

Below: SADF General Willie Meyer (left) explains an attack against the Cuban/Fapla forces in the War for Africa to the United States military attaché in Pretoria.

Gathered together before the onslaught, South African forces prepare for battle on Angolan soil.

Unita guerrillas preparing to enter battle © Fred Bridgland.

Bushmen of the SADF's 201 Battalion played an important role in the War for Africa. Although they operated as machine-gunners, drivers, signallers, medics and mortarmen, their most remarkable skill was tracking, following nigh-on invisible spoor at great speed.

South African missile crew with French-designed Crotale missile battery. It is known as the Cactus missile in South Africa. One of the missiles had been fired at an attacking Mig-23 without success.

Troops clamber over an Angolan Air Force, Russian-built Mi-8 assault helicopter shot down during the battles. This helicopter is codenamed Hip by NATO.

Opposite:

Top left: Tailplane of a Russian-built, Cuban-piloted Mig-23 fighter (codenamed Flogger by NATO) shot down by an American Stinger missile near the Cunzumbia River in Angola.

Top far left: UNITA troops prepare to demolish a rail bridge on the Benguela Railway.

Bottom: UNITA soldiers frequently moved on foot along the Benguela Railway, blowing up points systems as they progressed.

This page:

Top right: Some Russian-supplied radio equipment captured by South African troops during the Cuito battles appeared to date from World War II. Very little up-to-date electronic gear – apart from ultra-sophisticated missiles and aircraft tracking devices – was deployed by the Angolans.

Bottom right: Without Soviet weapons, the Angolan war would have ground to a halt; in the background is a Russian BM-21 'Stalin Organ' MRL system and, foreground, a BRDM amphibious scout car.

Above: South African
Olifant tanks moving
up to the front prior to
the big engagement near
the Cuito River with
Angolan and Cuban
forces.

Left: President Fidel
Castro of Cuba
addressed the nation
prior to Fapla's 1987
attacks in eastern
Angola.

Above: Cuban 'Tanquistas' in Angola.

Right: Civilian ammunition bearers pass through a village close to the front. UNITA copied the North Vietnamese Vietcong in its strategy to transport weapons. © Jim Hooper

Unita Soldiers crossing river.
© David Kane (left) and
Fred Bridgland (below).

Laying landmines on the approaches to a bridge on the road to Cuito Cuanavale. South African and UNITA Special Forces played a major role in disrupting Fapla supply columns.

South African Minister of Foreign Affairs Pik Botha with freed SADF prisoner of war Johan Papenfus.

Anti-aircraft Krimpvark gun developed by Armscor and deployed during hostilities in South Angola.

Above: Fifteen-year-old Fapla soldier Bernardo Ngulu (left) taken prisoner by UNITA. His second-hand uniform was bought for him by his father. UNITA interpreters claimed Bernardo had never been issued with boots. UNITA frequently captured Fapla soldiers: many were executed. © David Kane

Below: Ratels, Valkirie MRLs and supply trucks pull back across the Kavango River towards the end of the War for Africa.

Casspir vehicle. The *plofadder* detonates automatically, exploding and throwing aside mines for several metres on either side of it, thus clearing a safe path through the minefield. The *plofadder* was still at the experimental stage of development in South Africa and this was the first attempt at using it in battle.]

Several tanks had avoided the minefield and others had got through it unscathed. Retief lined them up in front of the minefield to lay down a protective field of fire while three tiffies went into the field in an armoured recovery vehicle (ARV) to rescue the badly damaged Olifant. It was a perilous task with bullets clunking from the armour all the time and mortar shells falling into the minefield and exploding at intervals. Retief became worried when no one emerged from the ARV after it had manoeuvred close to the Olifant and remained motionless for some time. He radioed Van Zyl to say he needed volunteers to go into the minefield and help with the Olifant recovery. Lieutenant Tobias de Villiers Vos volunteered and Van Zyl went with him.

'There was noise and chaos all around, but we reached the ARV,' said Van Zyl. 'There was huge relief all over the faces of the tiffies when they looked out and saw Vos standing there on the outside getting to work on hitching the tank up to the ARV's winch. Eventually one of them got out to help Vos. The vehicle's cab is very high and you are very vulnerable as you exit. The damaged tank track was jammed and the pair of them had to climb back to the top of the ARV, with bullets thudding around them, to get the cutting gear. They freed the track so that it would rotate, but the ARV couldn't pull the tank out of the clogging sand by itself. Another ARV and an Olifant had to be called in to tow it to safety where it could be repaired.'

[For his courage in crossing the minefield and taking the initiative in recovering the Olifant, Lieutenant de Villiers Vos was later decorated for courage on the field of battle with the Honoris Crux.]

While giving cover to the minefield rescuers the Olifant crews watched in astonishment as one Fapla commander, whose T-54 had been hit in its tracks, climbed out of the hatch and then sedately reached back to reemerge clutching a smart briefcase before strolling off with it under his arm as unflappably as a business executive going to the office. He was shot dead as he ambled away from his crippled tank. The Olifants had by now destroyed another two enemy tanks. Several other units had got forward to support the Olifants, including two platoons of 32 Battalion who, along with 4 SAI infantrymen, captured a line of trenches from which Fapla infantrymen had been firing intensively.

The momentum, lost when the Olifant got stuck in the minefield, was beginning to be regained when Major Retief ordered a retreat. Several things concerned him. Although Fapla infantry resistance was fading, the SADF infantry companies were running low on ammunition and they were separated from fresh supplies by the minefield. As its infantry withdrew Fapla began to concentrate heavy artillery fire on the South Africans. Retief also feared that an enemy air attack might catch his Olifants exposed in front of the minefield – and Olifants were not to be lost in any circumstances, the high command had made that very clear!

'Our infantry were very upset at being ordered to withdraw,' Van Zyl asserted. 'One of the 4 SAI corporals said he wouldn't retreat and they had to read the riot act to him before he obeyed. Personally, I think if we had fought on we'd have got 16 Brigade's base. By withdrawing we let them know that minefields hassled us. And they didn't forget it either.'

When Piet van Zyl's 32 Battalion men had withdrawn to the 'safe' southern side of the minefield he gathered his platoon leaders – Theron, Human, Wessels and De Villiers Vos – for reports on the state of his company. 'Besides those we knew to be dead, there were eight black soldiers missing,' he said. 'I went back with Vos looking for our lost people who had been in the thick of the fight with the Fapla infantry. We gathered up seven of them... They were OK. But when Major Retief gave the final order to complete the pullout there was still one missing. A 4 SAI guy came back who said he had seen a 32 Battalion soldier sprawled out in one of the Fapla trenches; he appeared to be dead.

'I told Retief I would have to recover the soldier. The Major said it was impossible. The retreat could not be delayed any further. I told him I couldn't leave until the missing guy had been recovered.' Another officer present at the time takes up the story: 'De Villiers Vos volunteered to go back with Piet. It was highly dramatic. They had to run forward 800 m, first crossing the minefield and then leaping into the forward Fapla trenches, all the time under rifle and machine-gun fire from remaining pockets of Fapla infantry. Vos would first sprint forward a few metres with Piet lying flat and giving him covering R-4 rifle fire. Then Vos would fling himself flat and give Piet cover as he ran forward for a few metres like a bat out of hell. Then it was Vos's turn to run again. They leap-frogged forward in this fashion all the way to the Fapla trenches where they engaged enemy infantry in a firefight while we all looked on in amazement as though watching a war movie.

'They found the soldier in the trench system. He was alive, but had a serious back wound made by a 14.5 mm shell. They made a stretcher for him with their rifles and a ground sheet and then started running back. They had made 200 m before one of the Ratels moved into the minefield to pick them all up under a belt of covering fire from the Olifants. They made it to safety and then we all got the hell out.'

Mike Muller's Combat Group Alpha was ordered into the fray to take over from where Leon Marais's Combat Group Charlie had left off. Muller's Ratels and infantrymen were to marry with the Olifant squadron. But Alpha was never really clear about its task, and the late notice meant that it was able to begin the attack only an hour before sunset, by when Fapla had broken contact and pursuit was inadvisable because of the thickness of the bush. Muller was therefore ordered to withdraw, along with Charlie, to rear laager areas.

Intelligence showed that more than 300 Fapla had been killed or wounded in that day's action and 14 enemy tanks had been put out of action. This compared with five South African dead, 19 wounded, one tank crippled and several Ratels lost – a clear victory by any numbers game. But again the action had to be judged a failure. 16 Brigade, despite its terrible casualties and severe equipment losses, still had not been destroyed and the Hube-Chambinga gap to safety for the Fapla brigades remained open. The SADF top brass went back into planning sessions to decide on an emergency plan to plug the escape hole.

Charlie's woes were not over, even as its weary fighters withdrew in darkness to its laager after getting the wounded to the field hospital.

'The supply convoys were rumbling in from the rear echelon to enable us to reorganise and refuel,' said Van Zyl. 'Officers got little sleep as the choppers and fuel lorries came in all through the night. Exhausted infantrymen and tank crews were sleeping on the forest floor around the tanks and Ratels. As the logistics vehicles came in they were meant to have someone walking in front of them to watch out for sleeping soldiers. But the system went wrong, and one supply truck ran over a tankman, who had survived two days of battle with T-55s, and smashed both of his legs. He joined the wounded being casevaced out by the choppers. His war was over.'

CHAPTER 25

'DESTROY THE G-5S!'

While Combat Groups Charlie and Alpha prepared for the 9 November attack on 16 Brigade, Commandant Robbie Hartslief's Combat Group Bravo on the Mianei was going about its foremost task of protecting the G-5s of Quebec battery, and afterwards Sierra battery, bombarding Cuito Cuanavale.

Hartslief's situation during the 16-day wait for his comrades' assault against 16 Brigade was extremely precarious. His small force faced two enemy brigades supported by the tactical armoured group of 16 Brigade. If Fapla had made a concerted and determined attack on Bravo in the last week of October, following Alpha's move to Mavinga, it is doubtful whether Hartslief's men could have held the line. The G-5 battery, in turn, would have had to retreat far southwards out of range of Cuito Cuanavale and the vital Chambinga bridge, over which logistics were coming to the forward Fapla brigades. When SADF reconnaissance commandos dug in around Cuito Cuanavale reported that three new TMM bridging vehicles had arrived at the town from Menongue, Hartslief sent scouts from 32 Battalion to identify potential crossing points on the Cuito River from which Fapla might try to get at the guns from the west.

But, just as the Fapla Command HQ at Cuito Cuanavale failed to appreciate that a strong SADF force was beginning to gather north of Mavinga, so it failed to appreciate how weak the South Africans had left themselves on the Mianei. Consequently 59 Brigade did not grasp the opportunity within its reach. Its will had been greatly weakened as a result of the serious casualties inflicted upon it by daily G-5, MRL and SAAF bombardments; under this pressure 59 Brigade's morale had been sapped much as 47 Brigade's had been at the Lomba. A symptom of its lack of heart was its feeble patrolling south of the Mianei where 32 Battalion's bush fighters had laid mines and set out devilish automatic ambushes triggered by tripwires and a variety of other nasty devices.

So grave were 59 Brigade's losses in the bombardments that the Fapla field command HQ, just north of the Vimpulo, permitted the brigade to withdraw and lick its wounds after it was noticed that Combat Group Alpha had moved off to Mavinga – precisely the time when Hartslief's Bravo had been rendered most assailable. Senior Fapla commanders at Cuito Cuanavale were aghast at the disengagement decision; they countermanded it and ordered 59 Brigade not only to stay on the Mianei but to move beyond it and press on with its task of wiping out the G-5s. Elements of 59 Brigade which had moved 20 km north to the source of the Hube River to hand over wounded men turned back with fresh supplies of food and ammunition brought in from Cuito Cuanavale across the Chambinga bridge by 25 Brigade. One of 25 Brigade's three battalions was detached to reinforce 59 on the Mianei.

The indecisive Fapla commanders were beset by further uncertainty when on 31 October a strong SADF force crossed the border from Namibia's Ovamboland, several hundred kilometres to the west of the southeast Angola war theatre, and struck 200 km into Angola to hit a big SWAPO base near the Angolan town of Cuvelai. More than 150 SWAPO guerrillas were killed in several hours of fighting in deep bush. The raid was a continuation of the SADF's long-running cross-border war with SWAPO whose military camps were in southwest Angola. But the attack was also designed to create fear among the Fapla commanders of the possibility of a major South African thrust from the west on Menongue and Cuito Cuanavale.

The Cuvelai raiders pulled out on 2 November, having succeeded both in destroying the SWAPO camp and worrying the Fapla high command. However, there was a high price to pay for the marauding. Twelve SADF soldiers were killed at Cuvelai – most of them in a single mortar-bomb explosion – and back in the Republic it was immediately widely assumed that they were casualties of South Africa's war against the Angolan and Cuban Armies on behalf of UNITA. Remarkably, the South African government was still denying at this time that its forces had anything to do with the Angolan fighting, although two British newspapers – *The Scotsman* and the *Sunday Telegraph* – had blown the gaff a few weeks earlier to international audiences.

UNITA's fiction, backed by Pretoria, that it alone was winning 'great' victories in southeast Angola was deeply resented by the SADF's fighting men. 'Hell, our guys were dying there and no one back home was being told how or why', said 61 Mech's Major Laurence Maree. 'On one of the occasions when President Botha and most of his cabinet visited the troops at Mavinga, with enemy Migs flashing high overhead, officers were telling him very bluntly how annoyed the troopies were that UNITA was claiming success while South Africa denied involvement. The soldiers saw nothing to be ashamed of in what they were fighting for. They were proud of what they were achieving and they resented risking their lives every day for a story that wasn't being told.'

Hartslief and Bravo on the Mianei bluffed their way through October – on few other occasions in the war would the SADF's situation be potentially so perilous – but out of the blue, on Sunday 1 November, 59 Brigade made its long-threatened big move towards the G-5s with explicit orders to raze the guns. Recces reported that several 59 Brigade units had advanced with tanks five kilometres south of the brigade's previously known position.

With only the G-5s themselves, an MRL battery, 400 infantrymen and Major Hannes Nortmann's eight Ratel-90s immediately available to Hartslief to stop a thrust by nearly 2,000 Fapla soldiers and 16 tanks (from the combined force of 59 and 21 Brigades, plus 16 Brigade's tactical group and the battalion from 25 Brigade), Colonel Roland de Vries (acting brigade commander while Ferreira was absent for a short break) quickly detached a company of 61 Mech infantry and a platoon of Ratel-90s from Combat Group Alpha in Mavinga as reinforcements.

The lead tanks of 59 Brigade came around the source of the Mianei in the late afternoon of 1 November to get among the big guns of Quebec battery. 'There were 36 sorties by enemy aircraft south of the Mianei that day trying to find and destroy the G-5s,' said Jean Lausberg. 'It made the task of the artillerymen more backbreaking than ever. Every time they got warning of the Migs coming, they had to lower their guns' massive barrels, camouflage the battery and drop into their foxholes, and then reverse the process after the all-clear to resume firing.'

Colonel de Vries, greatly alarmed by Quebec battery's sudden precarious predicament, ordered Lausberg to move it 24 km eastwards to a safer position about ten kilometres southeast of the source of the Mianei.

'It was a hell of an operation to move 50 big vehicles through rough terrain and bush,' said Lausberg. 'The gun tractors had to break their own paths through the trees and undergrowth. The tractors had been in Angola for more than three months. They had developed clutch problems, so movement was very slow. Quebec battery began its move eastwards at 11pm (on 1 November) and by first light (on Monday 2 November) it had only covered half the distance to its new position and was situated due south of 59 Brigade.

'I ordered the battery commander to keep moving even though daylight had come. But the first Mig sortie arrived shortly afterwards and neutralised the movement because the battery had to disperse and camouflage. They started up again, but by now the clutches of the gun tractors were burning out and the tanks of 59 Brigade were warming up their engines to begin moving south.

'We got four of the guns away, but the other four were lame ducks directly in the path of 59 Brigade's T-54/55s. It was then that Hannes Nortmann with his Ratel-90s and 400 infantrymen engaged the advance motorised infantry elements of 59 Brigade. They had almost a dozen contacts in the course of the day which stemmed the advance. Hannes had two Ratels damaged by direct hits, but no casualties. He only broke contact just before dusk when the enemy tanks began to come through. They were only slightly more than a kilometre from our stranded guns, but heavy mortar and MRL fire and an SAAF raid held the tanks up and they did not press onwards in the fast fading light.

'We sent in recovery vehicles during the night and pulled the other four guns to safety in the thick bush of our new position. The day was,

I think, both the worst and the nicest experience of my life. 59 Brigade came within a hair's-breadth of destroying the G-5s, in which case we would have been in real trouble with our generals. On the other hand, we had managed to attract the attention of the whole of 59 Brigade to the south when we were actually going to launch our main assault on 16 Brigade from the northeast; that was a proud achievement for such a small force.'

59 Brigade moved back to its original position just a few kilometres to the north where it was joined by 21 Brigade with the tactical group.

Another attempted Fapla push seemed inevitable. Hartslief established a defence line just to the southeast of the Mianei source, expecting an attack the next day, and then the next, but it did not come ... The tension became almost unbearable for the South African soldiers holding the thin Mianei line as they waited for Combat Groups Charlie and Alpha to get in position, some 50 kilometres to the northeast, and relieve the pressure by attacking 16 Brigade.

4 SAI's Combat Group Charlie at last moved northwestwards out of Mavinga on 3 November to Piet van Zyl's 'Club Mediterraneé' staging area. 61 Mech's Combat Group Alpha followed on 4 November. As Alpha began moving Hartslief was ordered by Ferreira to prepare Bravo for an exploratory attack against 59 Brigade on 9 November – the day of the scheduled Charlie-Alpha strike against 16 Brigade. Bravo's mission was to launch its foray three hours in advance of the main attack to divert Fapla attention so that the big punch to be slung from the east would be as devastating as possible.

Bravo began its diversionary assault, as planned, in the early morning darkness of Monday 9 November. But instead of being greeted with the expected fireworks when his combat group reached the enemy's plotted positions, Hartslief found that 59 Brigade had folded its tents and gone. Military intelligence discovered that the brigade had packed up and moved 20 km north over the Vimpulo during the night. When Fapla's armoured tactical group also moved north on 9 November to support its mother 16 Brigade against Charlie and Alpha, this left only 21 Brigade and the battalion from 25 Brigade on the Mianei.

Just before sunset on 9 November the 21/25 Fapla force attacked Bravo with ten tanks and two battalions of infantry. Hartslief, under strict orders not to 'mix it' with tanks, withdrew. But his paramount task of drawing attention away from Charlie's attack had been fulfilled. Hartslief's luck continued to hold because the 21/25 force withdrew to its laager areas just north of the Mianei instead of pressing on with the attack.

In the next 24 hours 59 Brigade continued its headlong retreat north. Radio intercepts showed that the brigade had been called all the way back to the Tumpo Triangle, a small area on the eastern bank of the Cuito River directly opposite Cuito Cuanavale. The Tumpo Triangle, bounded by two small tributary rivers of the Cuito called the Tumpo and the Dala, was the staging area for the Fapla brigades after they had crossed from Cuito Cuanavale and put their first foot into 'Savimbi-land.'

Bravo was called upon to make another diversionary foray against the 21/25 force prior to Charlie/Alpha's second attack on 16 Brigade on 11 November. Hartslief deployed a company from 32 Battalion north of 21 and 25 Brigades which proved sufficient to distract them during the battle between 16 Brigade and Combat Groups Charlie and Alpha.

By the night of 11/12 November 59 Brigade had reached the Chambinga bridge. Its escape was therefore assured, along with 16 Brigade which Combat Group Charlie had failed to annihilate.

The question now was whether the 21/25 force could be cut off and destroyed south of the Hube before it too reached the Chambinga bridge and then the haven of the Tumpo Triangle.

CHAPTER 26

FAPLA'S GREAT ESCAPE: THE CHAMBINGA GALLOP

To cut off 21/25 Brigades from sanctuary Commandant Leon Marais's Combat Group Charlie was ordered to deploy near possible crossing points on the Vimpulo to prevent the enemy getting north to the Hube. Commandant Mike Muller's Combat Group Alpha spread out in thick bush between the Mianei and the Vimpulo – where 16 Brigade's tactical group had earlier spent much of its time in concealment – to be ready to hit the 21/25 force from the flank or rear once it was stopped by Combat Group Charlie and to prevent it breaking out eastwards.

By 13 November 59 Brigade was safely back across the Chambinga River, but it had left its tanks behind to support 16 Brigade and its tactical group. With 20 tanks at their disposal, 16 Brigade and the tactical group were able to form two defensive lines – one on the high ground between the Chambinga and the Hube, and the other just east of the Hube source.

66 Brigade had two battalions at the Chambinga bridge. But it had sent its third battalion down to an area northeast of the Cuito-Mianei confluence; this posed a real potential problem for Hartslief's Combat Group Bravo. The G-5s began pestering the 66 Brigade battalion as well as pinning down the 21/25 force on the Mianei and making life as hellish as possible for the Angolan forces moving to and fro across the Chambinga bridge.

Though most of the tanks and a thousand or so men of 21/25 Brigades were still just to the north of the Mianei, a pioneer 21/25 unit with tanks had pulled back well north to the source of the Vimpulo. Its role was obviously to cover the impending retreat by the 21/25 force. So Ferreira decided the pioneer group would have to be destroyed before a big attack could be made against the main 21 and 25 Brigades concentration.

★ ★ ★

While Charlie and Alpha manoeuvred from the northeast towards their new positions, responsibility for keeping the heat on Fapla fell yet again on the SAAF and the artillery. The three G-6s moved onto the Chambinga High Ground just south of the Cuatir River on 13 November and began shelling Cuito Cuanavale, lying 28 km to the southeast. It was a grave shock to Fapla to discover that the South Africans' much dreaded heavy artillery had moved well to the north of Cuito Cuanavale. The first day of G-6 shelling damaged three Soviet radar installations in the Fapla-held town.

The two G-5 batteries were, however, beginning to suffer from severe stress. Three of the big guns were completely out of action because of fractures to vital parts, and nearly half of the batteries' support vehicles were beyond repair. The MRL battery had temporarily withdrawn from the Mianei for repairs and to replenish its ammunition. This put exceptionally heavy pressure on the remaining guns and equipment. Weapons fatigue and problematic logistics would from now onwards cause more and more headaches for the SADF.

Late in the afternoon of Friday 13 November 21/25 Brigades surprised the South Africans by unexpectedly beginning a rapid withdrawal northwards from the Mianei. '21 Brigade withdrew so fast that we couldn't stay with them,' said Hartslief. 'As well as moving rapidly, they were also going into territory which was relatively strange to us.'

Ferreira ordered Marais to accelerate Combat Group Charlie's redeployment to the Vimpulo. The Commandant's instructions were to deploy a big ambush force to stop 21/25 Brigades crossing the Vimpulo, and then to hit the enemy hard on its flank. Marais in turn ordered Captain Piet van Zyl's company of 32 Battalion bush fighters to lead the 4 SAI armour and infantry to ambush positions at possible crossing points across the Vimpulo. 'I asked Marais for a precise RV (map reference point) because I suspected it was where [Major Lourens] Du Plessis and I had had the problem with the mines in mid-October,' said Van Zyl.

Six possible crossing points had been identified on the Vimpulo. Two of the most likely were near a deserted hamlet called Sandumba, and these were indeed the fords where Van Zyl had had his adventures with the mines. Van Zyl's men began leading Combat Group Charlie into ambush positions during the night of 14/15 November and went on constant alert for the anticipated imminent arrival of 21/25 Brigades.

The SADF was now about to make one of its worst blunders of the war. Ferreira ordered Marais to deploy Charlie's main ambush force near Sandumba to hit 21/25 Brigades as they went for the crossing.

'Vos and I got to the Vimpulo late in the day [of 14 November],' said Van Zyl. 'We did a six kilometre reconnaissance and suggested that the main ambush should be laid two kilometres southeast of the Sandumba ford.'

But Combat Group Charlie, which had made a headlong dash of more than 20 km from the headwaters of the Cunzumbia to the Vimpulo, instead deployed some six kilometres southeast of Sandumba. 'During the night Vos and I went patrolling north of the Vimpulo and we met up with Piet Fourie and Frenchie during a terrible storm,' said Van Zyl. 'They said they couldn't understand our stratagem because the best crossings were clearly further west, as near as possible to Sandumba.' Then through the noise of the storm they heard tank engines. The tanks were *already* on the north bank and heading northwards. '21 and 25 Brigades had used the cover of that storm to cross the Sandumba fords and escaped unnoticed by Combat Group Charlie,' said Colonel Ferreira. 'They continued moving north rapidly towards the area of the Hube River source.'

There was a terrible storm also in the SADF brigade HQ as UNITA generals and SADF staff brigadiers and colonels demanded to know how 21/25 Brigades had been permitted to spring the trap. SADF spokesmen are reluctant to this day to say on the record where responsibility lay for the huge blunder. But the night's events provided rich fodder for those with deep faith in the cock-up theory of history. Whoever made the critical mistakes had cost the SADF the opportunity to wipe out another whole brigade plus a battalion of Fapla.

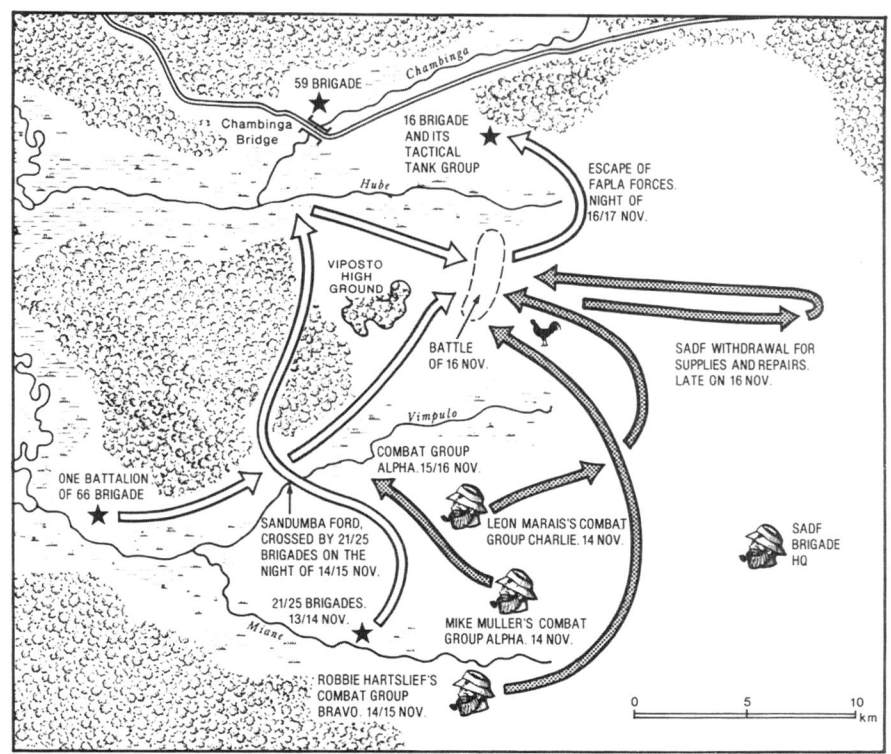

The Chambinga Gallop: Part 1 – The Escape of 21/25 Brigades, 13/17 November 1987.

Instead, 21/25 Brigades would survive to fight again yet another day and kill more South African and UNITA soldiers.

Combat Group Charlie now made an emergency high-speed traverse to the source of the Hube to prevent 21/25 Brigades from going around it and swinging westwards towards the Chambinga bridge. Combat Group Bravo was ordered to leapfrog up from the Mianei to support Charlie, while Combat Group Alpha stayed south of the Vimpulo to monitor any stray Fapla units left behind.

The game-plan of 21 and 25 Brigades was to manoeuvre around the western edge of the 1,270-metre-high Viposto High Ground (see map) and either cross the Hube or turn eastwards along the southern bank of the river, keeping to the treeline, until they could make a dash around the Hube source. Combat Groups Charlie and Bravo intended to squeeze 21/25 Brigades into the *anhara* between the treeline and the Hube River and destroy them there.

21/25 Brigades failed to find a crossing point on the Hube, and so came around the northern edge of the Viposto High Ground. Just after 10 am on Monday 16 November heavy fighting erupted as the Fapla forces began their bolt towards the river source and safety. Within 90 minutes three SADF men were dead and two of their vehicles had been destroyed. On the plus side the Commander of 21 Brigade, Captain Nguleica, had been seriously wounded when his BTR-60 armoured personnel command vehicle was shot from under him.

Little else was going well for Combat Group Charlie. It had deployed further south of the river than ordered by Ferreira and had given away its presence to the 21/25 force by using noisy *plofadders* to breach a minefield and had then fired mortar shell illumination flares to light its way into position, thus breaching basic SADF operational principles of silence and stealth. Back in Brigade HQ eyebrows were raised particularly high when Charlie ran into the minefield, because maps had been captured during the attack on 16 Brigade which showed precisely where the mines were between the Chambinga and Hube River sources.

'My company moved on foot between a squadron of armoured cars,' said Piet van Zyl. 'There was a company of 4 SAI infantry in front of us, the squadron of Olifant tanks to our right and Hannes Nortmann's Ratel squadron behind us. There were more units away to the right of the tanks. To the left of us was a UNITA infantry battalion.

'Soon after we made the first contact, heavy fighting had spread along the whole line. It was all very confusing and unnerving. Their Stalin Organs were really letting rip, and the rockets were hitting the ground in front of us and skidding between the men on foot and the tanks and armoured cars. We had to order our men to walk behind the tanks or they would have been blasted to Hell or Heaven. As it was, one of my troops got hit by shrapnel when an 82 mm mortar shell hit a tree right behind us. His face was covered in blood. We carried him back so that a Rinkhals armoured ambulance could come forward and pick him up. Then Vos got hit in the shoulder by shrapnel: he refused to go back, so we put him in a Ratel so he could watch the rest of the fight.

'Wessie (Corporal Wessels) and I steered our men towards Jurg (Human) and Thai (Theron). Two of their guys had been killed by a mortar shell, so we helped put their dead and wounded into a Ratel. To the left the 4 SAI infantrymen, all white national servicemen, were involved in a very heavy scrap and the Olifants started moving in to support them.'

The Olifants quickly shot out four T-54/55s and a BM-21 Stalin Organ which was little more than 200 m from the South African lines. 'The Stalin Organ started burning and exploding. Its rockets were flying everywhere. We were flat on the ground and the Olifants leapfrogged back a bit to avoid damage.

'By then we were still only at a point near the edge of the *anhara,* which was meant to have been our startline at the break of day. We began passing enemy dead and then we captured three young Fapla guys sitting in a trench shaking with fear. Their eyes were wide and they thought we were going to shoot them. But we sent them back in a Ratel to HQ for questioning.

'We at last reached the edge of the *anhara* way behind schedule some time in the early afternoon. The Fapla infantry began running across the *anhara* to get to the Hube, just as 47 Brigade had done on the Lomba. The Olifants and Ratels came forward and began to kill them with anti-personnel rounds. Browning light machine-guns were firing at them and our mortars were just beginning to pinpoint them when a message came through that there were enemy tanks to the rear (south) of us. Our tanks and Ratels turned around through 180 degrees to see what was happening. They chased back and we ran between them, but we couldn't see a thing. It was Hannes Nortmann, just to our southwest, who first confronted the Fapla tanks.'

With the exception of Nortmann's armoured car squadron, Robbie Hartslief had held most of his Combat Group Bravo back in reserve as the South Africans manoeuvred into positions from where they could force 21/25 Brigades out into the killing ground of the *anhara*. The Fapla tanks had advanced towards the *anhara* from just behind Hartslief's HQ area inside the treeline. When the alert was raised Nortmann raced back towards his mother combat group to give protection.

'Nortmann came through and engaged the tanks about 50 m in front of my command group,' said Hartslief. 'He shot out three of them. He obviously still had some of his nine lives in hand because to take on a tank with a Ratel is really quite something and Hannes had done it again and again in this war.'

Nortmann used up at least one of those lives during the encounter. He spotted a tank gun barrel moving in the treeline trying to acquire a target and thought it futile to try to silence the tank with the 20 mm gun of his own command Ratel. When the gunners of his nearby Ratel-90s failed to understand his radio instruction, he leapt out of his vehicle and walked, apparently oblivious to the danger from flying metal, to the nearest of the armoured cars, pointed out the tank by hand and then watched the 90 mm rounds slot home.

Hartslief too got in a few shots at the tanks, but then his Ratel-90 broke down with gearbox trouble and got stuck in a deep gully leading from the treeline into the *anhara*. 'I could see the tanks burning that Hannes had shot out. The other Fapla tanks broke contact and burst from the left through the middle of my headquarters area. The bush was so thick that I don't think they saw any of us as they crashed through. My Ratel was so comprehensively stuck that I couldn't exercise control and had to hand over command of Bravo to Commandant Marais (of Charlie).'

Hartslief's Ratel was jammed in the gully along with a Withings armoured recovery vehicle with a seized-up Rinkhals ambulance in tow. An enemy BM-21, desperate to get around the Hube source to safety, noticed the struggling SADF vehicles and fired a whole pack of 40 rockets at them horizontally from just 300 m, hitting only the Rinkhals. Two South Africans were wounded by shrapnel. Sergeant Willem Labuschagne, the Withings driver, carried the most seriously wounded man, medical orderly Lance Corporal Redelinghuis, 50 metres under heavy machine-gun fire to one of Nortmann's Ratel-90s. The Ratel driver dismounted to help Labuschagne lift Redelinghuis into the armoured car. A T-55 then opened fire and the driver dived for cover in the bush. Labuschagne, a 46-year-old regular soldier, got into the Ratel and drove it off to a medical post. Labuschagne had acted with high courage and selflessness, but Lance Corporal Redelinghuis died later from his wounds. (Labuschagne was subsequently decorated with the Honoris Crux for his bravery.)

'During the encounter with the Fapla tanks our Olifants and Ratels began to run low on fuel and ammunition. One Olifant ran out of fuel in mid-battle,' said Van Zyl. 'And UNITA units fighting alongside us had taken a terrible number of dead and wounded. Everywhere I could see them carrying their own corpses and wounded on improvised stretchers made from wood cut from the bush.

'In the late afternoon we were ordered by Commandant Marais to break contact with 21 and 25 Brigades. Then we withdrew eastwards for some 12 km to get new supplies and carry out repairs. There the tiffies were fantastic. They had been busy all day on and behind the battlefield fixing things. Now, as usual, they just settled down to work right through the night servicing the tanks, the Ratels and the trucks.'

'But we shouldn't have moved so far away,' said Van Zyl. The SADF had made yet another critical mistake. As Combat Groups Charlie and Bravo began withdrawing, so Fapla's 21/25 Brigades had themselves pulled back westwards to regroup and dig in defensively. On the basis of reports by commandos from 5 Recce Regiment the SADF intelligence analysis was that the Fapla consolidation exercise would take some six hours or more. But 21/25 Brigades sprang yet another surprise. Despite the abundant evidence that the enemy force had a full box of tricks, the South Africans were caught on the wrong foot again. As Charlie and Bravo were settling into their laager area, 21/25 Brigades quickly packed up their wares and sprinted for the source of the Hube and were round it during the night of 16/17 November, helped by another thunderstorm, before the South African combat groups reacted.

The 21/25 rabbit, penned in so that it was ripe for shooting and skinning, had with one mighty bound sprung free again. This headlong flight towards the safety of the Chambinga bridge, which had really begun with 16 Brigade, became known to the SADF men as the Chambinga Gallop.

Official SADF records so far made public do not record the scale of the consequent row at Brigade HQ where one field commander in particular caught most of the flak for not pressing home the attack more vigorously.

★ ★ ★

The fighting on 16 November cost Fapla 130 dead and seven tanks and several other vehicles destroyed, against four SADF men killed, 19 wounded and two Ratels, a Rinkhals and a Withings destroyed. But on balance of confidence Fapla had won the day. The South Africans' morale had been badly dented by the succession of errors; there were many long faces in the laagers. On the other hand, with its Great Escape now nearly completed, Fapla's mettle had been strengthened.

After their bolt during the previous night, the soldiers of 21/25 Brigades dug in on high ground on 17 November between the source of the Chambinga River and the source of the Hube River. They provided a defensive screen for 16 Brigade and its tactical armoured group which from first light began retreating northwards across the Chambinga bridge.

Colonel Ferreira decided that another attack must be made on the enemy on 17 November, this time with Mike Muller's Combat Group Alpha as the spearhead supported by the tank squadron and two 32 Battalion companies detached from Combat Group Charlie. The guess at SADF 20 Brigade HQ was that Fapla forces remaining southeast of the Chambinga bridge had very little resistance left in them. Faced with yet another South African attack they would break and retreat in disorder to the bridge; as the enemy funnelled towards the bridge, causing chaotic congestion, the G-5s, MRLs and 120 mm mortars would inflict terrible damage upon them.

Lieutenant Koos Breytenbach, the forward artillery observer at the Chambinga bridge, became known as the 'Murderer of the Chambinga' as he brought down endless G-5, MRL and 120 mm mortar fire on the crossing during the five weeks he spent there watching the Chambinga Gallop. The *anhara* floodplain on the southern side of the Chambinga crossing was about one kilometre wide. The retreating Fapla vehicles from 59, 21, 25, 66 and 16 Brigades were boxed up in a forested area of about six square kilometres just south of the floodplain awaiting their turn to approach the bridge.

The bridge consisted of one TMM mobile bridge across the main stream, with puckered wooden log roads approaching it over marshy ground and small rivulets. 'The concentration area was a perfect target for our artillerymen who settled in for a highly productive – or, rather, destructive – period,' said Jean Lausberg. 'When the Faplas moved out onto the *anhara* they made an even better target for Koos, who became very close to the UNITA troops guarding him. They brought him water, washed his clothes and cooked his food.'

The UNITA men also gave their own names to the SADF artillery pieces. The G-5 was christened 'Kafundanga' after UNITA's former chief of staff, Samuel Kafundanga Chingunji, who died in mysterious circumstances in 1974 during the war against the Portuguese but is still regarded by many UNITA followers as a man as mighty as Savimbi himself. The 127 mm MRL was dubbed 'chindungu,' meaning 'the red pepper that bites.'

★ ★ ★

It looked to Deon Ferreira as though everything would evolve according to his plan after the G-5s' opening early morning barrage. Koos Breytenbach watched in amazement as two companies of 16 Brigade's infantry marched from the concentration area across the *anhara* towards the bridge, providing a perfect target for long-range artillery. Breytenbach brought in ten G-5 airburst fragmentation rounds onto the foot soldiers, followed by an MRL airburst ripple. Reconnaissance Commandos counted more than 60 dead 16 Brigade soldiers on or approaching the bridge.

The SADF artillery's priority was to lay down patterns of fire which would keep the bridge blocked for as long as possible. An early G-5 salvo caught a vehicle on the bridge, forcing 50 or so other vehicles to pull back southeastwards while the obstruction was cleared.

The G-5s' timely success was an encouraging omen for Combat Group Alpha as it set out from its laager area southeast of the Chambinga source. Piet van Zyl linked up with Mike Muller, who was shocked by the 32 Battalion captain's refusal to ride inside the Ratel-20 armoured infantry carriers, or 'coffins,' as Van Zyl described them. Instead Van Zyl's men took turnabout in riding on top of the tanks and walking between the tanks and armoured cars. 'It had rained all night,' said Van Zyl. 'It was cold and every time we pushed through the trees we were showered from the wet leaves. The best place to be was on the flat area behind the turret of an Olifant above the exhaust. It was nice and warm. It was too noisy there to hear warnings of air attacks. But you could tell when the alarm had been given because you would see our infantry on the ground disappear into the Ratels at high speed.

'As we advanced the tanks began firing ahead speculatively. It was an amazing sight. After an Olifant unleashed a 105 mm shell you saw a path opening up through the forest just like the Red Sea divided for Moses. We seemed to be doing well, but then UNITA warned us that a major minefield stretched ahead for something like ten kilometres. We had to stop while the sappers checked it out. It turned out to be just a few scattered small mines. That lost us at least an hour.'

Mike Muller had decided to attack 21/25 Brigades on the high ground between the Chambinga and Hube sources from the northeast, with Combat Group Bravo deploying further south as his reserve. Muller's Combat Group Alpha found itself manoeuvring through unexpectedly continuous thick bush at snail's pace, causing further delay. The roar of the revving tank and armoured car engines gave the 21/25 Brigade force warning of the impending attack, and elements began slipping away from their defensive positions towards the Chambinga bridge. When at last Alpha was in position to smite the enemy an air raid warning forced its vehicles to take cover. By the time the all-clear sounded, the whole 21/25 Brigade force had decamped and extended the distance between it and Alpha.

Only in late afternoon, two hours before nightfall, did SADF forces catch up with rearguard units of 21 and 25 Brigades about three kilometres southeast of the Chambinga bridge. Even then it was not the main Alpha group but Bravo which made the contact, with the amazing Hannes Nortmann leading his Ratels yet again to shoot out two T-54 tanks before Fapla broke contact and fled towards the Chambinga bridge.

'We [Alpha] caught up with 21/25 Brigades about 1,500 m from the bridge,' said Piet van Zyl. 'Our Ratels had just hit one of their ammunition vehicles when UNITA gave us warning of another air raid. We took cover but the attack never came. By the time we began

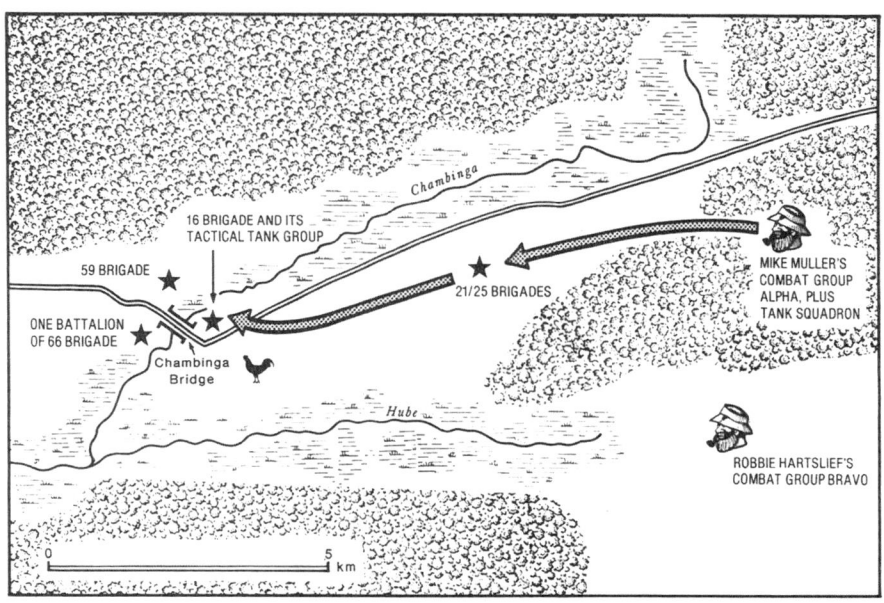

The Chambinga Gallop: Part 2 – The Pursuit to the Chambinga Bridge, 17 November 1987.

chasing them again it was getting dark and much of the 21/25 Brigade force had run for the bridge and crossed it. My infantrymen had made not a single contact all day. We were pulled back through the night many kilometres to the laager because they [senior officers] were afraid of attacks by Migs the next day. Fapla then just came from the north across the bridge and took out some of its vehicles. I felt despairing. We should have pressed on the following day and taken everything out. We just didn't go for it.'

Van Zyl was right. Fapla had slipped yet another noose. Although the G-5s destroyed in the order of 300 Fapla vehicles at the Chambinga crossing on that day of Thursday 17 November 1987, the most stirring performance came from Fapla's 59 Brigade which exercised impressive control, despite otherwise near anarchy at the bridge, and brought valuable equipment back north across the Chambinga River to safety.

The whole Fapla force was thus back across the river to safety at the end of the Chambinga Gallop. It was back in much the same position as it had started in July. A major phase of the War for Africa had come to an end. All Fapla's offensive capability had been drained. In the fighting from 9 to 17 November the Angolans had lost 600 dead and at least that number wounded against 17 South African deaths and 41 wounded. The MPLA, admitting major losses in the Cuito Cuanavale fighting for the first time in late November in a statement issued in Luanda, said 4,000 of its soldiers had been killed or wounded since July 'by the racist South Africans'. The SADF said more than 1,000 of this total were accounted for by deaths. SADF estimates of Fapla equipment losses in the same period included more than 90 tanks and armoured cars, 11 Sam-8 and Sam-13 missile systems, 20 BM-21 Stalin Organs and more than 300 assorted other vehicles.

In the numbers game the South Africans were the clear winners. But nevertheless 20 SA Brigade had not succeeded in its main aims of either destroying the Fapla brigades, before they could retreat to good defensive positions, or driving them from their last toehold on the east bank of the deep and fast-flowing Cuito River. SADF officers took comfort from the fact that Fapla had at least been pushed north of the Chambinga River. But the facts were that South African morale was low, equipment was failing with great regularity and SADF logistics were inadequate. For Generals Geldenhuys and Liebenberg and Admiral Putter, the question was what to do next.

★ ★ ★

20 SA Brigade had failed so many times to snare the Fapla brigades that it became necessary for the senior SADF generals and the government in Pretoria to do some fresh thinking. The enemy, capitalising on its series of narrow escapes, was now too well deployed and dug in over a limited area of good defensive ground to be chased off or destroyed by artillery alone. The generals decided there would have to be a deliberate attack on the Cuito River bridgehead. The politicians approved.

But that left a tricky question to be resolved. Would the new offensive be launched by troops already in the field, or would they be replaced with fresh soldiers?

For several reasons it would have been better to press on with the soldiers already in Angola. They knew the conditions; they were battle-hardened; and, because of November's frustrating failures, they had a thing or two to prove yet. But one of the limitations of the South African military system was coming home to roost. The South African Army is essentially a conscript force. It has only 18,000 full-time career soldiers, mainly comprising the officer corps and the regular soldiers of the black battalions. The backbone of the fighting force is made up of 60,000 young white national servicemen, each serving two years of compulsory full-time duty,[1] and about 140,000 Citizen Force members, civilians who on completion of their national service are obliged to report for a month or more of military service each year for the first ten years after their return to civilian life. Thus, the South African Army, while having only a small core of Permanent Force members, can mobilise the biggest army in Africa in time of trouble.

The Christmas holiday in South Africa is the most important of the year. It comes in the middle of the southern African summer. So, not only is it the time when families get together in the traditional Christian ritual, but businesses and factories close down for up to a month and mini-Great Treks begin to the beaches of Natal and the Cape, the game parks and the rest of the big outdoors. The Army releases as many national servicemen as possible for home leave, and those who have served their two years are demobilised in time to return to civilian life by Christmas. The whole process receives enormous attention from the South African press, and motorists are urged to give lifts to returning young soldiers who identify themselves at the roadsides with fluorescent orange sashes worn over army drabs.

Nearly all of the fighting men in Angola with 61 Mech and 4 SAI were national servicemen coming to the end of their two-year period of conscription. By Christmas they were due to be out of uniform and back home to resume their normal lives, studies and careers. Logically, in terms of the war, it would have made sense for their period of conscription to be extended so that the impetus of the SADF push was not drained too severely. But the South African public were still very badly informed about the War for Africa: disinformation, secrecy and censorship had combined effectively to hide the true scale of the conflict from the Republic's citizenry. True, there were occasional announcements of the loss of yet another young serviceman's life 'somewhere on the border'. True, many people either knew or suspected that their country's armed forces were involved in something very much bigger than the government was revealing. But it had ever been that way since the mid-1970s when the Cubans first entered Angola, the Western powers lost their nerve, and SWAPO began major cross-border raids from Angola into Namibia. An extension of the period of national service, against this surreptitious background, would set alarm bells ringing in Johannesburg's plush northern suburbs, in the dorps of the Transvaal, across the bleak plateau of the Orange Free State, among the vineyards of the Cape and the banana and sugar plantations of Natal and possibly trigger a political crisis. The idea of defeating Cuban- and Soviet-backed communism in Angola was widely favoured among the white electorate; but the deaths of those voters' sons in pursuit of the goal was deeply unpopular. The voters wanted victories, as long as they were easy; they could be expected to raise a hue and cry if the national service period was extended.

So in the end the generals and politicians decided it would be best if the national servicemen were stood down, as scheduled, and that others take their place. The decision was greatly resented by the field commanders, to whom it made no military sense at all. The replacement batches of 2,500 national servicemen scheduled to join 4 SAI and 61 Mech in Angola had all completed just one year of military service with training battalions. They had no experience of real warfare and each would need several weeks of special training and acclimatisation after their arrival before they would be ready for battle. It would give Fapla a big bonus window of time to organise its defences, build up supplies and rethink tactics.

'The training period in my Combat Group (Alpha) greatly reduced our momentum,' said 61 Mech's Commandant Mike Muller. 'My officers had to cope with a complete changeover of 1,100 men. From the time they began arriving from 30 November onwards, the new soldiers had to get used to a new climate and entirely new physical conditions. They also had to learn to fight at very much closer quarters than they had been trained for. In Angola, it was bushy terrain, but back in the Republic they had been tutored mostly in open veld. On the training ranges you shot out "enemy" tanks at 1,000 metres. In Angola we had been shooting them out for real as close as 10 to 15 m.

'Command control in the Angolan terrain was very difficult. We had to train the newcomers in the special kinds of co-ordinated formations we needed to keep: in that thick bush if one bloke made a slip then half of the combat group could be lost to the commander, and then you had to stop and re-group before you could go forward again. You lost precious hours that way. It was tough work training new men in what we had learned only by hard experience. It took time. We scheduled three weeks for training to get them battle-ready, but it took longer.'

So, although there would be scarcely a dry eye among South African *vrouens* and *moeders* (wives and mothers) as they rushed out onto their stoeps before Christmas to welcome home their husbands and sons from the war, the combat group officers were left gnashing their teeth with frustration.

Colonel Deon Ferreira had mixed feelings. 'I knew the commanders were against the hassle of changing troops at such a critical stage,' he said. 'The organisation and retraining needed a big effort. In terms of the hassle factor I was against changing the troops. Ideally we should have finished the job with the old troops. But, on the other hand, many of them had seen more action in three months than many South African soldiers saw in the whole of World War II. Fighting spirit was down. Leon Marais and his people in 4 SAI had had enough. A lot of equipment needed replacing. And anyway there was no real choice once the generals had told the troops they would be home for Christmas. It would have been very difficult to remotivate those guys.'

As a compromise between the desires of the field officers and those of the waiting women, the generals decided that 20 SA Brigade would make one last effort before Demob Day on 30 November to push the Fapla brigades from their remaining patch of territory on the east bank of the Cuito River. Such an idea ran directly counter to the recommendations of the combat group commanders who said Fapla's defences in front of Cuito Cuanavale were virtually impregnable to an attack from the east.

They argued, more potently than ever, that the logical way to achieve victory was to attack Cuito Cuanavale from the west, isolate all the enemy's eight brigades in and around the town, and then destroy them at the SADF's leisure. Their wishes, first expressed in August and then again after the 3 October victory over 47 Brigade, were again proscribed.

There were several reasons why the hard-headed pragmatism of Robbie Hartslief, Mike Muller and Leon Marais was overruled. The generals knew something that the commandants were not aware of. Fidel Castro, fearing a military catastrophe for the Fapla forces, had ordered Cuban diplomats and MPLA officials accredited to the United Nations to contact South Africa's UN mission in New York in order to explore the possibility of a negotiated settlement of the Angolan conflict. Such an agreement, Castro suggested, should be linked to a resolution of the problem in neighbouring South African-ruled Namibia. Since this was the sort of formula South African Foreign Ministry officials had been working towards for the best part of a decade, the ears of Foreign Minister Pik Botha in Pretoria naturally pricked up. From now onwards the foreign affairs mandarins would have an ever greater input into the conduct of the War for Africa. The negotiations ball would at first roll slowly, uncertainly and in an unclear direction – but, eventually, it would turn with ever greater momentum and certitude along the sound tarmac laid by the SADF's military successes until eventually the whole face of southern Africa would be transformed in a way that few people would once have thought possible.

Castro was also coming under severe pressure from Soviet leader Mikhail Gorbachev whose reforms would lead in 1989–90 to some of the most profound changes in world history as the Marxist-Leninist ethic disintegrated under the weight of its contradictions in eastern and central Europe. As early as late 1987 Gorbachev's policies of *glasnost* (openness) and *perestroïka* (reconstruction) were already beginning to have a major impact on Cuba. For nearly 30 years Moscow had underwritten Castro's communist revolution by buying Cuba's sugar at more than the world price and selling oil to it below the market price. Under Gorbachev such extravagant economic gestures, which had helped suck the Soviet Union dry, were being phased out. In a speech on 28 December 1987 Castro described the previous 12 months as one of the most difficult for Cuba since he came to power in 1959. 'A year of many obstacles,' was the euphemism he employed to describe the squeeze being put on him by Moscow. There were clear signs that Moscow was growing disenchanted with the burden of bankrolling the Cuban/MPLA war in Angola. On 11 November 1987, the 12th anniversary of Angola's independence, Soviet television journalist Valeriy Grigoryev, in a 30-minute film report from Angola, launched an extraordinary attack on Moscow's MPLA allies which could only have been sanctioned at the highest level. 'There is no question that the war has become a heavy burden that the [Angolan] working people have to shoulder,' Grigoryev told Soviet viewers. 'More than half the country's budget is spent on defence ... Corruption is at an unprecedented level. Inflation is rampant. Speculation and the so-called black market have become serious problems on a national level. The crisis can also be attributed to mismanagement. Because of the failure to reconcile government planning and the state budget, the deficit in the balance of payments continues to grow. Foreign debt is increasing. The state bureaucracy has been blown out of proportion, while the management of the economy and enterprises is terribly poor. Production discipline is very low. How can there be talk of fulfilling plans when more than one-third of the republic's enterprises are idle while the rest are working at minimum capacity?'

The SADF generals concurred reluctantly with their diplomats' views that a devastating attack on Cuito Cuanavale from the west would be foolish just as the Angolans and Cubans, urged by their Soviet bankroller, were beginning to seek a face-saving way out of the conflict. Yes, it would probably result in the destruction of the brigades at Cuito Cuanavale. But it might also lead to an uncontrollable escalation of the war on other fronts as the Cubans, impelled by the need to demonstrate Latin American *machismo,* and the Soviets – who, despite Gorbachev's accession, still needed to fan gently the dying embers of Brezhnevian socialist internationalist solidarity before finding a respectable moment to douse them finally – sought to demonstrate their 'unshakeable' commitment to the MPLA. Already South African military intelligence had learned from the CIA that Castro had ordered the soldiers and pilots of one of

Cuba's finest divisions, the 50th, to Angola in mid-November to join the fighting in the event of the military situation deteriorating further.

The SADF generals had no doubt of their forces' ability to take on the Cubans and beat them: but equally they had no doubt about the heavy cost this would involve in South African lives, equipment and domestic and international political controversy.

A kind of half-cock military plan was decided upon to conclude Operation Moduler before the national servicemen went home to their mums, wives and girlfriends. The troopies would not launch the ground attack from the west advocated so strongly by their field commanders. They would not, however, wait twiddling their thumbs in Angola before throwing away their uniforms and returning to civvie street. They would, the generals determined, launch one last attack from the east to try to drive the Fapla brigades back to the western side of the Cuito River, thus achieving the main aim of the hiccup-ridden chase of the enemy from the killing fields of the Lomba River: the generals reasoned – or, rather, Pik Botha's Department of Foreign Affairs reasoned – that if the attack was successful it would exert just enough pressure on the Cubans and Fapla to transform the pre-negotiations into substantive talks.

The 20 SA Brigade HQ at Rundu now had dual and incompatible duties – to plan the eviction of Fapla from Savimbi-land by the end of November *and* to arrange the return home well in advance of Christmas of men who knew they would be fighting the last battle of their national service careers.

A forlorn task was made more difficult by the fact that Fapla itself was learning a trick or two. For example, one SADF artillery observer directing fire on the Tumpo Triangle logistics base grew increasingly frustrated at his inability to exercise accurate control because the rocket and G-5 shells were falling in an inexplicably irregular pattern. It took the observer specialists some time to work out that Fapla sappers had bamboozled the SADF by placing explosive charges in the ground which they detonated at random as their enemy's shells fell.

Furthermore, the SADF generals *knew* that the forces at their disposal were inadequate in themselves to throw Fapla from its defensive positions. The hope was that an attack over the Chambinga High Ground might simply frighten Fapla into withdrawing right across the Cuito River in the belief that the SADF force was very much bigger than in reality. The reasoning at high level was that Fapla was so demoralised that it would have little fight left in it. Just the *threat* of one last major push by the SADF, with its formidable reputation enhanced by the Lomba triumphs, would be enough to make the Angolans cut and run.

To say that the field commanders were sceptical about this plan is to do scant justice to their bitter opposition to it. Time and again, as this book was researched, these officers, who are still serving loyally with the SADF, asked the author to switch off his tape recorder while they gave him their off-the-record opinions of what they had been asked to do. 'Fundamentally stupid,' said one highly decorated officer who argued that Fapla, despite its many shortcomings, had often fought with a degree of determination that South African soldiers in the field respected. The field commanders knew from their warfare textbooks and from hard, bloody experience that the Tumpo Triangle into which the Angolans were slowly being forced was ideal defensive terrain; that the enemy had used the time given to them, by the SADF's inability to attack immediately, to organise three defence lines between the Cuito River and the Chambinga High Ground; that the Fapla brigades would not readily give up the terrain they now held, especially as their confidence had been lifted by recent small-scale successes; and that there were two Fapla brigades, the 8th and the 13th, and several Cuban companies in reserve just across the river around Cuito Cuanavale. The SADF force, numbering scarcely 3,000 men at that stage, would be attacking more than 5,000 enemy soldiers on the Cuito Cuanavale east bank who had withdrawn into well-prepared defensive positions. Unanimously the commandants of the three combat groups continued to argue that, whatever the political and diplomatic considerations might be, attacking Cuito Cuanavale from the west was the only option that made any sense militarily.

The SADF attack was delayed until Wednesday 25 November, primarily because of the requirement that the tanks, G-5s and other bits of weaponry first be fully repaired and operational with adequate back-up spares, fuel and logistics in place. Commandant Mike Muller highlighted one of the many logistics problems that were being experienced: pins he needed for the tracks of the tanks arrived only just in time to enable the Olifants to take part in the fight with a degree of confidence that they would not be knocked out by their own lack of spares. This time the main attack was to be carried out by UNITA forces, with SADF units in support and follow-up roles. The main thrust was aimed against 25 Brigade at the Chambinga bridge. Robbie Hartslief's Combat Group Bravo received the tank squadron under Mike Muller. The early rules of Operation Moduler combat were that SADF forces were to destroy the Fapla brigades *before* the enemy crossed the Chambinga bridge, but that the South Africans themselves were *not* to cross it. Now the bridge would have to be traversed in contravention of the original operational guidelines.

The principal aim of the attack of 25 November was to drive the Fapla brigades from the east bank of the Cuito River by Saturday 28 November. Two days after that the 4 SAI and 61 Mech national servicemen were due to start demobilisation. The minimal aim was to achieve domination of the Chambinga bridge by the end of the young soldiers' last battle.

The attack, with Combat Group Alpha deploying to the northeast to distract 59 Brigade's attention from the main thrust against 25 Brigade, was launched with a series of hiccups. The initial artillery barrage was scheduled for 4 am, but began three-and-a-half hours late. The UNITA/ SADF ground assault also started late because UNITA recces failed to meet Combat Group Bravo's forward elements at the agreed rendezvous.

The plan called for UNITA's 3rd and 5th Regular Battalions to push over the Chambinga High Ground just to the north of the Chambinga River and then turn north to push into the Tumpo area with Combat Group Bravo following up close behind and Combat Group Charlie securing the Chambinga bridge.

Robbie Hartslief found that his Ratels of Combat Group Bravo and Mike Muller's tanks were able to advance at only a leaden pace because of the thickness of the bush. Vision was so limited that the armoured vehicles had to use electronic navigation, and the vegetation was so dense that the Ratels and Olifants were unable to rotate their turrets.

The noise and the pace of the South African advance enabled Fapla forward units to retreat to safety almost at leisure. At 11 am Bravo ran

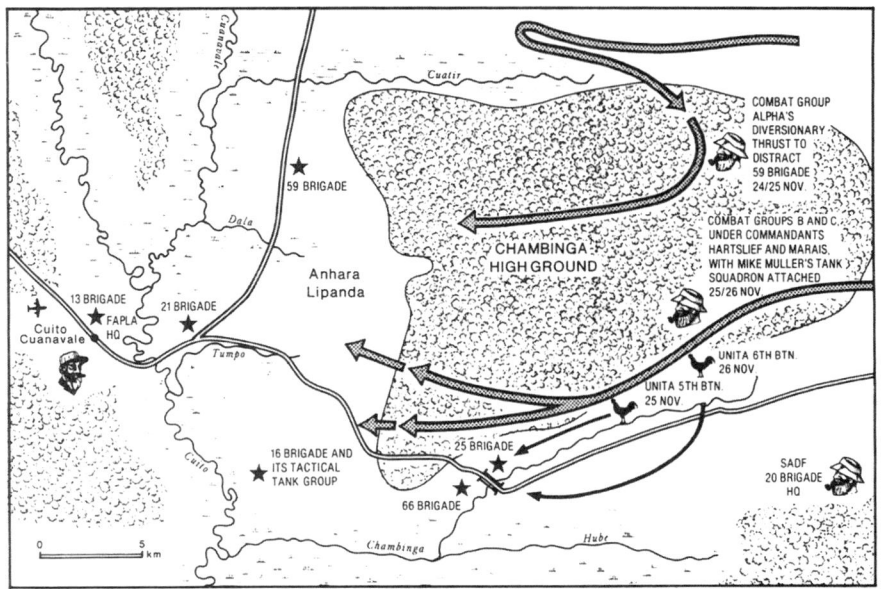

The Last Unsuccessful SADF Attack of Operation Moduler: 25/26 November 1987.

into a minefield which, while it inflicted no damage, robbed the advance of yet more momentum. Meanwhile, behind, Charlie had come under heavy 120 mm mortar attack and lost three men wounded.

By 3 pm Bravo was still struggling through heavy bush, having advanced only 800 metres in the previous four hours. For a while forward momentum stopped completely as the vehicles encountered vegetation almost as impenetrable as a brick wall. The tanks were pulled out to high ground to the northwest to function in a purely observation role.

It was only at 5 pm that Bravo reached Fapla's outer positions after UNITA had pushed the Fapla forward elements westwards at heavy casualty cost to Savimbi's 5th Regular Battalion. Bravo was at last ready to attack, but during a reorganisation halt the combat group suffered a particularly heavy and accurate Fapla artillery attack. One mortar bomb fell right through the open hatch of a Ratel, killing the gunner, and two other South African soldiers were seriously wounded by shrapnel.

Having sustained serious casualties, with Muller's Olifants unable to manoeuvre, the bush showing few signs of thinning out, and the light beginning to fade, Commandant Hartslief decided to call off the attack for that day.

Combat Group Charlie, with Mike Muller's tank squadron attached, became the main SADF attack force the following day, Thursday 26 November, with Bravo reverting to the reserve role.

Charlie was even more out of luck than Bravo. During the night Fapla reinforced its positions at the Chambinga bridge with another ten tanks. The South African force again moved off later than planned and was held up unexpectedly by a minefield. Then Leon Marais's men came under a fierce artillery barrage, particularly from big Soviet M-46 guns positioned at Cuito Cuanavale. Marais was forced to withdraw to the Chambinga source. The whole attack was called off with the South Africans having failed to achieve even their minimal aim of capturing and securing the Chambinga bridge.

The generals declared Operation Moduler at an end, with the enemy having been driven back all the way to its July starting point. The national servicemen in the front line began heading for civvie street. Staff officers began planning a full-scale attack on the Fapla bridgehead at the Cuito River with fresh SADF troops and weapons reinforcements. The new operation, designated Hooper, would begin officially on Sunday 13 December 1987.

★ ★ ★

It was not only national servicemen who exited the War for Africa with the conclusion of Operation Moduler. Others' war was over too.

Captain Piet van Zyl, who had been called back into action from his Natal farm by Colonel Deon Ferreira, had been worrying for some weeks about the way his big property was being managed in his absence. The key maize planting had begun on 20 October and had been handled inefficiently. As a result, both the sheep shearing and potato harvesting had fallen badly behind schedule, threatening Van Zyl with potential losses of many tens of thousands of rands. Van Zyl, essentially a man of action, was chafing at the bit at the prospect of a long period of inaction between the end of Moduler and the launching of Hooper. 'I got a message from the farm on 8 December saying a lot of things were going wrong,' he said. 'It seemed also to me that our generals had reached a point of indecision about the conduct of the war. It was obvious that the new national servicemen would need a lot of retraining before we would be ready to press on. Our tanks would need a lot of servicing, and there would be a long wait before reinforcement tanks arrived. So I asked Colonel Ferreira if he minded if I returned to the farm.'

It was almost a re-enactment of scenes from the Boer War when individual Afrikaner commandos would break off from battle when the mealie (maize) planting season came round. Ferreira willingly but sadly let one of the finest fighting officers he had known fly out by helicopter to put his farm back in order.

Ferreira himself, after more than three months of exhausting work directing 20 SA Brigade, was relieved by Colonel Paul Fouché for Operation Hooper.

Another comrade of Ferreira's from his days at Fort Buffalo as Commandant of 32 Battalion was also out of the war. Sergeant Mac da Trinidada, the black Angolan recce group leader, had continued to enjoy an exciting life after the decisive 3 October battle with 47 Brigade on the Lomba.

'My team was sent north after that to track Fapla's 59 Brigade on the western side of the Cunzumbia River and 21 Brigade on the eastern side,' said Da Trinidada. 'We were there for something like three weeks with our artillery bombarding their positions, and their artillery bombarding the SADF positions. With other recce teams and small infantry groups we were hitting their logistics routes from behind with mines, hit-and-run guerrilla ambushes and automatic ambushes.

'We reconnoitred possible crossing points on the Cuito River, scouted for Commandant Hartslief on the Mianei, and then after a short leave back at Fort Buffalo we were assigned to Mike Muller's Combat Group Bravo. On 11 November we led Commandant Muller's 61 Mech units into positions south of the Vimpulo while Combat Group Charlie tried to stop 21 and 25 Brigades crossing the river. There were lots of enemy patrols in the area because 21/25 Brigades were retreating fast from the

Mianei towards the Vimpulo. I went out with Corporal Branco on 12 November to try to locate the enemy concentrations, but we couldn't get to close quarters because of the heavy patrolling. The next day we got near and we brought in our Mirages to bomb them and then brought in G-5 fire. Branco and I followed 21/25 Brigades as they retreated, trying to bring 61 Mech in on their tracks from behind to complement the big Combat Group Charlie ambush on the Vimpulo.

'On 14 November 21/25 Brigades began another sprint towards the Vimpulo at about 4 pm. Branco and I followed their tank tracks for about four kilometres before I radioed to 61 Mech that they should get ready to attack. What I hadn't realised at first was that 21 Brigade had left some of their tanks behind at their old position to the south. We moved towards it and they shot at us with 12.7 mm guns mounted on top of the tanks. We were only two guys, so we weren't an easy target.

'We radioed Mike Muller to tell him not to come in after all, and then Branco and I started working our way eastwards with the eventual intention of moving northwards to link up with another recce team. We were wearing Fapla uniforms, and as we withdrew on the eastern side in the early hours (on 15 November) we ran into UNITA. Two hundred men were setting up an ambush there and we hadn't been warned about it. They opened fire on us. I felt my AK-47 fall down from my right hand as I was on the radio to my people telling them I was pinned down in a UNITA ambush and somebody had better order them to stop shooting. Then there was heavy shooting again all around me. Branco and I "bombshelled" away from each other and started running. I had to drop my heavy kit, including my radio. I stopped after I'd run about two kilometres. It was only then that I became aware of the pain. A UNITA bullet had gone through my forearm and shattered one of the bones. There was a lot of blood and several nerves had been cut, although I didn't know it at the time. I decided to treat myself from the medicine in the small emergency survival kit we carry in a special pocket in case you lose everything else. It ensures you can last for two days.

'I injected myself in the muscle with morphine to cut off the pain. I bandaged it and then assessed my position. All I had was my big pocket knife, my survival food, a small compass and my maps. So I knew where I was, but without the radio I couldn't communicate my situation to base. I ran south all day towards a 32 Battalion post 17 km from where I had had the contact with UNITA. All the way I was losing a lot of blood. I had to keep stopping to strip bark from *chimwanje* trees to use as rope to renew the tourniquet I had tied at the top of my arm. I wasn't too worried at first about the wound, but I didn't want to look at it. Later I began to get dizzy and I started thinking: when am I going to find people to help me?

'I reached the 32 Battalion post at about 5 pm. Captain Jako Potgieter (an artillery officer) was in command and I asked him for a cigarette. He had to hold it for me because I couldn't keep it steady. At first, the captain thought I was shot in the body because there was blood everywhere and my trousers were soaked with it. Then there was an argument between the captain and the doctor. Potgieter wanted me to tell him what had happened, but the doctor wanted to start work on me. The captain said: "Let me have a quick word with him before you put him under the anaesthetic." All I remember telling him was to change the radio codes because I'd lost my code booklet and that I'd left a flask of whisky in my kit. I always carried it to put in my coffee when it was cold.

'In fact, Potgieter already knew it was UNITA who had fired on us. UNITA had reported they were involved in a contact with a whole *battalion* of Fapla, although it was only Branco and me. UNITA had picked up my kit, weapon and webbing and then realised we weren't Fapla.

'The doctor put me under at about 7 pm and I woke up just before 6 pm the next day [Monday 16 November] with my right arm and hand entirely encased in plaster. I was in the military hospital at Rundu. They had flown me there by helicopter at about three o'clock that morning. The next day I was joined by the Lieutenant [de Villiers Vos] who had been wounded in his shoulder in the battle against 21/25 Brigades on the Hube. I was on a drip, but the Lieutenant sat talking to me. He said Sergeant Mendes [of the 32 Battalion recces] had got my kit back from UNITA but had drunk all of the whisky in my flask.'

On Wednesday 18 November Da Trinidada and De Villiers Vos were flown to military hospital in Pretoria for further treatment. Da Trinidada began an extensive course of surgery to mend the shattered bone in his forearm and to stitch together severed nerves, although the doctors quickly abandoned hope of restoring movement in the little finger of their patient's right hand. Two metal pins will stay in Da Trinidada's forearm for ever and, although the micro-surgery on his nerves will continue for years, he was back on active recce service with his battalion within nine months of the shooting.

'When Frenchie and Piet [Fourie] heard I'd been shot they flew down to Pretoria to see me in hospital,' said Da Trinidada. 'They got a pass for me to go out for a meal with them at the After Dark nightclub. I ordered a very big medium-rare steak. When the food came I found that although I could eat the chips OK I couldn't cut the steak because my arm and hand were still covered with plaster. I knew Frenchie and Piet would pretend not to notice my problem. And there was no way I was going to ask them to help; they would have had even more fun at my expense. There was also no way I was going to pick up the steak with my good hand to eat it. It wouldn't have been polite. In the end, I got a waitress to cut it for me. It was the first time in my life I'd thought about the possibility of taking a wife. Marriage doesn't really suit my type of work because I'm not often at home. But that evening I needed a woman to cut my steak and I began thinking about asking my girlfriend in Rundu to marry me.'

For Robbie Hartslief, who had spent more than four months at the front, the winding up of Operation Moduler meant the end of his war on the eastern front. But it was not the end of his war. He was about to embark on an entirely new adventure elsewhere.

Note

1   This was reduced to one year following President F W de Klerk's reform blitz of 1990.

PART 6

THE SIDESHOW

We were skilfully guided, for we slipped through a gap between two camps, passing so close that we could hear the murmur of voices and could see the forms of soldiers outlined against their fires.

Colonel Deneys Reitz,
in *Commando – A Boer Journal of the Boer War.*

Ben Battle was a soldier bold,
And used to war's alarms;
But a cannon-ball took off his legs,
so he laid down his arms.

Thomas Hood (1799–1845),
'Faithless Nelly Gray.'

CHAPTER 27

BEGGING FOR PERMISSION TO DESTROY THE ENEMY

Commandant Jan Hougaard, who had been sent back to Rundu in late October to prepare his secret mission, completed his planning and organisation by late November. The generals, having several times rejected attacks on Cuito Cuanavale from the west, had decided that *something* had to be done from that direction, not least because convoys of 300 vehicles or more were constantly arriving in Cuito Cuanavale with supplies and new weapons from Menongue, 200 kilometres to the west. The regular replacement from the west of weapons and spares simply mocked the sweat and blood SADF and UNITA troops had shed in the east in destroying great quantities of Fapla equipment. The knowledge of the convoys' arrivals was greatly undermining the morale of the South African soldiers, many of whom shared their officers' desire to attack Cuito Cuanavale from the west.

But though they had now conceded the necessity of a western operation, the generals' idea fell far short of what the field commanders were urging upon them – a full-blooded attack from west of the Cuito River to isolate the Fapla brigades in Cuito Cuanavale and across the river to the town's east. Instead, Hougaard's brief was to organise a clandestine military operation along the Menongue-Cuito Cuanavale road with minimal forces to disrupt enemy logistics severely while the main SADF force continued to press home attacks from the east. As usual, there was an additional stipulation: minimum casualties.

Hougaard first had to gather intelligence about Fapla along the Menongue-Cuito Cuanavale axis (see map) and then raise a suitable force to carry out the mission. There was no doubt in his mind that the men of his own 32 Battalion were the best suited in the SADF for the stealthy, deep-penetration task. It was how they had been earning their pay for years. However, most of 32 Battalion was tied up in the east in Commandant Hartslief's Combat Group Bravo. The winding up of

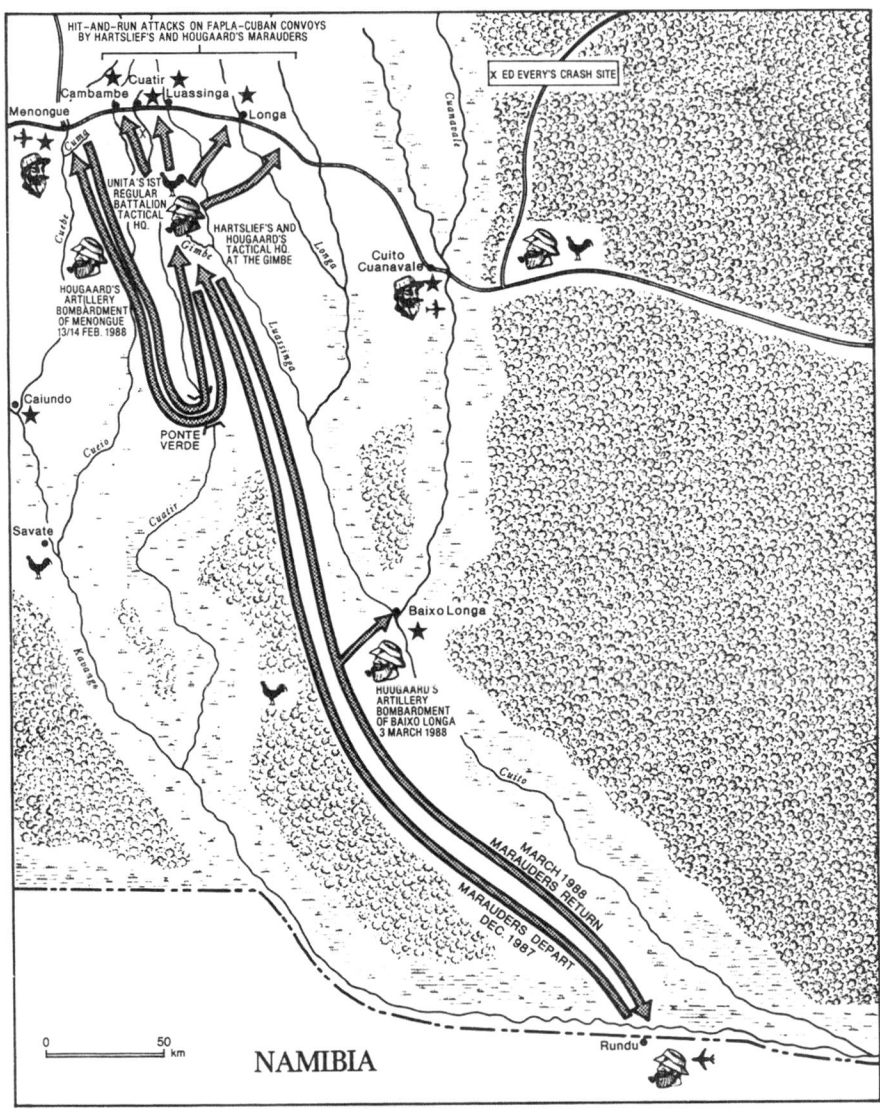

The Sideshow: December 1987 to March 1988.

Operation Moduler solved that problem. Hartslief and his 32 Battalion men would be stood down from the east and made available to Hougaard. However, they would leave their frontline positions in mid-December, and after resting, repairing, re-equipping and being briefed would only be ready to infiltrate the Menongue-Cuito Cuanavale area in mid-January 1988.

Hougaard's orders were to move a force into the area by early December. He needed soldiers to serve in the interim until Hartslief and his men could take over. Hougaard was given a company of 120 men from 101 Battalion, which was made up of black soldiers from Ovamboland in northern Namibia. The MRL battery which had been with Hartslief on the Lomba/Mianei since July 1987 was pulled out well ahead of the rest of Combat Group Bravo so that it could go in with Hougaard from the beginning of the new mission. From among sundry national servicemen and 32 Battalion elements who had been held back in reserve at Fort Buffalo, Hougaard put together a support company with 81 mm mortars, jeep-mounted 106 mm anti-tank cannons and Milan anti-tank missiles.

'During the planning phase I had to wait for some Special Forces guys from 1 and 5 Reconnaissance Commandos to join us,' said Hougaard. 'Our own 32 Battalion recces were really buggered by that time and so they needed additional support.

'This was a very high risk operation. With real determination the enemy could have cut us off there with battalions they had in Caiundo and Baixo Longa.

'On the plus side the whole area between the Cuatir and Luassinga Rivers was controlled by UNITA's First Regular Battalion, which many of us thought was one of Savimbi's finest units. They were everywhere. I found them a good source of information and early warning. Moving only at night, and with UNITA guiding us, we took the whole convoy north through the bush between Caiundo and Baixo Longa. We split the procession up so that we were only in small groups moving from point to point. Sometimes we laid up for 48 hours and sent out recce teams ahead to establish the next place where it would be safe to stay. By day we made no movement whatsover. We were heavily camouflaged and we lit no fires. It was dense forest all around.

'We were told we would be in there for two months and that we would have to take with us nearly all of the logistics we'd need for that period. There would be no regular airlift of supplies, as at Mavinga. Just very irregular helicopter forays at night. So before we could do anything we had to move in tons and tons of equipment, ammunition, food, fuel and so on and make big caches which we left UNITA to guard.

'The move north took us a long time, and while everyone waited for us to get into position the SAAF made several raids on the convoys. They were quite successful, but never strong enough to interrupt the logistics flow seriously and give our guys on the eastern side of the Cuito River a better chance.'

[In a typical SAAF raid by four Mirages on 22 December 1987, on a static convoy of 318 Fapla vehicles, including 35 tanks, at Longa, only eight were destroyed.]

Hougaard's first task after getting his supplies into the area was to gather as much intelligence as possible from along the Menongue-Cuito Cuanavale road. Recces from the Special Forces, 32 Battalion and UNITA quickly had the whole length of the road covered.

'It was December by then and the rains were heavy every day, which worked to our advantage. The road was only a narrow strip of tar. They couldn't move off it with the vehicles or tanks or they would have got bogged down. That made their progress tortuous, and because they were restricted to the road they were quite vulnerable. On the other hand, there was always a complete brigade of nearly 1,000 men – usually Fapla's 8 Brigade – protecting the convoy, while our force was never stronger than 120 men.

'Pretty soon we knew where the convoys were every minute of the day. And Fapla helped us by leaving in place all the kilometre stones placed there in the old colonial days by the Portuguese. So by reading the stones the recces knew exactly where they were all the time.'

Sergeant Piet Fourie and his team of three black recce colleagues from 32 Battalion spent two months on the Menongue-Cuito Cuanavale road. 'Sometimes I sat just 400 m from the road making coffee as I watched the convoys,' said Fourie. 'Massive convoys with hundreds of vehicles in them would stop right in front of me. The bush was very thick, and Fapla's typical reluctance to leave the road and come in behind us through the forest worked to our advantage. Only occasionally would they deploy flank foot patrols at the side of the road. Then we just moved back out of the way.

'We would sit there sending statistical information on a convoy by radio – how long it was, where the front was, the position of the back-marker, the types of vehicles in it. Then our guys would come in with the Mirages and bomb them. We were flat on our stomachs, because those bombs were bad news. Everything in the convoy was firing as they heard the Mirages come in. Then we saw the trucks burning and the firing went on for five to ten minutes after the planes had gone.'

Piet Fourie had a high opinion of the SAAF after seeing them fly many times over enemy brigades with missiles exploding all around them in balls of fire. His admiration was not shared by his fellow 32 Battalion recce leader Sergeant Frenchie, who complained: 'Many times we pinpointed the enemy convoys but when we sent the co-ordinates to the Air Force and called in a strike they often replied that they couldn't come because it was too dangerous. We used to feel: What about us then? Why have we been ordered to risk our lives for every minute of the day when others are not required to do the same? It was very frustrating. We knew we'd done our part of the job properly, but it was useless because other people weren't doing theirs.'

Frenchie's disillusionment extended also to the logistics supplies: 'Every night we used to lay landmines, tunnelling under the tarmac from the side of the road. But they had only limited effectiveness. They would destroy just one vehicle or throw the track from a tank. I wanted to lay automatic ambushes which cause much greater devastation. But the logistics were a big balls-up. I sent the message back for the equipment to be sent in on the next helicopter run. But when I checked the stuff that UNITA brought up by truck (from the helicopter night landing pad) half of the things were missing. There were many things like that. For me they all added up to an unsuccessful operation.'

In the operation's early days Hougaard relied on the Air Force bomb-ing raids and the recces' mine-laying to disrupt the convoys. Having set up his logistics base some 100 km south of the road, he had to scout for a forward base from which to launch ground attacks against the convoys which would not be detectable by Migs and helicopters during the day. Eventually he divided his force between two bases set up in dense forest near two small streams, the Bambi and the Gimbe, about 30 km south of the road. The SADF bases were completely separate from those of UNITA who had one particularly big base on the Cuatir River south of the tar road. But in all its major movements the SADF force was preceded by a protective screen of several hundred UNITA guerrillas who provided intelligence and early warning. With Hougaard at all times was a guerrilla liaison team headed by a UNITA brigadier and a major. Settlements in the dense forest between the Cuatir and the Luassinga were sparse, but Hougaard said such peasant people as there were had long ago thrown their support behind UNITA because of the movement's prolonged control of the area.

After the initial orientation and organisation phase, Hougaard began manoeuvring his artillery towards the road, deploying the eight MRL launcher vehicles in such a way that some 50 km between Cuatir and Longa were covered. However, Hougaard did not permit the MRLs to fire in the early weeks of the operation. Instead he used UNITA's 120 mm mortars to hit the convoys in liaison with the recce mining teams and the SAAF. 'I held the MRLs back because I knew the first time we used that stuff Fapla would know the South African Army was there,' he said. 'That might have caused problems for us because they had a lot of forces available in Menongue. They suspected something was going on because there were Migs above every day looking for something. We kept so still that we hardly breathed.'

While waiting for the right moment for a major ground attack, Hougaard's team worked on making the SAAF raids on the convoys more effective, again using the 'toss-bombing' technique to thwart the enemy's Mig-23s. 'The Air Force sent in two or four Mirages at a time, hugging the river valleys and forest canopy before pitching up to lob their bombs. We found that if we could radio the SAAF with precise references on the convoy's location and its mid-point the pilots could land their bombs slapbang on the road and take out that part of it.

'We had to wait for the right moment because although our guys came in low there were enemy Migs in the air at nearly all times, either going from Menongue to bomb our forces east of Cuito Cuanavale or coming back. Hanging around with them at very high levels were "top cover" Mig-23 air superiority fighters bristling with missiles which outmatched anything we had if engaged in straight combat. The answer was for our guys to sneak in while the enemy planes were still on the ground or fool them while they were in the air.

'My EW team was always listening to their frequencies. We also had recce teams near Menongue who radioed us every time planes prepared to take off or came in to land. One small problem was that we only had recces on the southern perimeter of Menongue. I wanted observation posts established on the other side as well, but that was north of the latest line that the politicians and generals had drawn as the limit for SADF penetration into Angola.

'On one occasion there was a flight of eight Migs coming in to land at Menongue after a mission to Cuito Cuanavale. As usual we were listening in on all their frequencies. The first two landed routinely. But the third guy had problems: every time he came in he made a bugger-up of it. The guy in the control tower kept telling him to go back and come back in. Then the controller started swearing at the pilot, saying, "You're keeping the other planes up. They're very low on fuel. If you don't touch down soon they'll have to ditch or go to another airfield."

'It was a stroke of luck for us. A big convoy had concentrated at Cambambe, just 15 km out of Menongue. It was the first overnight resting place for the convoys. They joined up with other elements there from Bie, to the north, and Cuchi, about 100 km to the west of Menongue. They used to sort themselves out and reorganise before pushing on again. They made a perfect target and we had already called in our planes. One had taken off from Grootfontein when the SAAF controllers called off the attack because they said it was too dangerous. They had spotted the eight Fapla Migs coming back from Cuito Cuanavale.

'The more the Mig pilot failed to approach his landing correctly the more he started to lose his cool and panic. I contacted brigade headquarters at Rundu and said the Mirages should take off from Grootfontein again and the raid should not be cancelled this time because the enemy was *hors de combat*. So our Mirages came in and took out a lot of vehicles from the convoy while they had Migs in the air just a few seconds flying time away.'

By mid-January 1988 the SAAF raids were inflicting much more comprehensive damage, either striking in the early morning or slipping in under the high-flying Migs heavy with armaments on their way to Cuito Cuanavale. On 9 January, in the early morning, four Mirages caught a 170-vehicle convoy protected by Fapla's 8 Brigade about two kilometres west of the Cuatir River. Recces counted 40 vehicles left behind burning. The time had come, Hougaard decided, to unleash his MRLs.

'By the afternoon of the following day the convoy was approaching a Fapla base at Longa, about 100 km out from Menongue. A tremendous thunderstorm broke, so I decided to hit them with UNITA's 120 mm mortars and several ripples from our own rocket launchers. Because of the storm the Migs were not able to provide protection, so we could afford to hit them for slightly longer than the five minutes we scheduled for attacks. Our philosophy was: Shoot and scoot. It was a direct derivative of the SADF doctrine for fighting in Africa. Having good intelligence, being highly mobile and never staying in one place, and hitting the target at the right time with maximum effort and firepower.

'When we stopped firing we didn't wait to find out how much damage we'd done. We packed up and withdrew out of the area as fast as the bush would allow to positions 100 kilometres south of the road out of range of inevitable follow-up counter-attacks. The recces stayed behind, and later they reported that we'd taken out 60 or more vehicles. It was not as destructive as I wanted, but it was a lot of logistics we'd destroyed and that was important. From that point onwards it was open season on the convoys, hitting them with everything we had whenever good opportunities arose, even putting in UNITA infantry ground attacks right along the road. We found that when we hit a convoy heavily with artillery part of it would move away. The rest was left behind with a protection element, and we hit that with a straightforward close-range infantry attack.

'That 10 January attack spelt the end of my field involvement in that theatre. Commandant Hartslief had his 32 Battalion guys ready to take over and press home the attacks much more regularly. I was back in Rundu by 21 January to begin planning new operations at brigade headquarters.'

Hougaard felt the Menongue operation was going reasonably well, given the severe limitations placed upon it by the generals. He may not have achieved all the objectives, but he *had* fulfilled one imperative – not to lose any equipment. Neither had he lost any SADF men in the frontline fighting. There were two deaths, however, and a tragically serious injury among a team of three national servicemen operating a 20mm anti-aircraft gun at one of the task force's logistics bases. One day, when the bulk of the force had left base to deploy near the road, they had grown bored and wandered out to inspect the nearby wreckage of a Fapla Mig out of curiosity. The Mig proved to be booby-trapped and in the resultant explosion two of the young men were killed instantly and the third lost both of his eyes and both arms.

Hougaard, despite satisfaction that he had set up the Menongue-Cuito Cuanavale operation reasonably effectively, still shared his fellow-officers' disappointment that no decision was forthcoming from on high to launch a major operation against Cuito Cuanavale. 'We were practically begging for orders to attack (from the west),' he said. 'The assault from the east looked more and more like a stand-off situation. Everybody was pretty frustrated because they wanted to go for Cuito Cuanavale. Everybody's hopes had been built up when the Cabinet came to see us at our tactical HQ north of Mavinga (in late November 1987) with the Migs flying overhead and bombing all around. The President (P W Botha) was there and (defence minister) Magnus Malan and Pik (the foreign minister, Pik Botha). P W said then that we would get everything we needed and he said: "You people must go on." But it didn't work out that way. There were limitations put on us all the time, and as a result a lot of enthusiasm drained away.

'Robbie Hartslief and I knew that with the kind of force we'd been given for the Menongue-Cuito Cuanavale operation we couldn't go on hitting the road indefinitely. But with a few extra men and resources and permission from on high we could have switched to other tactics which would have inflicted very serious damage. With bigger ground forces we could have attacked the convoy concentration points and taken them out completely, or we could have gone west and north of Menongue and taken out many of the supplies coming by road before they even reached Menongue.

'Robbie and I also asked for G-6s which with their firepower and great mobility would have inflicted terrible damage on the convoys. But at the time the top brass was afraid about that type of equipment getting captured. (The three pre-production G-6s which had bombarded Cuito Cuanavale from the northeast during Operation Moduler were withdrawn from Angola at the end of November 1987, never to return. One of the guns which had blasted the town was subsequently sent to an international arms exhibition in Chile, where several export orders were placed for the production weapon).

'With bigger forces and more weaponry we could also have begun taking out the big Soviet planes which were flying men and weapons into Menongue. The big Ilyushin-72 transports were particularly juicy targets. We knew we had the weapons and techniques to hit them. UNITA tried with their Stingers, but they weren't successful. However, a UNITA colonel managed to shoot an MI-24 (helicopter gunship) out of the air near Menongue with an RPG-7. The Ilyushins used to arrive very high right above Menongue. Then they spiralled down to land. It was impossible for us to penetrate far enough inside their defences to bring the Ilyushins down. But there were ways of doing it with more planning and latitude of manoeuvre.

'We had worked out one method with the Air Force and on one day towards the end of December (1987) several Mirages had actually taken off from Grootfontein to bomb Menongue, where there were up to 40 Migs on the ground at any one time as well as transport planes. But for some reason they were called back after they were on their way. We'd planned it well, so we know they would have got through. We believed it was a high-level political decision to pull them back at the last minute: someone up there (in Pretoria) said Menongue and other big targets must be left out. We heard that another possibility was that they were afraid of provoking bigger Cuban involvement, because there was a whole regiment of Cubans there in Menongue, and their planes and pilots would have been among those wiped out. We heard Cuban pilots all day long speaking Spanish and Russian on their radios. Aeroflot (the Soviet state airline) used to fly the logistics into Menongue. Once we heard a Cuban bringing in his Mig to land when he developed trouble with his undercarriage. There was an Aeroflot transport sitting over Menongue and the Soviet pilot started giving the Cuban precise instructions in Russian on how to sort out the problem. So obviously the Russian had flown Migs and wasn't a mere commercial pilot.

'The Cubans were much better pilots than the Angolans, and I doubt whether our leaders wanted to lure them into deeper involvement. The poor training of the Fapla pilots was working in our favour. Theirs was probably the worst trained air force in Africa. They had technologically more advanced planes, but the superior training of our guys closed the gap. But it seems that someone on high didn't want to escalate the war on another front at a time when the South African Army already felt stretched.'

PART 7

INTO 1988. OPERATION HOOPER – THE COUNTER-OFFENSIVE CONTINUED

The Boers observe the movements of a column from a long way off, only show-ing very few men. Then, having chosen some advantage, charge in with great boldness; and the result is a serious casualty list.

Field Marshal Lord Horatio Kitchener,
in a despatch during the 1899–1902 Boer War.

The green time has come
The rains invade
The listing masthead
tilts and tilts again
surrend'ring eighteen years
Heeling beneath mud
final arms laid down
rebuke life's brevity
No dry dust remains Nor sign Nor shallow mound
Angola's reclaimed
Unsung The boy from Cuba dies again

Kathryn Kane,
1976.

CHAPTER 28

THE ATTACK ON 21 BRIGADE: 13 JANUARY 1988

Operation Hooper began in rather less secrecy than Operation Moduler. Scarcely three weeks before Hooper's launch day – Saturday 13 December 1987 – the United Nations Security Council unanimously demanded that South Africa withdraw all its military forces from Angola.

South African Foreign Minister Pik Botha reacted to the Security Council's 25 November resolution by flatly rejecting the demand. 'South Africa will not be prescribed to in this manner,' said Botha. 'The South African government will decide for itself when South African troops will be withdrawn from the current battleground.'

The foreign minister then stipulated the circumstances under which Pretoria would consider ordering the SADF to withdraw from Angola: They would pull out only when Cuban and Soviet troops and military advisers were withdrawn, or when South Africa's security interests were no longer directly affected by the Soviet and Cuban presence there. [The *or* was important, in view of the fact that Angola and Namibia had become the focus of one of the most fascinating diplomatic chess games in Africa's history. In that game the military would be pawns – vitally important pawns, but pawns nevertheless – hogtied in what they could do by the politicians, but continuing to die, eat bully-beef and drink lukewarm contaminated water in the interests of the 'great game' while the diplomats sipped good wines and dined well.]

The furore had erupted at the UN before South African Defence Minister Magnus Malan finally admitted, in a statement released in Pretoria in mid-November 1987, that the SADF was indeed fighting in

Angola and had 'saved' Savimbi's UNITA from annihilation. Malan spoke out partly at the urging of Britain's MI-6 intelligence agency, which was deeply supportive of the South African adventure but appalled by the witless conduct of the accompanying public relations campaign.

A senior MI-6 officer responsible for Africa told the author at the time: 'The South Africans are going to spell out all that they're doing in Angola too late and miss the prime moment. They are notoriously introvert and secretive. It's very damaging that they're not spelling it out to the outside world, but on the other hand their furtiveness is not surprising in view of the way their "friends" have constantly reneged on them.'

Malan said South Africa had been forced to intervene because of the scale of Soviet and Cuban assistance to the Luanda government.

Admitting for the first time that four South African soldiers had been killed in fighting against Fapla and the Cubans in southern Angola, a South African Army communique said their deaths were the result of 'limited' support on 9 November to UNITA in operations against 'Cuban and other Communist surrogate forces.'

Having decided to come clean, the SADF PR men could not bear, for some reason known best only to themselves, to tell the truth fully. They said the four had died in an air raid. In fact, seven South African soldiers died in *ground* fighting on 9 November on the first day of Combat Group Charlie's clash with Fapla's 16 Brigade, which had *minimal* support on the battlefield from the Cubans. None of the men was named, and none of the many other South African deaths was immediately admitted.

Magnus Malan referred to 'a Cuban-Russian offensive which forced South Africa into a clear-cut decision – accept the defeat of Dr Savimbi or halt Russian aggression.'

Paradoxically, on the same day – Thursday, 13 November 1987 – that Malan was telling the world that the SADF had rescued Savimbi, the UNITA leader was claiming to journalists at his Jamba HQ that his movement had beaten off Fapla, the Cubans and the Soviets single-handed. 'There has not been South African intervention,' he told some 20 foreign correspondents who had been flown into Jamba from Pretoria aboard a 40-year-old twin-prop Dakota of the South African

Air Force. 'We've had aid from South Africa but not men fighting at our side. That is categorical ... There is no battle going on here that warrants the participation of the South Africans.'

If Savimbi had been allowed to claim victory for UNITA alone, it would undoubtedly have incensed the 2,000 or more South Africans to the north of him who had just fought a furious battle with Fapla over three days and had seen 11 of their comrades die in that time and a great many more maimed on UNITA's behalf. It was certainly with this in mind that Malan decided to spike the UNITA leader's propaganda guns.

Like the incident with the Sam-8 system at the Lomba River, it was indicative of the fact that the SADF's relationship with the UNITA President was rarely smooth, although Savimbi was less scathing about the South Africans behind their backs than he was about the Americans who had CIA specialists based in Jamba and who must, at times, have liaised with the South African military.

Savimbi was grateful that the South Africans had been consistent in their support. But he never lost an opportunity to express to non-Americans bitter cynicism about the United States which withdrew aid from UNITA in the movement's hour of greatest need in 1976 and only resumed it again in 1986 when it had become clear that UNITA could not simply be wished out of the Angolan equation.

★ ★ ★

It was against this background that the South African forces to the east of the Cuito River began preparing for the new round of heavy warfare which would mark Operation Hooper. General Liebenberg set 4 SAI and 61 Mech – the former Combat Groups Charlie and Alpha which for Hooper reverted to their normal battalion names – an initial target date of 31 December 1987 by which to destroy the Fapla brigades or drive them across the Cuito. Combat Group Bravo, meanwhile, reverted to its 32 Battalion persona and marauded towards Menongue. 61 Mech was reinforced by an additional squadron of 11 tanks, manned by Citizen Force men of the Pretoria Regiment led by Major Vim Grobler.

General Liebenberg's target date proved completely unrealistic. The new intake of national servicemen from the training regiments needed more than the allotted three weeks of instruction and rehearsal in Angola to prepare them for the warfare to come. Time and again they practised the art of tank-infantry-Ratel co-operation, first using blank ammunition in their tactical exercises and eventually live ammunition. Savimbi's public denials of SADF-UNITA co-operation notwithstanding, the regular battalions of his guerrilla organisation joined fully in these co-ordination drills.

There were other problems. Staff officers had not done enough detailed planning. Heavy rains were causing hold-ups. One of the new tank crewmen was severely burned by lightning. Land movements were very difficult, especially across the marshes lining the many streams and rivulets, and the Olifants had to be used as bulldozers to tow trucks through the mud.

Just before Christmas men began to fall ill with hepatitis and cerebral malaria. These were to become grave problems; within 48 hours of the birth of the 1988 New Year the first two SADF men had died from the malaria strain which was a particularly virulent one.

There were major troubles with logistics and supplies. Vital diesel filters for the tanks failed to arrive. By the time Operation Moduler was wound up, ten of the 16 G-5 guns from Quebec and Sierra batteries were out of action, mainly because the seven-metre long barrels of specially hardened steel had worn out. The field commanders were exasperated to find there were neither enough replacement barrels and other spares immediately available nor enough specialist technicians to carry out the complex refitting tasks. Colonel Jean Lausberg had terrible problems ensuring that his gun batteries had adequate supplies of shells, charge packs and fuel. On one occasion the Sierra G-5 battery fell silent. It had plenty of shells, but it had run out of charge packs whose detonations in the breech sent the shells arching towards their targets. Lausberg hitched a lift to Rundu aboard a Puma and made sure that the helicopter returned to Sierra battery the following night packed to its roof with charge packs.

This inefficiency was serious since the G-5s had proved one of the South Africans' key weapons, more than making up for the problems of technological lag encountered by the SAAF.

The generals, recognising the problems of their field commanders, set a new later date by which the MPLA's army was to be cleared from the east bank of the Cuito River – Tuesday 5 January 1988.

The SADF set about softening up the opposition, with the six serviceable G-5s playing the main role yet again. The big guns, each firing up to 200 shells a day, concentrated on two main targets – the bridge across the Cuito River from Cuito Cuanavale, and the Fapla brigades dug into defensive positions on the east bank.

The guns pounded the bridge so heavily that on occasions trucks were blown from it completely, and the external fuel tanks of T-54 tanks were set ablaze. By Christmas 1987 the bridge supports had been so thoroughly weakened that it was no longer possible for Fapla to put tanks or other vehicles across it. Supplies getting through by convoy from Menongue were being unloaded on the west bank and being carried across the rickety structure by troops who reloaded them on to trucks on the east bank.

The intensity of the shelling made it impossible for Fapla to carry out repairs by day. On Christmas night 1987 Angolan engineers attempted to close the gap in the middle with a mobile TMM metal bridge, but it fell into the river. However, the engineers persevered and within a few days tanks and trucks were using the bridge again. This made it more important than ever that one of South Africa's secret weapons be used effectively against the Cuito bridge. A heavy burden fell on the SAAF to perfect quickly its bombing technique with the newly developed H-2 laser-guided 'smart' bomb so that the bridge could be destroyed.

G-5 fire rained down upon the Fapla brigades arraigned in a fan-shape in front of Cuito Cuanavale. Between Cuito Cuanavale itself and the Cuito River Fapla's 13 Brigade was dug in along with one Cuban Army battalion to protect the town in the event of an SADF ground attack across the river. The commander of the Fapla forces had moved his underground bunker HQ from the airfield several kilometres to the northwest of Cuito Cuanavale.

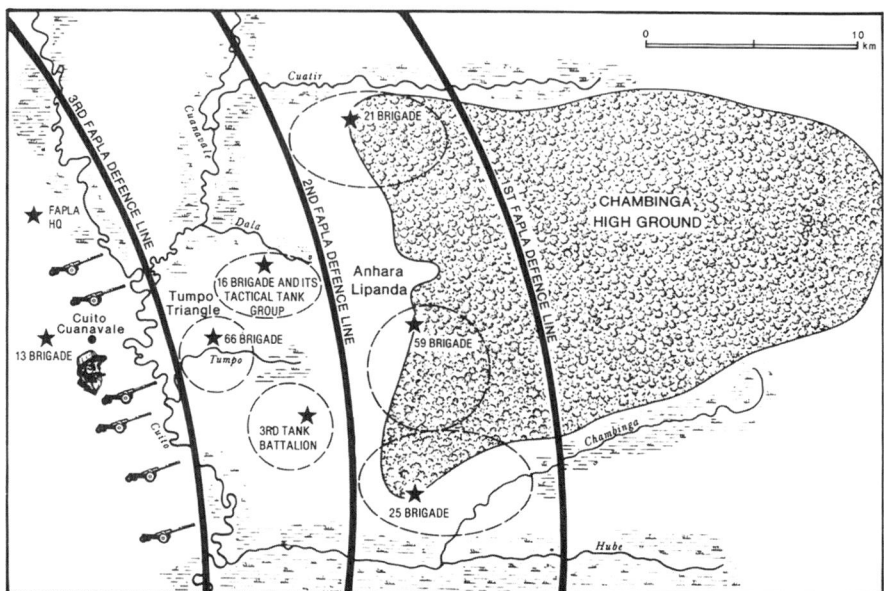

The three defence lines of the Cubans and Fapla east of Cuito Cuanavale at the beginning of SADF's Operation Hooper: January 1988.

Just across the river from Cuito Cuanavale 66 Brigade, 16 Brigade and its tactical armoured group, and 11 tanks of Fapla's 3rd Tank Battalion were dug in between the small Dala River and the bigger Chambinga River, about 15 km apart. This area of flat, low-lying ground encompassed the 'Tumpo Triangle', between the Dala and Tumpo Rivers, within which was located Fapla's main logistics base. Sixty or so Soviet-made heavy artillery pieces – D-30s, M-46s and BM-21s – were aligned around Cuito Cuanavale in such a way as to give maximum protection to the base.

Further east 21, 59 and 25 Brigades were aligned in an uneven defensive arc, some 17 km from north to south, on the western edge of the Chambinga High Ground between the Cuatir and Chambinga Rivers. 25 Brigade was just north of the Chambinga. 59 Brigade was some ten kilometres further north again – in a midway position between 25 Brigade and 21 Brigade, which was dug in just south of the Cuatir River.

It was 21 Brigade which had been singled out for elimination first by SA 20 Brigade HQ. It was to be attacked from the east; the plan was for the South African force subsequently to swing southwards and attack and eliminate 59 Brigade from the north.

21 Brigade was spread out over the most northwesterly spur of the Chambinga High Ground, about five kilometres north of the Dala tributary and three kilometres south of the Cuatir.

Just as Major Pierre Franken had played a critical role as a forward observer in the elimination of 47 Brigade on the Lomba River, so his Artillery Regiment comrade Major Robert Trautman was now selected to carry out a similar task against 21 Brigade on the Cuatir River. Trautman was infiltrated by recces into an OP just north of the Cuatir a week before Christmas. He spent most of the following five weeks in the top branches of a single tree identifying 21 Brigade positions and bringing down artillery fire upon them at opportune times.

Like Franken's role at the Lomba, Trautman's turned out to be a starring one. Through his binoculars he watched 21 Brigade infantrymen walk to the Cuatir to collect water in buckets, canisters and goatskins every morning at daybreak at precisely the same spot, five kilometres east of the Cuatir's confluence with the Cuanavale River. Trautman waited until one morning just before Christmas when nearly 50 young Fapla soldiers came down to the river together to gather water. Trautman brought in G-5 airburst shells and afterwards he counted more than 20 dead infantrymen.

The Pretoria Regiment tank squadron was pushed forward for its first action, not in direct combat but so that its 105 mm guns could act as support artillery to the Army's G-5s and 81 mm mortars. On one day just after the New year the Pretoria Regiment pumped nearly 900 shells into 21 Brigade's positions while the G-5s fired more than 300 shells and the 81 mm mortars launched some 500 bombs.

On the afternoon of Monday 29 December Trautman was surprised to see a big enemy infantry contingent crossing the Cuatir from north to south at the customary watering point. This, subsequent intelligence confirmed, was the advance guard of a 300-strong 21 Brigade battalion which had infiltrated north of the Cuatir, totally undetected by either UNITA or the South Africans, on a large-scale recce mission to the source of the river. Trautman brought in G-5 airburst shells and subsequently counted more than 60 enemy dead in the *anhara* lining the Cuatir.

Early the following day the artillery major was surprised to see an even bigger party of men begin to cross the river from north to south. Trautman waited until most of the infantrymen were strung out across the open *anhara* before bringing in a thunderous rain of 155 mm and 127 mm shells from the G-5s and MRLs.

Trautman reported that of those who survived only 20 made it to the south bank while the rest sought cover among the trees on the north bank. A thunderstorm temporarily obscured Trautman's vision, but when the rain stopped he saw the battalion attempting to cross the Cuatir once again. He estimated another 40 Fapla dead in the subsequent artillery bombardment. The rest of the battalion stole across during the following night under continuing bombardments lit up by phosphorus flares brought in by Trautman. The major's final report estimated 120 Fapla dead in the crossing of the Cuatir.

As at the Lomba, the SADF employed a variety of techniques to undermine Fapla morale before the main ground assault was finally launched against 21 Brigade. 'Ground shout' teams beamed loudspeaker messages to 21 and 59 Brigades during the night suggesting they retreat because all was lost. Propaganda pamphlets were scattered from special shells fired by the G-5s, which also fired phosphorus illumination rounds during the night over 21 Brigade's positions to give the Angolans the impression that the SADF had them under constant observation.

The South Africans' UNITA allies were considerably more impressed by the daylight flares than by the propaganda pamphlets written by the young psychology graduates at Defence HQ in Pretoria. The UNITA men were amused by the leaflets, pointing out drolly to South African troopies that if their psychological warfare experts had been really clever they would have realised that most of the poor bloody Fapla infantry were completely illiterate.

Several SADF psychological warfare teams also spread out to cut trees down with chain saws in the forests north of the Cuatir. Their purpose was twofold. First, to persuade 21 Brigade that an SADF unit was preparing bridges for an attack from across the Cuatir. Second, to select tree trunks the length and diameter of G-5 barrels to set up decoy gun positions, which would be given credibility by moving one or two G-5s up to them now and again to fire a few rounds.

The SAAF was also called upon to weaken 21 Brigade prior to the main showdown. For example, four Mirage F-1AZ fighter-bombers struck at 21 Brigade just after Christmas with a mixture of airburst and delayed action high-explosive bombs, destroying at least one mobile rocket launcher. However, the MPLA won the propaganda war, announcing in Luanda that 21 Brigade anti-aircraft units had destroyed three of the attackers.

While, in fact, all the Mirage raiders had returned unharmed to Grootfontein, the SAAF was finding life tougher than ever before. 'As far as the Air Force was concerned, Operation Moduler had been a 100 per cent success,' said Colonel Dick Lord. 'The air war had been well thought out within our technological possibilities and it had been well executed. Our MAOTs (mobile air operation teams) posted in the front lines with the Army had been invaluable in co-ordinating roles and bringing the planes in on attainable targets.

'We hit the enemy hard on the Lomba. It is always a good idea in warfare to try to finish a guy off when he is on his knees, so we also hit the Fapla brigades hard as they began their retreat. But for every day they fell back they swung the air war more in their favour. Once they were back across the Chambinga and were being herded by our ground forces into the Tumpo Triangle, our problems became very severe. By chasing them that far our fliers used an Afrikaans proverb to sum up the Air Force's problems: "*Ons speel met die leeu se eiers* (We are playing with the lion's balls)."

'We kicked the lion's balls hard. But ops had become much more difficult. A Mirage taking off from Grootfontein to bomb the brigades across the river from Cuito Cuanavale took 40 minutes to fly the 500 km distance, much of it hugging the treetops. It took the same time to get back.

'The distance meant that so much fuel was used that there was only enough spare to spend two minutes over the target area. This limited the amount of after-burn our pilots could use to give them extra speed in tricky situations. [Extra fuel is used in after-burn to set ablaze gases in the jet engine exhausts, thus giving extra boosts of speed.]

'The enemy on the other hand had more than 30 Mig-23s and 21s at Menongue, only 180 km from our ground forces opposite Cuito Cuanavale. Flying at height, the Mig-23s were only nine minutes away from the battlefield and they had enough fuel to be able to spend 45 minutes in the target area while using just about all the after-burn they liked.

'That wasn't all. The nearer we got to Cuito Cuanavale the more difficult it was to escape the Fapla radar net spread to catch us. They had scores of mobile radars of seven different types (Barlocks, Spoon Rests, early warning Flat Faces, Side Nets, Odd Pairs, Squat Eyes and Thin Skins), with frequent duplication as back-up. The range of the net extended across the Angolan border into Namibia. East German Army units guarded the radars and maintained the electronic equipment.'

Coupled with Fapla's extensive system of ground-to-air missiles, Lord claimed that the SAAF flew in a more hostile environment than any air force had ever faced. 'The Israeli Air Force has never faced such a full range of missiles,' he said. 'And when its pilots have carried out deep penetration raids it's been on a one-off basis. Our pilots had to go in deep day-in, day-out. During Moduler they had to fly to avoid Sam-8s, Sam-13s and Sam-9s as well as the normally expected shoulder-launched Sam-7s, 14s and 16s. During Hooper they also came in range of Sam-6s (computer-controlled missiles with ranges of up to 30 km which can lock on to aircraft as close as 100 m to the ground and up to a height of 18,000 metres) and Sam-3s (guided missile used in short-range defence against low-flying aircraft).

'The more distant our planes were from Cuito Cuanavale, where there was an array of enemy radars, the narrower was the height range within which our pilots could be tracked. By the time they got back to Grootfontein they were right out of enemy radar range at any height. But north of the Chambinga River they were in a "red radar" area which meant they appeared on the enemy screens anywhere down from 7,500 m to 50 m. They were only really safe hugging the ground, because above 7,500 metres they were within the enemy missile envelope or were prey to the Mig-23s.

'More than ever we had to rely on the superb training and discipline of our pilots, the forward observers and recces, the level of maintenance of our aircraft and the improvements we had managed to make to many of the shortcomings of the Mirages' French advanced electronics.

'Air-to-air combat was now completely out of the question for us. The FAPA (Angolan Air Force) had too many advantages in terms of speed, range, radar and survivability, in the shape of numerous little airstrips they could lob into in the case of emergencies.

'One thing that worked for us was that FAPA, despite the high quality of its Mig-21s, Mig-23s and Su-22s, was among the worst trained air forces in Africa. And it operated according to rigid Soviet doctrine. Our pilots had freedom of initiative while working within carefully conceived plans. The Angolan Air Force guys were given fixed radar and distance vectors on which to fly from Menongue. As they approached the target they were still directed from Menongue Control: "Steer 145 degrees, hold it steady for 46 nautical miles, now drop your bombs," that sort of thing.

'It led to such inaccurate bombing from high levels that although they were launching up to 60 sorties a day against our ground forces only four SADF men and two UNITA guerrillas were killed in air attacks throughout the whole of the war in the east. They used all sorts of weaponry – rockets, high explosive bombs, retard bombs, and phosphorus bombs – but they rarely got us. Only occasionally did they come in low to the target, but those ground attacks were mostly unsuccessful as well because they didn't have forward observers in place to bring them on to the objective. Sometimes they bombed their own positions.'[1]

[The UNITA Stingers were clearly a factor in forcing the Angolans to fly high, although the SADF was constantly frustrated by UNITA's poor handling of the American missiles and its low kill rate with them. Although a condition attached by Washington to supplying the weapons was that the SADF be allowed nowhere near them, South African recces helped UNITA Stinger teams to acquire targets and operate the missiles. It would be stretching credulity too far to suppose that the worldly-wise Special Force reconnaissance men did not ensure, in the course of these acts of philanthropy, that one or two examples of the missile did not find their way to Pretoria. Certainly SADF men the author interviewed asserted on occasions that South Africa had its own advanced ground-to-air missiles, though Pretoria has never admitted any such developments. When pressed further on the issue, the military men invariably became coy.]

Despite the best and worst (to wit, the psychologists' propaganda pamphlets) efforts of the South Africans, Fapla morale did not crack. SADF commandants admired their enemy's defensive operations and its disciplined control of its artillery – big M-46 130 mm guns delivering 33 kg shells over distances of more than 25 km; highly manoeuvrable D-30 122 mm field guns firing 22 kg shells over distances up to 21 km; and the Stalin Organ BM-21 multiple rocket launchers, firing volleys of forty 78 kg 122 mm rockets at a time over distances of up to 20 km.

Although Fapla's movements, like those of the South Africans, were now restricted entirely to the hours of darkness, the enemy's morale had risen greatly and it used the long SADF delay in launching the new offensive to build up its equipment supplies. However, it was not possible for Fapla to make up for its thousands of dead and maimed experienced soldiers with the illiterate teenage recruits who were being drafted ever more rapidly and pushed through their basic training.

Despite its overall lack of success, the Angolan Air Force did force the South Africans to keep their heads down and stay very still most of the time during daylight. The Migs scared the SADF men more times than the most macho of the soldiers were willing to admit.

D-Day for the attack on 21 Brigade was set for 2 January 1988. But 4 SAI, trying to get to the start line, had manoeuvred into a heavily camouflaged position north of the Cuatir River when seven Mig-21s bombed the area. The attack was immediately called off. One bomb fell right inside the 4 SAI laager near a ten-tonne water tanker truck. 4 SAI's Sergeant-Major Jacques de Wet radioed the tanker driver after the massive explosion, but received no reply. He rushed to where the bomb had exploded only to find the driver making the best of a bad job: shrapnel had punched holes in the bowser and the driver was stripped taking a shower in the precious water before it soaked away into the endless sands of southern Angola.

★ ★ ★

The second D-Day for the attack on 21 Brigade (5 January) also passed as the South African command waited for low cloud and rain so as there would be no harassment from enemy planes. The attack was finally launched on Friday 13 January by 4 SAI, 61 Mech and UNITA's 3rd Regular Battalion. 4 SAI was led by Commandant Jan Malan, who had replaced Leon Marais in command. 61 Mech was under the temporary command of Commandant Koos Liebenberg, relieving Mike Muller who had been given six weeks leave to move his family and furniture from the Republic to 61 Mech's permanent staff HQ at Tsumeb in northern Namibia. UNITA's Chief of Staff, General Demostenes Chilingutila, a tough little soldier who had once been a sergeant in the Portuguese Army, had taken direct control of the 3rd Battalion for the strike on 21 Brigade.

The plan was for 4 SAI and UNITA's 3rd Battalion to carry out the main attack, coming from east of the Cuatir River source over the Chambinga High Ground. 61 Mech would manoeuvre between the defensive works of 21 and 59 Brigades and position itself on a densely forested hill, which became known as 61 Koppie, three kilometres south of the 21 Brigade perimeter and just north of the Dala River source. 61 Mech had a dual flank force role – to prevent Fapla reinforcements reaching 21 Brigade from the south; and to hit 21 Brigade if it broke and started running for the safety of the Tumpo Triangle. Once the battle was over, UNITA would permanently occupy the abandoned 21 Brigade position.

21 Brigade had two outposts on the crest of the Chambinga High Ground to the east of its main position – one just two kilometres south of the Cuatir River and the other three kilometres further south again. UNITA's 3rd Battalion was to eliminate the northern outpost while 4 SAI wiped out the southern one.

4 SAI began its approach past midday after the usual early morning softening up of the enemy by the G-5s and MRLs. Together they fired some 300 rounds into the main 21 Brigade positions, and this was followed by the 81 mm and 120 mm mortars and then the SAAF whose bombs set a bush fire raging near the enemy HQ.

4 SAI comprised the most formidable South African combat group to go into battle since World War II – a central column of every variety of Ratel, with nearly 1,000 infantrymen mounted, and support vehicles, and two flanking columns each comprising 11 Olifant tanks.

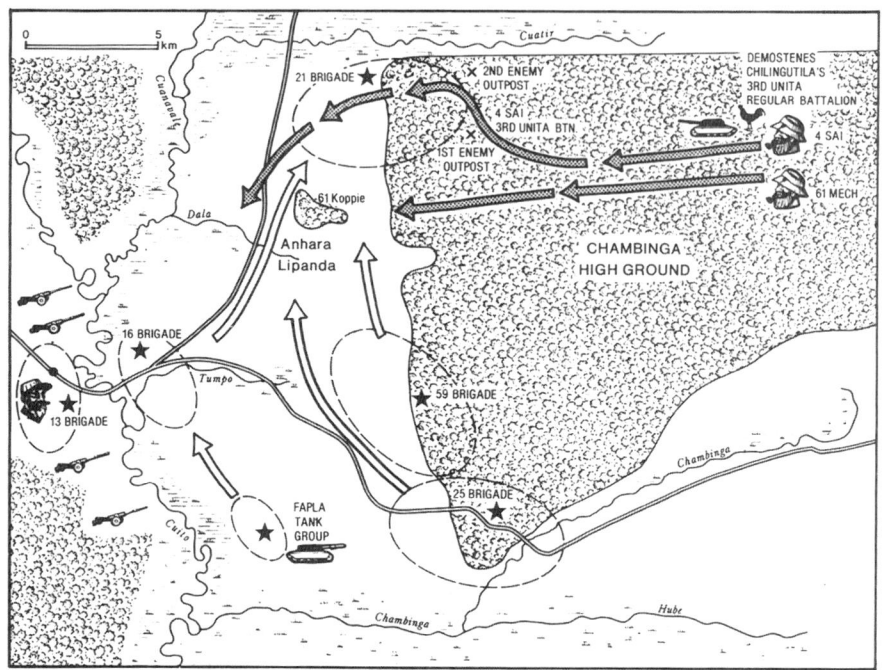

The Attack by 4 SAI and 61 Mech on Fapla's 21 Brigade: 13 January 1988.

Yet again, an SADF force was surprised by the density of the Angolan bush. Progress was slower than had been planned in the neat exercises fought by staff officers at tactical HQ on their forest floor sand models. The roar of engines as the Olifants and Ratels ploughed through the tangled trees and undergrowth quickly alerted Fapla to the fact that an attack was underway. Heavy artillery and mortar fire began to rain down among the South African armour, causing no casualties but forcing all the Ratels and Olifants to fasten their hatches.

4 SAI met little opposition at the southern outpost so it turned north to help UNITA on the northern objective where life proved tougher. The battalion first ran into an anti-tank minefield – a Ratel lost a wheel when it detonated one of the mines. Then the small Fapla force fought with unexpected grit and courage, retreating in orderly fashion from bunker to bunker and maintaining a steady stream of fire as the Ratels

and Olifants advanced in 200 m bounds. An Olifant drove right up to one bunker containing 20 or so Fapla infantrymen who had fought with particular valour and fired into it a high explosive shell which killed all of them instantly.

By mid-afternoon 61 Mech had reached its protective position on the flank and 4 SAI and the 3rd Battalion were ready to attack the main 21 Brigade position. 4 SAI's progress was tortuous. Three tanks lost their tracks swinging across the uneven terrain and had to be taken back to the laager area by recovery vehicles. A Ratel lost a tyre when it ran over an anti-personnel mine. Then a Mig-21 raid put another Olifant out of action when flying shrapnel from a Mig bomb shattered the sight periscope of the South African tank.

Only an hour of daylight remained when 4 SAI finally moved into the attack on the main enemy position under very heavy artillery, mortar and small-arms fire.

While the Olifants were taking out bunkers systematically the thinner-skinned Ratels were suffering under a deadly hail of fire from Fapla's 23 mm guns, each firing hundreds of armour-piercing slugs per minute which exploded from the gun muzzle at a speed of 3,500 km per hour. Two Ratels were quickly put out of action – one when a 23 mm round destroyed the driver's periscope and the other when one of the solid metal projectiles penetrated a turret and slammed out through the opposite side, narrowly missing the head of a crewman on its journey.

The Citizen Force tankmen of the Pretoria Regiment won their first scalps when enemy tanks attacked from the flank and the Olifants' guns knocked out two of them. Progress was now rapid for the first time in the day as the Olifants and Ratels drove over anti-personnel minefields to clear a passage onto the target for the infantry.

A fusillade of direct rocket fire at a range of just 150 m from a Stalin Organ threw the track off another Olifant, but now the battle was virtually over as the South African tanks ran over the Fapla bunkers and took out the deadly 23 mm guns one by one. Just before sunset the Pretoria Regiment shot out another two tanks and 21 Brigade began to break and run towards the Cuanavale River.

Commandant Koos Liebenberg was surprised to find enemy tanks, trucks and infantrymen fleeing for safety between his own 61 Mech vehicles at the flank position. The Ratel-90s shot out three of the retreating tanks and four armoured cars, but were so shocked by the appearance of a platoon of nude Fapla soldiers in their midst running at high speed that they failed to react in time and the streakers got clean away.

When darkness fell Commandant Jan Malan tried to press home the South African advantage by the light of illumination rounds fired by the G-5s and 120 mm mortars. But the dust of battle and gathering thunder-clouds reduced visibility drastically. 4 SAI had to pull back and returned at first light to clear up and confirm that the whole of 21 Brigade had retreated.

4 SAI swept down from the Chambinga High Ground and reached a point just ten kilometres from Cuito Cuanavale on a road running north eastwards from the Cuito Bridge. From there Colonel Paul Fouché ordered Commandant Malan to clear the east bank of the Cuito River north of the Dala of all Fapla soldiers. 4 SAI encountered little resistance and shot out four enemy armoured cars and a field gun and gathered up a lot of intact Soviet equipment, including five tanks and two M-46 field guns. UNITA anti-aircraft units operating alongside 4 SAI with captured ZU-23 guns had a conspicuous success when they shot down an enemy Mig-21.

4 SAI and 61 Mech withdrew to their laagers to the east of the Chambinga High Ground on the evening of Saturday 14 January 1988. By any normal method of tallying, they had reason to feel they had done a good job. Seven enemy tanks had been destroyed and five captured intact; four armoured cars had been destroyed and two captured intact; rocket launchers and various field guns had been destroyed and three more Sam-8 missiles (not entire systems) had been captured. Fapla had lost an estimated 150 dead and wounded. Against that only one South African had been wounded, and he shot himself accidentally, and UNITA admitted in one of its regular press communiques to four dead and 18 wounded.

And yet the SADF knew that by its own standards it had flopped yet again. It had failed to annihilate 21 Brigade; the majority of 21 Brigade's personnel escaped to the Tumpo Triangle, where they began reforming and were made up to strength again by the addition of units from other brigades. The SADF did not follow up and immediately destroy a demoralised enemy because its own numbers on the ground were extremely limited, as a result of the transfer of 32 Battalion to the Menongue operation and because the logistics support was inadequate.

The two tank squadrons desperately needed new tracks and back-up spares. Some vital spares ordered ten weeks earlier had still not arrived in the forward areas by mid-January. For the first time the Ratels also suffered a serious spares crisis. Clean overalls requested by tiffies in early December 1987 did not arrive until the end of the first week of February 1988, by when they were very niffy tiffies indeed. There was also a desperate shortage of fresh rations. Some artillerymen had seen no fresh meat or fruit for ten weeks: this was not only demoralising but also extremely debilitating in a hostile environment of sweaty heat, alternate dust and pounding rain, and dense clouds of black flies by day and whining mosquitoes by night. It was little wonder that disease began claiming men at an even faster rate. Cerebral malaria posed a terrible problem and hepatitis was sapping the South African strength dramatically: by early February more than 100 men had been evacuated with severe hepatitis from 4 SAI alone.

Morale was further dented when a 61 Mech serviceman was killed in a stupid accident. As his Ratel sought cover during an air raid alert he was crushed to death between the open hatch and a heavy overhanging tree branch. And towards the end of January Robert Trautman, still up his tree north of the Cuatir, reported that 21 Brigade was re-occupying the positions from which it had been driven in the 13 January battle.

Major-General Willie Meyer, the Commander of the South West Africa Territory Force (the Namibian extension of the SADF), was seen as a Job's comforter when he visited the front and tried to lift the troops' low spirits by suggesting that it was sometimes desirable to let an enemy retake a position so that it could be destroyed completely in a later attack!

21 Brigade dug into its old positions along a two kilometre-long north-south line and began laying protective minefields, as did 59 Brigade further south. Meanwhile, another battalion of Fapla's 66 Brigade was sent across the Cuito River to reinforce units already defending the

Tumpo Triangle logistics base. Other reinforcements followed, and by early February there were nearly 50 Fapla T-54/55 tanks on the east bank of the Cuito River. In addition, units from Fidel Castro's elite 50 Division, normally assigned to guarding Havana, began to arrive in Cuito Cuanavale after embarking from Cuba two months earlier.

50 Division was under the command of General Arnaldo Ochoa Sanchez, head of Cuba's military mission in Angola.

Castro, while sending his precious 50 Division to Angola, also asked Angolan President Eduardo dos Santos if Cuba could take over responsibility for defending Cuito Cuanavale, with Fapla forces there coming under Cuban command. Dos Santos said yes, and Castro set up an operations room in Havana from which he could follow the progress of the Cuito campaign, often issuing his own direct orders on how things should be conducted.

Ochoa Sanchez, a man of striking appearance who was popular with his troops, felt that he was being asked *not* to make a Homeric defence of Cuito Cuanavale but to cover a retreat that Castro had already decided would be necessary. He was gloomy about the task which had been set him and Fidel's brother, defence minister Raúl Castro, quoted Ochoa Sanchez as telling him: 'I have been sent to a lost war so that I will be blamed for the defeat'.[2]

It took until 25 January for the SADF high command to decide what the next target would be. 59 Brigade, the strongest of the defending enemy units, would be directly attacked in the belief that its collapse would force 21 and 25 Brigades to fall back towards Cuito Cuanavale without additional fighting.

Notes

1   Deon Ferreira said Brigade HQ had confirmed evidence of the Angolan Air Force bombing its own frontline infantry on at least six occasions.
2   *Business Day* (Tuesday 18 July 1989).

CHAPTER 29

THROWING SOMETHING AT THE CUITO RIVER BRIDGE

East of Cuito Cuanavale, in the southeastern theatre of the War for Africa, there were only two centres of substantial modern construction which hinted that the Land Beyond the End of the Earth had heard of the twentieth century.

One was Mavinga, where a score or more of spacious, Mediterranean-style bungalows were spread out down two dirt roads which crossed each other and were lined by orange trees which gave abundant harvests in June. The houses were lived in by colonial district officers, traders and big game hunters who brought rich clients from the United States and Europe to what was until the mid-1970s perhaps the biggest and richest wild animal paradise in Africa. The exquisite little town was abandoned in 1975 when civil war intensified following Angola's independence; by the end of the century, it may well have been entirely engulfed by the surrounding bush.

The other was the strong, steel-reinforced concrete bridge across the Cuito River. It provided access from Cuito Cuanavale to the only 'road' in the Land Beyond the End of the Earth, the sand track which wound some 160 km through the bush and across the rivers and *anharas* to Mavinga.

The Cuito River bridge was crucial to Fapla's logistics operation in the War for Africa. And so from the very beginning the SADF was making plans to destroy it. Jan Hougaard's early plan to send in 32 Battalion to blow up the bridge was vetoed because of fears of heavy South African casualties.

From mid-October, when the G-5 guns got into position south of the Mianei, the Cuito bridge took constant heavy punishment from the

155 mm shells. 'The bridge was one of our top priority targets,' said Colonel Jean Lausberg. 'One problem was that it was narrow, and only direct hits on it were effective. The bridge was very strong and covered in tarmacadam, so normal high explosive shells were totally ineffective in weakening the structure. We got round that by using penetration shells with a delay detonation fuse which set off the explosion not on impact but half a second later, after the shell had penetrated.

'Another difficulty we faced was getting observers close to the bridge. Forward observers were critical to the success of accurate bombing by the G-5s. But the area around the Cuito Bridge was crawling with Fapla soldiers and, later, Cubans. One of my artillery observers, Lieutenant Charles Fuch, got to within 600 m of the bridge and was able to make a very useful sketch of it. But it was too risky for him to stay there for long and guide our shells on to the target.'

The closest Lausberg could infiltrate a forward artillery observer was on high ground at the source of the Dala River, eight kilometres north-east of the Cuito bridge. 'Major Cassie van der Merwe sat there for three weeks in November as we tried to seal off the Cuito crossing after the battle with 16 Brigade,' said Lausberg. 'He had a lot of UNITAs for protection. After a while Cassie reported that he thought he had malaria, but he point-blankly refused to return to base. He got through the fever after the doctor instructed him to take a hell of a dose of malaria tablets.'

The G-5 bombardments left the bridge in tatters but not down. Men died and tanks and supply trucks were destroyed on the bridge. But still the Fapla convoys continued to move across.

It was not only the G-5 artilleryman who tried to destroy the bridge. After 32 Battalion was denied permission to attempt its demolition, 4 Reconnaissance Commando came up with its own plan. Recce officers have refused to give an account of how the attack was planned and carried out, but some outlines of the operation from official sources have been published.[1] Seven commandos were dropped by helicopter 40 km northeast of Cuito Cuanavale in late August. As night fell on 25 August 1987 they entered the river 24 km north of the Cuito Bridge and let the current sweep them downstream towards their target. The author can vouch personally for how straightforward this part of the operation must have been, for I have swum extensively in the same river further north with UNITA soldiers as my companions; the river is clear, deep and fast-flowing. No effort is needed to swim downstream. It is simply a matter of steering, which must have been a relief to the commandos with all the explosives, weapons and other equipment they were carrying on rubber dinghies.

How they avoided detection at the bridge and placed their charges may not be known for a long time. What is known is that the resulting explosions caused tremendous damage but failed to bring the bridge down completely. It did however limit the volume of traffic which could move across. All the men got out alive, although one missed the rendezvous, according to the one available account, because he had an encounter with a crocodile and had to stab the reptile in the throat in order to escape. He was picked up later at a reserve rendezvous point. The man has since been known to his comrades as Crocodile De Wet, after a small Cape Province town in the hinterland of Saldanha Bay, where recces undergo frogman training. They also train in Lake St Lucia, in Natal, and in its surrounding crocodile-infested lagoons.

The SADF high command grew desperate to bring down the bridge completely and make the enemy's resupply operations more difficult. Armscor had at pre-production stage a highly secret 'fire-and-forget' air-to-ground missile, so called because it is released at a distance from the target and then identifies the target and engages it by itself while the pilot and his aircraft are scooting back to base. Such weapons, incorporating state of the art microchip and sensor technology, are also known as 'smart' or 'intelligent' weapons. Nothing is known about the Armscor H-2 project, which remains classified to this day. A sister programme has developed laser-guided bombs for the South African Army's mortar batteries.

Though no specifications have been released of the H-2, it must have an initial rocket system to take it to within a certain range of the target. At a set distance and height the bomb's own 'intelligence' automatically takes over and independently searches for the kind of specific target it has been programmed to seek out. Once the target is identified, the bomb veers unerringly towards it under its own guidance system, with millions of computations passing through the microchip by the second.

The technology is difficult and takes years to perfect, so the Air Force could not have been confident of success when the H-2 was dragged prematurely from its Armscor womb and delivered to Grootfontein to be fired in anger.

The Buccaneer, a British warplane which had seen more than 20 years of service with the SAAF, was selected as the launch platform for the H-2. The aging Buccaneer's great virtue was that it could fly fast, far and easily at the very low level at which the H-2 would be launched. The Buccaneer would be accompanied by other Buccaneers and Mirage F-1AZs to act as decoys and give protection.

Six planes, including the Buccaneer, took off on the first H-2 raid just before dusk on 10 December 1987. The planes returned without releasing the bomb because of unspecified technical problems. Further raids on 12 and 13 December went even more sadly wrong. On both occasions H-2s were launched which proved to be 'unintelligent'. Both plopped into the Cuito River well short of the bridge.

The New Year brought a change of luck. On 3 January an H-2 Buccaneer and its escorts, four Mirages and another Buccaneer, took off from Grootfontein early in the morning but had to return without launching the smart bomb when it was reported that enemy Migs were already flying dawn patrols around Cuito Cuanavale.

The same team took off from Grootfontein four hours later to try again. Two patrolling Mig-23s acquired the raiding party on their radars, but for some unaccountable reason broke off and returned to Mcnongue. The strike Buccaneer pressed onwards and released its H-2 which this time acquired the target and homed in on it relentlessly. A 20 m length of the bridge disappeared in the resultant explosion. The Fapla command reported to Luanda that the bomb had been delivered by a remote piloted vehicle.

The Cuito Bridge was not rebuilt during the War for Africa. However, Fapla was still able to get trucks and tanks across the river using TMM bridging equipment and pontoon ferries.

Note
1   Helmoed-Romer Heitman, *War in Angola* (Ashanti Publishing Ltd, Gibraltar, 1990).

CHAPTER 30

THE ATTACK ON 59 BRIGADE: 14 FEBRUARY 1988

Hepatitis claimed as new victims the Commandants of both 4 SAI and 61 Mech, Jan Malan and Koos Liebenberg. Commandant Cassie Schoeman took over from Malan, and Mike Muller returned early from leave to take over from Commandant Liebenberg. Mike Muller arrived at the tactical HQ and received orders to prepare 61 Mech as a flank defensive and reserve force for the attack on 59 Brigade. Cassie Schoeman would lead a thrust by 4 SAI on 59 Brigade's main positions.

'Our base area was on the eastern side of the Chambinga High Ground, about 30 km from the nearest outposts of 59 Brigade,' recalled Mike Muller. 'I trained there with my men, practising co-ordination between tanks, Ratels, infantry, artillery and UNITA battalions. Our job was quite a big one. We had to be ready to protect 4 SAI from attack by Fapla's 25 Brigade, immediately to the south, and 21 Brigade, immediately to the north. 25 Brigade was the bigger danger, since UNITA was scheduled to make a feint attack on 21 Brigade. We also had to cover against 16 Brigade and its tactical armoured group and Fapla's Third Tank Battalion in the Tumpo Triangle. Unknown to us at that stage was the entry of elements of Castro's prized 50 Division to bolster Fapla.

'My first task was to lead my battalion between 21 and 59 Brigades, whose outer pickets were about five kilometres apart, and take up position in dense bush on the northeastern edge of the *Anhara Lipanda* [an area of flat, featureless, sparsely vegetated land fanning out eastwards from the Cuito Bridge to the Chambinga High Ground]. Once we were in position we would be about 13 kilometres from the Cuito Bridge and would be able to scrutinize all the enemy brigades.

'We faced three big problems in getting into position. The obvious one was that we had to sneak in without Fapla cottoning on to just how big was my force. I had been assigned a tank squadron, two companies of mechanised infantry, two armoured car squadrons, a mortar platoon and an engineer troop. The second hard nut to crack was Heartbreak Hill, which began at the crest of the Chambinga High Ground and fell sharply about 60 m through thick bush to our delegated flank position just inside the bushline from the *Anhara Lipanda*. What made it especially difficult was the looseness of the sand on the steep slope. Our recces said it would be tricky to descend and even trickier to climb back up, especially towing vehicles that would be damaged or have engine failures.

'The third problem was that our delays had enabled Fapla to bring up a new heavy mobile bridge to Cuito Cuanavale to span the gap in the Cuito Bridge. Fapla moved lots of heavy equipment across the river again, and they supplemented the bridge with a mobile flat-bottomed metal ferry. So we knew we were in for a big fight.'

Mike Muller's and Cassie Schoeman's men prepared to attack 59 Brigade on the D-Day of 27 January 1988. But the attack was postponed because inadequate supplies of diesel fuel had been brought in by convoy to sustain a prolonged battle. This reduced the odds favouring 4 SAI and 61 Mech since it gave Fapla even more time to reinforce and improve its defences. 59 and 21 Brigades began busily laying minefields and 21 Brigade received tank reinforcements.

Colonel Paul Fouché reset D-Day for 5 February, but it had to be postponed yet again when Artillery Regiment commander Jean Lausberg reported two of the G-5s were beyond repair, except back in the Republic. 'They needed precision engineering on certain parts which could not be carried out in bush workshops,' said Lausberg. 'They had to be flown out, and this meant that only four of my 16 G-5s were available for battle. The spares situation had become very serious. Spare parts for the G-5s were being collected as they reached the end of the factory production lines.'

The G-5 predicament meant such a severe delay that Colonel Fouché left early for his next assignment – to form a new operational brigade in South Africa to take over eventually from 20 SA Brigade – and Colonel Pat McLoughlin assumed command.

The enforced delay also gave the SADF time to make modifications to its battle plans. The SAAF Air Defence Group moved French Cactus-Crotale low-level surface-to-air missile systems to the front to give extra protection against the Migs. The 20-year-old Cactus-Crotales, whose technology was archaic and whose transporters were much too dainty for bush warfare, were supported by other Air Defence teams with captured Soviet Sam-7 shoulder-held ground-to-air missiles, Soviet Sam-9 low-level surface-to-air missiles mounted on BRDM-2 armoured cars, and Soviet ZU-23 guns, much admired and respected by the South African fighting men. Colonel Deon 'Falcon' Ferreira, by now senior staff officer in charge of operations in Windhoek, continued to fret to be in the thick of action. He was therefore spending nearly all his time alongside McLoughlin at tactical HQ, seven kilometres north of the Cuatir, for the attack on 59 Brigade.

D-Day was re-scheduled for Sunday 14 February 1988. But McLoughlin was deeply anxious throughout the Saturday beforehand as Muller and Schoeman geared up their men for the attack. With him in his heavily camouflaged bunker there was the reassuring presence of Ferreira, plus an intelligence officer, an operations officer, a national serviceman keeping records, a Medical Corps doctor, a padre and an Air Force liaison officer.

Two things were critical for the attack. On 13 February Robbie Hartslief's 32 Battalion marauders planned to launch an artillery attack on Menongue Airport in an attempt to prevent Fapla warplanes from taking off to bomb eastwards of Cuito Cuanavale. Then McLoughlin needed cloud to ensure double protection for his battalions against air-craft as they manoeuvred down the western slope of the Chambinga High Ground.

When news came through that Hartslief had made a successful attack against Menongue, McLoughlin ordered Muller and Schoeman to begin moving 61 Mech and 4 SAI from their base areas late at night over the

Chambinga High Ground towards 59 Brigade's positions. The two SADF battalions, accompanied by UNITA's 3rd Regular Battalion, which had won grudging respect from professional South African officers who applied exacting standards, were in the forward assembly areas by 2 am on 14 February.

As light seeped in at the dawn, there was fog and a low layer of cloud. The Migs would be out of action. 'We waited for the "go" command from Colonel McLoughlin at tactical HQ,' said Muller. 'At 8.45 he said "go" and our artillery immediately opened up. At about the same time two UNITA semi-regular battalions attacked outposts of 21 Brigade from the northeast. That was a successful feint, because for several hours the Fapla command HQ thought 21 Brigade was the main objective and 59 Brigade was ordered to move north to help 21 Brigade.

'61 Mech led most of the way through the thick bush, with 4 SAI following in our tracks. We moved in three columns so that we were not strung out too far. By 11 am the fog had lifted and the clouds had cleared. The Migs were in the air in swarms. That held us up further because we had to keep seeking cover in the densest bush. It was not until after midday that we reached the crest of the Chambinga High Ground. Recces there who had plotted routes for us guided me into 61 Mech's position and Cassie Schoeman onto 4 SAI's first target, the northernmost battalion of 59 Brigade. [Three battalions, each of 400 men, made up 59 Brigade.] Now we split up. 61 Mech slithered down Heartbreak Hill, sneaking between 21 Brigade and 59 Brigade.

'We were in position on the edge of the *Anhara Lipanda* by 2 pm, and now it all depended on Cassie and 4 SAI who swung south about a quarter of an hour later three or four kilometres behind us to hit 59 Brigade,' Muller said. Cassie Schoeman's tank squadron and supporting Ratel-90s, Ratel-20s and Ratel-81s made their first contact just after 3 pm when an Olifant gunner by the splendid name of Spikkels Terblanche slammed a 105 mm shell into a 23 mm gun emplacement and silenced its sputtering. Meanwhile, the UNITA battalions in the north continued to do a fine job and, despite taking heavy casualties, hit 21 Brigade's main positions at the same time as 4 SAI's attack began.

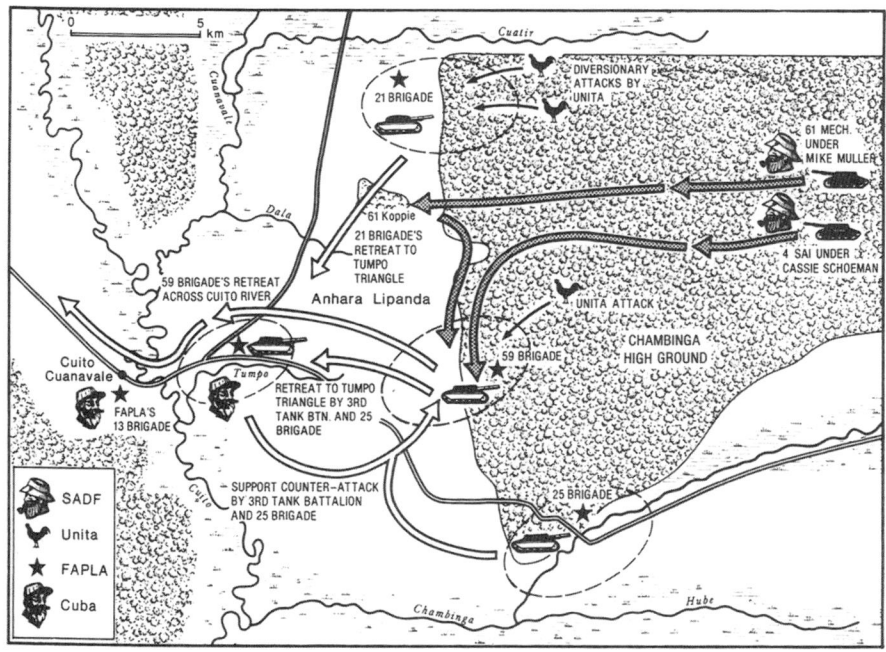

The Attack on 59 Brigade by 4 SAI and 61 Mech: 14 February 1988.

Cassie Schoeman moved his force forward in 100 m spurts, stopping to lay down concentrated fire and reorganise. Soon after Spikkels Terblanche's early success the Ratel-90 again proved its remarkable worth in African conditions when one of the armoured cars shot out a T-55 tank with its 90 mm gun. The only early mishap was a 'cook-off' in the gun of an Olifant which reduced the big 105 mm barrel to a jagged and blackened metal stub. Fortunately none of the crew was injured, only the pride of the castrated tank as it limped out of the battle.

4 SAI's Olifants and Ratels were soon in the main enemy bunker area. Many Fapla soldiers were mown down as they climbed out of their dug-in positions and tried to flee. By 4.15 pm 4 SAI had destroyed another four T-55s and had reached 59 Brigade's HQ only to find that it had been abandoned. 4 SAI's main task was achieved: 59 Brigade was in full flight back to the Tumpo Triangle.

'When 59 Brigade realised it was in trouble, its commander asked Fapla's 3rd Tank Battalion to move up and provide support,' said Muller. 'The 3rd Tank Battalion first moved southeast to link up with elements of 25 Brigade and then northeastwards inside the treeline along the edge of the *Anhara Lipanda* to attack 4 SAI from the west.

'Our recces and EW teams alerted me to the manoeuvre and so I shifted my main force due south in fighting formation, leaving behind a flank force of one armoured car squadron and a company of mechanised infantry. After we had gone about two kilometres we came to the edge of a longish *shona* which intruded from west to east into the treeline (see map). It was slightly more than 1,000 metres wide. We had no time to manoeuvre all the way round – it was well past 5.30 pm – so we had to expose ourselves by crossing it to get to the combined force of the 3rd Tank Battalion and 25 Brigade.

'My headquarters troop consisted of three Ratels – a Ratel Command vehicle with radios and map tables inside, and mounted with one 12.7 mm machine-gun in the turret and three 7.6 mm machine-guns; an EW Ratel; and a Ratel-20. We moved about 20 to 30 metres behind the front line of tanks.

'We poked our noses out of the *shona* and stopped to do some observation. We saw movement in the bush on the southern side, but we didn't know at that point that it was Fapla's 3rd Tank Battalion trying to get in position to attack 4 SAI on its western flank. I ordered a fire belt drill [in which tanks fire one shot each, all at the same time]. Two enemy forward observers fell dead out of the trees and later on we discovered they were both Cubans. We then detected that the force on the other side of the *shona* was beginning to retreat southwards. I ordered my force to move fast across the open *shona* in battle formation – tanks in front followed by Ratel-mounted infantry with Ratel-90s on the flanks.

'We hit the southern bush line at high speed, and barely 50 m into the trees we confronted the first enemy tank with most of 61 Mech still strung out across the *shona*. The tank was parked in an ambush position in deep bush at a right angle to our line of advance. It had lurked there quietly and safely because I had ordered my eight 81 mm mortar crews to lob their bombs 1,000 m into the southern bushline where my intelligence team estimated 59 Brigade to be fleeing westwards. Four smoke plumes showed mortar hits on 59 Brigade.

'It was Captain Christo Terblanche (a 61 Mech infantry company commander) who first noticed the ambush tank. That tank commander was a Cuban, and I think his plan was to take out my HQ group because he let our first line of tanks go past him when he could have knocked out one of them easily. My intelligence officer told me that as we crossed the *shona* he had intercepted a message from the 3rd Tank Battalion to the Cuito Cuanavale HQ saying they had located 61 Mech, and HQ replied with instructions to kill the 61 Mech commander.

'My command group never saw that tank until we were just past him. It had started moving towards us at speed, with its commander standing up with his head through the open hatch, when Christo Terblanche in a Ratel-20 on my right flank spotted him. It was impossible in that bush to move the Ratel into reverse in time to intercept the tank, so Terblanche leapt down intending to take the tank out by dropping a hand grenade through the hatch. But he couldn't get near because all the 20 mm guns on the Ratels and other machine-guns were pouring fire at the tank. Terblanche turned back and asked his gunner for his R-4 rifle, but by the time he began to go forward again one of the other gunners had shot the Cuban commander dead as he turned to the right to knock me out.

'As the commander fell dead during the turning manoeuvre he must have slumped on the controls because the gun barrel drooped and at the same time fired a 100 mm shell which shot out the rear axle of the Ratel next to me. No one was injured, but the Ratel was completely out of the battle because lots of metal and other rubbish from the axle was forced up into its engine.

'I had two spare tanks behind me, so I brought one of them up to destroy the T-55. It had been a close experience. I think the Cuban was on a kamikaze mission to hit our HQ; he must have known he was going to die. Maybe he was on dagga [marijuana]. I don't know, but the Cuban and Fapla troops loved that stuff. Sometimes they did crazy things which were difficult to believe. We suspect they smoked dagga to give them guts before a fight.' [Christo Terblanche was subsequently awarded the Southern Cross medal for outstanding bravery in the course of battle.]

The fighting now swirled ferociously as the Olifants encountered more T-55s of Fapla's 3rd Tank Battalion and 25 Brigade which were concealed in thick bush near the *shona*. They fought valiantly to protect 59 Brigade as it fled westwards, some 1,000 m behind 25 Brigade towards the safety of the Tumpo Triangle.

'It was a very close fight in the dense bush,' said Muller. 'We were destroying their tanks at only 10 to 30 m range while many infantrymen were being killed on the ground with machine-gun fire. About 25 minutes into the battle we had advanced only 400 m into the bush but had shot out seven of their tanks; four were burning like hell and exploding all the time for an hour or two. That made things very difficult for our infantrymen on the ground, so they were having to take cover or get back into the Ratels.

'59 Brigade began to direct 23 mm fire on us from the southwest. The ZU-23 is a hell of a good weapon. You don't hear the shots during battle because there is so much other noise from bombs falling and your own weapons firing. You only see the 23 mm tracers coming at you at four shots a burst. My HQ Ratel came under heavy fire at one time. Luckily we were behind a row of tanks, and one tank at my right front acted as a shield. It was a fantastic sight. The 23 mm shells come at a hell of a speed and there was a kind of white heat with showers of sparks as they hit the tank. But they can't penetrate a tank's armour and they just left a pattern of white dots. One slug took off the radio aerial just above my head: six inches lower and I was dead. After that I ordered all hatches closed. Later there were 'bruises' all over my Ratel where 23 mm shells had struck at too sharp an angle for penetration.

'The crew of one of my Ratels weren't so lucky. A burst of four 23 mm shells hit their vehicle directly: the holes were 20 cm apart. All four men were killed instantly by flying metal and by the speed of the shells which cause a massive displacement of air. They were badly wrecked up. They weren't human beings any more, just a hand here and a head there and a piece of rib there.'

Further disaster followed. The SADF had encountered Cubans before in the War for Africa, but at the earlier battles on the Lomba, Mianei, Vimpulo, Hube and Chambinga Fidel Castro's warriors had restricted themselves to advisory and planning roles and the operation of high technology equipment. They had not got involved directly in ground combat. Colonel Ferreira's intelligence team had identified a pattern of seven Soviet and 30 Cuban advisers attached to each Fapla brigade. The Soviets were with the brigade commander's HQ while the Cubans manned sophisticated anti-aircraft, radar and heavy artillery equipment; but whenever serious danger loomed both the Soviets and the Cubans were helicoptered to safety. Now, in the 14 February battle, Cuban troops were fighting in the front line for the first time and they were dying for the first time. The commanders and gunners of the 3rd Battalion's T-55s were Cubans while the drivers and gun loaders were Angolans. Some of the infantrymen and forward artillery observers also were Cubans.

Once it was clear that men from Havana were heavily involved, the order came from Pat McLoughlin to Muller and Schoeman: 'Get one of them – alive!' A Cuban PoW was desperately needed for intelligence and propaganda purposes. The media highlights of the Cuban–South African tussles since 1975 had not derived from the frontline fighting, in which foreign editors around the world showed little interest, but from the occasions on which either side could produce a captured Boer, Fidelista or Ruski at a well-attended press conference.

'Having been ordered to get one, I could hardly believe my luck when a Cuban soldier without a weapon appeared right next to my Ratel at the height of the battle with his hands in the air,' said Mike Muller. 'But my delight immediately turned to dust when a small UNITA infantry unit attached to 61 Mech cut the Cuban boy to pieces with small-arms fire.

'There wasn't time to remonstrate. You see the shellbursts, the flames, the contacts, the dying, but strangely you don't hear the shooting although there's hellish noise all around. As commander keeping control of the tanks and armoured cars you have always to stay cool and calm and talk steadily on the radio as you work with the troops on the ground. All the while I was watching out of my observation window (a tiny square of reinforced armour-glass) I had my headphones on listening to all the different radio nets. I was concentrating so hard on all the talking that was going on that I didn't even notice one tank shell which passed within feet and mowed down a tree right next to us. It was only when my crew pointed it out after the battle that I knew about it, although I could see whole trees falling next to our people elsewhere.'

For the first time since the October 1987 fighting on the Lomba River the South Africans had achieved a reasonably unambiguous victory. McLoughlin and Ferreira had defined limited but clear aims – the destruction of 59 Brigade and the driving of 21 and 25 Brigades back into the narrow confines of the Tumpo Triangle. By the end of the day on 14 February the survivors from 59 Brigade were pouring into the Triangle. But they didn't stop there. They passed over the TMM bridge on the Cuito. Fapla generals were only able to halt the retreat and reorganise 59 Brigade at Longa, more than 120 km northeast of Cuito Cuanavale. 21 and 25 Brigades and the Third Tank Battalion also began pulling back into the Tumpo Triangle on the night of 14 February after the battering they had taken. Tallying enemy losses, Deon Ferreira estimated that four Cuban tank commanders and gunners and more than 400 Fapla had died during the day's battle. Fourteen T-54/55 tanks were destroyed, in addition to eight Soviet armoured cars, one BM-21 Stalin Organ, one mobile radar-guided Sam-13 anti-aircraft missile system, and seven ZU-23 guns. On the other hand, Ferreira had bad news for niggardly politicians in Pretoria who while desiring victories on the battlefields also wanted them achieved with no casualties in order to protect themselves to their white electorates. Besides 61 Mech's four deaths, another three of the battalion's young national servicemen had been seriously wounded.

After overrunning 59 Brigade, 4 SAI swung round to help 61 Mech in the encounter with 25 Brigade, the 3rd Tank Battalion and 59 Brigade's retreating tail. Schoeman moved his force parallel with Muller's but about two kilometres further eastwards along the lower part of the slope of the Chambinga High Ground, shooting out another two enemy tanks. 'After the fog and cloud cover lifted in mid-morning the enemy aircraft were permanently in the air dropping thousands of tonnes of bombs all over the show,' said Muller. 'What we had always feared then happened. With a lot of skill and several slices of luck we'd held out against the planes and lost no one in the course of hundreds of bomb attacks. But late in the day a Mig dropped a bomb right among a group of 4 SAI national servicemen and four of them were killed.'

The deaths notwithstanding, Mike Muller, Cassie Schoeman and Demostenes Chilingutila ranked the 14 February defeat of 59 Brigade and the 'burning' of 21 Brigade, 25 Brigade and the 3rd Tank Battalion at the edge of the *Anhara Lipanda* with the destruction of 47 Brigade on the Lomba. 'It was a very good fight,' said Muller, a 35-year-old who had served 18 years with South African armour since leaving school and had taken part in every cross-border action into Angola, including the first, Operation Savannah, in 1975. 'We destroyed 59 Brigade almost completely. We had to do a lot of manoeuvring to get at them. They had concentrated in a good defensive position and they had a good Cuban reserve.'

Muller, Schoeman and Chilingutila had broken the pattern of equivocal, questionable South African/UNITA victories on the way north from the Lomba to Cuito Cuanavale and had given the generals a fresh opportunity to press home the military ascendancy which had been so nearly thrown away. They had also created a new 'space' in which the politicians could manoeuvre to gain diplomatic advantage.

Muller and Schoeman were particularly delighted with the performance of the Olifants against the Soviet T-54/55s. 'It was tough for our guys to look down the barrel of a T-55 from only 10 or 30 m,' said Muller, whose nervous tic in one eye suggested stress from endless border warfare through the 70s and 80s. 'It takes guts to go into dense undergrowth where you know there are tanks which you can't see. The T-55 is a very good tank. It has a good gun. It's easy to maintain and operate, and it has a very low silhouette. It's small: looking down from the gun position of a Ratel it looks something like a Porsche sports car.

'But Fapla's gunnery was very poor. They got a lot of shots off but they weren't very accurate. There were a lot of trees falling around our people, but for the most part their shells were falling short or went over our heads. Part of our tankers' training is in eye sharpening: if you see a target you go for it with maximum aggression and precision. As soon as one of our Olifant commanders had identified a T-55 target it usually only needed one shot to take it out. The Ratel-90s also destroyed tanks, but with their smaller guns they usually needed at least five shots before they found the "soft" spot just beneath the turret.

'The Olifants were using very deadly HEAT (high explosive anti-tank) shells developed in South Africa. The shell contains a tungsten steel slug in its nose cone. On impact, explosives concentrated in the cone force the tungsten shot through the armour at a hell of a speed. It literally burns a hole through the armour and all the heat, flames and gases that are released set off all the ammunition inside. The slug rattles around inside the tank, knocking shrapnel off everywhere and slashing the crew to pieces. But Russian armour is not very good – it's notoriously soft – and sometimes the tungsten would go through the front and right out again through the back: the tank was still knocked out because the impact force and air displacement is so great that the crew can't survive. It's very good ammunition.'

As a result of the 14 February victory the SADF now had most of Fapla penned into a box just across the Cuito River from Cuito Cuanavale. The box, about five kilometres from north to south and six kilometres from west to east, was bounded in the east by the Cuito and Cuanavale Rivers; in the north by the Dala River; in the south by the Tumpo River; and in the east, between the sources of the Dala and the Tumpo, by the narrow base of the fan-shaped *Anhara Lipanda*. The Tumpo Triangle was the name loosely applied to this 30 sq km quadrilateral of dusty Angolan soil which no one had ever considered to be worth fighting over before Cuban, South African, Soviet, American, MPLA and UNITA fortunes clashed there. The Triangle denotation arose because the main Fapla/Cuban logistics base was tucked into a sliver of land where the Tumpo tributary enters the Cuito River at an acute angle.

The SADF objective now had to be to drive Fapla and the Cubans from the Tumpo Triangle and to destroy the logistics base. But before the big assault could begin one mopping-up operation would be necessary. UNITA had detected a 400-strong battalion from 21 Brigade with three tanks sitting on Highpoint 1251, a small forested hill just north of the Dala. Highpoint 1251 would have to be cleared before all would be ready for the big push into the Tumpo Triangle.

CHAPTER 31

THE ATTACK ON HIGHPOINT 1251

Commandant Mike Muller put together a special unit to clear out Highpoint 1251. Before dawn on Saturday 20 February 1988 Muller's combat team, consisting of an Olifant squadron, a Ratel squadron, a UNITA infantry battalion and a mortar platoon, was ready in the assembly area about six kilometres east of Fapla's 21 Brigade battalion and its three tanks.

'We moved off just before dawn with very good guidance from UNITA who knew the area well', said Muller. 'As soon as the enemy heard the roar of our engines we began to draw very heavy enemy artillery fire. Then we ran into an anti-tank minefield and one of the Ratels lost its front axle.

'On UNITA's advice I retreated two kilometres and readjusted the line of advance further to the south, but we were held up again by bombing runs by Mig-23s which forced us to take cover in the bush. They made several raids and progress was slow. When we were able to move, the UNITA infantry, riding on top of the tanks, took several casualties in the Fapla artillery bombardments.

'We got held up yet again when an Olifant hit an anti-tank mine and lost a track which had to be replaced. There were more air attacks and it was only by about 4 pm that we began approaching the enemy's half-prepared hillside positions. When we had advanced to within about 1,000 m of the battalion's outer trenches they suddenly began to run and cross the Dala and Cuanavale Rivers. We brought in G-5 fire as they ran across the open *anhara* and many of the Fapla guys were killed and wounded. When we moved through the 21 Brigade positions we discovered that all the enemy tanks and vehicles had gone.' Muller took his force down to the north bank of the Dala, from where the Olifants wiped out an enemy mortar position to the south of the river.

Muller's men had taken Highpoint 1251 without any real fight. They were then ordered to pull back to 61 Mech's laager position to the east of the Chambinga High Ground. During the retreat they again came under heavy bombardment from Fapla artillery on the western bank of the Cuito River and Mig-23s dropped bombs within 50 m of some of the tanks and Ratels. Muller's men came through without injuries and the SADF was now ready for the first vital attack into the Tumpo Triangle.

PART 8

THE SIDESHOW (CONTINUED)

If the enemy were superior in numbers, they would provoke the enemy's attack, dismount, take cover and shoot, remount and ride away. In European military manuals it was a formula known as 'strategic offensive, tactical defensive.' The Boers had never seen the manuals.

Thomas Pakenham,
The Boer War.

CHAPTER 32

THE ATTACK ON MENONGUE

Commandant Robbie Hartslief, having taken over from Jan Hougaard, directed 32 Battalion's marauders from late January 1988 onwards in regular attacks on Fapla supply convoys inching uncertainly along the 200-km road from Menongue to Cuito Cuanavale.

'We had established that we could get our MRL teams within range of convoy concentration and rest bases at Cuatir, Luassinga and Longa,' said Hartslief. 'Between 1 and 28 February we hit convoys on 16 separate occasions with the MRLs and mortars. Each convoy contained between 150 and 250 vehicles, but sometimes there were more than 300. Three convoys were purely Cuban, each guarded by a battalion of infantry. We would attack just about every second day, firing about 10 MRL ripples – some 250 rockets in all. We scooted out from our bases at Gimbe and Bambi, hit them hard and then scampered back fast to safety. We co-ordinated with the SAAF who would hit the convoy just before or after us with four, six or sometimes eight Mirages. On one occasion the planes left sixty Fapla trucks burnt out along the road.'

Captain Herman Mulder, 32 Battalion's intelligence chief, working with UNITA liaison officers at Hartslief's Gimbe HQ, 50 km south of the road, plotted the minute-by-minute movements of every Fapla convoy. His information sources were recces from 32 Battalion; 1 and 5 Reconnaissance Commando; UNITA Special Forces staked out along nearly the whole length of the road; artillery forward observers; and the mass of radio intercepts picked up by his EW warfare team in their specially equipped Ratels.

'Within minutes, sometimes seconds, of a convoy setting off, I knew,' said Mulder. 'After another hour I knew its entire composition.'

Hartslief recalled the tedium of waiting through the hot, fly-infested days for night to fall and the action to begin. 'We sat around in the Gimbe area in foxholes, under trees, under camouflage. We just slept or planned operations, watching Migs fly overhead on their way to Cuito Cuanavale. We couldn't bombard the convoys every night. The big rockets and charge packs for the MRLs together weighed 60 kg each and we needed several trucks to push through the forest just carrying ammunition to the attack area. Each time it was a big effort, so we had to wait until we knew the enemy had concentrated.'

Satisfaction came when recces reported that for many kilometres along the road wrecked and burnt-out Fapla vehicles had been pushed off to the side. A correspondent for *The Independent* of London, who was taken by the MPLA to Cuito Cuanavale, reported seeing 'more than 400 tanks, troop carriers and supply lorries pushed down the road from Menongue, weaving in and out of the charred remains of vehicles which bear testimony to relentless strafing runs by South African jets and UNITA attacks.'[1]

Among Hartslief's problems was his men's inability to manoeuvre the MRLs within firing range – 21 km – of Cambambe, the first halt for the convoys some 30 km out of Menongue. It was also difficult for the SAAF to put in regular attacks at a point so close to the big Menongue airbase. The big dust clouds kicked up by the MRLs provided another headache for Hartslief. The powdery billows could be seen by the Migs constantly moving out of Menongue a short distance away. This ruled out their use by day, so Hartslief sent one troop of four MRLs back to Rundu to be replaced with a troop of smaller and more manoeuvrable 120 mm heavy mortars which when fired left only small, temporary dustclouds, making possible daylight forays.

★ ★ ★

To coincide with the big attack by 4 SAI and 61 Mech against 59 Brigade on Sunday 14 Febuary 1988, Deon Ferreira urged that his old battalion,

32, be let off the leash to strike at the Menongue airbase. The idea, he told Colonel Pat McLoughlin, would be to prevent the Cuban and Angolan Mig-23 and Mig-21 squadrons from taking off and interfering with the SADF's fight with 59 Brigade. McLoughlin agreed, and on 6 February Hartslief was instructed to prepare his men for perhaps the most daredevil mission of the entire War for Africa.

As soon as Hartslief received the order to attack he sent two 32 Battalion companies with UNITA recce teams ahead on foot, with only two navigation Buffels, to reconnoitre the area of the Cuma, a small stream about 20 km southeast of Menongue. It was from Cuma that he planned to launch the South African bombardment. (See map, chapter 27.) Hartslief followed the advance party with 65 vehicles, including 16 ten-tonne trucks carrying MRL and mortar ammunition, two-tonne 'Jakkal' trucks carrying the 120 mm mortars, the whole Ratel-90 anti-tank squadron, plus the command Ratel and other logistics and recovery vehicles.

'We moved towards Cuma only at night without lights,' said Hartslief. 'It was wild country and it was raining, so there was no natural illumination whatsoever. We had a lead Ratel fitted with navigation equipment for night movement. The rest followed. It was all part of our training. We were blind, relying entirely on instruments. Every kilometre I stopped the procession to check that no one was missing. We managed to keep everyone together even though we were the size of a small brigade.

'There were no bridges, so every time we crossed a river we had first to build fords with tree trunks and rocks. We often got stuck, but we had a very good small team of engineers with us who got us through. It took four days to infiltrate without detection into our attack positions, which I regarded as a major success in itself, especially as there were a number of small farms between the Cuma River and Menongue whose peasant owners were all MPLA supporters as far as we could tell.

'The attack we had been asked to do was extremely risky because of the big size of our force. Quite apart from the farmers, enemy reconnaissance patrols were constantly in the area. Just ten kilometres across the Cuma River from our deployment area there were enemy tanks. Just to the west there were heavy enemy movements along the road south of Menongue to Caiundo.'

By the evening of Monday 13 February Hartslief's force was in position for the attack. Major Pierre Franken, of Lomba River repute, took command of the artillery barrage. 'I had to rely on the MRLs,' said Franken. 'We couldn't get near enough to bring the 120 mm mortars into play. We had the four MRLs ready by 10.30 pm and fired a ripple of 96 rockets into Menongue airbase. I was given the bearings by recces dug in just beyond the base perimeter.

'We waited a short time to see whether anyone had located us. When there was no reaction, Commandant Hartslief ordered us to fire another ripple. It took time to reload. It is physically demanding to load MRLs with 60 kg shells and then the charge packs for firing. There were no stars or moon that night, so we were groping around almost sightless.

'We fired the second 96-rocket ripple at 1.30 am and then moved away as fast as possible towards Gimbe. We didn't halt until 6.30 am when the first light glimmered in the east. By 6.45 am the whole convoy was camouflaged, and just after 7 am the first two Mig-23s flew over us. We assumed they were from Lubango because we were confident we must have inflicted a fair amount of damage on Menongue.'

The 32 Battalion force, protected by heavy rain clouds from air attack, made it back in only two days to Gimbe, where Mulder, Hartslief and Franken began collating intelligence reports to assess the effectiveness of their assault on Menongue. Given the scale and sheer daring of the effort, their conclusions were dispiriting. Seven Cubans and 37 Angolan Air Force personnel were killed when their sleeping quarters at the side of the runway were hit and one Mig-21 was put out of action, but by midday of 14 February the base was functioning again and aircraft were taking off to attack 4 SAI and 61 Mech east of Cuito Cuanavale.

'We fell far short of what we had hoped to achieve', said Hartslief. 'Our objective was to inflict so much damage to the airstrip that no aircraft would be able to take off on 14 February for the Chambinga High Ground battlefront. We just might have fulfilled our aims if we had got near enough to use the 120 mm mortars which fire shells which can penetrate a tarred airstrip. It was impossible with the MRLs and their high explosive and airburst shells: no penetration shells had been designed for that weapon at that time. What we really needed were the G-5s and their heavy 155 mm penetration shells.'

Throughout the rest of February Angolan Migs bombarded the Gimbe and Bambi areas three or four times a day. 'They knew we were there somewhere, but they didn't know exactly where.' said Hartslief.

Captain Herman Mulder recalled one day when eight Migs came to hunt and destroy the men of 32 Battalion. 'Two Mig-23s flew top cover while six Mig-21s in pairs flew lines from the southeast, south and southwest towards where they estimated our Gimbe base to be. They poured out streams of 30 mm cannon fire on each pass. Three successive times they came in, each pair from a different direction; it's a very difficult manoeuvre, and no one does it unless they're sure of the target. We were all deep in our foxholes. I was scared shitless. I thought we were going to be cut to pieces.'

In fact, no one was hurt. The 30 mm slugs only tore up and shredded bush between 32 Battalion's camp and the UNITA camp, about a kilometre away. By the end of the month none of the well camouflaged South African vehicles had been hit and only one soldier had been wounded, a black mortarman who was burnt on the back from a white phosphorus bomb.

However, the relative failure of the Menongue attack meant the SAAF had to step up its bombing raids on the Angolan convoys. It was during one of these raids, on Friday 19 February, that disaster struck for the South African Air Force.

★ ★ ★

On the morning of 19 February four Mirage-F1AZs prepared to take off from Grootfontein to hit a Fapla road convoy where it had concentrated at Cuatir, 40 km east of Menongue. Major Ed Every was flying the rear aircraft, and as usual a young operations clerk, who had adopted Every as his hero, was on the hard pan beyond the hangars watching the Major taxi towards the end of the runway. Ed Every was known as Never Ready because almost invariably he forgot something – his map, flight authorisation documents, or gloves – and the ops clerk would rush to fetch it like a Labrador puppy. On this day, Every forgot nothing and soon the formation was flashing across Angola at treetop level to wreak destruction on the Angolan convoy.

At Cuatir the first three Mirages 'tossed' their bombs into the midst of the convoy. They had soared up, twisted down and were on their way back home as Every flashed in to toss his bombs. An SADF recce team on the ground saw the bombs lob from under the Mirage's bomb racks and then saw black smoke pour from the plane as it reached the top of its pitch-up to begin its twist down. The plane had clearly been hit by one of Fapla's arsenal of anti-aircraft weapons. The recces, having watched the plane lose height and then disappear, radioed the information to Hartslief at Gimbe.

From Gimbe, Hartslief and his men saw a huge black pall of smoke fill the air where Every's plane hit the ground some 15 to 20 km south of the road and just to the west of the Cuatir River.

'In Every's Mirage we knew there were a lot of maps, including details of 32 Battalion's deployment,' said Hartslief. 'If the enemy got those maps it would be a turning point in our Menongue operation. By about 6 pm our recces had located the precise crash site and had detected a column of enemy vehicles, including tanks, going towards it. So they seemed certain to get the maps if they had not been burned.

'We had been planning that night to follow up the Mirage attack on Cuatir with an MRL and mortar bombardment. But we cancelled that and decided to wait until the enemy were grouped around the aircraft and then bring the MRLs down on them.'

UNITA recces reported that they had seen a parachute stream from the stricken Mirage and that later a white man in a green pilot's uniform had been spotted running through the forest. SADF recces had seen nothing similar and were pretty sure Ed Every was dead. They suspected the UNITA men were suffering from excessive use of their imaginations. Hartslief, also certain that Every was dead, was nevertheless ordered to patrol intensively in case the pilot was staggering around hurt and confused trying to survive and not knowing the difference between the combat uniforms of the Cubans, Fapla, UNITA or 32 Battalion.

After night fell the SADF recces reported that a whole battalion of Cubans were at the crash site. Their tanks and vehicles were parked and they were walking around with lamps and torches searching the wreckage and the surrounding bush. Pierre Franken manoeuvred his four MRLs into position and just when the recces reported that the Cuban concentration was particularly intense he let loose a ripple of 96 rockets right on top of Every's destroyed Mirage.

'Our recces reported that the enemy took away two truckloads of bodies.' said Hartslief. 'Military intelligence later reckoned 143 Cubans and Fapla had died. So we got our own back for Every.'

★ ★ ★

Back at Grootfontein Captain Reg van Eeden sat, as he did every time a mission was flown, with other Air Force men waiting for the four Mirages to return. 'We saw the formation come back,' he said. 'They flew straight in. We saw one, two, three, but there was no fourth. We shrugged and said it must have diverted. But then as they were taxiing back to the hard pan the radio reports began to filter in that one of the aircraft had been hit.

'I'll never forget the expression on the face of Ed's little ops clerk. There were tears in his eyes. He had read the registration number on each of the three returned aircraft and knew the missing plane was Ed's. For days after he went about saying: "Who am I going to run around after now?" That night we all got drunk in the pub and I was full of regret that I had never apologised to Ed for telling him to shut his mouth.'[1]

★ ★ ★

Fapla pushed a whole infantry brigade with tanks and M-46 guns into the forest south of the Menongue-Cuito Cuanavale road after the Mirage incident in an attempt to flush out and destroy 32 Battalion. 'We were sure they had located us,' said Hartslief,' and on 3 March Brigade HQ at Rundu said it was getting too hot for us to hang around there. So we started moving out in a series of fast night hops. On the way south we said a special farewell to Baixo Longa (on the Longa River), the MPLA's most southerly outpost in the war area, where a battalion of Fapla infantry was based. We infiltrated 45 of the vehicles to within eight kilometres of the town and put in one 96-rocket ripple from the MRLs and 350 120 mm mortar bombs.'

★ ★ ★

Although both Hougaard and Hartslief had enjoyed the sheer adventure and derring-do of the Menongue enterprise, they were bitterly disappointed that its possibilities had been exploited to only a limited extent because of considerations and intrigues at high command and political levels which they were unable to understand.

'We were begging for orders to launch an attack on Cuito Cuanavale itself with a bigger force,' said Hougaard. 'With the limited force we had we couldn't have kept hitting that Menongue-Cuito Cuanavale road indefinitely. We had lots of options available to us which we spelt out to higher commanders. We could have used bigger ground forces to hit their concentration areas along the road. We could have gone west of Menongue and hit convoys before they even reached that town, but the rules of engagement strictly forbade us to move men to the north or west of the town. We wanted to take the G-6s in, which would really have buggered the convoys. Their great mobility would have made it difficult for the enemy to capture one, but at that time the top brass was really afraid of that type of equipment being seized.'

Hartslief said there was deep frustration among battlefield officers that the great SADF war effort was not put into the Menongue area to attack Cuito Cuanavale from the west. He said: 'All the combat group commandants wanted to launch an attack from the west as early as November 1987. Even in December we could have attacked the Menongue-Cuito Cuanavale road in strength and cut all their logistics. The war would have been over. The enemy couldn't have stayed there [in Cuito Cuanavale].'

Herman Mulder said that even the limited force sent in west of Cuito Cuanavale was held back in the early stages of the operation by top generals. 'We didn't get the authority to do what we wanted.' he said. 'We were unable to use our element of surprise.' One instruction, totally ignored by the recces, was that no SADF man was to approach the Menongue-Cuito Cuanavale road any closer than 1,000 m.

Hartslief said that by hesitating the generals lost the opportunity to inflict catastrophic damage on Fapla. 'When we got into the area in December the enemy deployments were very weak at Longa, Luassinga and Cuatir. It was only after our bombardments in January that they started to strengthen those positions with ten tanks at Longa, ten in Luassinga and four at Cuatir. Our limited force couldn't attack them so effectively any more.

'I think we succeeded in slowing the logistics operation down. But that's all. We could have destroyed it, but we weren't given the means or the latitude to do so.'

Notes

1   Karl Meier, reporting from Cuito Cuanavale for *The Independent* (1 March 1988).
2   Despite MPLA claims to have shot down more than 40 warplanes during the War for Africa, in all my interviews with soldiers downward from commandant level to troopie I only gathered evidence of one Mirage, Every's, being destroyed, plus one Bosbok and three unpiloted RPVs.

PART 9

THE THREE BATTLES FOR THE TUMPO TRIANGLE

There is this turbulent land,
a storehouse of pain and trouble,
confused mother of fear,
Hell in life.

Seventeenth-century Portuguese poem about Angola.

War is the unfolding of miscalculations.

Barbara Tuchman,
American historian.

Half a league, half a league,
Half a league onward,
All in the valley of Death
Rode the six hundred.

Alfred, Lord Tennyson (1809–92),
The Charge of the Light Brigade.

CHAPTER 33

MIKE MULLER LEADS THE FIRST TUMPO ATTACK: 25 FEBRUARY 1988

The battle of 14 February against Fapla's 59 Brigade and the skirmish on Highpoint 1251 of 20 February had forced the Angolans and Cubans back into their last 30 sq km bastion on the east bank of the Cuito River, the Tumpo Triangle.

The SADF's enemies had built strong defences, with two lines of intricate infantry trenches and sandbag bunkers running north-south between the sources of the Dala and Tumpo Rivers. Breach one stout trench line and there was the dispiriting prospect of another one to go. Fapla had also laid extensive anti-tank and anti-personnel minefields in front of the trenches. For Fapla riflemen and artillerymen there was a clear field of fire out across the almost treeless flatland of the *Anhara Lipanda*, which varied in width from west to east from about four to six kilometres.

Fapla's M-46 and D-30 guns and BM-21 Stalin Organ MRLs were placed on the west bank of the Cuito River, where the land was considerably higher than that stretching from the Tumpo Triangle across the *Anhara Lipanda* to the foot of the Chambinga High Ground. It was like a shooting gallery in which the guns had all the fun because the odds were stacked entirely in their favour. Suddenly, the Cuban/Fapla artillery, which further south had been ineffective compared with the G-5s because of its lack of range and poor use of forward observers, was on equal terms with the South African artillery.

Fapla's big guns and BM-21s – some 60 of them in all – had been widely spread in ones and twos. This gave their crews multiple lines of fire and meant it was difficult for the South African gunners to select priority counter-bombardment targets. Despite all the best efforts of Hougaard's and Hartslief's marauders south of the Menongue-Cuito Cuanavale road, big quantities of supplies had got through with the convoys and there was no shortage of ammunition for the enemy gunners.

The SADF objective now was to drive the Fapla/Cuban forces from the Tumpo Triangle and let UNITA take over the abandoned positions. This would deprive Fapla of the bridgehead it needed for any future offensive against UNITA's Mavinga and Jamba strongholds.

On staff officers' and politicians' maps it all looked so very simple. But the field officers knew they faced a formidable task. Get through the minefields and the trenchlines and then you would become sitting ducks for the artillery. At the same time the enemy warplanes would be overhead all the time, and your own Air Force would be unable to help out because, despite all the skills, ingenuity and courage of South Africa's pilots, the Mirage obsolescence factor outweighed all the qualities the SAAF's men could bring to bear in the Tumpo Triangle. If the SAAF had tried to fly into the Triangle too often in close ground support its planes would have been swallowed up as though in some evil black hole.

It would be left to the infantrymen and the tank and armoured car soldiers on the ground to assault the enemy stronghold. Some men had begun to see similarities between their situation and that of the Light Brigade in the Crimea, but the charge would have to go ahead if the generals so ordered.

Commandant Mike Muller of 61 Mech drew the first short straw.

★ ★ ★

Muller's battle plan was passed up through all the layers of command, including the Chief of the Army, General Kat Liebenberg, to Defence Minister Magnus Malan – another illustration of how every move the SADF attempted to make was subject to diplomatic and political factors outside the battlefield officers' knowledge or control.

Muller's combat group was formed around his own 61 Mech Battalion, which was to be the main attack force consisting of 20 Olifant tanks, a mechanised infantry company in Ratels, the troop of four anti-tank Ratel-ZT3s, a team of 120 mm mortars, a Parachute Regiment assault pioneer platoon, a group of anti-aircraft specialists with Sam-7 missiles and 20 mm guns, a strong party of engineers and UNITA's 800-man 5th Regular Battalion.

For support Muller also had a flanking force made up of a Ratel squadron, a troop of three tanks, a mechanised infantry company and a 120 mm mortar group; three companies of more than 300 infantrymen from 32 Battalion; and UNITA's 3rd and 4th Regular Battalions totalling some 1,400 men.

4 SAI, which had lost its commander, Cassie Schoeman, to yet another dose of hepatitis, was held in reserve.

Muller, a thin, wiry man with a dark moustache, had to take his force across the Chambinga High Ground to launch the attack. There were only two viable routes across the hilly terrain. The first was up the long gentle eastern slope and then down the short, steep Heartbreak Hill, from where the attack against 59 Brigade had been made on 14 February. The second lay further south, where the western slope of the High Ground was somewhat longer and not so severe as at Heartbreak Hill. The route led down to an area where the old Portuguese 'road' from Cuito Cuanavale to Mavinga stretched out across the *Anhara Lipanda*.

'Road' is something of a euphemism, because the grandest highway east of the Cuito River consisted of nothing more than a deeply rutted track through the sand, which was abandoned for another course each (frequent) time it became unmanageable.

It was the second route that was chosen for the attack.

Muller wanted to attack the first defence line, formed by Fapla's 25 Brigade, from the south and work along it, destroying installations, and wiping out troops, before turning south again to attack the second defence line from the same direction. The 32 Battalion companies, led by Major Tinus van Staden, would launch the opening assault from the south, leaving 61 Mech to press home the main attack. UNITA's 5th Regular Battalion would attempt to distract Fapla by pressing home an attack further north along the defence line and Savimbi's 4th Regular Battalion would launch a feint attack to the west of 32 Battalion on the Tumpo River.

The whole combat group assembled to the east of the Cunzumbia River source, some 45 km from the first Fapla defence line, on the evening of 24 February ready to launch the attack on Saturday 25 February 1988.

Through the night, moving up the eastern slope of the Chambinga High Ground, Muller's battle group was led by a navigation Ratel. The 32 Battalion companies began infiltrating towards Fapla positions at the source of the Tumpo River from the southeast before the sun rose. But when they reached the objective they found that all the Fapla soldiers of 25 Brigade were abandoning their positions and running away.

'Then our G-5s and 120 mm mortars opened up and the enemy artillery replied,' said Muller. 'Their air force appeared shortly afterwards and subsequently there were Migs in the sky all day.

'My command vehicle was an incongruous sight. I was using the Olifant which had lost its gun barrel on 14 February. If the enemy had ever seen it we might have won before lunch: they would have died from laughing at the exploded stump.

'Recce commandos took us along a path they had marked through a minefield until we were just 1.5 km from the enemy's first outlying positions which were being tackled by 32 Battalion. At this stage I was keeping just inside the treeline for cover at the eastern edge of the open *Anhara Lipanda*, manoeuvring slowly southwards and waiting for the right moment to attack.

'We opened into tactical formation, but after another 100 m we ran into another minefield laid just inside the treeline that our recces had not discovered. I was about 20 m behind the first line of Olifants, but my tank was the first to be hit. It was one of the new Soviet M-57 anti-tank mines, much more potent than the M-58s or M-49s. It took the track off my tank and damaged the suspension unit and shock absorbers. I switched to a Ratel as my command vehicle for the rest of the battle.'

The mine explosion gave away Muller's position to the enemy. 'Soon we were engulfed by the biggest Fapla artillery barrage of the war,' said Muller. 'It was bloody hellish. They put down M-46, D-30, BM-21 and ZU-23 fire on us. They knew where the minefield was and they could

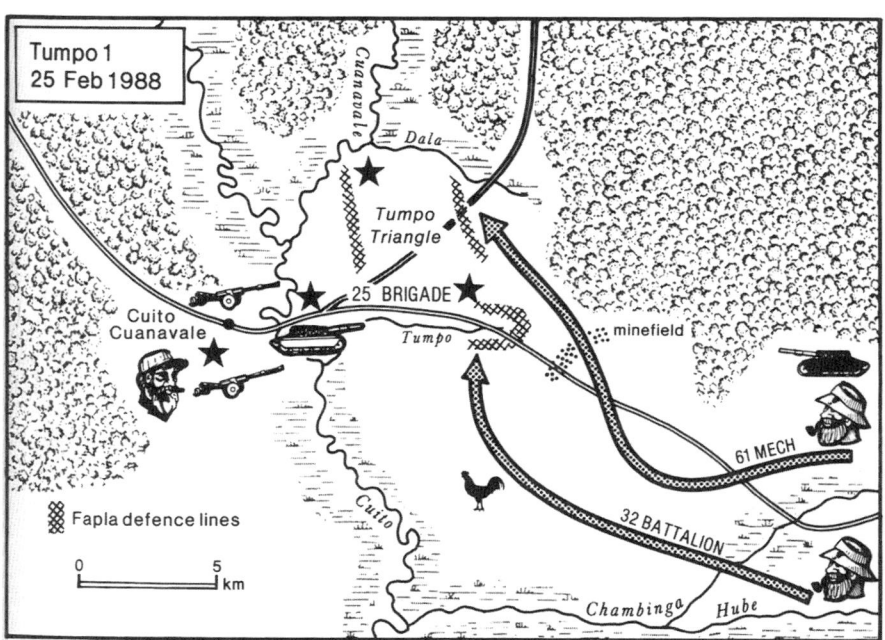

Tumpo 1
25 Feb 1988

Cuanavale

Dala

Tumpo
Triangle

25 BRIGADE

Cuito
Cuanavale

Tumpo

minefield

61 MECH

Fapla defence lines

Cuito

32 BATTALION

0   5
km

Chambinga   *Hube*

see us in the edge of the forest. Our G-5s had stopped firing because there was always two, three or sometimes four Migs in the air and our artillery could not afford to betray their position. The UNITA Stingers should, in theory, have brought down as many as four Migs that day, but for reasons I've yet to understand the missiles weren't available.'

Soon three other tanks had lost tracks to mines and suffered damage to their suspension units as Muller tried to withdraw in 20 m leaps only to discover that the minefield was much more extensive than he had first realised.

The combat group then took its first casualty. 'My anti-aircraft troop was deployed 1,500 m to my north,' said Muller. 'It fired at some Migs. Enemy forward observers picked up the position and laid down M-46 fire, whose shrapnel killed one of my Sam-7 corporals, Hendricks, as he was trying to shoot down a Mig. One of the Withings recovery vehicles trying to pull out the stricken tanks to the rear was struck directly by a 130 mm round from an M-46; it burned out completely.'

Muller's situation was so desperate that he called up one of the Casspir-launched mine-breaching *plofadders* which had so far failed every time they had been used.

The string of explosive sausages again failed to explode. A Ratel tried to detonate the *plofadder* with a hail of fire from its 20 mm cannon. When that failed the only thing to do was to call up a section of nine men from the assault pioneer platoon and ask them to go forward to the far end of the *plofadder*, detonate it there and open a safe lane through the minefield for the combat group.

'Lieutenant Louwtjie Louw led the assault pioneers through the minefield, using sticks and mine-detectors to feel their way forward under heavy artillery bombardment, marking each mine they found with a flag,' said Muller. The tension was so great it was almost visible. It was a very difficult and very slow action. Every metre they advanced took five minutes. They detonated the *plofadder* at about 11.30 am and by about 12.30 the tanks were moving through the cleared lane towards the objective. We had lost more than five hours stuck in that minefield.'

[Louwtjie Louw and all the members of the section were awarded the Southern Cross Medal for this action.]

Muller's force advanced across the *Anhara Lipanda* towards the outer positions at the source of the Tumpo held by a battalion of 25 Brigade which 32 Battalion had attacked and found deserted. 'The trenches were freshly dug,' said Muller. 'There was an intact BTR-60 (armoured car) standing there and knapsacks, webbing and water bottles abandoned and scattered all over the ground.

'UNITA's 3rd Regular Battalion moved up the trenchline ahead, but they sent back radio signals saying that they too, like 32 Battalion, found that the Fapla soldiers had gone.

'Everything seemed to be going so smoothly that, instead of continuing the sweep along the first defensive line, I decided to push on to the second which began a little way further westwards where a tributary ran into the Tumpo. An advance company of 32 Battalion put down yellow smoke to mark their position so that we could integrate. That was a mistake because it drew heavy and accurate artillery fire.

'By 3pm five of my Ratels had received direct hits. One M-46 bomb explosion ripped off the door of a Ratel-90; the commander had both his legs sheared off and his gunner was wounded. Five 32 Battalion blokes had also been wounded. All our ambulances and recovery vehicles were busy taking the dead and wounded to medical posts in the rear.

'Later, one of the tanks still stuck in the minefield with a damaged track came under heavy M-46 fire as the crew was trying to get it ready to be pulled out. The crew dived back into the Olifant. But the corporal driving the tank didn't get his hatch closed in time. A shell hit the sloping armour just in front of the hatch and he was killed outright.'

Muller's force reached the southern end of the second defence line, more than one kilometre into the enemy objective, but the Fapla troops had fled from there as well. 'Since I couldn't call in our artillery to counter theirs, I told Colonel Pat McLoughlin it would be difficult to press on with the attack. We had cleared out the first line of their defences. But we had taken losses and the delays meant the setting sun was now in my gunners' eyes.'

McLoughlin gave permission for Muller to pull his force back. But as it crossed the Chambinga High Ground in darkness an M-46 scored a direct hit on a big mine-proof truck carrying mortar shells. The whole truck and its ammunition burnt out in a series of spectacular explosions.

'The driver, Sergeant Koekemoer, started steering the truck away from the rest of the column after the shell hit it,' said Muller. 'Thanks to him, no one was hurt. But when all the mortar shells began to cook off he had to drop out of his cabin into a deep foxhole and let the truck burn.'

Muller later discovered from a forward SADF observer, who had watched the whole action, that he had counted some 1,350 'accurate' Fapla artillery shots on Muller's combat group in the course of the day. Some 1,000 of these had come from the big M-46s.

The army definition of an 'accurate' artillery shot is one that falls inside a military formation within 20 m of a vehicle or fixed position. 'They certainly hammered us that day,' said Muller. 'Seven of our vehicles were knocked out and two were burnt out completely.'

★ ★ ★

In the early days of February 1988 Major Tinus van Staden, training commander of 32 Battalion, gave more thought to his second job as the unit's nature conservation officer than the war in Angola. Most of the battalion was absent on the Menongue operation with Commandant Robbie Hartslief. Other companies, held in reserve, were only in light training in case they were asked at any moment to expend their energies on one of the Angolan battlefields.

Van Staden was able to spend his afternoons and early evenings at the Buffalo Battalion's infantry training base on the banks of the Kavango watching marsh harriers and white and chocolate fish eagles sweep the great river's wide waters. It gave him time to think about new projects for the further ecological upgrading of the battalion's 650 sq km base, set in thick forest at the western end of Namibia's Caprivi Strip.

One of the finest nature reserves in southern Africa had gradually been created since Colonel Jan Breytenbach, the battalion's founder, took the forest over in 1976 as a base in which to mould 2,000 ill-disciplined guerrilla refugees from Angola into one of the finest fighting units of the SADF. Breytenbach, younger brother of the exiled poet and African National Congress member Breyten Breytenbach, was an ardent conservationist who grew increasingly appalled by the alleged elephant poaching activities of some SADF units inside Angola in co-operation with UNITA's trade officials.

Major van Staden, a career soldier in his early thirties from the Orange Free State, was the latest in a succession of battalion conservation officers who had built up the wild elephant population of the Fort Buffalo base from less than 100 in the late 1970s to some 900, one-fifth of the entire Namibian population, by 1988. The wild buffalo population had grown from less than 50 to more than 600. Impala, which were absent from the forest before Buffalo Battalion arrived, were returning. A population of just three rare sable antelope had grown to 27.

It was a brave poacher who stepped into the reserve in pursuit of meat, hides or ivory. Van Staden trained his men in tracking and other arts of warfare by sending them out on anti-poaching patrols throughout the base. It was not easy to convince the black troops that buffalos should be preserved, not eaten.

'Our guys had been brought up so close to nature that they believed it was their privilege to hunt,' said the Major. 'But they got better year by year. Back in 1981 they themselves poached seven elephants and sold the tusks. After that they found it more and more fun to stop Botswana and Kavango poachers. We used to hand them over to the civil authority. I had to restrain our guys at first from taking the law into their own hands: they would have ended up spending more time in Namibia's civil courts than doing the job in Angola they were paid for!'

Van Staden's big contribution to Buffalo Battalion's conservation programmes was the drilling of boreholes to create watering places in dry areas, financing them from battalion funds for 'training purposes'.

Van Staden particularly loved one waterhole his 'notorious' black infantrymen had created ten kilometres from the Kavango. 'We finished it in June, in the middle of the dry season,' he said. 'By the end of the second day of pumping there were eight centimetres of water in the pan. I watched a lesser jacana [a long-legged lily-trotting bird] come in, and I had never seen one at the river. I went back on the third day and there were two types of duck, a yellow-billed duck and a red-billed teal, resting on the water. Later there were dabchicks on the water and a purple roller drinking at the waterside, and I watched lion, kudu, spotted hyena, steenbok, civet cats, warthog, red lechwe and bushbuck go there to drink.

'I was like a little child. It was a conservationist's paradise, and I know that properly managed the area could take ten times as many animals.'

But much as Van Staden liked ducks and big mammals, his greatest love was tiny feathered birds. If anybody would listen, he waxed ecstatically about the white-browed sparrow weaver or more especially about the enchanting beauty of the tiny jet black and virgin white Bontpiek, or Arnot's Chat, which he spent most of his spare time observing. There was not a single black Angolan soldier who passed the training programme of Tinus van Staden, much feared by his underlings, and entered skirmishes and battles in Angola without knowing there were 400 species of bird in their home base, of which nearly 200 had been spotted by their Major and 50 of which were unique in southern Africa to the Caprivi Strip.

But Tinus van Staden, a lean man of medium height with a long wound down one cheek resembling a duelling scar, had attributes other than a Franciscan tenderness towards birds. In August 1981, during the SADF blitzkrieg named Operation Protea into southwest Angola, the then Lieutenant van Staden had leaped on to an enemy T-54 tank, discovered it was empty and begun to draw fire from bush at the side of the road. Van Staden and other soldiers in his patrol returned the fire.

From the treeline emerged Soviet Sergeant-Major Nikolai Pestretsov with his hands raised above his head ready to be taken to South Africa as a prisoner-of-war. Behind Pestretsov lay the still warm body of his dead wife clad in Soviet Army uniform. Next to Mrs Pestretsov lay two dead Soviet lieutenant-colonels and one of their wives, also in uniform. One of the lieutenant-colonels was in charge of the Soviet-Fapla-SWAPO garrison at Ongiva, which had attempted to evacuate northwards but had been overtaken by South African ground troops.

It came as no surprise therefore to Van Staden, with his combat reputation, when his bird-watching activities on the Kavango River were interrupted by an order to move three companies of his black infantrymen into Angola and prepare them to take part in a major battle.

From Fort Buffalo Van Staden's force of more than 300 men was flown the 250 km to Rundu by C-130 transport planes. At Rundu Van Staden transferred to a Puma helicopter, which took off just before dusk on 16 February and crossed the Angolan border and flew him at 50 m to Mavinga. It landed after dark by the light of one paraffin-soaked cotton wick implanted in a sand-filled baked bean can.

'That scared me more than any lion at a waterhole or any fighting I ever did in Angola,' Van Staden told friends.

Van Staden moved by truck to the Brigade tactical HQ, east of the Chambinga High Ground, to join Pat McLoughlin and Mike Muller in planning and co-ordinating the Tumpo One attack.

Van Staden's infantrymen flew into Mavinga three nights later through bad weather in darkness at 150 m on the cabin floors of two Transall-160s and a Hercules C-130. The Hercules shaved off the tops of two trees as it lined up to land with the guidance only of dimly lit paraffin pots at the side of the runway.

The soldiers were disoriented when they stepped out of the plane into pitch blackness: the 'landing lights' had been extinguished within a second or two of the plane's wheels touching the red laterite of the airstrip. They were led by UNITA soldiers holding their hands to overnight bunkers. The planes, their engines still running, loaded casevacs, broken equipment and personnel for the return trip across the black treetops to Rundu.

When his men joined him at the tactical HQ, Van Staden told them their main task would be to go in ahead of Mike Muller's main force, attack the trenches and bunkers of Fapla's 25 Brigade at the source of the Tumpo and create a bridgehead through which 61 Mech's tanks would penetrate the enemy lines.

The 25 Brigade trenches curved around the Tumpo headwaters in the shape of a scorpion's tail, with the tip on the southern side of the river's source at a low rise known as Hill 1208. Van Staden decided his men would make an approach on foot to the target from the Viposto High Ground, 16 km to the southeast of the Tumpo source. The 32 Battalion men would hit the scorpion's tail at its tip and then move along the defence system clearing it out until they were at the Tumpo source and could signal to the Olifants to come through.

Van Staden sent out a team of three 32 Battalion recces to establish exactly where 25 Brigade's point positions were. He wanted to move up from the south inside the western treeline of the *Anhara Lipanda* for as long as possible before he exposed his men on open terrain. At the Chambinga River the recces liaised with UNITA's 4th Regular Battalion at its forward base just north of the river.

'The recces needed someone from the 4th Battalion to guide them in towards the Tumpo,' said Van Staden. 'My men wanted only to be taken to within range of the enemy. They would then have moved in by themselves under cover of darkness to plot exactly where the enemy lines started. But UNITA refused to take them and in the end my men couldn't get close enough to give precise co-ordinates.'

Van Staden and his 300 moved out on a Ratel and eight trucks from tactical HQ in the late afternoon of 23 February for the Viposto High Ground. Two of the trucks broke down on the way, and Van Staden had to leave them behind with a captain and 70 fighting men. The trip

through the lush tropical vegetation to the south of the Chambinga High
Ground gave Van Staden time to indulge in some game viewing.

There were several troops of baboons and a lot of small buck. But the
major was most interested in the abundance of birds. The binoculars he
always carried slung around his neck were as much for bird-spotting as
Fapla-viewing.

'In a trailing branch I saw a bosloerie, a narina trogon, perhaps the
most beautiful bird in Africa, metallic emerald green with a scarlet breast,'
he said. 'I had never seen one before. I ordered the Ratel driver to stop
and reverse a bit so I could train my binoculars on it.'

But soon it was back to war. 'We knew we would have to cross the
Chambinga River swamps that night to avoid detection by the Angolan
Air Force,' said Van Staden. 'We left the remaining vehicles under
heavy camouflage at Viposto and walked towards the swamps lining the
Chambinga. We arrived there at about 5 am on 24 February just as the
first tinge of grey was appearing in the east.

'There was only one way through the swamps, and that involved walking in single file. It was a very dangerous time with 230 people spread
out in line without cover in an area of open water and thick mud two
kilometres wide. For the most part, the route was knee to waist-deep
mud, but we had our fun when people disappeared completely beneath
the sludge from time to time in unexpected holes.

'I took 90 minutes to get across. I was near the front, and when
I reached firm ground to the north of the Chambinga it was fully
light and the last people were just starting to go into the swamp. I
prayed that no aircraft would appear, and luckily none did. Quickly
afterwards we moved into the treeline to lay up and wait for the
attack the next day.'

On the morning of 24 February Van Staden asked the commander
of UNITA's 4th Battalion to attack and destroy a small but troublesome
Fapla forward post about five kilometres south of the Tumpo which lay
directly in Van Staden's planned line of advance.

Again UNITA refused to help. 'Instead I called in a bombardment
from our G-5 artillery at about 4 pm,' said the Major. 'At 5 pm I ordered
my guys to start marching towards the Tumpo. I said we had to take

a chance, and if the Fapla forward post was still there we would have to go right over it. But luckily the Faplas had withdrawn after the bombardment, and we went past without any trouble.

'At that stage I don't think the Faplas realised what was going on. Over a period of about two weeks beforehand UNITA had staged a series of small pestering attacks, so I don't think they understood a big assault was building up.'

UNITA's 4th Regular Battalion had by now spared two of its scouts to guide 32 Battalion towards the target. Van Staden marched his men through the night until the scouts estimated they were about three kilometres south of the tip of the 'scorpion sting,' on Hill 1208, of 25 Brigade. Van Staden told his men to rest, and to sleep if they could.

He roused them at 3 am on Saturday 25 February to begin the attack. 'It was very dark. There was no moon. It was very difficult to control the movement of 230 men spread out over 500 to 1,000 m in extended line in very thick bush. I was moving by compass only and I had to believe in it. My biggest worry was that we wouldn't hit the sting at the end of the curve. If we missed it we could find ourselves walking parallel with enemy fortified positions without knowing it.

'I had calculated direction and distance as much as I was able the day before. I also had an Artillery Regiment forward observer with me to help bring in heavy bombardments if we needed them. He was a captain. When I estimated we were at the target I asked him to bring in white illumination 120 mm mortar shells which released flares on little parachutes. They gave a lot of light. It was like daylight and I saw that we had hit exactly the spot I had aimed for.

'We were about 600 m from the enemy lines and we could actually hear them scrambling and running. Soon there was a hell of a noise as they started up vehicles and began moving away. They were too far off for us to use our small arms, so we carried on moving forward in the darkness with the 120 mm mortars continuing to fire the parachute daylight flares. The whole time we could hear the Faplas running and driving away in front of us.

'When daylight appeared we were out in open *anhara*. We could see Cuito Cuanavale just eight kilometres away. But we were still short of the Fapla lines on Hill 1208. We knew there had been several hundred Faplas in the defensive positions. The only thing to do was to charge Hill 1208 as fast as we could run. Anyone who was still there would see clearly and get in lots of accurate fire against us. But we had to complete our task of securing the position to let the tanks come through.

'My men all ran like cheetahs. They had no idea what weapons the enemy might have. I felt like a general that morning watching 230 men run at top speed in extended line across open space towards the objective inside the bushline on the hill. It was unbelievable! 230 men may not sound a hell of a lot, but it was exhilarating to watch them. I told them that if we hit the enemy running we might be able to go right through them.

'We came round the base of the hillock, because that's all it was, and saw a truck moving on the other side. I ordered a staff sergeant to take it out, and he destroyed it with an RPG-7 from 400 m. Soon we were in the Fapla trenches, but there was nobody left there. Other than the shot-out truck, there was a BTR-60 abandoned intact. We could see they had left in a hurry. There were shoes and clothing lying around where they had been sleeping and boxes of ammunition stacked up all over the place. When the guys realised what they had done they started whooping and cheering like crazy. They had stormed an enemy position of several hundred men and taken it with just one RPG-7 shell and without losing any dead or wounded!'

Van Staden settled down his men – ten whites and 220 blacks – in all-round defensive positions to await Mike Muller's Olifants and Ratels, scheduled to arrive at 7 am. 'We could hear our tanks coming,' said Van Staden, 'but when I spoke to Commandant Muller he said he was having trouble getting through the minefield. We must hold our position and wait.'

The Fapla artillery on the west bank of the Cuito River began to lay down fire on 32 Battalion. At first it was light and inaccurate, but as the D-30s and BM-21s found their range it became very heavy.

'Although our orders were that we mustn't take shelter in the Fapla trenches because they might be booby-trapped, we took a chance and dropped into them,' said Major Van Staden. 'I reckoned that the Faplas had run so quickly that they could have had no time to lay explosive charges. It turned out to be the right move. We were pinned down in the artillery bombardments for nine hours that day. It was just bombs, bombs, bombs all day.

'I had a hell of a headache, and everyone else must have had as well, especially from the D-30 shells passing overhead through the sound barrier. But the worst were the BM-21s which never seemed to stop firing. They went on and on and on. I understood why they scared the African troops so much in the first round of Angolan fighting back in 1975–76.

'If you could hear whistling you knew you were OK – their 122 mm shells had gone right over. But if there was no whistling you knew the shells were on target or falling just in front of you. At first it was terrifying, but there came a stage when the terror faded because you'd just got used to the constant noise. We took casualties, but they would have been much heavier if we had not taken to the enemy trenches.

'At one stage I was crouched with a signaller in a very narrow part of the trenchline about two metres deep when a huge high explosive bomb landed and detonated just a metre from the lip of the trench. We were talking on the radio at the time, and, although we were half-buried and our ears were singing for weeks afterwards we weren't hurt. If the trench had been wider and more shallow we might not have been so lucky. The sand absorbed a lot of the bomb's force.

'Bombs landed within three metres of soldiers out in the open and they were uninjured. A bomb would penetrate, and the compacted sand around it would force the explosion upwards. Within a metre, out in the open, it would get them. Further away they were OK; but if it had been hard ground they would have been dead. And if the enemy had had our type of airburst shrapnel fragmentation bombs, I'm sure we would all have been wiped out.

'We were bombed from all sides and from the air that day. The Fapla Migs crossed our positions 56 times dropping bombs, but they were very high and the closest their bombs fell were about 100 m away. We were lucky. We had no support from our own Air Force, but every time a Mig swept low the Fapla anti-aircraft guns tried to clobber it on the assumption that it must be one of our planes.'

While half of Van Staden's force was sheltering in the Fapla trenches, the other half was spreadeagled on open ground and beginning to take casualties. Three men, one of them seriously maimed with leg and abdomen wounds, were treated by the battalion doctor and his medical assistants.

One lieutenant, out in the open with his troops, later related how the soldiers complained all the time that they should move into the trenches. The lieutenant in his heart agreed, but hid his desperation as he waited for an order from Van Staden by affecting the utmost imperturbability by sitting against a tree with his hat over his eyes and pretending to be sound asleep.

'But tranquil he was not,' said Van Staden. 'I organised the trenches to make room for those outside, and when I gave the order for his company to take cover he was suddenly very wide awake and running as fast as any of his men.'

When 61 Mech's armour finally moved through the minefield in the afternoon, Van Staden fired two red flares to indicate his positions to Mike Muller. The main force was to move through the 32 Battalion area to press home the attack, leaving Van Staden to prepare his withdrawal.

As the armour passed through, things began to go wrong. 'Infantrymen from UNITA's 3rd Regular Battalion were sitting on the tanks, and as they drove between the trenches they started shooting at us,' said Van Staden. 'It was very dangerous. Our black guys had no great love for UNITA, but they knew they couldn't shoot back. The lieutenant who had been stuck out in the open was struck on the front of his helmet by a bullet; luckily, it didn't penetrate, but ricocheted away.

'There was lots of yelling and screaming to try and get the UNITAs to stop shooting. And then some of our guys followed a standard drill and threw yellow smoke grenades to indicate that "own forces" had come together. But they didn't do any lateral thinking: it was a stupid move at that time. The smoke just hung there for several minutes and was a good target indicator for the Fapla artillery on the other side of the Cuito River.

'Soon all the enemy artillery was shooting at us. It was worse than bad. They hammered us. The armoured people just closed their hatches, but a lot of the UNITA guys got swept off the tanks by the enemy fire. We were packed into the bottom of the trenches like tinned anchovies, but only two more of my men received wounds.'

In normal 32 Battalion operations the soldiers wear cloth bush hats. For this battle they had been ordered to wear reinforced steel helmets which saved the lives of the lieutenant and one of the troopies. The troopie was struck on the side of the helmet by a piece of flying shrapnel the size of a fist. The soldier had a few cuts on the face, but without the helmet he would have been dead.

Muller told Van Staden to withdraw his men. The 32 Battalion commander also heard Muller telling Colonel McLoughlin by radio that the armour was pulling back too: it was by now 5 pm, and, with the main force only at the beginning of the objective, there was no chance of going right through the target area before darkness. Major Van Staden asked Muller to take his five wounded men and the Artillery Regiment captain in his Ratels to the main medical post.

'The captain was in a very shaky state,' said the Major. 'He was freaking out as though from some kind of shell shock. He had been at or behind the front line for three months without a break. That's too long, and the day's concentrated shelling finally proved too much for him.

'He was very good at his job, but battle fatigue had got to him. There was no way I felt he could last the tough 16 km walk back to our vehicles.'

After some three kilometres of walking, the exertion and tension of the day and the previous nights began to work on some of the Major's men. 'We had drunk hardly any water all day,' said Van Staden. 'It had been very arduous and exhausting. Some of the guys began to drop from heat exhaustion. It was still light, about 6 pm. We had another 13 km to go, including re-crossing the Chambinga swamps. So I allowed the really shattered people to rest for a while and drink.

'The problem was that we had gone into the attack with very light gear; each troopie had only a litre of water in his pack, and most of them had drunk all their ration. I allowed them to break open their transfusion solution bags and drink from them. It was against the rules, but I decided the chances of anyone getting wounded in artillery or Mig attacks that late in the day were fairly low.' [The solution, rich in essential body salts, was carried in polythene bags to be used in an emergency as a substitute transfusion for blood plasma.]

A military intelligence major attached to 32 Battalion for the Tumpo operation was delirious with exhaustion and dehydration. 'He was so bad that he couldn't stand and he didn't know where he was,' said Van Staden. 'The guys made a stretcher for him with tree branches and carried him for four kilometres. We slept that night on the north side of the Chambinga and crossed the swamp next morning just before first light when everybody had rested.

'My Angolan troops made me laugh so much that night: they have a good sense of humour. All night our artillery was bombarding the Fapla positions. The shells were coming over our heads making the same whistling noise as we'd been hearing all day from the Fapla artillery shells. Eventually they were all making the whistling sound together when they heard a shell coming. And then they broke into fits of giggles and started slapping each other's hands, thighs and backs. They were just showing me that their spirits weren't broken after spending all day under fire from artillery and airplanes in terrible heat.'

Major Van Staden and his troops walked to their camouflaged vehicles on the Viposto High Ground on 26 February and drove back to tactical HQ without mishaps or interruptions – except for those caused by Van Staden reaching for his binoculars to identify some eagle which had landed and other feathered birds.

'We were pretty pleased with ourselves when we got back to the tactical HQ,' said Van Staden. 'We were the only unit which had achieved its goal, and we did it with only one shot fired in anger. I'm sure that if the armour hadn't got stuck in the minefield we could have finished the whole Tumpo thing that day, because the Fapla infantry just ran. They weren't willing to fight.

'I was pretty proud, too, of how cool and sane the men had stayed during the artillery barrage. There were nearly 60 heavy guns and rockets firing on us all day from across the Cuito. Brigadier Fido Smit, at brigade staff HQ in Rundu, had made academic studies of warfare and he told me later that more artillery and aircraft bombs had fallen around us that day than in the whole battle for Delville Wood.' (Some 2,700 South African soldiers died in the five-day First World War Battle for Delville Wood, in northern France, in July 1916.)

CHAPTER 34

MIKE MULLER LEADS THE SECOND TUMPO ATTACK: 29 FEBRUARY 1988

Colonel Pat McLoughlin decided that next time the way to overcome the problems encountered on 25 February would be to launch a night attack against the Tumpo Triangle. McLoughlin again asked Mike Muller to lead the assault.

McLoughlin's rationale was that the SADF's greatly superior night fighting techniques and training would at last achieve the final SADF military goal of driving the last living Fapla soldier from the east bank of the Cuito River. Night combat would enable the South African artillery to come into play and would neutralise Angolan Air Force superiority over the Tumpo battlefield.

[Although the SAAF was balked at Tumpo, it continued raids elsewhere. On 19 and 25 February waves of Mirage F-1AZs, flying low over dried-up river beds, broke through the formidable Fapla radar and missile defences in southwest Angola and struck at the important airbase town of Lubango, 300 km inside Angola, and at Ongiva, further south.

The targets were SWAPO bases – in revenge for the planting of a bomb by SWAPO at the First National Bank at Oshakati, the SADF's northwest Namibian HQ, which killed 20 people and badly injured six others, including the daughter of the pro-SWAPO Lutheran Bishop of Ovamboland, Cleophas Dumeni.

The prime target for the SAAF was the Tobias Hanyeko Training Centre, SWAPO's most important military training institution ten kilometres from Lubango, where more than 20 people were killed. The SAAF seems to have broken through a 'window' when much of the enemy radar system was out of action for routine checking. Captain Banca Armindo Fraternidade, commander of Fapla's 35 Brigade, admitted to Jan Raath, a southern Africa correspondent with *The Times* of London, that the radar was sometimes 'rested' for maintenance.][1]

Muller this time was to take the northern attack line, coming through from the laager area 40 km east of the Chambinga High Ground, up the gentle but thickly forested High Ground eastern slope, and then down Heartbreak Hill towards the Tumpo Triangle. At his disposal Muller had two squadrons of Olifant tanks, a Ratel-90 squadron, a company of mechanised infantry in Ratels, two 32 Battalion infantry companies, an engineer section, a mortar platoon, an EW team, a medical unit and two battalions of UNITA infantry. 4 SAI was again kept in reserve, except for four Ratel-90s and a platoon of 30 mechanised infantry who were to deploy southeast of the Tumpo Triangle as a deception tactic.

McLoughlin scheduled the attack for the night of Monday 29 February 1988, to continue into the Tuesday.

'We began moving out of the laager later than scheduled because the mine rollers (special flails attached to the front of a tank to detonate land mines) had not arrived,' said Muller. 'Eventually they found two of the rollers and by 9 pm we were on the Chambinga High Ground approaching the summit of Heartbreak Hill. Soft rain was falling and it was very misty, with visibility only 20 to 30 m. Five of my tank drivers reported faulty night periscopes, and when the rain fell harder I requested permission to delay the attack until first light.'

McLoughlin reluctantly agreed to the delay. Muller's main force began moving again before first light and by 10 am had crossed the *Anhara Lipanda* and had pushed about 1,000 m along the southern bank of the Dala River from its source and entered an area of very thick bush inside the Tumpo Triangle.

'I was puzzled and uneasy about how quiet everything was,' said Muller, who had denied permission to his tank gunners to fire at identified Stalin Organ positions on the Cuito west bank for fear of giving away the position of his advancing force. The Fapla artillery was inactive except for a few Stalin Organ ripples which posed no threat to us. I slowed our movement down, going forward in bounds of just 100 m at a time and, later, even less.

'By late morning we were about four kilometres northeast of the Cuito bridge and were very nearly at the edge of the bushline bordering the Cuito floodplain. It was then that our friend, the cloud cover, began to lift, and just before midday we were warned that the first wave of Mig-21s and Mig-23s was on its way. Fortunately, they bombed their own positions and ZU-23 emplacements opened up to frighten off their own planes. One of the Mig-23s was hit and crashed. I thought it had been hit by one of Fapla's 23 mm guns. UNITA thought it had been hit by a Fapla ground-to-air missile. Our SADF intelligence blokes were convinced it was taken out by a UNITA Stinger.'

As Muller continued to probe forward his lead tank, equipped with a mine roller, began to detonate mines in the bushline. The noise drew very heavy ZU-23 and 120 mm mortar fire.

'The M-46s were not involved because by then we were within their minimum range. I ordered my tank and Ratel commanders to spread out for a fire belt action against the Fapla gun emplacements. That lasted for fifty minutes with support from our G-5 artillery who picked off some of their gun positions. We advanced to within about 3,000 m of the Cuito bridge. Other weapons, including 82 mm B-10 recoilless anti-tank guns, AGS-17 fragmentation grenade launchers and Sagger anti-tank missiles, opened up against us until we had fire from some 20 gun positions coming at us from in front and on both flanks.

'I can't begin to describe to you how incredibly heavy the encounter was, but I was assured afterwards by senior officers that in terms of shell volume it was one of the biggest and toughest engagements fought by the SADF since World War II. We fired many hundreds of rounds from the Olifants, the Ratels and our mortars, and gradually we began to pick off their gun positions.

'The enemy's 23 mm guns were again particularly daunting. UNITA suffered very badly. They were our main infantry, responsible for killing enemy infantry carrying RPG-7s on the ground within range of the Olifants while our tank and Ratel guns concentrated on the enemy tanks and artillery emplacements.

'Those 23 mms were just wiping the UNITA blokes off the tanks. If I close my eyes now I can still see it clearly. The first 23 mm fire we drew came from the west bank of the Cuito and it went over our heads. Then a burst came between the Olifants and the Ratels. You only *see* the 23 mm tracers. There's so much other noise that you don't hear the shots. In front of my command Ratel there was an Olifant with five UNITA infantrymen sitting on its engine plate. When that 23 mm burst came they began leaping off to take cover. As they jumped off one of them was hit in the face with a 23 mm shell. His head just disintegrated.'

All through the fire belt action Muller's force was standing in the middle of a heavy minefield. It was a big headache for him, but plenty of other problems were developing. He had set out on the Tumpo Two adventure with only 16 of the 22 Olifants in the two tank squadrons available because of maintenance problems and logistics incompetence.

Even before the force had drawn enemy fire five of the tanks had broken down and been removed to the assembly areas by ARVs. 'Their oil and fuel filters were clogging and the engines were overheating,' said Muller. 'They had fought for more than 800 hours through several battles without servicing, mainly because none of the heavy jack and lifting equipment had arrived, equipment the tiffies had been continually requesting from Pretoria.

'No other tank in the world could have gone on for that long in those conditions and with all that dust without major servicing. We were very proud of them, but it was unfortunate that they began going through their threshold of endurance during this battle. The tiffies got no rest. They worked all night fixing up the vehicles. Then they fought all day with us in the ARVs ready to repair vehicles or pull them out. They performed miracles, but some marvels were beyond their powers.

'Our logistics were very stretched. Some spares were too heavy to be brought in by aircraft or helicopter. Our replacement power packs (engines, plus the attached automatic transmission) for the Olifants had to be brought in on transporters all the way from Rundu for hundreds of kilometres by night through the bush. By the time they reached us most of the power pack units were badly damaged. Sometimes the units had fallen through the floor of the transporter because of the bad terrain and the poor driving.

'The control was poor. There were no senior officers with some of the convoys. The young blokes just got in and drove like they were in stock cars. It needed old heads to remind them all the time to slow down, and to jump on them if they took no notice.'

Muller decided to pull back for 700 m out of the minefield to regroup and try to find a route for bridging the obstacle with a minimum aim of destroying all the 23 mm gun positions. During the withdrawal one Ratel detonated a mine, but the tiffies repaired the damage and had it back in action after 30 minutes.

By the time Muller had regrouped, his tank commanders were reporting to him that only five of the Olifants were now working as one after another they passed through the 'serviceability' threshold. To add to Muller's woes, the artillery commanders were reporting similar problems with the ailing G-5s.

Muller withdrew a little further to consider his options. Taking into account his intelligence briefing of the night before that there were at least 10 tanks inside the Tumpo Triangle to be dealt with, Muller

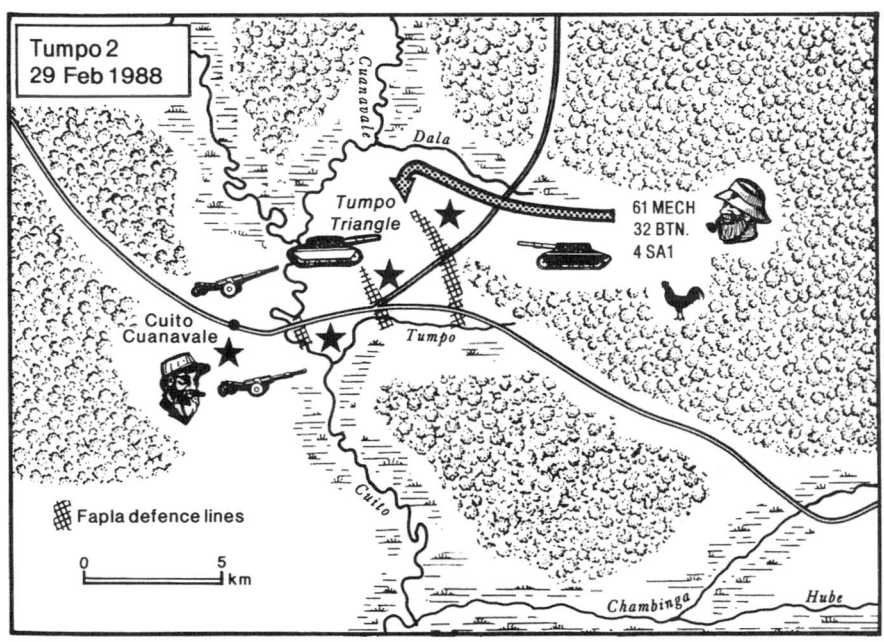

decided to ask permission to break off the engagement. The odds were too much in favour of the enemy.

On return to the laager, military intelligence gave Muller an updated report that sent his spirits plunging. 'They said they had discovered there were not ten enemy tanks but only two in the Triangle. If I had known *that* we would have continued right through and settled the whole matter.'

Note
1   *The Times,* London (29 February 1988).

CHAPTER 35

JAW-JAW BEGINS TO SUPPLANT WAR-WAR

The first two Tumpo failures contributed to a major joint reassessment by the SADF generals with the battlefield commanders at colonel and commandant levels on how to proceed next. Tumpo One probably failed because, inexplicably, no follow-up night assault was ordered from brigade level when the Fapla infantry were clearly in a state of panic and on the run. Tumpo Two failed because military intelligence gave the SADF's fighting men an over-estimate of the enemy tank strength and because of serious logistics problems as different major weapons, which had been at the battlefront for months, began to fail.

The national servicemen from 4 SAI and 61 Mech were in need of a rest from the physical and psychological punishments of the war zone. Toleration limits vary dramatically between men. But, denials notwithstanding at the highest levels of the SADF, the nervous breakdown of the Artillery Regiment captain with Major Tinus van Staden's 32 Battalion infantrymen was just the tip of a very complex iceberg at the beginning of March 1988.

Dust, dirt, heat, disease, flies, mosquitoes, lack of fresh fruit, vegetables and meat, and the sheer strain, fatigue and tension of constant presence in one of the most remote and unpleasant war zones on earth were taking a toll of the fighting men. They were passing through the same kind of critical thresholds as their weapons and machines. To this day young men who fought opposite Cuito Cuanavale are being treated by psychiatrists for a severe nervous condition called post-traumatic stress syndrome.

To surmount the problem of excessive wear and tear on men and machines, the generals decided to replace the 4 SAI and 61 Mech men of 20 SA Brigade with fresh soldiers and equipment from 82 SA Brigade which Colonel Paul Fouché had been sent back to form in the Republic from among the bank clerks, car mechanics and farmers of the Citizen Force.

20 SA Brigade began its withdrawal on 4 March 1988 with the arrival of the first Citizen Force units of 82 SA Brigade – elements of a Ratel squadron from the Regiment Mooi Rivier and G-5 gunners from the Potchefstroom University Artillery Regiment.

On Tuesday 8 March, 20 SA Brigade's Colonel Pat McLoughlin handed over to 82 SA Brigade's Colonel Fouché. It marked the end of Operation Hooper and the beginning of a new phase in the War for Africa, Operation Packer. But, more far-reachingly, it served as a major landmark in southern African history, presaging changes of breathtaking scale and speed throughout the subcontinent.

★ ★ ★

Forces were now at work way beyond the control of the battlefield commanders and barely within the mastery of the Chief of the Defence Force, General Jannie Geldenhuys, and his senior generals. In much the same way as South Africa's fighting men and war machines were passing beyond vital limits of potency, so many external forces were reaching critical junctures.

The deepest secrets of international imperatives underlying and suffusing the War for Africa at this crucial stage will only emerge once personalities like Chester Crocker and South Africa's Director-General of Foreign Affairs, Neil van Heerden, write their memoirs and when Castroist conformist orthodoxy crumbles in Cuba to allow that side's true story to be told. But enough evidence and clues already exist to show that diplomacy was beginning to shape the War for Africa rather more than the conflict was influencing the art of lying for one's country.

★ ★ ★

The tentative Cuban knock on the door of South Africa's New York UN Mission in late November 1987 to explore a possible negotiated end to the War for Africa opened the way to something more substantial. A major breakthrough came in late January 1988 when Angola and Cuba told the United States at a meeting in Luanda that they accepted the necessity for all 50,000 Cuban troops in Angola to be withdrawn.

Following the meeting between Chester Crocker, Angolan Foreign Minister Afonso Van Dunem Mbinda and Cuban Politburo member Jorge Risquet, US State Department spokesman Charles Redman told reporters on 1 February 1988 in Washington: 'The Angolan delegation for the first time affirmed its acceptance of the necessity of the withdrawal of all Cuban troops from Angola in the context of a settlement. Cuban officials concurred in this decision.'

The Crocker–Van Dunem–Risquet act was an interesting one. Risquet, a smiling, bearded man, was one of Fidel Castro's most senior lieutenants. He was in charge of foreign affairs in the Cuban Communist Party Politburo and was one of the small group of guerrillas who had fought with Castro and Che Guevara in the Sierra Maestra in the 1950s against the Batista regime. Risquet, however, was not an unbending dogmatist. Within the narrow limits of permitted debate in Cuba, he had demonstrated a certain independence of mind. On one occasion, during a spell as Minister of Labour, Risquet had dared to voice the 'bourgeois' viewpoint that it was logical for a worker, even 'of a complete revolutionary outlook,' to be concerned about the family budget!

As the talks progressed over subsequent months, Risquet became known as Oom [Uncle] Kaspaas to the South African negotiators after a popular Afrikaans cartoon character.

Van Dunem was reputed to be a 'moderate' in the MPLA government, willing to consider talking to UNITA rather than pursuing endlessly an elusive 'ultimate' military solution. He demonstrated his subtlety by bringing to subsequent talks his Justice Minister, Mr Fernandes van Dunem, a former law professor in Belgium who surprised the South Africans with his knowledge of Afrikaans poetry.

Chester Crocker, in his sombre suits and behind horn-rimmed spectacles and conservative moustache, looked more like a dull and dowdy English country solicitor than a man who was perhaps the finest conceptual thinker ever to have served in a United States presidential administration. The Reagan Administration in which Crocker served had indicated right from the beginning, in January 1981, that Washington would never recognise the MPLA government as long as a single Cuban soldier remained on Angolan soil. But pressure on Angola to get rid of the Cubans would have to be part of a more complex game-plan for the whole southern African region.

The rough outline was that South Africa should be offered conciliatory and feasible terms for getting out of Namibia. That prospect would be used as a lever for a Cuban withdrawal from Angola to be followed by an MPLA/UNITA power-sharing arrangement. The co-operation of black Organisation of African Unity states with all of this was to be secured with a promise of open elections in Namibia, a talisman for OAU pride.

The Reagan Administration's policy was christened 'constructive engagement' because it involved South Africa as a legitimate participant in a general process of change in southern and central Africa, rather than as the accused in the dock. The original author of 'constructive engagement' was the then Professor of African Studies at Georgetown University, Washington – Dr Chester Crocker, Reagan's nominee as his government minister in charge of Africa.

Crocker was seen as intelligent but conservative by Jimmy Carter/Edward Kennedy-inclined liberal Democrats. On the other hand, he was regarded as a dangerous liberal by the Republican right wing in Congress, who withheld confirmation of his nomination for several months.

Crocker was too cerebral by half for many of the right-wingers, but if they had read carefully his writings on southern Africa the more discerning ones should have been able to see that his proposals for the region were by no means conventionally liberal. In the particular case of Angola, they spelled problems for the MPLA and Cubans for years to come.

In one article on the Namibia-Angola problem Crocker noted that Namibia was top of the Western calendar for most liberal democrats while the Angolan war was hardly on it at all.[1] Somehow, according to this mindset, the Cuban and Soviet presence in Angola was legitimate or justified until Namibia was settled and UNITA defeated. Crocker argued differently.

'Angola is the logical focal point for policy,' he said. 'It is in Angola, after all, that anti-communist forces are effectively engaged in trying to liberate their country from the new imperialism of Moscow and its allies.

'This process should be encouraged with the aim of getting the Cubans out so that a genuine political reconciliation can take place. As for Namibia, while a settlement is important there, it will not by itself end the Angolan strife, because Savimbi is by no means the tool of South Africa. He could continue to operate with the active support of other African states and governments elsewhere.

'Accordingly, the West should back UNITA until such time as the MPLA is prepared to negotiate and expel the communist forces from Angola. Namibia, according to this argument, is a separate and less important issue.'

Unlike so many of his Western contemporaries at that time, Crocker was prepared to see and understand the rich complexities of central and southern Africa. 'The region will be shaped by forces more substantial and concrete than journalistic conventions like "racist regimes" and "Marxist guerrillas",' he observed.

Crocker played his cards long and cogently. Many years later, when the situation had been transformed, Crocker said one of the considerations, or principles, which had imbued his strategy was realism. Namibia could not be treated in isolation from its regional context; it needed to be linked to the problem of neighbouring Angola.

After the January 1988 Luanda meeting, more responsibility fell on Crocker than anyone else to devise a level-headed, face-saving frame-work that would enable Cuban good intentions to be converted into sound practice.

There were plenty of obstacles. Angola's MPLA government took the line that it would accept a timetable for the withdrawal of 'all' Cuban troops provided South Africa and the United States stopped giving aid to UNITA; South African troops were withdrawn from Namibia; Namibia was granted independence under the terms of United Nations Resolution 435; and international guarantees were given for the security of Angola.

The MPLA proposed no timetable for Cuban withdrawal, but Crocker asked that it prepare one as soon as possible. Crocker declined to give any undertaking on behalf of Washington on the suspension of

US aid to UNITA. President Reagan and his supporters in Congress were unwilling to sacrifice UNITA as part of a Namibia deal linked to Cuban troop withdrawal.

The initial hostility of most South Africans towards the new MPLA position was tempered at key high levels of the Ministry of Foreign Affairs by a message that the Soviet Union, for years the MPLA's main patron and bankroller, was firmly behind the plan for the Cubans to leave Angola. The intermediary from the Soviets was the flamboyant rightwing West German politician Franz Josef Strauss, Prime Minister of Bavaria, who had managed remarkably over the years to maintain close relationships with both the Moscow and Pretoria governments.

Strauss, visiting southern Africa in late January 1988, immediately after meeting Soviet Foreign Minister Eduard Shevardnadze in Bonn, told South African Foreign Minister Pik Botha at a secret meeting place in the Kalahari Desert that the Soviet Union wanted to find a political solution to the Angolan problem because it had concluded that a military one was not possible.

Botha's ears pricked up particularly sharply when Strauss told him that Soviet Leader Mikhail Gorbachev, who with his philosophy of 'new thinking' was rigorously reassessing every aspect of Soviet policy, no longer considered South Africa was 'ripe for revolution' and believed that a peaceful negotiated settlement of the country's internal problems would be in everybody's best interests. At about this time Neil van Heerden established a specialist Soviet desk in Pretoria for the first time since the early 1960s and organised a conference to examine the possibility that the Soviets could be trusted in negotiations.

In early February Crocker and Pik Botha met each other at the South African Embassy in Geneva, Switzerland, soon after the former had again met Van Dunem and Risquet in Luanda and the latter Strauss in the desert. Significantly, an unnamed representative of the South African Defence Force, probably General Geldenhuys, was also present at the Geneva meeting.

Crocker told Botha and the high-ranking SADF officer that the MPLA and the Cubans were now ready to talk. A senior official of the South African Ministry of Foreign Affairs present at the Crocker-Botha meeting said: 'We came home and examined the whole thing at many different levels and we concluded that, yes, we should explore the new opportunity.

'The cabinet took the final decision, and the matter was also discussed in the National Security Council, but it was our (the Foreign Ministry's) recommendation that we go ahead.'[2]

In March 1988 Neil van Heerden and one of his top men at the Ministry of Foreign Affairs, Mr Derek Auret, flew to Washington to meet Crocker secretly and ask him for more clarity and firm details on how he intended to proceed. A few days later a letter was delivered to Pik Botha in Pretoria from Crocker proposing exploratory formal talks in London between the MPLA, the Cubans and the South Africans with the Americans playing the role of 'facilitator'.

Meanwhile, Cuban and Angolan officials in Luanda presented a paper to visiting American State Department officials suggesting that all Cuban troops leave Angola over a *four-year period*. The proposal included provisions for phased redeployment of Cuban troops towards the north during the withdrawal process. Although the offer was still conditional on the US and South Africa stopping all aid to UNITA, South African troops withdrawing from Angola, and Namibia being granted independence under United Nations supervision, the US negotiators saw the proposal as an encouraging development.

The US followed up the Luanda meeting with a fresh round of talks with Pik Botha on a chilly winter's day, 14 March, in Geneva. Botha subsequently presented a tough posture in public, saying the Cuban/ Angolan proposal lacked 'numbers, figures and timetables'. At the same time, President P W Botha, reacting to the Luanda demand for the withdrawal of the SADF from Angola, said: 'We are staying in Angola until the Cubans leave.'

Pik Botha, however, was privately delighted by what Crocker told him in Geneva. The two men agreed that the way was now undoubtedly open for the Cubans to leave Angola in exchange for the independence of Namibia – a far cry from the early *machismo* days of Cuban involvement in Angola, when Castro said his forces were on a sacred internationalist mission in support of Cuba's co-ideologues, the MPLA, and that there could be no trade-off over Namibia.

Botha left Geneva for Pretoria believing that he was on the verge of a diplomatic triumph. The Cuban departure would amount to a *de facto* South African victory in Angola after one-and-a-half decades of warfare. The Cuban withdrawal would enable him and other 'reformers' in the cabinet to sell to the Republic's white electorate the idea of throwing off the Namibian millstone. In turn, without a Cuban military threat in the region, it might then become possible for the South African government to embark upon the difficult task of internal political reform. But, meanwhile, the War for Africa went on.

Notes

1   Chester Crocker, with Mario Greznes and Robert Henderson, 'Southern Africa: A US Policy for the 80s', *Africa Report* (January–February 1981).
2   *Sunday Star*, Johannesburg (9 April 1989).

CHAPTER 36

GERHARD LOUW LEADS THE THIRD TUMPO ATTACK: 23 MARCH 1988

Commandant Gerhard Louw was appointed a tank and armoured car instructor at the South African Army Battle School at Lohatla in the dry brown expanses of northern Cape Province in early January 1988. Tall, erect and broad-shouldered, Louw was a highly disciplined career officer in his early thirties who took his soldiering very seriously. In his intensity, he bore more resemblance at first acquaintance to an officer of the British school than the more anarchic and quarrelsome Boer tradition.

Battle School's main responsibility was to keep the Citizen Force, comprising almost 80 per cent of total army strength, up to scratch with modern warfare techniques during its periodic call-up sessions. Citizen Force tank soldiers from the Orange Free State's Regiment President Steyn were mobilised in Bloemfontein at the beginning of February 1988 for Colonel Paul Fouché's 82 SA Brigade. Louw moved to the School of Armour in Bloemfontein for a fortnight to help resident instructors prepare the Citizen Force men for battle. They were helped by men from 4 SAI and 61 Mech who had already fought in the front line of the War for Africa.

Louw and the team of instructors flew from Lohatla to Rundu at the end of February to await the overland arrival of Regiment President Steyn with its pristine tanks. Louw established a training area six kilometres inside Angola from Rundu and continued preparing the Citizen Force men there until 10 March, when 61 Mech and 4 SAI passed them on the way out with their battle-fatigued Olifants.

'We didn't really have enough time to train the men thoroughly,' said Louw. 'In the nature of things, it takes more time to get men who have been back in civilian life ready for battle than it does career soldiers or national servicemen.

'Our life wasn't made easier by logistical problems. One of the two tank squadrons of Regiment President Steyn came all the way from Bloemfontein to Angola without its mounted 7.62 mm machine-guns. We had to get the men used to the terrain, the climate and the equipment and train them in drills, tactics and co-ordination in a very short time. When the time came to move deep into Angola they still weren't fully operational, mainly because we'd been hampered by ammunition shortages and equipment shortfalls and failures.'

Louw had travelled to Rundu and across the border to put the Regiment President Steyn through more intensive training before waving them off to the warfront and returning to his instructor's post at Lohatla. But in January and February 1988 South Africa was hit by its heaviest rainfall and worst floods in decades. The farm and home of President Steyn's Citizen Force commandant were seriously damaged by the floods.

'His business was virtually swept away,' said Louw. 'He faced terrible financial troubles, and so he was unable to assume command. As the man on the spot, I was asked to take over command of the two Citizen Force tank squadrons and lead them into battle, even though I was Permanent Force.'

While the training continued, Louw heard that Mike Muller's second attack on Tumpo had failed. It did not surprise him. In his capacity as an armour instructor, he was deeply sceptical about the wisdom of sending tank forces into open ground sown with minefields and enfiladed by a formidable array of heavy artillery overlooking the battleground.

Louw sent the A and B Olifant squadrons of Regiment President Steyn off to the Brigade tactical HQ east of the Chambinga High Ground. The Citizen Force men got their taste of the harshness of the Land at the End of the Earth as they ploughed day and night through the deep sand of the vague tracks in the forests and across the grasslands of southeast Angola. Louw himself moved back to Rundu in a Ratel, and was flown from there with his training team to the tactical HQ to receive his orders for a third tank attack on Tumpo from Colonel Paul Fouché.

Louw now had to overcome a typical problem thrown up by the half-cock conduct of the latter phases of the War for Africa, with the battlefield officers never quite knowing from day to day what new limitations or expectations might be placed on them by the politicians and diplomats.

'When South Africa called up its first troops for the campaign, they were committed piecemeal, with mechanised infantry designated for the primary role,' said Louw. 'Thus 4 SAI was committed with a tank squadron attached under the command of a mechanised infantry commandant and his infantry battalion HQ. The same went for 61 Mech.

'As operations evolved it became clear that the "subordinate" tanks were the most effective weapons in bush that, theoretically, was infantry terrain unsuitable for tank warfare. The enemy fought with tanks, and the UNITA infantry couldn't face them effectively. The enemy infantry had the same problem with the Olifants.

'As it became clear that our tanks and Ratels were achieving more successes – the armour of the Olifants was not penetrated once by enemy fire – and as our artillery demonstrated its superiority, the South African infantry took a less and less prominent role, especially in view of our orders to keep casualties to an absolute minimum.

'But something was wrong with the analysis when 82 SA Brigade was formed. The Citizen Force units called up did not constitute a full tank regiment, even though it was perceived the battle would be based on a tank regiment-led assault. The units called up were structured in the same way as those which had just been withdrawn. I was a whole squadron of 11 tanks short to be able to form a proper regiment. I had no proper regimental HQ, only two infantry battalion HQ structures as provided for 61 Mech and 4 SAI. That made my tactical problems very complicated and involved. I had to form a makeshift regimental HQ with only one tank and with the rest of the staff supplied by a De La Rey Citizen Force infantry battalion. It was frustrating and time-consuming.'

Once Louw had established his rough and ready HQ, he began last-minute training of the President Steyn tank squadrons in regimental tactics, marrying up with the De La Rey infantrymen and the soldiers of UNITA's 5th Regular Battalion. Louw was shocked to find that the UNITA battalion was way below its ideal strength of 700 men because of combat attrition. 'By the time HQ personnel, signallers, cooks, bottlewashers and the rest had been taken into account, they only had about 200 fighters.'

The generals, having wind of Crocker's and Botha's ambitions, pressed Colonel Fouché to get on with Tumpo Three before the military were overtaken by diplomatic events. Fouché, plagued by similar logistics problems to those which had bedevilled Pat McLoughlin, secured one postponement of the attack. But in due course he was able to signal Brigadier Fido Smit in Rundu that Tumpo Three would be launched in the early hours of Wednesday 23 March 1988.

Commandant Gerhard Louw's mission was to drive the enemy out of the Tumpo area; hold the captured terrain until last light on 23 March; and allow field engineers, two companies of infantry from 32 Battalion, UNITA's 5th Regular Battalion and recces from 4 Reconnaissance Commando to move in to blow up, once and for all and comprehensively, the bridge across the Cuito River.

Louw's force to deliver the final SADF blow in the battles east of the Cuito River was assembled and moving into its positions by the afternoon of 22 March. Louw's own main attack formation comprised the A and B Olifant squadrons of Regiment President Steyn, plus the Regiment Mooi Rivier Ratel squadron and two mechanised infantry battalions of the Regiment De La Rey and Regiment Groot Karoo.

The Artillery Regiment Potchefstroom University provided support in the form of one battery of G-5s and one battery of World War II-vintage G-2 guns with a maximum range of scarcely 16 km. The mobilisation of the G-2s was an indication both of the degree of punishment the G-5s had undergone and of the limited production of the weapon to that date.[1] 44 Parachute Brigade provided a 120 mm mortar battery and 19 Rocket Regiment a troop of four MRLs.

Besides its 5th Regular Battalion, UNITA also sent into battle its 3rd and 4th Regular Battalions and two semi-regular battalions on the east bank of the Cuito. Another two semi-regular battalions were deployed on the west bank to launch hit-and-run attacks on outlying Fapla positions around Cuito Cuanavale.

Major Tinus van Staden's three 32 Battalion companies operated over the Chambinga High Ground and down Heartbreak Hill, to the south of Louw's planned northern attack line, towards the *Anhara Lipanda*. Van Staden was reinforced by an infantry company and anti-tank and anti-aircraft units from the Regiment Groot Karoo.

In the days leading up to Tumpo Three, 32 Battalion and Groot Karoo troops were assigned various tasks. 32 Battalion, assisted by UNITA's 4th Regular Battalion, deployed on the steep western slope of the Chambinga High Ground with the dual responsibility of sweeping the area for mines in advance of Louw's attack and stopping any Fapla reconnaissance patrols from moving east of the *Anhara Lipanda*.

The UNITA 4th Battalion performed impressively, lifting more than 200 mines in early March. Liaising with them was 32 Battalion's Lieutenant Thai Theron, Captain Piet van Zyl's friend who had vowed the previous November at the "Club Méditerranée" lagoon that if he ever lost a leg in warfare he would commit suicide.

On 9 March Thai Theron, on night patrol on the *Anhara Lipanda*, stepped on a Soviet anti-personnel mine and his right foot was blasted away. Theron was removed quickly by helicopter. After surgery he was fitted with an artificial foot. Theron did not take his own life, and after extensive physiotherapy he returned to 32 Battalion to become Van Staden's second-in-command in the training unit.

The Regiment Groot Karoo units attached to 32 Battalion were very active southeast of the Tumpo River in an attempt to distract Fapla's attention from the direction of the main attack. The Groot Karoo men built simulated bridges, made obvious movements and generally made a lot of noise.

The SAAF went into action again in an attempt to soften up the enemy. Mirage F-IAZs made two bombing attacks right into the Tumpo Triangle, but after another raid on 19 March on the Fapla battalion stationed at Baixo Longa, 80 km southwest of Cuito Cuanavale, fresh tragedy struck. Ed Every's flying colleague and friend from 1 Squadron, Major Willie van Coppenhagen, crashed and was killed in northern Namibia on his way back to Grootfontein. He had reported no problems or damage after the attack, and the Air Force inquiry team concluded that he had developed a technical problem, temporarily lost orientation while trying to deal with it, and crashed before he could make good.

★ ★ ★

Louw's force moved out from Brigade tactical HQ about 4 pm on Tuesday 22 March and reached the assembly area on the eastern slope of the Chambinga High Ground just before dusk at 7pm. 'Logistics had been a constant nightmare while we were getting prepared.' said Louw. 'A lot of vital equipment I had been asking for reached us only just in time, things like night vision periscopes which were needed for the movement we faced in darkness, heavy machine-guns for one of the tank squadrons and "chest boxes" for the signallers.'

In the assembly area Louw established a logistics supply point and rearranged his tanks and the trucks carrying UNITA infantry into a column consisting of two 'line ahead' formations moving parallel to each other. It fell dark as the column moved forward. Louw established a surgical post as his force went down Heartbreak Hill, heading for the 'waiting area' on the eastern edge of the northern lobe of the *Anhara Lipanda*, due east of the source of the Dala River.

'We got lost once on the way,' said Louw. 'A recce group had gone out and plotted the route, and they actually led the advance. But the terrain was all sand-dune hills covered with trees, and we came to one point where a lot of sandy tracks met and then split. The recces got confused in the dark and took the wrong route. They realised after about a kilometre, but you can't turn around an armoured column in most conditions, let alone those.' The recces scouted south to find the lost track, and then led the column through dense bush to rejoin the appointed route.

A 32 Battalion company was at the 'waiting area', about six kilometres from the forward Fapla trenches manned by 25 Brigade, when Louw's column began moving in at 4 am on 23 March. The black Angolans of 32 Battalion had marked the final part of the line of attack for Louw with 'close sticks', which are implanted in the ground and, once their tops have been broken off, glow with a greenish phosphorescence from the chemicals inside.

'I was supposed to start moving at 6 am, but the sky was overcast and it was still dark,' said Louw. 'I decided to postpone my advance until 6.15 when we could see better to change our night periscopes for day periscopes. The night periscopes are heavy and it's not a simple action. I wanted to move out with day periscopes so that we weren't faced with the problem of changing them in the middle of the battle itself.'

UNITA's infantrymen took position on the engine plates of the Olifants as the tanks moved out onto the *Anhara Lipanda*. After about a kilometre the first enemy artillery fire began. 'For those of us in the tanks, it was no hassle,' said Louw. 'An artillery round only really endangers a tank with a direct hit. The UNITA men were OK at that stage as well because the artillery fire was very inaccurate and sporadic.

'Then as we moved forward we received a radio warning of an enemy air raid. The drill on such occasions is for tanks to scatter on order from the commander. But they dispersed like cockroaches in a floodlit kitchen without waiting for the command. I bawled them out on the radio, not least because the planes proved to be our own Mirages trying to bombard 25 Brigade. They had to pull out of the attack because the cloud was too dense. I pulled the tanks together again in double column, and we were going along quite well on Mike Muller's earlier tracks when our artillery opened up on the enemy positions.

'Once we were across the *Anhara Lipanda* we could just see Cuito Cuanavale itself to the southwest across the Cuito River. It was then that we hit our first minefield. We were still in columns of two, but only one mine roller had arrived and the right-hand column had to enter the minefield without an advance roller. There was a bang. A mine had blown a track from one of the tanks and a bogey wheel came flying over my head.'

Louw halted the advance and called field engineers forward to clear a way through the minefield. It was now about 9 am. One of two *plofadders* with Louw's force was moved forward. Five hundred kilos of explosive in the *plofadder* sausage string shot out. But the braking mechanism did not release the rocket properly, so the sausage failed to stretch right across the minefield, and, yet again, the *plofadder* failed to detonate automatically.

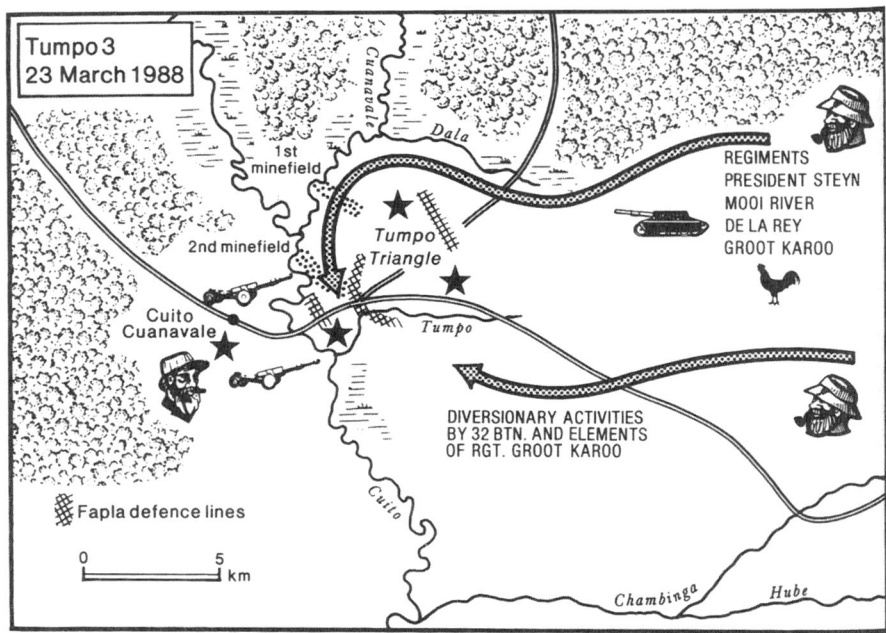

The engineers prodded their way forward to the front end of the *plofadder* and detonated it manually. But they reported back to Louw that because it had not deployed right across the minefield the obstacle had not yet been properly breached.

'I ordered the other *plofadder* forward,' said Louw. 'It fired from the same position and deployed properly, but once again it did not detonate automatically. The engineers went forward this time in a Ratel to detonate from the front. The Ratel hit an anti-personnel mine, which blew one of its tyres, so the engineers went the rest of the way to the front on foot with mine-detecting equipment, plucking out a few more anti-personnel mines by hand on the way. Then they detonated the *plofadder* manually.

'All this held up the advance for two-and-a-half hours. Enemy artillery, particularly BM-21s, fired at us all the time. But everyone was quite calm. We weren't in real danger at that stage. We were on a slight slope coming up from the Dala River towards Cuito Cuanavale. We weren't visible and the rockets tended to pass over our heads and fall into the

Dala Valley: the *anhara* lining the river there became heavily pockmarked with blackened shell craters.'

Louw's tanks had encountered a 'warning' minefield of a very sophisticated defence system organised by Cuban General Ochoa Sanchez's top field commander, General Cintra Frias, in the Tumpo Triangle and Cuito Cuanavale area.

Cintra Frias had planned according to Soviet Army landmine operations doctrine. This states that the key purpose of a minefield is not so much to inflict damage on attacking vehicles as to channel them into predetermined kill zones covered by massed artillery fire and anti-tank missiles. The minefields, containing a variety of explosive devices, are sown in several belts, usually up to 300 m wide and 50 m or more deep.

Fapla's 25 Brigade had lost more than 150 men in the Tumpo Two battle, but the unit had not been destroyed. Cintra Frias made the survivors dig in deeply in well-prepared trenches and bunkers behind the minefield belts. They were supported by a formidable array of different artillery pieces immediately behind them within the Tumpo Triangle and on dominating higher ground on the west bank of the Cuito.

Directly behind 25 Brigade, in the Tumpo Triangle, was Fapla's 66 Brigade and 16 Brigade's old tactical armoured group, now dominated by the Cuban-manned 3rd Tank Battalion. Spare tanks had been brought across the Cuito on metal ferries until there were a dozen or more in firing positions behind 25 Brigade's lines. Any attacking force which reached Fapla's forward trenches would inevitably face a torrid reception from an enemy which had prepared skilfully in advantageous terrain, and whose confidence was high after beating back both the Tumpo One and the Tumpo Two attacks.

Louw moved the President Steyn tanks in single file across the minefield through the lane cleared by the two *plofadders*. They were led by the lone Olifant with a mine roller attachment. The Ratel squadron of the Regiment Mooi Rivier stayed back at this stage in a covering role.

'I sent A Squadron through first,' said Louw. 'I followed in my own command tank. B Squadron followed behind me. As we came over the rise above the Dala it was still overcast, but there was sun getting through and we could see the whole of Cuito Cuanavale spread out before us.

We now had to move down a slight slope and up another to get to the Tumpo area itself.

'We started drawing heavy fire because, for the first time, the Fapla could see exactly where we were. The dust clouds from the *plofadder* explosions had given them the first target pinpoint, and now they were firing at us with just about everything they had, including some Sagger anti-tank missiles passing overhead at more than 400 km per hour. It got heavier and heavier and more accurate.

'It was about midday. Despite the artillery barrage, I managed to get the A Squadron commander to get his tanks into combat formation. B Squadron to his left was having difficulties forming up. A Squadron started to move forward, but because the bush was very dense at that point I couldn't establish a link between the two squadrons. We had to stop A Squadron just as they were beginning to emerge from the trees into open area, which was Tumpo itself. The open area used to be subsistence farming land years ago: many trees had been cut down, so all that faced us from that point was open grass on sand on the east bank of the Cuito.

'Eventually I got B Squadron formed up and I ordered both squadrons to begin moving forward again in extended combat line abreast. Each tank was firing intensively at speculative targets as it advanced. The poor UNITA guys were beginning to take hideous casualties, especially from the 23 mm guns. Soon after the Olifants started moving three of them hit mines almost simultaneously. Fapla must have sown boosted mines because this time I saw not only bogey wheels but whole suspension units sailing through the air.

'I told everyone to stop and we went into a "fire girdle" action in which each tank commander fires independently whenever he thinks he has seen a target. The enemy had us pinned down in the minefield for the time being, and they had the chance of shooting out the Olifants one by one. Fortunately the minefield was just inside the treeline. If it had been on the open ground they would have knocked out more of us.

'One of our ARVs managed to tow out one of the tanks. A second ARV attached itself to another tank but couldn't move it. I moved my command Olifant to see what the problem was. A boosted mine had blown off the whole rear suspension unit and the tank had tilted and fallen into a hole, where it was stuck fast. I got out of my tank and directed the driver so that the ARV was towing the crippled Olifant and my tank was towing the ARV.

'By now the enemy seemed to be throwing everything towards us, including phosphorus bombs. Out of the corner of my eye, I saw missiles whistling over our heads. They had BM-14s and BM-21s firing horizontal rocket salvos at us from the opposite bank. Fortunately all the rockets landed in front of the tanks and the rocket boosters and motors tumbled over our heads and caused no losses. It was a big noise, of course, lots of noise and so much smoke and dust that I could barely see my tanks.

'Mortar shells landed all over the place and 23 mm slugs crashed through the sound barrier. We were in danger of being well and truly pinned down in a sea of mines, so I gave A Squadron permission to withdraw for a distance but then to stand firm and give cover while we extracted B Squadron.'

As Louw's Olifant and the ARV took the strain of attempting to pull out the tank with the destroyed suspension from its hole, they detonated several anti-personnel mines. 'It was strange that none of us had stepped on any of these, because we had been crawling all over the show to get the tows fixed,' said Louw.

The disabled tank proved impossible to move. 'The more we pulled it the deeper it dug into the sand.' said Louw. 'I decided we would have to cut loose and leave the tank in the minefield for the time being. I got out of my Olifant and ran to the damaged tank, rapped on the hatch and told the guys there to get out and run to my tank and the ARV.'

Louw returned to his command Olifant to make radio contact with Brigade HQ which was now in a state of high anxiety about the progress of the Tumpo Three attack. Louw told them to hold fast: he was trying to get the Olifants back into combat line. He leapt out of his tank again and ran between exploding mortars, rockets and bursts of 23 mm fire to the ARV, which was not on his radio net, to tell the tiffies to unhitch their tow from the Olifant.

'I got my own tank untied,' said Louw. 'That was no problem. But the ARV was attached to the stuck tank with an iron bar and shackle which had been under such strain that the bar buckled, leaving the Olifant virtually fused to the ARV. None of the tiffies' tools worked, and in the end they had to use a metal saw to get free.'

Louw turned his attention to the third damaged tank, the one with the mineroller attached. One of its tracks and a bogey wheel had been blown off. It was hitched up to three tanks in line from B Squadron, which were dragging the Olifant away at snail's pace as it scraped a deep furrow in the sand.

'The mineroller made the damaged tank extra heavy,' said Louw. 'We had techniques for disconnecting the roller quickly, but apparently nobody was willing to get out of the tank to do it. The towing was very difficult, and the squadron commander was concentrating so hard on the problem of maintaining movement that he was going in the wrong direction. He should have been moving northwards into the treeline away from the Fapla artillery. Instead, he was drifting eastwards, moving parallel to the enemy positions and offering a maximum target area.

'When you've got four heavy tanks moving tied together in that way they can't change direction quickly. If you turn at a sharp angle you can't drag 56 tonnes of armour and steel with you. The turn has to be gradual and smooth over a long distance. I ran across to the squadron commander and he reckoned it would take another kilometre and two hours, at the rate they were travelling, to change the formation's direction, by when they would be well past the entrance to the cleared lane through the first minefield.

'It was now about 2 pm. The artillery barrage had not let up at all, and, with the unexpected exertions the tanks had been guzzling fuel faster than expected. I asked for permission to break off the attack, and Colonel Fouché granted it.'

Louw decided that the tank in the hole and the mineroller tank could not be recovered without seriously endangering the withdrawal. All the shackles anchoring kinetic towing ropes to the mineroller tank had also bent so severely that they could not be detached. 'I gave orders to cut the towing ropes, but they were too tough for our military knives,' said Louw. 'Finally, we severed the ropes with machine-gun and automatic rifle fire.'

Louw walked to the now abandoned mineroller tank and, as he had with the other beleaguered Olifant, beat heavily on the battened hatch and ordered the crew to get out and scramble fast to the other tanks.

'There was no time for them to grab personal items,' he said. 'Bushes and the tops of trees were being swept away by the artillery and 23 mm fire. One shell hit my tank. I didn't know where at the time. I just heard a clang and the explosion. I drove it back and forward for a while, and since nothing seemed wrong I concluded that it couldn't have been a proper hit. But days later it was pointed out to me that the shell had hit my gun barrel and there was a big dent on the inside. If I had tried to fire, I would have ended up with a drastically shortened barrel!'

Louw now asked Colonel Fouché for permission to destroy the two crippled tanks since there was a real danger they would be captured by Fapla. General Kat Liebenberg, who was with Fouché at the Colonel's forward tactical HQ about 20 km from the battlefield, stepped in with an order that the Olifants were not to be wiped out but left in the minefield for recovery later.

'As we moved out we rolled over anti-personnel mines everywhere and detonated them,' said Louw. 'We carried several UNITA casevacs who had been wounded by artillery and mine shrapnel. At first, I couldn't find the entrance into the lane back through the first minefield. We wandered around in the bush and I was really scared that we were going to veer into the minefield and lose more tanks.

'I radioed for one of the Mooi Rivier Ratel-90s to move along the cleared lane and fire signal flares to mark his position so that we could move up to him.

'As we approached the entrance one of the Olifants threw its track. It had nothing to do with the mines. It was purely a mechanical mishap. We had no kinetic ropes left, so we had to leave that relatively undamaged tank behind for collection later while the rest went single file along the path cleared earlier by the *plofadders*.

'We moved through to a former hamlet called Cabarata, on the south bank of the Dala, where UNITA stayed more or less permanently. It was about 4.30 pm and the Fapla Migs were in the air for the first time that day. I don't know why they had been so inactive. They used the SAAF's "toss-bombing" technique, but the bombs landed far away from us. We put the tanks under the trees and camouflaged ourselves to the best of our ability. We were still within enemy artillery range, and when shells started landing among the tanks I thought, hell, let's get out of range, air warnings or no air warnings.'

Louw's force moved through the 'waiting area', dropped off the UNITA casualties at the surgical post and then moved to a point further north, where it spent the night out of artillery range before moving back on 24 March to its training area near Brigade tactical HQ.

Tumpo Three was the only clear defeat the SADF suffered in the War for Africa. The assault had achieved nothing for the South Africans. Many UNITA soldiers had been killed and wounded. Five Olifants were damaged, and only two of those had been recovered.

'We got orders on 25 March to destroy at all costs the three Olifants we had left behind, as we had wanted to do before we withdrew from the battlefield,' said Louw, who was subsequently decorated with the Honoris Crux for bravery for his conduct in the enemy minefields. 'But it was too late. A 4 Recce commander and UNITA special forces reported that Fapla and the Cubans had pushed out a company of infantry immediately after we withdrew to dig in around our tanks. We tried to devise all kinds of plans to penetrate their defensive perimeters and recover the Olifants, but we weren't able to implement them.'

The capture of the Olifants was a major propaganda and intelligence coup for Fapla and the Cubans. It enabled them to offer solid evidence for the version of history they were giving to the world – that they had won the War for Africa. They were aided and abetted in the propaganda war by the South African government which remained reluctant to come clean about the fighting and which shrank from the task of fully explaining the complex justifications for SADF involvement in Angola.

The Cubans and their Eastern Bloc allies no doubt found it interesting to analyse just which countries theoretically honouring the international arms embargo against Pretoria had helped develop the Olifant's classified advanced electronics and its modern fire-control system incorporating a laser range finder.

The loss of the Olifants was a classic example of one of the major blemishes of the SADF campaign – the failure of the generals, whether or not because of political pressure, to respect fundamental SADF doctrine that battlefield initiative should rest with the field commanders free from interference by higher officers. It was failure to respect this doctrine, and not any failure of the fighting men, that delivered South Africa's Olifants to its enemies.

All attempts at displacing Fapla and the Cubans from the last postage stamp of land on the east bank of the Cuito River had failed. With some 800 Cuban troops now dug in around Cuito Cuanavale, even the SADF high command was finally convinced that it was impossible to destroy the enemy bridgehead from the east without a massive increase in South African forces and the loss of hundreds of South African lives. Such a high death toll would of itself have been politically unacceptable in the Republic. But it was out of the question for another reason also – the first round of formal peace talks between Cuba, South Africa and Angola was imminent, and General Jannie Geldenhuys had been appointed a member of his country's official negotiating team.

The government and the State Security Council decided to demobilise the Citizen Force units of 82 SA Brigade which had been formed for the Tumpo Three battle. Under the Defence Act, no Citizen Force soldier could be compelled to serve for more than 120 days in each two-year cycle. Since the emphasis now was to be on maintaining the status quo, this could be achieved with a reduced body of Permanent Force soldiers abetted by national servicemen units.

'From the end of April we kept only a very small force of about 1,000 men in southeast Angola to stop any enemy build-up on the east bank of the Cuito,' said Colonel Deon Ferreira. 'Tumpo Three was our last offensive effort in that war theatre. Our forces worked until the end of August (1988) laying a massive minefield between the Cuatir and the Chambinga Rivers to keep the enemy pinned down at Tumpo.'

Sapper teams from 13 Field Engineer Regiment and, later, 24 Field Engineer Squadron had the task of laying thousands of anti-tank and antipersonnel mines over a period of nearly five months. It was dangerous work. Major Piet Kock, the commander of 24 Field Squadron, lost his foot when he trod on a Soviet POM-Z anti-personnel Stakemine. POM-Zs, mounted on wooden spikes driven into the ground, have been sown so liberally across the face of Angola by Fapla and SWAPO that peasants and their children will be losing their feet and legs to them well into the next century.

The death of a sapper when detonating a booby-trapped POM-Z led to perhaps the greatest act of courage by an SADF man in the whole War for Africa. A team from 13 Field Regiment was laying and arming a defensive minefield south of the Tumpo River on 23 April 1988 when there was a violent explosion. Four South African engineers and seven UNITA soldiers were scythed down.

Sapper Johannes Jacobus Badenhorst, who was working with another team, walked towards the stricken men even though he had not worked in that part of the minefield and knew nothing about the pattern in which devices had been sown. He carried out one severely wounded man and then walked back to fetch another, who proved to be dead. For more than an hour Sapper Badenhorst worked on defusing mines which surrounded the dead man. He then walked out of the minefield to fetch a ground-sheet, and went back again to wrap the body and carry it out.

The following day Sapper Badenhorst was one of a party of engineers being taken back by a Ratel to the 13 Field Regiment base east of the Chambinga High Ground when the vehicle's engine caught fire. All the sappers, except Badenhorst, abandoned the vehicle when it became clear the fire was out of control.

Badenhorst stayed aboard the Ratel, loaded with weapons and ammunition, throwing off mortar bombs, R-4 rifles and other equipment until rifle bullets, discharged by the heat, began flying around and drove him out. Badenhorst was treated for severe burns on his hands and was cited by his commanding officer for an 'extraordinary deed of bravery in the face of mortal danger'. He later received the highest decoration awarded for valour during the War for Africa, the Honoris Crux Silver. Badenhorst's Silver was the only one given, although 21 slightly lesser ranking Honoris Cruxes were awarded.

The sowing of the minefield began in mid-April. Its pattern was to be roughly horseshoe in shape – beginning south of the Tumpo River; stretching eastwards north of the Chambinga; turning northwards along the eastern edge of the Chambinga High Ground; and turning westwards once more between the Dala and Cuatir Rivers. The intent was to prevent Fapla from pushing eastwards again during 1988 as the SADF wound down its presence in southeast Angola and trained UNITA teams in the use of the vast quantities of weaponry captured during the War for Africa.

The South African sappers laid mainly Armscor R2M1 anti-personnel and No.8 anti-tank mines, but also used Soviet mines captured during the war or dug up from Fapla minefields. In one outstanding operation UNITA's sappers recovered more than 600 Fapla-sown Soviet TM-57 anti-tank mines and gave them to the South Africans for re-laying against Fapla. Mines were also laid outside the horseshoe along the eastern banks of the Cuito and Cuanavale Rivers where UNITA and SADF thought Fapla might attempt crossings.

Operation Packer formally ended on 30 April 1988 with the departure of Paul Fouché and the demobilisation of the Citizen Force units which had served in his 82 SA Brigade. The new phase, christened Operation Displace, featured scarcely 1,000 troops compared with the 3,000 SADF personnel who were in southeast Angola at the height of the fighting. However, the new force endeavoured by a variety of actions to give Fapla the impression that the SADF was still there in strength.

All the radio nets of the departed units were kept open and very active as part of the deception exercise. Dummy targets were built for Fapla Migs to bomb. Vehicle movements similar in pattern to and as intense as those of 82 SA Brigade were simulated. Ratel training exercises were carried out in such a way as to give the impression that a new armoured attack was being prepared. During one such exercise, on 3 July, the Ratels drew heavy enemy artillery fire as they moved across open ground. One man was killed by shrapnel. He was the final SADF casualty in the southeastern theatre of the War for Africa.

One battery of G-5s, the SADF stars of the war, was brought back to strength and continued a barrage against Fapla targets for months after the men of 82 SA Brigade were back at their desks in insurance offices and behind the wheels of farm tractors.

Peter Honey, southern Africa correspondent of the *Baltimore Sun*, visited a forward UNITA position on high ground overlooking Cuito Cuanavale and described how the shells from the South African G-5s were still going into Cuito Cuanavale in April 1988 at the rate of about 20 per hour: 'Binoculars draw closer the stark vista below; scorched craters gaping across the countryside and in the town itself. Only the water tower and a few houses on the northern edge of town seem relatively intact. To the west the airstrip, a vital factor in this protracted siege, seems pocked and scarred with shell holes, although from ten kilometres out it is difficult to assess the damage.'[2]

The key components of the small Operation Displace team were a squadron of anti-tank Ratel-90s and Ratel-ZT3s led by 32 Battalion's Major Hannes Nortmann; a multi-racial battalion of motorised infantry of the South West African Territorial Force; a company of trackers from the 201 Bushman Battalion; the sapper teams; and one battery of eight G-5 guns and an MRL battery, operated by both Permanent Force and national service artillerymen.

UNITA deployed three of its battalions to the east of the Tumpo Triangle, with the job of observing the enemy and stopping Fapla reconnaissance patrols from moving beyond the *Anhara Lipanda*.

Notes

1   In fact, the main cause of the G-5 shortage was more likely its export popularity. Armscor had big export orders to fulfil, including an order from Iraq for some 100 G-5s and thousands of tonnes of ammunition.
2   Peter Honey, 'Siege keeps Angola town in never-ending nightmare', The *Baltimore Sun* (Sunday 24 April 1988).

PART 10

THE DENOUEMENT

War is much too serious a thing to be left to military men.
Charles Maurice de Talleyrand (1754–1838).

Question: *What's the largest country in the world?*

Answer: *Cuba. Its heart is in Havana. Its Government is in Moscow. Its graveyards are in Angola and Ethiopia; and its people are in Miami.*

People's Daily, Peking.

CHAPTER 37

MORE JAW-JAW

With the Tumpo Three battle out of the way, the belligerents were shepherded slowly towards negotiation by Crocker for the United States and by the Soviet Union's Deputy Foreign Minister Anatoly Adamishin, who played a critical role behind the scenes in putting pressure on the Cubans and Angolans and conveying messages to the South Africans to ease their anxieties. At one stage in 1988, Adamishin even paid a secret visit to South Africa and made a helicopter trip over the gold mines of the Witwatersrand with Pik Botha.

The first official round of talks were held in London on 3–4 May 1988 in one of those slightly shabby 'George Smiley' clandestine settings in which the British specialise. The South African negotiating team which sat down at a U-shaped table in a characterless basement conference room at Durrants Hotel, in a side street in the centre of the British capital, was led by Neil van Heerden. His team included General Geldenhuys, Major-General Neels van Tonder of CSI, and Dr Niël Barnard, head of the civilian National Intelligence Service.

The Cubans and MPLA fielded a joint team. It was led by Cuba's 'Oom Kaspaas' Jorge Risquet. His top assistant was General Ulysses Rosales del Toro, the Cuban military's Chief of Staff, who inevitably became known to the South Africans as 'Ulysses the Bull'. Foreign Minister Afonso van Dunem was there for the MPLA together with Justice Minister Fernandes van Dunem and the Fapla Chief of Staff, General Antonio dos Santos Franco.

Chester Crocker was in the chair, but before the talking began he had a meeting with Adamishin, who was in the wings throughout 3 and 4 May to be 'helpful' if needed. The superpowers had clearly reached agreement that there was a 'window of opportunity' for a settlement from which everyone could gain something.

The Cubans would stop losing young men in a lost cause. The Soviet Union and South Africa would be saved the cost of an expensive and unwinnable war. The South Africans would be rid of the Cubans from Africa. The international community would secure the independence of Namibia. But the biggest carrot for the South Africans was a secret one offered by the Americans: the chief prize resulting from a comprehensive agreement would be the expulsion of South Africa's banned opposition African National Congress from its East European-financed military training camps in Angola and the delivery of the ANC to the negotiating table to reshape South Africa internally by peaceful process.

US State Department officials in Crocker's weighty team said black African 'Frontline' states 'bought' the idea of South Africa's withdrawal from Namibia followed by free multi-party elections there on the understanding that they had to take a tough line with the ANC. One State Department man said the message from Crocker to the Frontline states was: 'If you keep your nose clean and don't provoke South Africa, we will back you. But if you harbour ANC guerrillas and the South Africans come over the border and kick arse, don't look to us.'[1]

An American official advising Crocker throughout the London meeting told the author of this book: 'The Cubans want out. They have suffered too many health problems and deaths. The Angolans are bankrupt and not paying their fees. But Castro wants to get out without appearing to lose face and without being seen to abandon an ally. That will make it tricky, because we're dealing here with something to do with *machismo* which, let's face it, we don't fully understand.'

Given that the sides regarded each other as Beelzebub, the London talks went remarkably well. Van Heerden, with Geldenhuys at his shoulder, pledged that South Africa would implement UN Resolution 435 on Namibia if the issue of Cuba's withdrawal from Angola could be resolved. The Angolans repeated their March offer on Cuban withdrawal.

As grey English rain poured relentlessly down outside, the 60 or so negotiators from Angola, Cuba, South Africa, America and the Soviet Union – crammed into a room so ungenerous that it was difficult for them even to push back their chairs – began discussing in hypothetical terms the necessary ingredients for a comprehensive settlement.

There was a coffee bar outside the conference hall where the delegates, many of whom had been knocking hell out of each other physically and verbally for years, found they had no choice other than to mingle during breaks. The atmosphere was stilted and thick with dislike and suspicion. It took the military men to break the ice. Jannie Geldenhuys, dressed in a blue-grey business suit set off by an SADF red, white and blue 'Border War' tie, walked over and introduced himself to General Rosales del Toro, dressed in a uniform covered with more medal ribbons than South Africa has gold mines. Later that day the two men went off for a 90-minute private meeting, at which Geldenhuys told Rosales del Toro that a four-year period for the withdrawal of Cuban troops from Angola was too long. Del Toro, growing increasingly relaxed with his fellow soldier, replied: 'OK, we're open to offers.'

The essential process of establishing professional and personal contacts had begun. The shape of future negotiations had been established. Chester Crocker had written a detailed paper setting out Angolan-Cuban viewpoints and proposals as he had understood them in his talks in Luanda and elsewhere. The proposals included the four-year Cuban withdrawal period and a suggestion that the South Africans get out of Namibia within seven months. Neil van Heerden delivered a detailed, point-by-point written response to the Luanda-Havana proposal.

The Angolans and the Cubans did not like what they read. But, although there seemed to be irreconcilable differences, everyone agreed there should be another meeting, this time on black African soil, at which Crocker would begin the proceedings with a detailed paper setting out South Africa's view of how a settlement should be reached.

South Africa and the other parties now embarked upon a period of intense secret diplomacy to iron out minor problems, explore new ideas, sort out misunderstandings and seek clarity on each other's positions.

Derek Auret, Deputy Director-General in the South African Ministry of Foreign Affairs, found he hardly had time to visit home between missions around the world and reporting back to the negotiations team working round the clock for days at a time at the Union Buildings in Pretoria on the options open to South Africa.

Van Heerden felt, since he had rejected most of the Cuban-Angolan proposals in London, that a heavy responsibility rested upon him to produce a detailed and coherent set of South African proposals for the next round of negotiations. When Auret finally had time to look at his diary he found he had flown out of South Africa 38 times in the course of the first six months of 1988 to gather information to bring back to the Angola-Namibia working group.

Planning for the next talks got bogged down in a prolonged argument over the venue. The MPLA got cold feet about the agreement reached in London on the next location, arguing that Pretoria was more interested in using the talks as a 'Trojan horse' for achieving a major policy goal of opening gates into black Africa.

Crocker's team proposed a number of sites worldwide, each of which were rebuffed by one or other of the protagonists. Then a Crocker man had the bright idea of Cairo. Egypt could be considered part of Africa by Pretoria and part of the Middle East by Luanda, which would enable both to save face. The proposal was accepted.

While Luanda and Pretoria squabbled about which luxury international hotel they should meet in, Crocker and Adamishin met privately in Lisbon and reinforced their countries' commitment jointly to pushing the Cuba-South Africa-Angola talks to a successful conclusion.

Speaking to reporters immediately after the Crocker-Adamishin meeting, US Under Secretary of State for Political Affairs Michael Armacost said it had been so successful that there was likely to be more agreement on southern Africa than any other issue when Mikhail Gorbachev and Ronald Reagan met for their fourth superpower summit in Moscow from 29 May to 2 June 1988. 'There has been probably more extensive preparation for these discussions on regional issues than at any previous summit meeting in history,' said Armacost.

In Moscow Gorbachev and Reagan set 29 September 1988, the 10th anniversary of the adoption by the United Nations of Resolution 435 on Namibian independence, as the target date for a settlement of the Angola/Namibia conflicts. 'The 29 September date is important,' Chester Crocker told the *New York Times* Moscow correspondent. 'Whether it's realistic is another question.'

Anatoly Adamishin, who continued his relationship with Crocker in intense behind-the-scenes talks at the Moscow summit, publicly committed the Soviet Union to playing a more active role in the negotiations and offered its services as co-guarantor of an eventual peace settlement.

It was clear by then that the Soviet Union was eager to settle the southern African conflict both to enhance Gorbachev's image as a peace-maker, already emerging since Soviet troops began their withdrawal from Afghanistan just before the Moscow summit, and to plug yet another expensive drain on the Soviet military budget.

Mr Adamishin declined to discuss with reporters how much aid the Soviet Union was giving Angola, although American officials said it was at least US$ 1 billion a year. 'Of course, it is not cheap [for us],' said Adamishin. He added that the MPLA's resources, based entirely on oil from its Cabinda fields, had been depleted by falling world petroleum prices and for the time being they were paying 'not a kopek' for the Soviet Union's military help.

The Cairo meeting was finally convened from 23 to 25 June. It proved to be the most dramatic and acrimonious round in all the negotiations.

The South African delegation, which flew in low over the Pyramids to the theme tune from Lawrence of Arabia, was this time led by Foreign Minister Pik Botha, wearing a flashy white tropical suit, and Defence Minister Magnus Malan. Botha and Malan were the front men. In the engine room were more than a dozen officials led by Neil van Heerden and Jannie Geldenhuys. World traveller Derek Auret was also there.

Botha and Malan were received warmly by the Egyptians and they larked like little boys as they donned Bedouin head-dress to ride camels near the Great Pyramid, visit the Tutunkhamen collection, sample superb Middle Eastern food, including kebbe and hummous from Lebanon and spit roast lamb accompanied by exotic sauces. They shopped for expensive souvenirs in the souk and applauded raucously an amply constructed belly-dancer whose whirling navel made the South African foreign minister's hyper-active eyeballs gyrate faster than normal.

Reports of their leader's activities on the Nile did not go down well with Hannes Nortmann and the thousand other womenless and wineless South African soldiers sitting among flies and mosquitoes in the bottom of dirt trenches opposite Cuito Cuanavale eating corned beef with fat turned runny by the heat. Their tempers had not been improved when Ministers Botha and Malan sent a message with strict instructions that the Operation Displace team was not do to anything to jeopardise the Cairo talks. Nevertheless, they were still obliged to 'hold the line' while losing neither men nor machines.

The talks opened with Crocker presenting the Cubans and Angolans with South Africa's proposals for a comprehensive settlement, drawn up by Van Heerden and his team. While Jorge Risquet, Afonso van Dunem and others digested Pretoria's ideas, Botha, Malan and Geldenhuys travelled to the British Commonwealth War Cemetery at Heliopolis to lay a wreath, hastily made by a Cairo florist from a bowl of proteas in the first class lounge of the South African Airways Boeing 747 which had brought the Pretoria delegation to Egypt. Their visit was to commemorate the thousands of South African soldiers killed fighting Axis forces in North Africa in World War II.

Back at the conference hall, in the Hyatt el Salaam Hotel, the South Africans found the Cubans and Angolans in angry mood. 'Oom Kaspaas' Risquet was in danger of bursting a blood vessel as he reviled and mocked the South African paper which proposed, among other things, that the Cuban withdrawal from Angola should be completed over seven months, instead of the four years suggested by Havana, and that Jonas Savimbi be brought into an Angolan coalition government within six weeks of the adjournment of the Cairo talks.

Risquet grew more churlish as he denounced and rejected the proposals. He demanded that apartheid in South Africa be added to the agenda. This provoked a fierce broadside on human rights abuses in Cuba and Angola from Pik Botha. Chester Crocker, who believed both sides were intent on provoking the other to fold their tents and walk out, diplomatically called an adjournment.

There was no social intercourse between the delegations that night. The South Africans, believing their rooms were bugged, retired to a corner of the hotel gardens to talk about how they could contribute to keeping the talks going on the final day. Huddled behind giant coloured umbrellas to confound directional microphones, Botha, Van Heerden and the rest of the team worked late into the night trying to identify some principles which might be acceptable to both sides as a basis for further discussion.

The Soviet Union honoured its pledge from the Moscow summit to play an active role in keeping the negotiations on course. Chester Crocker approached the Soviet representative in a side room at the talks and told him about the crisis. Vladilen Vlasev, the top civil servant in the Soviet Foreign Ministry responsible for Africa, summoned the Cubans and Angolans to another late night meeting behind giant umbrellas in another corner of the garden and proceeded to read the riot act. It is not known what threats he made, but he saved the Cairo talks.

The next morning the South Africans were surprised to find the Cubans and Angolans had done a lot of overnight homework and had come up with proposals for resolving the deadlock. In a final day free from aggressive rhetoric, Crocker persuaded the two sides to leave both their papers on the table. Some proposals were acceptable to both sides, but there were also cavernous differences. Crocker suggested that officials try to marry the two documents in a series of informal discussions prior to the next round of official negotiations. Both sides agreed.

Over the couscous and sweetmeats war had been avoided in Cairo. But elsewhere blood was about to be shed again in the War for Africa.

Note

1   Richard Dowden, 'Collapse of ANC: The prize for Pretoria in Namibian deal.' *The Independent*, London (Wednesday 11 May 1988).

CHAPTER 38

FIDEL'S LAST HURRAH!

In the days following the first round of peace negotiations in London, Fidel Castro concluded that it would be just a matter of time before the 'internationalist mission' in Angola of Cuba's Revolutionary Armed Forces would have to end. 'The peace process has become irreversible,' he later explained to his national Council of State.

Pressure from the Big Powers, the cost of the Angolan War in Cuban lives, diminishing confidence in the purity of the MPLA's revolutionary fervour, recognition that UNITA had sufficient support, determination and guerrilla skills to go on fighting for decades more, and the accelerating deterioration of the Cuban and Angolan economies had convinced him that it was necessary to get out or face eventual disaster.

But it was not in the nature of Fidel Castro to quit anything with a whimper, let alone the Angolan mission which from 1975 had been the equivalent for him of a sacred Crusade.

Both he and General Rafael Del Pino had been appalled by the Soviet decision in early 1987 to encourage the MPLA's desire to launch another military offensive into the 'great black hole' of southeastern Angola. As the Fapla force suffered the inevitable reverses that both he and Del Pino had foreseen, the Cuban leader realised that defeat for the MPLA would also be seen as defeat for his Revolution, even though his military men had been involved in the early stages mainly in advisory and technical roles. The Cuban Revolution could not be defeated; therefore, the MPLA could not be allowed to face defeat while Cuban troops remained on Angolan soil.

In Moscow on 7 November 1987 Castro met Angolan President Eduardo Dos Santos and the two decided to increase the Cuban troop presence in Angola and replace inexperienced soldiers doing compulsory service with crack regular troops, in particular those of the 50th Division which acted as Castro's personal force and had never served in Africa.

'We ourselves understood that even though we were in no way responsible for the errors that had led to that situation,' Castro later explained, 'we could not sit still and allow a military and political catastrophe to occur.'[1]

By 15 November 15,000 Cuban reinforcements, including the country's best pilots, had begun arriving in Angola. The most prestigious generals within the Revolutionary Armed Forces, Major-General Arnaldo Ochoa Sanchez, Major-General Leopoldo Cintra Frias, Brigadier-General Patricio De Laguardia Font and Brigadier-General Francisco Crus Borsao, who had all been involved in the 1975–76 fighting, directed the counter-offensive, with Fapla's commanders forced into a subordinate role to the Cuban generals.

The first Cuban fighting men entered combat in defence of Fapla's 59 Brigade on 14 February 1988, and by the time of the third Tumpo battle on 23 March Cuba had a whole regiment stationed around Cuito Cuanavale and a tactical tank group positioned inside the Tumpo Triangle. With the aid of SADF mistakes and Pretoria's refusal to escalate the war beyond a specific level, Castro and his generals helped ensure that Fapla held the line in front of Cuito Cuanavale.

But Cuba did not send its troops into Cuito Cuanavale only. Ochoa Sanchez, in daily communication with Castro, also began moving units southwestwards down towards the Namibia border opposite Ovamboland, more than 400 km from the fighting in the east.

By late January 1988 some 3,500 Cuban troops had deployed into southwest Angola. This began to worry the SADF. The Cubans had stayed north of a line roughly 300 km north of Ovamboland since 1984, when South Africa withdrew from southern Angolan territory it had captured in the big Operation Askari between December 1983 and February 1984.

The SADF withdrawal was made to allow the MPLA to reoccupy the region, provided both the Cubans and SWAPO stayed 300 km to the north. In practice, SWAPO returned and the South Africans made regular raids across the border to hammer its camps. The Cubans stayed away, but their return southwards at the beginning of 1988 threatened the opening of a western theatre of the War for Africa should they get mixed up in one of the regular SWAPO-SADF scraps.

The Cuban force in the south grew slowly, but the situation deteriorated badly in April when Cuban units began to intervene in SADF cross border raids on SWAPO concentrations. In one clash about 50 km across the border from Ovamboland on 18 April an SADF major was killed by a Cuban unit which intervened on behalf of a SWAPO group which was being pursued by the South Africans. During the fighting a medical orderly, Corporal Du Toit, lost contact with the SADF 51 Battalion force. On returning to search for Du Toit, soldiers found his body in a shallow grave.

The decision had already been made that something would have to be done about increased SWAPO activity, made possible by the Cuban advance southwards, when, on 4 May, the final day of the first peace talks in London, a Cuban force again attacked a South African unit inside Angola.

Neither South Africa nor Cuba said anything in London, but once they returned home details of the serious fighting began to emerge. The South African force from 101 Battalion had been reconnoitring some 50 km inside southwest Angola, near the Cunene River, when they were ambushed by the Cubans. A lance-corporal, Henrik Jacobus Venter, was killed and another, Private Johan Papenfus, was missing.

The Cubans later announced that Papenfus was a prisoner-of-war in a Havana military hospital where he was being treated for serious wounds to his left leg. The Cubans had scored a propaganda goal, but also provoked the SADF into speeding up preparations for major retaliation.

Commandant Jan Hougaard was again ordered, as he had been in the east and at Menongue, to do the preliminary planning and scouting for the attack on the Cubans and SWAPO in the western theatre of the War for Africa.

'The people who came back from the 51 Battalion and 101 Battalion contacts all said they had run into armoured cars, tanks and artillery,' said Hougaard. 'They were only in platoon strength in Casspirs and trucks. They were surprised, because we thought we controlled the area opposite Ovamboland. Whenever we detected SWAPO guerrillas moving south into that area we used to go in and sort them out, and the Faplas stuck to their bases and avoided contacts with us during the operations.'

After flying 450 km westwards from Rundu to Oshakati – the Brigade HQ of SADF forces operating in Ovamboland and across the border directly opposite – in late April, Hougaard was briefed by military intelligence. The assessment was that a big SWAPO force was concentrating in and around Techipa, a small Angolan town to the west of the Cunene River and about 50 km north of the border, before attempting to infiltrate into Namibia.

'We were ordered to go and attack the place,' said Hougaard. 'But I persuaded the Brigadier [Chris Serfontein, in charge of the Ovamboland sector] to let us put in a couple of recce groups first to get a more accurate picture of what was happening on the ground. I felt it was important because we knew the Cubans were pushing even more men into the area. They were upgrading the airfields at Cahama [125 km north of the border] and Xangongo [65 km from the border]. They were also rebuilding a 300 m bridge across the Cunene at Xangongo which we had blown up during Operation Protea in 1981. These were exactly the essential kinds of things they needed to do to reactivate their 5th Military Region and open up a western war front.' [Fapla and the Cubans had divided Angola into ten military regions. The 6th Military Region took in the whole eastern front war zone, stretching from Menongue, through Cuito Cuanavale into 'Savimbi-land.']

The SADF high command had long speculated that Fapla and the Cubans might open up a new front in order to divide South Africa's military capabilities while it was busy fighting alongside UNITA in the east. The runway at Xangongo was upgraded sufficiently to allow heavy transport planes to land. But Cahama gave the most cause for alarm: Mig-23s could now operate from there instead of from Lubango, the main southern Angolan warplane base 300 km north of the border.

'For the first time, Cuban Mig-23s and Mig-21s were flying across the border over Namibia,' said Hougaard. 'They were coming within 20 km of Oshakati and Ondangwa [the SAAF's airbase in Ovamboland]. They were too high to intercept with our [French Cactus] ground-to-air missiles. They never attacked, but people were asking why the SADF was not reacting.'

Colonel Dick Lord, speaking to the author after the war, said 26 enemy aircraft approached Oshakati and Ondangwa during April and May 1988. 'Although we did think they might attack the bases, the high altitudes they were flying at were not conducive to surprise. They were always within our radar cover,' he said. 'I think we made the correct analysis of the extent of the threat. We decided that they wanted to test our pilots' reaction times. For that reason we were reluctant to scramble, but often we couldn't because we didn't have any suitable fighters situated there!'

Hougaard moved to Ruacana, on the Angolan border, on 9 May to set up his tactical HQ and make preparations for infiltrating two four-man teams of 32 Battalion recces towards Techipa. Sergeant Piet Fourie and the three regular Angolan members of his squad made up one team. Hougaard decided to drop Fourie and his team by helicopter in the Devangulo mountain range, about 20 km southwest of Techipa; from there the recces were to move around Techipa and approach it from the north to gather intelligence.

'I gave Piet six days to do his job, and told him that the capture of one or more of the enemy should be high in his priorities,' said Hougaard. 'The going proved much rougher than we had expected. The mountain terrain was very difficult. It was semi-desert, with lots of rocks and sparse bush cover. Since the local population there was hostile to us, it made the chances of going undetected very slim. The recces had to be completely self-dependent. They carried everything they needed on their backs, including enough food and water for six days.

'I sat in the tactical HQ at Ruacana throughout the operation, keeping in regular touch by radio. Piet found he could only move at night. During the day the team had to split up and lie low; they couldn't move at all. After three days Piet said to me that by the time they reached

Techipa they would be completely buggered and be too tired to do their job properly. Also they were running low on water.

'I agreed with Pict that the risk had become too high. After the Papenfus incident, we couldn't afford to have *anyone* captured, let alone a recce. So I told them to get to a safe place in the mountains and sent two Alouettes there to get them out.'

Hougaard was disappointed with the failure of the first recce mission. Hard intelligence was desperately needed. Information from other sources suggested that the Cuban and SWAPO build-up was reaching alarming proportions. There seemed to be even more forces around Techipa than originally thought and the Cubans were pushing down the Cunene Valley. They had advanced to within 25 km of Calueque, the site of an incomplete dam 12 km inside Angola which the SADF had controlled since 1975 and from where water was drawn to supply the whole of Ovamboland.

A crisis within the ranks of Cuba's own generals in Angola also made the SADF fearful that Castro would launch a major attack to restore his wounded pride.

On 27 April Major-General Francisco Crus Borsao was killed in Angola as he attempted to follow in Brigadier-General Del Pino's footsteps and defect with several other military officers to the United States. In an operation called Camilo Cienfuegos – after the best loved hero of Cuba's revolution (other than Castro) who disappeared in mysterious circumstances in 1970 – Crus Borsao took off from Huambo in an aircraft, probably an Antonov-24 transport plane, on a routine flight which diverted towards Namibia.

American intelligence had made arrangements for the general and many of the other 26 people aboard to be taken from there to the US. However, a senior defector from Cuban intelligence said in Washington that the radio frequency used for Operation Camilo Cienfuegos' communications had been detected and the pilot was ordered to land soon after take-off.[2] He refused and the plane was shot down, probably by Mig-23s.

On 28 April Fidel Castro announced the general's death and said his plane had been shot 'accidentally', making no reference to the Washington reports that Crus Borsao had been trying to defect.

General Del Pino, however, felt SADF fears were exaggerated. Through intelligence channels from his 'safe house' in the southeastern USA he told SADF generals that the Cuban Army was not capable of mounting a successful full-scale attack. In his carefully argued assessment, Del Pino said the Cubans did not have the training, the organisational ability, the communications system or the logistic capacity to carry out a full-scale frontal attack.

Fidel Castro was fully aware of the reality underlying his own bluster. His adoption of an imperious and aggressive stance was an attempt to give military weight, albeit ephemeral, to the Cuban negotiating position at the peace talks. Del Pino said there was no doubt in his mind that if the Cubans mounted a full-scale offensive against the SADF they would be very heavily defeated. The consequences at home would be very serious, because casualties would be on a scale unacceptable to the Cuban people and military leaders.

The SADF should be confident of its ability to defeat Castro's army, said Del Pino. However, he warned that Castro had defeated the previous Cuban dictator, Sergeant Fulgencio Batista, and had maintained the Cuban people's revolutionary fervour for more than two decades because he was an audacious swashbuckler. He enjoyed taking risks and for a long time many Cubans had enjoyed the adventure despite the hardships. Therefore, Del Pino said, a Cuban attack could not be ruled out despite the fact that it would be a grave gamble for Castro.

Military victory against the odds would give the Cuban public and military, weary from 13 years of Angolan warfare, something to show for it at last; it would breathe new life into Castro's increasingly banal, cliché-ridden charisma and put off the day of reckoning for Cuba's economic, moral and social decay.

While Piet Fourie and his team recovered from their gruelling experiences in the Devangulo mountains, Hougaard prepared to send them towards Techipa from another direction. 'I decided to put them in through the flat, rolling country to the southeast of Techipa,' said Hougaard. 'The problem was that although there was some bush cover, it was in isolated clumps. Recce teams who had been into that kind of country before said there was no question of moving during the day; you just had to lie up in the bush.

'But it was dangerous. The enemy knew we had recce teams in there almost permanently, so they moved tanks in a platoon formation of four and whenever they saw an isolated clump of thicker bush they would send two of the tanks to drive backwards and forwards through it over and over again. A recce, no matter how well he was camouflaged, could end up as flat as a swatted mosquito.'

Fourie and his team were taken across the Cunene River by truck, over a low-level, concrete bridge, just downriver from the Calueque Dam. Two Mercedes-Benz trucks drove as far towards Techipa as they dare, simulating a mobile patrol. At last light Fourie and his three men jumped off. The trucks headed home while the recces walked through the night towards Techipa before laying up in undergrowth for the day.

It took three days for the patrol to reach a point about four kilometres east of the town from where Fourie intended manoeuvring around Techipa and approaching it from the northeast. At about 9 am on the fourth day Fourie's men noticed there were two enemy soldiers behind them, apparently unaware that there was anybody else ahead.

'We flattened ourselves in the long grass to check them as they approached,' said Fourie, still under orders to take enemy prisoners. 'My heart was pounding. There were a lot of huts scattered around with local population living in them. As the two guys walked past we jumped up and told them in Portuguese to raise their hands.

'We were scared, but we looked more horrifying then they did. I looked like a devil with my hair long and my face blacked. They were Faplas. One guy was so scared that he shot off like Ben Johnson and we couldn't stop him. The other guy was rooted to the spot with terror.

'It was a problem. Since one guy had escaped, it was just a matter of time before patrols came searching for us. We questioned the other guy a bit, in a military kind of a way. At about 4 pm artillery opened up from Techipa on the position where we had taken the prisoners, but since then we had been moving south all day.

'That night I and one of my guys made the prisoner lead us into the enemy base. We followed the bed of the Techipa River (which flows eastwards through the town). It was quite dark. The moon was just new. The prisoner kept quiet because he was really scared. We told him: "Make one false move and it's your last day on earth". He had no difficulty in believing us because we were really tensed up. I was shaking with tension at times.

'Soon we could hear Cubans talking. That was important intelligence. They hadn't been in Techipa before. Then we could see them. They were eating, making a lot of noise as conventional forces do, especially with tins. We were able to creep around several of their vehicles and check them out. We absorbed as much as we could and then started moving out with the prisoner. On the way back we hit a deep trench system and I realised we had gone through their outer defence perimeter without knowing it. I found myself thinking "Oh shit, what now?" We had a quick look at it and then got out.

'We joined up with the others and moved back through the night to the southern side of a big *shona* about 10 km southeast of Techipa. I checked in with HQ and I could hardly believe it when they told me to let the prisoner go – I won't go into this, I don't think it's wise to talk about the reasons I was given. So we let him go after we had checked the *shona* for any enemy presence.

'There were tracks of a big patrol which had passed recently and I thought "Hey man, this is not a healthy place to be." We pulled out another four kilometres south and stayed there for the rest of the day. In the evening we started moving south again, moving parallel with a dirt road from Techipa to the Cunene. We picked up an enemy outpost at a waterhole just off the road and got near enough to hear Spanish voices and see some of their vehicles.

'I got through on the radio and at HQ they seemed to think I was talking shit because they didn't believe that the enemy could be that far south. As a recce, you always know that they've got other sources of intelligence. But it's quite depressing when they don't want to listen to you because you're telling them something entirely different.'

Fourie was suffering from the normal paranoia of someone coming to the end of yet another high-risk mission, feeling unappreciated and knowing that men in starched uniform at HQ were downing the occasional ice-cold beer while he and his men tried to make their final litre of warm drinking water last out.

Hougaard sent in Alouette helicopters to pluck the Fourie team out by night. The recces' work was esteemed more than they realised. Their work, coupled with other intelligence information, had enabled the SADF to put together a very full picture of the scale of the threat.

★ ★ ★

Until November 1987 the Cubans had no more than 2,000 soldiers stationed in southwest Angola, and the nearest significant concentration to Namibia was more than 180 km north of the border. By early June 1988 more than 11,000 Cuban infantrymen were stationed in the southwest and some were patrolling to within 20 km of the border. The infantrymen, from Castro's elite 50th Division, were backed by more than a hundred T-55 and more advanced T-64 tanks. A full array of Soviet mobile radars had been moved south. An anti-aircraft regiment equipped with a whole family of high-altitude anti-aircraft missiles, including Sam-8s and Sam-13s, and a full artillery regiment had also moved into the southwest.

The South Africans had detected three integrated Cuban-SWAPO battalions. One, consisting of 200 Cuban soldiers and 250 SWAPO guerrillas, had moved into Techipa; it was the one into whose midst Piet Fourie had wandered. The battalion was supported by tanks and artillery. The other battalions, similarly composed, were based at Xangongo and Mupa, further to the northwest.

The integration of Cuban units with SWAPO meant war, as far as the SADF was concerned. The Cubans were providing a shield for SWAPO to move back into an area from which the guerrillas had been driven. The Cubans were also breaking the unwritten code that SWAPO and the SADF should be left alone to fight their own battles.

★ ★ ★

Hougaard was ordered to attack Techipa. Military intelligence believed the HQ for the whole Cuban operation in the southwest might be located in the little town because of the sprouting of antennae and the presence of other specialist equipment. Subsequent harder information confirmed this.

Hougaard was initially given a force of only 500 soldiers – three companies of 32 Battalion infantrymen. Much as he admired the fighting qualities of his own battalion, Hougaard knew they could not engage in a conventional battle against the weight of armour and the number of infantrymen the Cubans had assembled. He told Brigadier Serfontein in Oshakati that the best he could do with the 32 Battalion force was to fight a holding operation while a bigger conventional force was being prepared and moved to Ruacana.

Commandant Mike Muller had taken his 61 Mechanised Battalion out of southeast Angola in late March after the Tumpo Two battle. The battalion returned to its training headquarters, at Omuthiya in Ovamboland, where its weary tanks were subjected to comprehensive repairs and servicing before the crews flew off for several weeks leave in the Republic.

It had looked as though 61 Mech's war was over, but now, as the only full conventional battalion permanently posted in Ovamboland, it was ordered to get ready to do battle once more.

On 8 June General Geldenhuys said a general mobilisation from their workplaces of Citizen Force soldiers, numbering more than 140,000, had begun as the Cubans crept to within 12 km of the border in some places. 'We have the forces to handle the situation, although the situation is more serious than it was,' Geldenhuys told reporters in Pretoria. 'The Defence Force is ready to cope with any eventuality.' The SADF chief said it was vital that the Ruacana Falls hydro-electric scheme, on the Cunene River 55 km south of Techipa, be protected against Cuban attack. It provided electricity for the whole of Namibia and water to Ovamboland.

Jan Hougaard could have been forgiven a raised eyebrow in the direction of Geldenhuys as he went about the task of holding off more than 11,000 Cubans and perhaps 2,000 SWAPO guerrillas with his 500 'ruthless killers' from 32 Battalion.

Shortly after General Geldenhuys had made his 'they shall not pass' remarks to the press, Hougaard sent his three 32 Battalion companies across the low-level Calueque bridge aboard ten small Mercedes Unimog trucks tightly packed with men who swayed like stands of ripe wheat during the bumpy ride. Besides rifles, each company had 81 mm mortars, 14.5 mm machine-guns and a 106 mm recoilless anti-tank gun as support weapons. All in all, the composition of the force was very similar to those on countless other 32 Battalion raids into Angola through 12 years of warfare. But this time they were up against something altogether bigger than they had tackled alone in the past.

'I ordered each company to work independently on the enemy's flanks, in its lines and behind its lines,' said Hougaard. 'I wanted information and prisoners. Their orders were to engage in the kind of guerrilla warfare 32 Battalion is good at, interrupting logistics, taking on small groups of enemy, especially SWAPOs, and laying mines. I told them: "Just maintain the situation until 61 Mech gets here."'

Two of the companies were deployed south of Techipa, from where they began reconnaissance patrols. But at that time the general staff believed the main Cuban thrust might come from Xangongo down the Cunene River valley to Calueque. So the third company was sent to an area 20 km southwest of Xangongo overlooking the Cunene River.

In fact, the Cubans proved to be most active at Techipa, moving out frequently with tanks and armoured cars to within 12 km of Calueque and Ruacana. 'The probes were quite careful and cagey,' said Hougaard. 'Their artillery would lay down a barrage in front of them just in case there were SADF men there. But sometimes 12 or 13 tanks supported by infantry would push southwards with Mig patrols overhead.'

The 32 Battalion companies gradually extended their activities. Reconnaissance teams north of Techipa watched Cubans moving freely and confidently along the dirt road to Xangongo, sometimes in single jeeps or tanks, or a diesel tanker or two, almost as though they believed there was no possible SADF threat.

'Our recce teams also picked up the Cuban advance posts,' said Hougaard. 'Following typical Russian doctrine, 100 to 200 infantrymen supported by three or four tanks would dig in four to five kilometres in front of the main force concentration. So you would have to deal with that outpost first, which would give the main force early warning.

'Once our companies had located all the enemy positions, I decided we must start giving the Cubans some headaches. If we could rough them up a bit, then maybe they would react and we could help build up the intelligence picture for 61 Mech.'

There were two main Cuban outposts, both about 15 km from Techipa, one to the southwest and the other to the southeast. Southwards from Techipa between the outposts ran the dirt road towards Calueque. Hougaard and the commander of one of the 32 Battalion companies, Captain Maurice Devenish, decided to provoke the southwestern outpost with some mortar fire in the hope that a relief column would be sent from Techipa which Devenish's men would then ambush.

'The company did its reconnaissance and moved in at night because enemy vehicles moved every day between Techipa and the outpost,' said Hougaard. 'Devenish took 90 men on two Unimogs. They had two 81 mm mortars, two heavy machine-guns and a 106 mm recoilless gun. Early in the morning the mortars were in position to start firing on the outposts and the roadside ambush had been laid. As they waited for orders to fire, they saw five white engineers walking towards them sweeping the dirt road with mine detectors. They could hear vehicle noises, but they were far away. So they decided to hit those Cubans. They killed them with one sustained burst, and then saw a big patrol of Fapla infantry coming along the road. They charged the Faplas in a typical 32 Battalion "avanca".

'The engagement had just begun when they heard armoured cars moving towards them from nearby. They pulled back. They knew they were in trouble, but they didn't panic. They had the mortars about two kilometres behind them, and they began calling in a curtain of shells between them and the armoured cars while they sprinted back to the Unimogs. After a short while four BRDM-2s erupted from the bush. Our guys killed the white commander standing up in one BRDM turret with rifle fire. That made the BRDMs pull back to reorganise, but then things really began to go wrong.

'As they ran they could hear tanks starting up not far away. There was another Cuban outpost there which the recces hadn't discovered, and Devenish had set up his ambush within 1,000 m of it without realising! They were in big trouble because most of the country was fairly open with only small clumps of trees here and there.

'Devenish's aim was to get back to the Unimogs, fling all the kit on the trucks and let them go, and then split up in different directions. The kit we carry is very, very heavy, and with it they wouldn't have been able to run as fast and as far as they were going to need to do. As they came to the Unimogs the BRDMs and the tanks were coming at them from two different directions.

'They were busy throwing their kit on to the vehicles when the first one was hit at the back and began burning. The driver moved off and the Unimog fell into a warthog hole. The second Unimog was behind. The driver couldn't brake in time and smashed into the one in front. The radiator was spurting water. It was like something out of Fred Karno's Army, so they decided to leave both vehicles and everything in them and bombshell in different directions. They obeyed the old 32 Battalion dictum: when necessary run faster than a lily-livered cheetah.

'Devenish had run almost ten kilometres before he stopped to contact me by radio. He had to break off and start running again and his next contact was in early afternoon. I asked him if anybody had been killed or captured, because I knew that was the first thing Brigadier Serfontein was going to ask me. Devenish was a very experienced company commander, and I knew he would have arranged things to get his men back together again. He told me he was unable to account for 11; they were missing and he wasn't sure where they were because no one had been able to hang around when the tanks and BRDMs came with supporting BM-21 rocket fire.

'At that stage neither Devenish nor I knew whether they were alive or dead. The government was very sensitive at that time. Papenfus had just turned up in Cuba, and the last thing Pretoria wanted was to have to announce that 11 South African soldiers had been killed in southwest Angola. I was ordered to give priority to recovering them, which was unnecessary because we do that as a matter of principle in 32 Battalion.

'I think the order from Pretoria was something like: you *will* get those people. Then they asked me to confirm who was dead and who was alive. I said: "I don't know. Give me a chance. These people are in trouble in a foreign country fighting a conventional force. Let me concentrate on getting the guys I know about to a safe area, and then we can sort things out about the guys who are missing."'

'I had my third radio contact with Devenish in late afternoon, by when his party had outrun the Cubans. I suggested to him that since 11 of his men were missing some of them must be dead. He replied: "No, definitely not." He'd talked to all the guys in his group and by radio to other groups, and they confirmed that they had not seen anyone killed or stuck behind with the trucks. They were sure everybody had got away.

'I believed him because I knew him and his troops. Escape and evasion are things we practise day in, day out because you must know how to look after yourself, how to disperse and then come together again, in that kind of situation.

'I wasn't too worried about the men. I knew they could handle themselves. But I was worried about the stuff they had left behind. There was a lot of state-of-the-art frequency-hopping signalling equipment our Armscor people had developed which we didn't want falling into enemy hands. Devenish actually doubled back to the scene of the contact to scout for his missing men. He found none, but did report that both Unimogs were completely burnt out, much to my relief.'

Hougaard ordered Devenish to get the men who were with him, or he was in contact with, back to safety. 'I was convinced by then that the others would find their way out,' said Hougaard. 'Brigadier Serfontein was very calm about it, but there were a lot of other people on my back. I put a Bosbok 3,000 m up above Ruacana to try to pick up radio signals from the lost guys. There was nothing. We waited all night and then the first group of six arrived at Calueque about six in the morning. They were totally exhausted. They all had their rifles but only had ten rounds of ammunition left between them.

'All day I had to keep telling people to keep calm and that the other five would return in due course. Then, as sure as hell, they turned up at Ruacana at about six that night. They had run north around the Cuban positions and then westwards into the mountains to avoid the local population. It was quite some journey: in two days and a night they had trailed 100 km. It was good to show the top brass that our training paid off, but it was a bigger relief that the nagging stopped!'

★ ★ ★

Serfontein had by now decided that the Cuban force was too big and powerful for even 61 Mech to attack it successfully in its Techipa stronghold. There was also the big Cuban force in Xangongo, 70 km further east, which could, if necessary, come to the rescue of the Techipa garrison. Instead, it was to be back to old Boer commando tactics: 61 Mech would come in and try to take out the Cuban forward posts one by one and hope to draw the main force out of Techipa into the open.

As the SADF's main task force assembled south of the Calueque Dam under the command of 32 Battalion's officer-in-chief, Colonel Michau Delport, Hougaard wondered what to do about intelligence a recce patrol had brought back from east of Techipa on the road to Xangongo. They had seen big missiles. They hadn't been able to get close enough to identify them precisely, but they were obviously anti-aircraft ground-to-air missiles.

'The recces radioed the intelligence to me at four o'clock one afternoon,' Hougaard said. 'I told the Air Force and they said the missile system must be destroyed as soon as possible. We agreed on seven the next morning.

'I told the recces to carry out a final reconnaissance and be ready to bring in the air attack by radio the next day and mark the target direction with flares and mini-beacons. They did all the preparation and then the Air Force came to me and said it was too dicey. There were too many Migs in the area and there was a ban on air-to-air combat which might escalate the war.'

Hougaard told the recces to retrieve the flares and beacons and get out of the area. Then the SAAF came back to him and said they had made a fresh assessment. They would attack the missiles that night. Hougaard said it was impossible; the recces they needed to guide the planes in had left the area and were out of contact because their main high-power radio net was inactive while they were on the move.

However, Hougaard knew the recces kept their smaller ground-to-air radios turned on at all times and he volunteered to go up in a Bosbok to call the men on the ground in an attempt to rescue the mission against the missiles. The SAAF approved the idea, but gave the pilot strict instructions that he was not to climb above 1,000 metres or go too far north into Angola where he might enter the 'effective envelope' of known enemy missile systems.

'So I went up in a Bosbok, sitting in the back seat, from the airstrip at Ruacana,' said Hougaard. 'It's a light little thing weighing scarcely more than a tonne. I just about doubled its mass! We stuck to the SAAF rules at first, keeping under 1,000 m and only pushing 20 or so kilometres into Angola north of Calueque. It was night and I was sitting with my book of radio frequencies reading it with a torch and calling my guys over and over again.

'I couldn't raise them, so I kept urging the pilot to go higher. He refused, so I said "Man, go higher for God's sake or we're wasting our

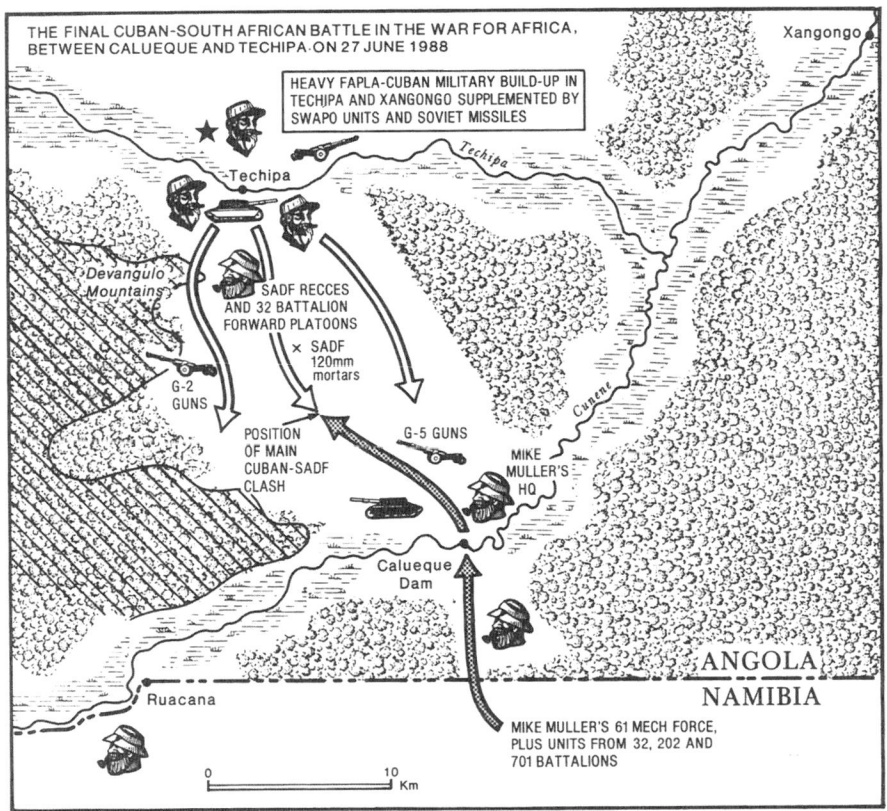

The final Cuban-South African battle in the War for Africa, between Calueque and Techipa on 27 June 1988.

time." So he went higher, and then higher, and all the time he was drifting further north over Angola, although I didn't realise it. I still couldn't contact our guys, so I urged him even higher. And he did so, although it was right against standing procedures.

'I remember asking him where we were, and just as I asked he said "Look, there's a flare." I looked out and said "That's no flare, it's a Sam." I didn't know where it had come from, but I saw it shooting in the air and then turn and come for us. By that time the pilot was diving straight down like mad. My binoculars, torch, map and everything were flying around the plane and hitting me in the face.

'Through the perspex canopy I could see this thing coming directly at us. If you've ever been driving on a road and seen a car coming straight at you with its headlights blazing, that was the kind of feeling I had. I kept yelling, "It's coming for us." Then it passed over us – I don't know how – by, I would guess, about 20 m. And then we heard a big "vroom" as it exploded over Ruacana and broke a lot of windows on the ground.

'There was a panic in Ruacana because they thought we had been shot down. We landed in quite a state of shock. The pilot was in double shock because he knew he had flown beyond permitted limits and he would have to answer for it.'

After Hougaard's dice with death, that night's planned air attack with Impalas on the missile site identified by the recces was cancelled and rescheduled for the following morning. Hougaard sent the Bosbok up again, with the same pilot, but this time with 32 Battalion's intelligence officer Captain Herman Mulder in the communications hot seat at the back.

'My task was to co-ordinate communications with all the companies in the bush and Commandant Hougaard and the Air Force,' said Mulder. 'I established communications with all our teams except for the most forward observation post, who could see the target with naked eyes. The higher you go the better your VHF communications. So we kept pushing higher and higher. We were about 40 km from Techipa, and we knew the enemy would pick up the plane possibly with binoculars but certainly on radar. But despite the Commandant's adventure the night before we believed the most powerful missile they had was a Sam-3 and we knew we were ten kilometres outside its effective range. The first two Impalas took off from Ondangwa to hit the missiles and we climbed to more than 4,000 m to maximise communications with the ground. We'd smashed all the rules and authority we'd been given.

'We were flying west to east into the sun when I saw the sun flash on metal or glass in the southern part of a big *shona* surrounded by little koppies [hills] 35 km to the north. I told the pilot to change course so I could show him what I thought were two vehicles.

'Next moment I saw a blue welding flare which seemed to hover above the ground for a split second. Then it was coming in our direction like a streak of lightning. I screamed to the pilot to go down. He just dived vertically and I think we free fell from more than 4,000 m to less than 2,000 before we levelled out a bit. Everything was flying around. The missile flashed past us. It was only the Hand of God that saved us. Then I saw that the Bosbok's canopy was riddled with gaping cracks. I looked round and two of the flare rockets carried by the Bosbok to mark ground positions had jerked out of their pods during our dive and embedded themselves in the canopy.

'We did two short circles at low level and by the time I landed I was trembling like a butterfly. That pilot was in real trouble again. The Impalas rolled in for their attack, but several missiles were fired at them, so they broke off. We have good early warning electronics, so they got away.

'At Ruacana we evaluated all the evidence and realised we were up against Sam-6s, powerful long-range missiles which are effective at distances of up to 60 km. This was serious. Those missiles had given the Israelis a lot of problems in Lebanon and Syria. All our aircraft movements were stopped for quite some time while our Air Force guys worked out the implications.'

★ ★ ★

The Cuban use of Sam-6s helped General Geldenhuys decide that 61 Mech must move with urgency across the Cunene at Calueque towards Techipa.

After their exertions opposite Cuito Cuanavale and their long leave in April, Mike Muller's men were worked hard through May to get them battle-fit again. By early June both men and machines were ready and Muller began flying regularly from 61 Mech's training headquarters at Omuthiya, in southeast Ovamboland, to Oshakati for planning meetings with Brigadier Serfontein, Commandant Hougaard and Colonel Michau Delport.

An early decision to take 61 Mech's tank squadron across the Cunene meant a big engineering job had first to be undertaken. The problem was that the low-level concrete bridge 200 m to the west of the Calueque dam was strong enough to take only one Ratel or one G-5 at a time; an Olifant tank was too heavy for it.

There was a seven metre-wide road across the top of the 30 metre-high dam. But work on the project had stopped when civil war broke out with Angola's independence in 1975 and approach roads at either end of the bridge had never been completed. Since Muller intended putting most of his complete combat group across the river in one night to catch the Cubans unawares, ramps sufficiently strong to take a whole squadron of tanks and all the other vehicles in convoy would have to be built at both ends of the bridge. However, surprise would be sacrificed if the Cubans detected the construction work.

The problem was handed to the Commandant of 25 Field Engineer Squadron, whose men had laboured manfully throughout most of the eastern theatre campaign building wooden river bridges, laying mines, drilling waterholes, building defensive earthworks, demolishing stricken vehicles and sweeping constantly for enemy mines.

The Commandant sat in his Oshakati HQ thinking through the problem beneath an adage on his wall of American World War II hero General George Patton: 'I want you bastards to remember that no damn fool won a war by dying for his country. The aim is to make the enemy damn fools lose by dying for their country.'

The Commandant presented his plan: his engineers would move into Calueque with bulldozers and earthmovers under cover of darkness and begin constructing massive earth ramps strong enough to allow the tanks and the rest of Muller's mechanised column to cross. By first light each day all work would stop and the ramps and heavy equipment would be camouflaged as though nothing had changed since 1975.

While the engineers built the bridge Muller gradually assembled his 61 Mech force. Finally it consisted of one squadron of 11 Olifant tanks plus a command Ratel; two companies of infantry in Ratel-20s; a platoon of eight anti-tank Ratel-90s; twelve mortar-mounted Ratel-81s; and a troop of four 120 mm mortars.

Units from other battalions were added to Muller's force. The Artillery Regiment provided a battery of G-5 guns. From 51 Battalion came four G-2 heavy guns. The Parachute Regiment sent a company of its crack fighters to protect Muller's headquarters group. There were two companies of infantry from 202 and 701 Battalions of the South West Africa Territory Force. Several infiltration and observation teams from the Reconnaissance Regiment implanted themselves in forward areas.

32 Battalion, as always, had men in the thick of things. It provided Muller with the troop of the SADF's only four anti-tank ZT3 guided missiles mounted on Ratels, plus one lone Ratel-90; a troop of four MRLs to support the G-5s and G-2s; two recce teams; and four companies of infantry and a light artillery support company.

The Ratel-ZT3 troop was commanded by the amazing Major Hannes Nortmann, who at times seemed to be fighting the War for Africa almost single-handed. His troop was pulled out from its protection role on the eastern front in mid-June to be a spearhead of the attack on the western front.

'We were never sure of the precise Cuban strength in Techipa,' said Muller. All we knew was that they were in a very aggressive frame of mind. 'Their armoured patrols pushed 25 km and more south of Techipa, keeping within the range of their artillery cover, but they avoided approaching nearer than 20 km from Calueque.

'The local population was not well disposed towards us, but some, realising that something big was coming, moved south into our area of control. They said the Cubans were saying to the local people: "Tell those Boers to come and get their arses kicked." It was all part of the cat-and-mouse game. We wanted to lure the Cubans as far away from Techipa as possible.

'In working out a strategy I had to take into account the fact that the vegetation was not so dense as in the east. And since it was winter there were no leaves on the trees, so the natural camouflage against Migs was not there.

'A major problem was that (subsequent to Piet Fourie's foray) few of the reconnaissance teams were able to get really close to the enemy lines at Techipa, so "eyes on the ground" observation posts were thin, which is not the way we like to operate.

'Early on I thought there was only a Cuban battalion at Techipa. Then we got information about a Cuban military convoy that moved 400 km down from Lubango to Xangongo, and it was so long that it was passing all night. Finally, when Herman Mulder drew a Sam and it was identified as a Sam-6, we abandoned any lingering idea of attacking the Cubans in Techipa.

'The priority became preventing the Cubans from taking Calueque. I was also pressed to inflict maximum Cuban kills as quickly as possible if they came right out of their stronghold fighting.'

Mike Muller may have been unhappy with the inadequate intelligence from inside Techipa, but he did know the Cuban HQ was inside the tiny town and that there was a Sam-6 battery at a water-pumping station three kilometres to the east of it. Muller had drawn up several alternative battle plans, but he finally decided to commence with a massive artillery barrage from the G-5s, G-2s and 120 mm mortars.

The aim was to inflict devastating damage on the HQ area to incite the Cubans so much that they would finally make their big move south and find three lines of armour and motorised infantry lying in wait for them in terrain of the South Africans' choosing.

On 16 June 1988 the G-5 battery moved across the low-level bridge at Calueque to deploy eight km further to the northeast where there was some reasonable tree cover for Muller to establish his forward HQ. Three 120 mm mortar teams established themselves 12 km south of Techipa, within range of the Cuban outpost to the southwest of the town. Two 32 Battalion companies moved up to the south of Techipa to carry out intensive reconnaissance missions as near to the town as possible.

Major Pierre Franken, who moved up with a 32 Battalion recce team to establish an observation post near Techipa from where he would be able to bring in artillery fire on the town, found the journey extremely irksome and disagreeable. 'The population was so hostile that when we passed too near to their kraals and the donkeys brayed the villagers would beat on drums and cooking pots to give away our position to enemy patrols,' Franken said.

'On one occasion we had to pass a horse at night and we knew there was a Fapla patrol lying up in a dip just to our left. The horse kept still until we were past it, and then it whinnied and galloped away. We pushed on a bit, stopped and then we heard people running at us from behind.

'We froze, slipped the safety catches on our rifles and waited standing up straight in the open. It was quite dark and four or five Fapla soldiers went straight past us. The nearest one must have been about ten metres from us, but they didn't see us.'

On Wednesday 22 June one of the forward 32 Battalion reconnaissance platoons reported big dust columns moving south. It looked as though the Cubans were moving out to do battle. 25 Field Engineers had only just completed the giant earth ramps at the Calueque dam. Muller moved his tanks and the rest of his main force, named Combat Group Charlie, across the dam that night.

Muller divided the force into three combat teams. They deployed forward to designated positions. Combat Team One, with a Ratel-90 squadron, two mechanised infantry platoons, and six Ratel-81s as its core, moved up to within 12 km of Techipa. Combat Team Two, with a core of one mechanised infantry company, three Ratel-90s and six Ratel-81s, deployed four kilometres further south. Combat Team Three, with the tank squadron, the four Ratel-ZT3s, two 32 Battalion infantry companies protecting Muller's HQ Ratel group, and a mechanised infantry platoon as its core, was yet another six kilometres to the south.

On 23 and 24 June Muller's forward observers reported Cuban artillery bombardments which seemed to be designed to mask the latest cautious move southwards of the enemy armour. On 25 June Muller did his final planning and co-ordinating and at first light on Sunday 26 June all three Combat Group Charlie teams and the artillery batteries began advancing towards the Cubans.

'The most forward elements, from 32 Battalion, were spread out along a 12 km front,' said Muller. 'My plan was to open proceedings with a massive artillery barrage just before darkness. So we moved forward very slowly to avoid kicking up dust and betraying our positions. In the middle were the Olifants flanked by two infantry companies. In front of them were eight Ratel-90s and four Ratel-ZT3s. Right out in front the infantry blokes from 32 Battalion were to monitor Cuban movements. Everybody was in position by just before 6 pm.'

It was almost time for the artillery barrage to begin but first Jan Hougaard, on a hill just north of Ruacana, had to implement a planned ruse.

'First the Impalas took off from Ondangwa in combat formation to activate the enemy anti-aircraft positions,' said Hougaard. 'As they approached the border the G-5 battery inside Angola and another gun position at Ruacana released weather balloons dragging aluminium foil tails. As the balloons rose the Impalas climbed high as though preparing to attack and then broke off southwards. The Cubans fired six Sam-6s at the balloons. Our artillery observers immediately plotted three Sam-6 launchers and the barrage began from the G-5s, G-2s, MRLs and 120 mm mortars. The Cubans in Techipa were blasted non-stop for about six hours.'

The enemy reaction was desultory. Despite the presence in Techipa of a whole Cuban artillery brigade, it fired only ten artillery shells in response. 'We inflicted very heavy casualties on the Cuban HQ and its personnel,' said Hougaard. 'Its communications were completely cut off and in the morning we could see black columns of smoke from Techipa and targets we had pinpointed to the east and southwest of the town.'

Hougaard was deeply satisfied with the effects of the artillery bombardment. But up front near Techipa his 32 Battalion men were having a torrid time.

Lieutenant Tshisukila Tukayula ('TT') De Abreu, a veteran Angolan member of 32 Battalion, and the 36 men of his infantry platoon had led an Artillery Regiment observer into a position two kilometres southeast of Techipa to identify bull's-eyes for the SADF guns. Just before the artillery opened up on the evening of 26 June, TT's platoon moved east and spotted tanks on the ground.

'They seemed to be waiting for me, because they started their engines,' said TT. 'I radioed Commandant Hougaard and told him that in ten minutes we could be in trouble. It was open ground and we could be cut off. The Commandant replied "*Nao problema* [no problem]. Just give us the co-ordinates and we'll bomb them with the G-5s".'

Covered by the heavy guns and with dusk falling, TT moved two kilometres away during the night. But at first light one of his patrols reported, to TT's horror, that the tanks had picked up the tracks and managed to follow the platoon.

'I radioed HQ and someone there told me "They must be South African tanks." I told him not to give me shit, they were Russian and we needed help. It was completely open country for three kilometres to the south, so we couldn't go that way. When they started shelling all around our last temporary base I decided we had to split up, so I told my sergeant to take half of the platoon northwards while I decided which way to take the others.

'The sergeant complained that he would be moving deeper into Angola away from ultimate safety, so I said "Look man you can't go south or else you'll be shot to pieces; you can't go west because there's a lot of nasty T-54 tanks there; if you go east that's the direction in which they're already following our tracks; they won't expect you to go north, in which case you might get out alive".'

'Then some of the guys wanted to stand and fight, but I told them 36 men with rifles and two RPG-7s against tanks had no chance. I ordered: "No shooting. We're going to have to rely on God and the speed of our legs".'

Back in Ruacana Jan Hougaard feared that TT, whom he had fought alongside for many years, and his platoon would soon be destroyed and killed. 'TT kept calling me on the radio, out of breath and saying in Afrikaans, English and Portugese: "Commandant, please help us",' said Hougaard.

'We had the G-5s ready, but the tanks came up on him constantly and he had to move on again before we could consult and get his position. All we knew was that he was moving northeast towards the Techipa River. At the same time I was trying to dissuade the captain, a white guy, commanding the company from going in to help TT's platoon. I told him to pull out. We had plenty of other problems that day we needed him to attend to! But he went nonetheless and tried to distract the tanks.

'It went on for hours with TT coming on the radio briefly and then saying he had to move on because the tanks were cutting him off. He had run something like 20 km when he came on and said that this time they were in big problems, they were completely surrounded by tanks and armoured cars and they were finished, please bring in the planes.

'But we couldn't do that with only Impalas available and Cuban Migs in the air. I said: "For God's sake, give me your position and we'll blast the place with the G-5s so you can make a run for it!" So he gave me the reference and said: "Start shooting right on it or we're dead". So we let go with the G-5s and when the first rounds fell TT came on the radio and I asked him what correction was needed. He said "Never mind that, just sweep and search".'

'So we pounded the hell out of that position and somehow they got out because of it and we didn't lose one of them. It was amazingly hairy. They ran for hours and hours, always hearing the tanks and occasionally seeing them behind.

'You may wonder how anyone can find the energy and strength to run like that all day. But when you're running in front of unfriendly tanks you're a very worried man. Somehow you find enough adrenalin at the time to do it, I can assure you.'

Mike Muller moved his artillery batteries a tactical leap southwards when the massive barrage of the evening and night of 26 June came to an end in case the enemy armour deployed aggressively to destroy them. As the sun rose on Monday 27 June there seemed to have been no Cuban reaction, so Muller ordered Combat Group Charlie to move cautiously northwards again.

'At about 4 am I had heard the distant sound of engines to the north,' said Muller. 'But I knew 32 Battalion was up front to give early warning, so I thought the noise was from the G-5 battery still moving south. At 5 am one of 32 Battalion's platoons picked up tanks moving south but suffered a radio failure and was unable to warn me.'

Meanwhile Hannes Nortmann was leading a big group of Ratels northwards through slightly undulating country to the east of the Techipa-Calueque road. Before gaining each crest, Nortmann clambered onto his turret and peered over the top of the ridge to ensure that no foes lay in wait. By about 9 am he was 18 km south of Techipa and, having carried out his routine lookout task, was taking his hunting pack of eight Ratel-90s, 12 Ratel-20s, four Ratel-ZT3s and eight Ratel-81s down the grassy northern slope of a hill towards the bush-covered valley floor before creeping up the next rise.

'When the Ratels were at the bottom of the dip, several RPG-7s were fired from a range of 25 m just inside the bushline,' said Muller. 'One rocket destroyed the gearbox of a Ratel-90 and totally immobilised it. The crew had to abandon it. There were armoured cars in the bush with Cuban and Fapla infantry. A company of T-54 tanks shot over the top of the hill from the north to join in the rumpus. It was at that moment that the forward 32 Battalion platoon at last made radio contact to say enemy tanks were on the way. I replied "I know. We've been busy fighting them for the last 15 minutes!"

'It was a big enemy force. More kept coming. There were a lot of Cuban tanks, 26 BMP-2s (mechanised infantry armoured cars mounted with Sagger anti-tank missiles), and many Cubans on foot carrying RPG-7s. They were very aggressive. We were outfired in terms of armour. Nortmann had real problems getting his force organised. The Ratel-ZT3s, in a bush-covered valley, were in the worst possible position to fire their missiles, so the Ratel-90s had to pit themselves against the tanks. They shot out a T-54, two ZU-23 guns on tracked armoured chassis and several trucks.

'Machine-gunners on the Ratels were shooting the enemy infantry between the tanks. They killed at least 60 of them. But a 100 mm shell fired from a T-54 hit another Ratel-90, killing one of our blokes, Lieutenant Meiring, and wounding three of his crew.'

Second Lieutenant Muller Meiring, from the little Orange Free State market town of Verkeerdevlei, was aged just 19.

Mike Muller continued: 'I redeployed the Olifants to strengthen the combat team. The Ratels began to pull back. Nortmann, despite being wounded by shrapnel in the neck and left hand, manned the machine-gun on top of his turret to give them cover. The Olifants arrived as the Cubans, too, were breaking contact. Two Olifants fired together at a T-54 with a dozen infantrymen on top. Both shots hit, destroying the tank and killing all the enemy infantry.

'The Cubans began to withdraw. I didn't give chase because I received intelligence that another two enemy tank companies [11 tanks to a Cuban company] were heading towards us, one to the west and the other to the east. And the middle one started to come forward again after it had regrouped.

'We were not strong enough to combat the enlarged enemy force head on. The secret in such a situation is to disengage neither too early nor too late. We zig-zagged backwards tactically for several hours, keeping the enemy in sight all the time. Platoons of 32 Battalion mechanised infantry provided cover for our withdrawal and acted as observers to bring G-5 and G-2 fire on the enemy all the time.

'The middle column was stopped when the G-5s knocked out two support vehicles. But the 32 Battalion guys opposite the eastern column drew fire, and it became clear that the third column was driving aggressively to cut us off in the west. I received permission from Brigadier Serfontein to move southeast to establish a compact front on the high ground ten kilometres to the north of Calueque. It was just before 3 pm. I was about to order the movement to Calueque when we picked up eight Migs, two flying top cover and six flying low towards us. We gave early warning to HQ.'

★ ★ ★

Minutes later Jan Hougaard, seated in his tactical HQ at Ruacana, got a radio message from a nearby hilltop observer post that several Mig-23s had flown low over them in the direction of Calueque. 'I flashed a warning by radio to Brigade HQ and then ran outside to see eight Mig-23s turn over Ruacana and then six of them levelled out south of the river towards the Calueque dam. Then I heard explosions and saw palls of smoke and dust.'

The Cuban Migs had hit their target with precision bombing in the most successful Cuban/Fapla bombing raid of the War for Africa.

'It was a very deliberate, well-planned, attack,' said Colonel Dick Lord. 'All eight Mig-23s had come from Cahama, 120 km north of Calueque. Two flew very high looking out for possible SAAF fighter interception. The other six hugged dirt roads at 100 m until they hit Ruacana where they flew past the airfield before lining up in pairs southwest to northeast along another dirt road on our side of the river towards Calueque.

'The first pair overflew the dam at just under 300 m to "acquire" the target and then climbed up to high altitude to call the other guys in. The other four attacked the dam wall in pairs straight and level at 400 m, first from southwest to northeast at a cross-angle and then from east to west.

'Each plane dropped two 250 kg parachute-retarded bombs on each pass. They flew very slowly. It was a very academic attack in which they ignored any threat from our air defences, and in fact it was only as they made their second pass that our 20 mm anti-aircraft guns and Sam-7s opened fire.

'They placed six of their 16 bombs on the dam wall and the ramps leading up to the road across it, which is not a bad percentage. There were two soldiers on top of the dam during the attack. One was quite badly hurt by flying concrete and shrapnel, but the other had a miraculous escape. He leaped something like 15 m to get away. He only sprained his ankle and was able to carry on running to safety.

'On the second attack run one of the bombs fell short of the dam near a Buffel standing next to the big steel pipeline which takes water off from Calueque to Ovamboland. There were 11 guys from 8 SAI (8th South African Infantry Battalion) on a supply mission sitting around among their vehicles under the trees eating their lunch. The blast was massive and they were all killed instantly'.

It was the SADF's worst single loss in the War for Africa. With the death earlier that day of Lieutenant Meiring, seven of the 12 dead were aged 19, four were aged 20, while the veteran among them was 23-year-old Lieutenant Noah Tucker, from Germiston on the East Rand.

In South Africa it caused waves of wrath, anguish and fear as international newspapers blazoned such headlines as 'Angola War: Pretoria's Plans Go Awry,' (*International Herald Tribune*, 13 July 1988), 'Military Balance

Shifts Against Pretoria,' (*The Times* of London, 16 June, 1988), '12 South Africans Die in Angolan Border Clash,' (*Washington Post*, 29 June 1988) and 'The nightmares of Pretoria's generals are coming true ... South Africa's whites for the first time are starting to feel the effect of casualties in a distant war of which they are told very little,' (*Africa Confidential*, 15 July 1988).

Heated questions were asked about why the SADF had allowed the enemy to make such a deliberate attack on a vital installation.

'They maintained radio silence and so achieved surprise,' said one 'senior SAAF officer' to Mr Willem Steenkamp, the doyen of South African military correspondents. 'Very few air forces can withstand this sort of attack; you can do very little but provide ground air defence. Their bombing accuracy was very good under the circumstances, very accurate.'[3]

That was not quite how Commandant Mike Muller saw it. His official report later said local warning to the anti-aircraft crews had been too slow. In the eastern theatre Muller and every other unit commander had attached to them senior Air Force officers at the head of Mobile Air Operations Teams.

'One member of the MAOT was an operations officer and the other bloke was an SAAF intelligence officer,' said Muller. 'Whenever a Mig took off from an enemy airfield our MAOT guys would know and they would tell us: "There is a channel active."'

'We immediately went to a state of readiness and when the enemy planes came within range we were already on "red alert", camouflaged and ready to fire at them as necessary. At Calueque-Techipa we had no MAOTs on the ground, so the warnings of enemy warplane take-offs went through ordinary operations channels which took a critical three to five minutes longer.'

It is probable therefore that South African anti-aircraft guns and missiles would have been ready for the Cuban Migs on their first slow and deliberate approach to the dam had there been MAOTs with Muller's Battle Group Charlie to the north of Calueque. As it was, the 20 mm guns hit one of the Mig-23s on the second bombing run. After several of the smoking Mig's systems had petered out, it crashed just north of Techipa, probably after the pilot had ejected.

Hannes Nortmann could not help being involved in this action too! He was being treated for his wounds in a Rinkhals ambulance parked near the 8 SAI vehicles at the dam site which moved off with the 32 Battalion major aboard only minutes before the Migs made their attack.

★ ★ ★

Back in Angola, Mike Muller's Combat Group Charlie now had another problem. Some of the Mig-23 bombs dropped at Calueque had destroyed one of the earth ramps leading to the road at the top of the dam. The Olifants could no longer get out of Angola that way.

'I was about to give the orders for the withdrawal to a tight laager ten kilometres north of Calueque when the Migs went in to bomb the dam,' said Muller. 'Now the only way out for the tanks was across a bridge at Swawek, 40 km to the southwest. It was in that direction that the western Cuban tank column was trying to cut us off.

'I redeployed the Olifants slightly to the west. I left the Ratels and mechanised infantry to keep an eye on the central and eastern Cuban force while I concentrated the whole of our artillery on the western column. The G-5s shot out eight of the enemy vehicles and they stopped advancing.

'I then ordered the G-5s to Calueque to cross the low-level bridge one at a time under cover of darkness followed by the Ratels and other vehicles. Then I moved westwards with the Olifants along a dirt mountain road with one motorised infantry company and a mortar group for protection. We had no problems and crossed the Swawek bridge into Namibia.

'It was lucky the Cubans didn't know Swawek was strong enough to take tanks or they would have bombed it as well. Then I would probably have had to dump the Olifants in the River Cunene.'

From Swawek Muller moved eastwards through Namibia to take up position south of Calueque while 25 Field Engineer Squadron reconstructed the earth ramp at the dam to allow the Olifants to move north again to re-engage the Cubans. Just before midnight on Monday 27 June 1988 Muller received orders to withdraw all his forces from Angola.

Commandant Jan Hougaard, on whom responsibility fell for getting the last protective and wandering 32 Battalion platoons back to Namibia, said: 'I was told in no uncertain terms that from that night onwards not a toe was to be put across the border into Angola.'

★ ★ ★

More suddenly than it had begun, the War for Angola was over.

Sixteen days later, on an island in New York harbour, South Africa, Angola and Cuba agreed on 14 principles as a basis for peace in Angola and Namibia requiring the linked withdrawals of the SADF from Namibia and the departure of the Revolutionary Armed Forces of Cuba from Angola.

All was solemnly sealed at the UN headquarters in New York at 10 am on 22 December 1988 when South African Foreign Minister Pik Botha, Angolan Foreign Minister Afonso Van Dunem and Cuban Foreign Minister Isidor Malmierca Peoli signed the trilateral New York Accords which would transform a continent.

By November 1989 the last SADF troops had left Namibia and the country became independent in March 1990 after UN-supervised multi-party elections. The last Cuban soldier was due out of Angola by 1 July 1991.

Notes

1 Speech to Cuba's Council of State in Havana, 9 July 1989.
2 Major Florentine Aztilloga Lombard, former Cuban intelligence officer, made the remarks in a radio interview in Washington on 29 June 1988.
3 Willem Steenkamp, *South Africa's Border War*, 1966–1989 (Ashanti Publishing), p.165.

EPILOGUE

A peace is of the nature of a conquest;
For then both parties are nobly subdu'd
And neither party loser.

William Shakespeare,
King Henry the Fourth, Part One.

Better a lean peace than a fat victory.

Seventeenth-century proverb.

And when the war is done and youth stone dead
I'd toddle safely home and die – in bed.

Sir Siegfried Sassoon.

So who won the War for Africa? Opinions – and there are many! – are sharply divided. Cuba was victorious, according to Fidel Castro. South Africa was the clear winner, according to the former Chief of the SADF, General Jannie Geldenhuys. Others have declared it a draw. But then again: 'Truth is the first casualty of war.'[1]

The most simplistic Cuban version, in print and video, is that the South African Army over-extended itself and became surrounded by Fapla and Cuban forces at Cuito Cuanavale. South Africa therefore entered negotiations brokered by the USA from May 1988 onwards to extract its beleaguered troops, tanks and armoured cars from what was Pretoria's own Dien

Bien Phu. 'A debacle' was how the Soviet/Russian commentator Vladimir Shubin described the outcome for South Africa at Cuito Cuanavale.[2]

'They will write about "before Cuito Cuanavale" and "after Cuito Cuanavale", because the power of South Africa, the whites, the "superior race", has come unstuck in a little parcel of land defended by blacks and mulattoes,' Fidel Castro proclaimed. In a public speech marking Revolutionary Armed Forces Day,[3] he went on: 'The resounding victories in Cuito Cuanavale by the powerful Cuban contingent spelled the end of foreign aggression. The enemy had to set aside its usual arrogance and sit down at the negotiating table ... Rarely in history has war, the most terrible, heartrending and difficult of human actions, been accompanied by such humanism and humility on the part of the victors, despite the near-total absence of these values in the ranks of the vanquished.'[4]

The Cuban narrative was taken at face value by Castro's sympathisers around the world and repeated so often that even among many beyond the true believers it became received truth.

But the assertion that the SADF had been 'surrounded' at Cuito Cuanavale was unreal: it does not stand up to objective analysis. No army could physically 'surround' another in southeastern Angola. The vastness of the sparsely inhabited wilderness, the tangled trees and vegetation, the clogging sand and the sucking swamps and laced river networks made such likelihood the stuff of fantasy. The limited numbers of troops committed to battle by the SADF, Cubans, Fapla and UNITA – in relation to the huge area of forest and swamp over which the fighting took place – made the idea even more far-fetched.

In speeches in Havana on 26 July 1988 and 9 July 1989 to the country's Council of State [Cuba's 31-member ruling body], Castro gave a more rational version of events at Cuito Cuanavale. In these domestic homilies, he referred only to the 'thwarting' of the South Africans. Castro said 'a complex and critical situation arose [at Cuito Cuanavale] as a consequence of an enormous military escalation by South Africa.' Intervening with tanks, infantry, aircraft and 'Namibian mercenary forces', the South Africans had dealt Fapla a number of military blows on the Lomba River, he said. The Fapla forces then began retreating because they were suffering grave shortages of food, fuel and ammunition.

Disaster followed, Castro admitted. The South Africans on 14 February 1988 crashed through a five-kilometre gap between Fapla's 21 and 59 Brigades and routed them. 'A very difficult situation emerged,' he said. 'They [the SADF] could have gone as far as the bridge [across the Cuito River] back into Cuito Cuanavale and cut off three Angolan brigades – more than 3,500 soldiers.'

In an implicit criticism of the Soviet military advisers, mirroring that of General Rafael Del Pino Dias,[5] Castro said: 'One day history will reveal it all, where the mistakes lay, why those mistakes were made. I shall only limit myself to saying that Cuba was not responsible for those mistakes.

'There were thousands and thousands of men from Angola's best units (besieged east of Cuito Cuanavale and the Cuito River) and *they were in danger of being wiped out.*[6] That would have been disastrous for Angola; it would have meant the possibility of destroying the independence and the revolution of Angola.' At this point, said the Cuban leader, Fapla requested greatly increased Cuban assistance. 'Help was essential not only to collaborate with Angola to get out of a difficult situation, but also for the security of our own troops,' said Castro. 'If South Africa were allowed to wipe out the Angolan troops the situation could become dangerous for our own troops as well. Therefore, without hesitation, the leadership of the [Cuban Communist] Party decided to help the Angolans to solve the situation.'

But, Castro added, Fapla could only be bolstered by reinforcing those Cuban troops already in Angola with more forces from Cuba. 'The troops that had been in Angola for years were not enough to guard a long strategic [logistics] line and also solve the situation that had been created in Cuito Cuanavale. That's why we had to reinforce the troops.'

In a significant phrase, Castro said: 'It was necessary to be strong enough to *avoid*[7] defeat.' He went on: 'We had to get into Cuito Cuanavale to support the Angolan forces and, at their side, wage the historical actions where the enemy was stopped, where it really crumbled ...

'We were not looking for military glory, or military victory. We were looking for a just political solution to the conflict. That was the main objective, and that's why the possibilities of negotiation were not discarded … Based on the principles and the points included in the (preliminary Namibia–Angola) agreement,[8] our military presence will no longer be needed in Angola.'

Chester Crocker said he met Castro in 1989, when the war was over and the New York Accords had been agreed, and quoted the Cuban leader as telling him: 'We respected your diplomacy and we were prepared to contribute to a settlement: it must be an honourable one and it must provide security for our people as they departed and for Angola as well.'[9]

Crocker also said: 'The Angolans, Cubans and South Africans wanted assurances that an "honourable" settlement could be achieved.

'No one had won on the ground. Therefore, everyone would have to win at the table. This fact would have to be fully reflected in the language, symbols and political imagery of the deal.'[10]

General Geldenhuys said that the SADF had strictly limited objectives when its fighting men became substantially engaged alongside UNITA in southeastern Angola in July 1987. 'It was not our intention to start a war that might end in Luanda and go on for ever. We did not want to establish a permanent presence. We did not want to make Angola our Vietnam. Our aim after crossing into Angola was to achieve certain limited tasks and then get out.'[11]

Geldenhuys denied that Cuito Cuanavale was ever an objective of strategic importance for the SADF. 'Cuito Cuanavale was put into the limelight by the Cubans. I actually forbade the Chief of the Army (General Kat Liebenberg) to take Cuito Cuanavale. I made just one concession: If our operations so developed that Cuito Cuanavale fell into our lap (then it could be occupied): additionally we had to be sure we would be able to defend it, because there is no point in capturing a place if you cannot hold it.'

There were several ways in which to argue about who won the War for Africa, said Geldenhuys, who stepped down in 1990 as head of the Defence Force. The best way, he said, was to look at the *initial*[12] objectives of each side: 'The Cuban-Fapla objective was to capture Mavinga and Jamba. They didn't accomplish it. Our objective was to prevent them from taking Mavinga and Jamba. We succeeded.

'The turning point was the Lomba River battles. They were a severe blow to the morale, thinking and image of the Cubans and Fapla. We destroyed a whole enemy brigade (47 Brigade) on the Lomba. History will prove it to be one of the most glorious and successful actions that South African forces ever took part in. There were heavy things flying and moving around – missiles, planes, tanks, guns. To destroy that brigade with minimal South African losses was remarkable.

'The Cubans and Fapla had to do something subsequently to shore up morale, so they presented the war to the outside world as though it was a matter of who captured or who held Cuito Cuanavale.'

Geldenhuys rejected the conventional wisdom that because of the creeping technological obsolescence of its aircraft – as a result of international anti-apartheid arms sanctions – the South African Air Force lost the war in the air. He claimed that for most of the war the Angolan Air Force, equipped with increasing state-of-the-art Soviet warplanes, was not a serious or decisive factor. 'It is true that they were more active,' he said, 'but they were not more effective. If they had been more effective we could have lost the war.

'We placed emphasis on local air superiority for limited periods when we wanted it. One of our senior Air Force commanders, Brigadier Carl van Heerden, made calculations as scientifically as possible about tonnages of ammunition dropped by both Air Forces. After the Angolan Air Force had delivered a million tonnes of ammunition we had lost only one man in air attacks. We were simply more operationally efficient: any one of our sorties was more effective than scores of theirs.'

Geldenhuys claimed also that the undoubted superiority of the Soviet-manufactured top cover aircraft proved a blessing in disguise for the SADF. Recognising that the arrival of Mig-23s in Angola had accelerated the push of the South African Air Force Mirage F-ICZs towards obsolescence, Geldenhuys had therefore made the development of night fighting capabilities an important part of South African military doctrine from the early 1980s. 'The motto was: When the enemy sleeps we begin to move. Fapla and the Cubans never really knew where we were.'

In addition, the superior range of the G-5 heavy artillery, claimed as the finest long-range gun of its kind at that time and exported to several countries, compensated for the erosion of South African air superiority. Geldenhuys said that during the Sal Island round of negotiations,[13] one of the Cuban officers in the military negotiating team led by General Ochoa Sanchez told him: 'Those fucking guns give us terrible fear.' Geldenhuys struck up a thoughtful relationship with Ochoa Sanchez, and one morning towards the end of the negotiations a wooden box containing Cuban rum and canned fruit was delivered to the South African general's home in Pretoria: it was a gift from his Cuban opposite number.

The War for Africa ended abruptly on Monday 27 June 1988 after the final bloody spasm in southwest Angola in which both Cuban and South African soldiers suffered terrible deaths and casualties.[14]

Castro and Geldenhuys maintained that the other side blinked and backed off. In reality, both armies disengaged to safe distances before they became embroiled in a series of battles that would have resulted in more carnage. 'Both sides realised that they stood on the verge of a devastating all-out war which neither wanted nor could afford,' wrote one military historian. 'Besides, peace talks were already underway. A tacit agreement was reached not to escalate the fighting. The war was over, bar the shouting.'[15]

The South Africans claimed to have killed 300 Fapla and Cuban soldiers on the morning of 27 June in a last armoured attack on an enemy column near Techipa, about 80 kilometres inside Angola. The Cubans conceded the loss of ten men and the South Africans said one of their armoured officers, 19-year-old Lieutenant Muller Meiring, was killed when his Ratel was shot out by a T-54 tank. The Cubans immediately responded, bombing the South African-occupied Calueque hydro-electric dam, on the Cunene River, 13 kilometres inside Angola, which supplied water and electricity to northern Namibia. Seven Mig-23s swept continuously over the dam, killing 11 South African infantrymen and inflicting such heavy damage that by 2016 the dam had still not been fully repaired. One Cuban pilot flew his plane in a low-level victory roll over the dam.[16]

'We had never been bombed like this by enemy aircraft in Angola,' said one veteran armoured officer. 'They (the Cuban pilots) shot with continuing accuracy … It felt like an eternity, and the Migs turned again and again and came back to us standing next to the dam wall. They hit the wall with bombs that fell left and right of us. Their 23 mm cannon moved us and shots rang out left and right ….

'Slowly and shivering, full of dust, we crawled from under the Ratels. We started running and saw the damage caused. I do not believe that any South African force or groups had been attacked so aggressively before by the enemy's aircraft.'[17]

Castro, after arguing in his speeches of July 1988 and July 1989 that the South Africans had 'smashed themselves against the Angolan-Cuban resistance' at Cuito Cuanavale, went on to describe the big Cuban push into the Techipa-Calueque area in June 1988 as 'extraordinary' and 'really impressive.' By that time it was clear that the 'peace process had become irreversible,' Castro further said. That was probably true. The second of twelve rounds of peace talks, brokered by Chester Crocker, had just ended in Cape Verde: there Cuba's military intelligence chief said his country's forces in Angola intended returning home – and that would require some reciprocal *quid pro quo* from the South Africans. General Geldenhuys saw merits in many of the arguments raised by the Cubans, but said he had no mandate to discuss possible concessions by South Africa.

However, the talks in Cape Verde prepared the ground for the next round of much more positive talks in Geneva from 2 to 5 August 1988. A powerful South African negotiating team, led by two sharp-witted career civil servants, Neil Van Heerden, Director-General of Foreign Affairs, and Niël Barnard, Director-General of the National Intelligence Service, took the Cubans and the MPLA aback by saying Pretoria was willing to withdraw all its forces from Angola and Namibia by June 1989, paving the way for the latter country's independence, in return for a Cuban withdrawal from Angola. A scarcely noticed part of the Geneva agreement, drawn up in a protocol, was that African National Congress military bases in Angola would be closed: this was a development of enormous future importance. 'So sensitive were the reciprocal military undertakings that the protocol was classified "confidential" at Angolan-Cuban insistence,' commented Crocker. 'This was not surprising: the South Africans got a lot by giving a lot at Geneva.'[18]

Castro said he was hugely concerned that the South Africans would counter his own show of strength at Calueque *not* by ignoring the provocation but by re-engaging in battle: Calueque was really a last flourish of *machismo* before he broke the news to the Cuban people that their soldiers would be coming home from Angola. Just in case the South Africans did not follow the script that he had prepared for them, Castro said he cabled General Ochoa Sanchez on 7 June 1988 with the following instruction: 'News of a possible South African surprise air attack should not be underestimated. Be ready to counter-attack with as many aircraft as possible. Do not wait for orders to carry out the attack if there is a strong enemy attack against our troops.'

The counter-attack never came. The war ended, and under the New York Accords, signed in the city of that name on 22 December 1988, the Cubans agreed to leave Angola, the South Africans withdrew their support from Savimbi's UNITA and prepared to begin leaving Namibia. The signing ceremony was held at United Nations Headquarters and was presided over by UN Secretary-General Perez de Cuellar, US Secretary of State George Shultz and the youthful and charming Soviet deputy foreign minister Anatoly Adamishin.

Adamishin's involvement in the negotiations was welcomed by Crocker, who had spent eight years patiently trying to bring all sides together to achieve a remarkable regional peace settlement.

Soviet involvement in the process was hugely important. Mikhail Gorbachev, the last Secretary-General of the Soviet Communist Party – before the Soviet Union was dissolved – had made clear to the MPLA and the Cubans that the billion dollars he assigned to finance and equip the 1987–88 assault on Mavinga and Jamba would be Moscow's final contribution if the offensive failed – as it did, on the banks of the Lomba River. The Soviets, some of whose military advisers died at the Lomba, were interested thereafter only in peace.

'It is a pleasure to work with an old African wolf like you,' Adamishin told Crocker on one occasion, and on another: 'Don't worry, Chet, I've got everything under control.'[19]

The joint commitment of the Americans and the Soviets undoubt-edly grew stronger and stronger to end the Angola–Namibia crisis: they combined blandishments with enormous pressure to persuade both the South Africans and the Cubans to step back from what would have been a catastrophic intensification of the conflict.

The concern of South Africa's leaders about further losses of its young men on Angolan soil – running in parallel, however, with a determina-ton to fight with unprecedented ferocity should the Cubans dare probe into Namibia – was expressed by Foreign Minister Pik Botha: 'I am personally of the opinion that, if the enemy is dug in over a broad front and equipped with a deadly arsenal, you must think twice before you simply allow hundreds of your sons to be killed.'[20]

The apartheid government's fear of 'excessive' casualties was especially great because the white population in South Africa had been given few details of the fighting. 'For all practical purposes it was a "secret war",' said one Special Forces soldier who fought in Angola. 'Relatives and friends had no idea what their loved ones were going through while serving on the border.

'For many South Africans who sacrificed their lives, the undertone of a "forgotten war" is a bitter pill to swallow considering the sacrifices they were expected to make. For the duration of the war, [everyday] life in South Africa continued almost unhindered.'[21] The 'troopies' were sworn under oath to secrecy about operations. 'In all history there cannot be many instances of a country going into a foreign war without the knowledge of its people,' remarked the veteran South African journalist Allister Sparks.[22]

David Mannall, who fought on the Lomba River as a 19-year-old and saw his teenage friends blown to pieces in the huge armoured battle there against Fapla's 47 Brigade, recalled returning home to Durban: 'We were re-entering "normal" society, but our reality and outlook was a very different shade of normal. They asked what we'd been up to. "We were in some big battles and got bombed by enemy aircraft," was about all I could say. Somehow it seemed impossible to find the words to accurately convey the humour, heartache, trauma, fear and bravery that are life at war.

'Society at large seemed uninterested, the government equally so … For most of us the experience resonated deeply, for ever re-shaping completely our outlook on life, death and the world in which we live. The baubles of our material world were no shield from which to shelter a scared kid still shivering with fear.

'We were still very young men, abandoned to make sense in a world without the brutal high-octane, high-stakes adrenaline-fuelled camara-derie and candour we'd become accustomed to during 90 days at war. Prospective employers placed no value on talents earned at such high cost. Courage and commitment in the face of Russian Main Battle Tanks counted for nothing in a "normal" world separated from the killing fields of death. The cost? A generation of cannon fodder soldiers.'[23]

The story became lore of South African soldiers hundreds of kilometres inside Angola listening with incredulity to radio broadcasts from back home in which government spokesmen denied their presence in that country. The war was waged far away from the public eye. Censorship and disinformation served to create a conspiracy of silence. 'The Nationalist Party government did not take the media, the soldiers or their families into their confidence,' said Gary Baines, Professor of History at Rhodes University, Grahamstown, who has written and lectured extensively on the Border War. 'The government often treated the general public with sheer indifference. It repeatedly refused to disclose the truth about the number and nature of South Africa's casualties.'[24]

Baines quoted the final stanza of a poem about a mythical teenage South African soldier who died and was buried in Angola:

> And all this time he lay
> womb warmthed in the curve of the Angolan earth
> with a hole in his head in which
> the starmoondarkness and veld stood vigil
> without even as much as a simple letter
> to tell them
> the uncensored bloody truth.[25]

General Geldenhuys firmly maintained that Castro, having decided that he and his Fapla allies could not win at Cuito Cuanavale, decided on an all-out attack in the southwest to save face before going to the negotiating table to agree on a withdrawal of Cuba's expeditionary force

from Angola. 'They were crack troops that Castro sent to Techipa,' said
Geldenhuys. 'We killed 300 of them on 27 June in that first and only
scrap (in southwest Angola).[26] We dealt a crushing blow to any ideas they
might have had about crossing the border.

'We had decided that if there was going to be a major war on the
southwestern front, then let's have it, but on South West African soil.
We in the SADF were enthusiastic about that possibility, because then we
would have really gone to town in a way we had never done throughout
the entire war. The psychological drive would have been there and we
would have had the political backing. We would have had the advantage
of a boost to morale and fierce motivation fighting on our own rather
than foreign soil. In northern South West Africa we would have been
fighting from our permanent bases, whereas at Mavinga and Cuito
Cuanavale we had very long supply lines. Logistics were excellent in
northern South West Africa, and we would have thrown several more
combat groups into battle. In southeastern Angola ninety percent of the
infantry was supplied by UNITA: in South West Africa the infantry
would have been purely South African Defence Force formations.'

If the Cubans had dared to cross the border into Namibia they would
have entered a 'killing field,' was Chester Crocker's opinion.[27]

General Geldenhuys told me that at the first round of peace talks, in
the cramped basement of Durrants Hotel in the West End of London,
from 2 to 4 May 1988, he gave the main Cuban negotiator, Havana's
armed forces chief, General Ulysses Rosales del Toro, a gift of South
African brandy. Rosales and his delegation brought huge Cohiba cigars.

The early stages of the clandestine London talks, undiscovered by the
British press, degenerated into open threats. Rosales warned Geldenhuys
that unless South Africa cut off all aid to Savimbi's UNITA and made
a commitment to leave Namibia, then nothing would stop Cuba from
invading Namibia.

Geldenhuys replied that if the Cubans dared 'to set one foot across the
border it would be the blackest day in Cuban military history.'

The bloodshed at Techipa and Calueque followed soon afterwards,
but Crocker rescued enough from the London talks to be able to organise another round in Cairo on 24 and 25 June 1988. The Cairo meeting

also began with verbal fireworks. This time the Cuban delegation was led by Jorge Risquet, Castro's right-hand adviser on Africa, and South Africa by foreign minister Pik Botha.

It was like watching scorpions in a bottle, observed Crocker, who spoke sympathetically about General Geldenhuys, who was in the South African delegation in Cairo. 'Geldenhuys thought he understood this game and how to respond to it,' said Crocker. 'His conversation with Rosales in London convinced him that an equitable deal could be achieved if escalatory military incidents could be avoided and if the political leadership in Havana and Pretoria wanted one. But he knew it would not be easy to persuade his own leadership.'[28]

Botha began in Cairo by proposing a timetable for a phased Cuban withdrawal from Angola. To which Risquet replied that it was a 'tasteless joke' delivered with typical South Africa 'arrogance.' Risquet said Cuba had refrained from interfering in South Africa's internal affairs, even though its apartheid philosophy was 'a crime against humanity.' Crocker said Botha, in reply, launched a 45-minute tirade in which he demanded to know from Risquet whether a Cuban citizen could take his or her communist government to court. In apartheid South Africa, he said, white doctors had successfully separated black Siamese twins. On a per capita basis, more South African blacks owned cars than did ordinary Soviet citizens. Angola's foreign minister Afonso Van Dunem threw his own firecracker into the talks by demanding US$ 12 billion in reparations from South Africa for damage wrought in Angola; to which Botha threatened to submit damage claims for Angola's support of SWAPO and ANC terrorism, and these would be higher than the Angolan claims since 'our property is more valuable than yours.'[29]

This kind of wrangling was pretty futile because in the previous month Ronald Reagan and Mikhail Gorbachev had already decided in principle at one of their historic summits – in Moscow between 29 May and 1 June 1988 – that Cuban troops would be withdrawn from Angola, and Soviet military aid to Angola would cease, as soon as South Africa withdrew from Namibia. It was hardly noticed amidst the general euphoria of East-West détente and the beginnings of talks about reductions in strategic nuclear arms arsenals. But the die had been cast. It remained *only* for the details of a Cuba–South Africa deal to be hammered out by armies of diplomats and other civil service 'experts', although, as General Geldenhuys observed: 'It is more difficult to make peace than to make war.'

However, Risquet and Botha settled down after their opening skirmishes and by the end the Cuban was asserting that he and his delegation would not cause a breakdown in the negotiating process. Likewise Botha refused to be provoked by 'your provocations' and promised to study the final Cairo document and not respond 'abusively as you have done.'[30]

Geldenhuys said that above all else South Africa wanted the Cubans out of Angola. 'That was our chief objective,' he said. Nothing could help more to stabilise the situation in the whole southern African region than the withdrawal of Castro's soldiers. 'We agreed that we must not make statements that would humiliate the Cubans. We had studied and come to understand their *machismo* thought processes. We saw that they could not afford to go out of Angola a defeated force.' Geldenhuys also told me that he advised General Ulises Rosales del Toro in London that he did not mind Cuba claiming victory at Cuito Cuanavale 'as long as every last Cuban in Angola either sails or flies home across the Atlantic.'[31]

Geldenhuys said that government silence, meanwhile, had caused problems with the fighting men. 'Good or bad, right or wrong, the South African government's position was that it [the conflict in Angola] was Savimbi's war, not ours. It tied our hands in dealing with the media. Savimbi was issuing the press releases: we only began to issue statements when we began to take casualties. It was then that we began to claim victories. Savimbi took exception and got very annoyed.'

Geldenhuys said he met his field commanders in Angola in January 1988 and told them: '*You* know who is winning the war and I promise you the records will be set straight in the future. We do not want to say we are defeating the Cubans because we will have to negotiate with them. They want the implementation of 435 [United Nations Resolution 435 calling for South Africa to grant independence to Namibia]. We want the Cubans out of Angola. We are happy to give 435 if the Cubans leave Angola.'

★ ★ ★

Ultimately the trouble with asking who won the War for Africa is that it might be the wrong question. It is of course the most obvious query. But a better question to ask might be: What new opportunities did the war, and the consequent New York Accords of 22 December 1988, open up for all the different belligerents?

The answer is: many.

For SWAPO it paved the way to victory – in a November 1989 multi-party general election, followed by independence from South Africa on 21 March 1990 – which the movement had no hope of achieving on the battlefield. General elections have since been held a further four times and the country is widely regarded as one of the most stable in Africa.

For Angolans it offered the opportunity to settle their 13-year civil war at the negotiating table free from internal interference by Cuban or South African military forces.

UNITA and the MPLA, both exhausted by the prolonged conflict, began peace talks in 1989: these resulted in a cease-fire in June of that year. In 1990 the MPLA abandoned Marxism-Leninism and declared social democracy to be its official ideology.

In September 1992 Angola's first multi-party general election was held since independence 17 years earlier. The MPLA won 54 percent of the votes and 129 of 227 seats in the Luanda parliament. UNITA returned 70 members to parliament. In the parallel presidential election the MPLA candidate, Eduardo dos Santos, was elected with 49 percent of votes cast against 40 percent for UNITA's Savimbi.

Savimbi declared the elections rigged and violence between MPLA and UNITA soldiers erupted in Luanda in the aftermath and spread to other parts of the country. Savimbi withdrew his forces to the interior to begin the civil war once again, despite objections by some of his senior officers who said ordinary people craved peace after years of warfare in which hundreds of thousands of fighters and civilians had died. Many massacres and purges, politically and tribally motivated, were perpetrated by both sides in the wake of the election. By one estimate, some 120,000 people were killed in the first eighteen months following the 1992 voting, nearly half the total number of deaths in the previous seventeen years of war.[32] The United Nations reported that as many as a thousand people were dying daily from conflict, starvation and disease in mid-1993 – more than in any other country in the world at that time.

UNITA quickly captured several provincial capitals, including Angola's second largest city, Huambo (formerly Nova Lisboa), after battles in which an estimated 10,000 people, many of them civilians, died. As many as 20,000 to 30,000 people died when UNITA laid siege to the city of Bie over a period of 21 months.[33]

But the tide began to turn when a number of senior UNITA officials resigned and defected: among them was UNITA's outstanding guerrilla commander, General Geraldo Nunda, who was immediately appointed Chief of Staff of Fapla, with the special task of tracking down Savimbi and either killing or capturing him. With the help of Israel and South African soldiers who had once fought against the MPLA in Angola, and with increasing support from Washington DC, Savimbi and his bodyguard were trapped by government soldiers against the banks of a tributary of the Zambezi River on 2 February 2002 and riddled with bullets. Savimbi died immediately. UNITA's new leaders quickly agreed to surrender their arms and sign a peace deal with the MPLA which holds to this day. In Angola's latest general election, on 31 August 2012, the MPLA was returned to power with 175 of 220 parliamentary seats against 32 for UNITA. Angola's next parliamentary and presidential elections are scheduled for August 2017.

The Angola war and the New York Accords provided Cuba with cover for sloughing off with honour a commitment to the MPLA that had become too expensive and too hot to handle. Crocker said Fidel Castro had the clearest strategy of any of the parties at the rounds of talks in 1988: he set aside other business for much of the year. 'Our Cuban counterparts made clear just how closely "the Beard" was following each move – at the table and on the ground,' said Crocker. 'Invisible but omnipresent, he kept his delegation on a short but well-defined leash. Aldana and his team knew that Castro wanted a deal.'[34] (Carlos Aldana Escalante, the Cuban Communist Party secretary for ideology, replaced Jorge Risquet Valdes in July 1988 as head of Havana's nego-tiating team).

'In one conversation over lunch, Aldana offered me an eloquent description of how much Cuba would gain from an honourable end to the conflicts in southern Africa,' recalled Crocker. 'Neil van Heerden, Jannie Geldenhuys and Niël Barnard are the guys who need to hear your message, I responded. Tell *them* that Cuba wants a settlement.[35]

Castro's man went from the lunch table with Crocker in New York on 11 July 1988 to tell the South Africans at the negotiating table that Cuba wanted a 'peace without losers' that would reflect 'the legitimate interests of all' and lead to an honourable withdrawal of Cuba from Angola 'of our own free will.' The South Africans were so taken aback and impressed, said Crocker, that they were still talking about Aldana's intervention three years later.

In 1975, when the Cuban adventure in Angola began, the 'internationalist' and 'scientific socialist' tide flowing from Moscow to the MPLA looked powerful. By 1988 the surge had lost much of its strength. Despite 13 years of ideological support from Havana, the Angolan economy lay in ruins, with the MPLA about to flip flop from Marxism-Leninism to a fairly extreme form of exploitative capitalism. The MPLA's leaders were casting off their military uniforms for Savile Row suits.

The opportunity to escape from the Angola entanglement gave Fidel Castro's government the opportunity to concentrate on Cuba's looming domestic challenges. The country had been left much exposed by the collapse of the Soviet Union, which ceased to exist on 25 December 1991 when the Soviet hammer and sickle flag was lowered for the last time over the Kremlin and replaced by the Russian tricolour. It meant isolation and great economic hardship for Cuba. Mikhail Gorbachev had already begun steadily running down Moscow's aid to Cuba from 1988 onwards – including the withdrawal of a 3,000-strong Soviet military training garrison stationed on the Caribbean island – but the subsequent dissolution of the Soviet Union had a further immediate and devastating effect. All Cuba's valuable special client trade and aid privileges were withdrawn: Havana's trade with the new Russian state plunged by more than 90 percent compared with the era of close relations with the Soviet Union that had endured for more than three decades.

At the height of Moscow's relationship with Havana, the Soviet Union provided Cuba with 90 percent of its oil at rates well below the world price and threw in extra supplies for the Cubans to sell for hard currency. Moscow also supplied Castro with military hardware free and bought Cuban sugar at three to five times world market price levels: the Soviet Union alone imported 80 percent of all Cuban sugar and 40 percent of all Cuban citrus.[36] Soviet subsidies to Cuba were estimated overall to be worth more than US$ 10 million a day.

Hungary, while still a communist country, also had long been a supplier of goods to Cuba. But as Hungary exited the Soviet empire it cut off the supply of spare parts for Hungarian buses in Havana and instead opened trade relations with Pretoria!

As the new Russia established increasingly cordial accommodation with the United States, Cuba's leaders and their people found themselves caught up in momentous changes that were almost beyond their capacity to control. The disarray and distress plunged Cuba into a crisis that threatened to undo thirty-five years of social gains and economic achievements. It found itself increasingly unable to import consumer goods and without markets to export the goods it produced. A new regime of austere rationing was introduced. Castro announced plans for what he described as 'a special period in peacetime' – a euphemism for a drastic austerity programme that placed the island state on a wartime economy, freezing social programmes and stopping the building of schools, hospitals, day-care centres and houses. For a while, the country could no longer afford surgical sutures, and doctors were using a homemade thread manufactured from a cactus-like plant called *henequen*. Industrial plants and factories reduced weekly work hours; some closed altogether.[37]

Cuba remained a Marxist-Leninist state, but limited reforms were gradually introduced, including initially the permitting of some self-employment in retail and light manufacturing sectors and the legalisation of the use of the US dollar in business and tourism.

In 2008 an ailing Castro stood down as president at the age of 81 in favour of his younger brother Raúl, then aged 76. By the early years of the 21st century Canada and China had become Cuba's main export partners, taking nearly 40 percent of the island's sugar, nickel, tobacco, fish, medical products, citrus fruit and coffee. By 2016 three million foreign tourists were visiting Cuba each year and a private property boom had begun. US President Barack Obama ordered the restoration of full diplomatic relations with Cuba and the opening of an embassy in Havana for the first time in more than a half-century as he vowed to 'cut loose the shackles of the past' and sweep aside one of the last vestiges of the Cold War.[38] Obama's decision eased travel restrictions for family visits, public performances, and professional, educational and religious activities. It also allowed greater banking ties, making it possible to use credit and debit cards in Cuba, and American travellers were allowed to import up to US$ 400 worth of goods from Cuba, including up to US$ 100 in tobacco and alcohol products.

Some 400,000 Cuban troops had been rotated through Angola over a period of 15 years, bolstering Fidel Castro's pet project. Nearly every Cuban family in a population of only ten million had been affected directly or indirectly by the war. The pledges of special employment privileges that Castro promised for all those who did their 'international-ist duty' were difficult to honour because of the depths of the post-1988 economic crisis.

Fidel Castro found it hard to adopt the extent of reforms that were being embraced in other countries that had recently deserted com-munism. He accused reformists in former hardline Marxist states of succumbing to 'the evils of capitalism.' When asked whether he too would move towards the kind of multi-party democratisation that was sweeping across swathes of the communist world, Castro said: 'We only need one political party, in the same way as Lenin needed only one.' On 4 August 1989 Castro banned the distribution in Cuba of *Sputnik* and the *Moscow News*, two popular Soviet publications that carried the message of Mikhail Gorbachev's liberalising *glasnost*.[39]

Nothing illustrated Cuba's post-Angola angst more dramatically than the decision of a 47-man revolutionary military tribunal to execute General Arnaldo Ochoa Sanchez, the soldier Castro had chosen to pull his chestnuts out of the fire in the War for Africa. For his efforts in Angola and elsewhere over the years Ochoa was one of only five officers to have been made a Hero of the Republic of Cuba.[40] But scarcely a year after the Cubans and South Africans fought their last battle in Angola, Ochoa was led before a firing squad on 12 July 1989 and shot dead, ostensibly for drug-smuggling offences for which he was found guilty at an eight-day hearing that had all the trappings of a show trial, including a four-hour diatribe by Fidel Castro against the general. Before sentence was passed Ochoa was stripped of his Hero of the Republic title.

Those who have investigated Ochoa's demise say it is unlikely that the truth behind his trial and execution will ever be known. 'On the one hand, the details of the case are tangled up in government cover-up and propaganda, and on the other in unrestrained rumour and hearsay,' wrote one author about Cuba's intervention in Angola.[41]

The main written charge against Ochoa was one of drug trafficking. The evidence was complex and shrouded in ambiguities, but the Castro brothers both also asserted in long statements that Ochoa's biggest crime was one of treason: they alleged that he had been planning to defect. Raúl Castro accused Ochoa of having said in Angola to fellow officers: 'I have been sent to a lost war so I can be blamed for our defeat.'[42] Ochoa and three other officers tried and shot with him said their activities had been authorised by Fidel and Raúl Castro: they said they sold diamonds, fish, sugar, rum and electronic equipment on the black market in Angola to obtain hard currency for the Cuban treasury.[43]

Describing one black market operation, Ochoa said he had been ordered by Castro to extend the airstrip in a southern Angolan town, Xangongo, prior to the final Cuban aerial attack on the Cunene River dam at Calueque on 27 June 1988. But, Ochoa testified, the Cuban finance ministry did not make available the half-a-million dollars he needed to do the job. He was forced instead to improvise to meet Castro's tight deadline. He instructed his aides to sell one hundred tonnes of Cuban sugar warehoused in Luanda for Angolan kwanzas, and then used the cash to buy local building materials for the airport and some basic supplies for his troops, little suspecting that this would form part of the later corruption indictment against him.[44]

'This was a public assassination dressed up in judicial clothing,' said Elizardo Sánchez Santa Cruz, the leader of Cuba's tiny human rights movement. Two days after the banning of *Sputnik* and the *Moscow News*, Sánchez was arrested, charged with 'disseminating false news' and sentenced to four years imprisonment, bringing to a close a two-year period in which the Cuban government had showed some limited tolerance towards human rights activists.

In a country where the Castro personality cult was supreme, Ochoa also had emerged as a megastar, recognised and cheered in the streets of Havana. Furthermore, he was sympathetic towards Gorbachev's reforms, for which Fidel Castro had nothing but contempt.

All the evidence suggests there was a cataclysmic falling out between Ochoa and both Castros over the defence of Cuito Cuanavale, even though the precise details remain impenetrable. Raúl Castro said at Ochoa's trial: 'We can't have people going around like that promoting themselves and saying, "That war in Angola, we made lousy decisions there."'

Fidel Castro had insisted on micro-managing the defence of Cuito Cuanavale from behind his desk in Havana. 'One can only imagine what it must have been like for Ochoa to try to manage a war against South African tanks and artillery with tens of thousands of Cuban troops in a vast, war-weakened country under the incoming barrage of instructions from Fidel Castro a hemisphere away. From the cables it appears that Ochoa simply ignored some of Castro's demands', wrote *The New York Review of Books'* Julia Preston. 'The "reality" of Cuba is that the Castros do not allow anyone they do not strongly control to question their policies,' she said. 'The evidence indicates that Ochoa was executed because of his impatience with this reality, not because of specific acts that he committed.'[45]

In a closing statement at his trial, Ochoa declared that if he faced execution, 'My last thought will be of Fidel and the great revolution he has given our people.' One widely accepted account tells how, as he was led before the firing squad, he asked not to be blindfolded and to be permitted to give the final command to his executioners himself. Both wishes were granted. Another version details the Chief of the Military's Special Troops, General José Luis Mesa Delgado, putting a final bullet in Ochoa's head. A statement in the *Granma* newspaper the next day announced his execution to the Cuban public. His wife was later informed of an unmarked grave in Havana's cemetery.[46] Ochoa was 58 years old when he died.

★ ★ ★

Perhaps the most astonishing and important section of the December 1988 New York Accords, scarcely noticed initially by the media, was the buried paragraph that spelt the end of Angola as a haven for the military wing, *Umkhonto we Sizwe* (the Spear of the Nation), of South Africa's African National Congress. All the ANC's military camps in Angola were shut down and throughout 1989 and 1990 the guerrillas and trainees were transported to Uganda, Tanzania and Zambia away from the front line with South Africa. It marked the end of any possibility of South Africa's white-ruled government being toppled by force from outside. The much romanticised armed struggle was over.

The decision to expel the ANC's fighters can be read in the dry diplomatic language of the fifth provision in the New York Accords.[47] Chester Crocker explained that the idea of an absolutely precise written provision was rejected in favour of a gentlemen's agreement, permitting the ANC itself in January 1989 to 'facilitate' the Accords by announcing from Lusaka the closing of its guerrilla bases in Angola and the expulsion of its fighters. The ANC communique described the development as 'an advance of great significance for our region.'[48]

Crocker added: 'This side agreement contained potent symbolism, and it would set new standards of regional conduct. UNITA would lose its regional military ally at the moment when the MPLA was losing the Cubans. The ANC would lose its last remaining sanctuary within reach of South Africa.'

The withdrawal of the Cubans and the neutering of any ANC military threat opened up entirely new opportunities for South Africa to tackle its grave internal problems.

It was always inconceivable that South Africa would embark upon *serious* domestic and democratic reform of Verwoerdian apartheid while the Cuban Revolutionary Army was encamped just beyond its borders. Castro had sent his armed forces to shore up a one-party state in Angola, whose leaders allowed the independent country's first multi-party election only 17 years after independence, in 2002, and after the ruling MPLA party had switched almost overnight from hardline Marxism-Leninism to a particularly aggressive capitalist philosophy.

The South Africans, for all their shortcomings, were nonetheless not soft in the head. The Cuban demand for the realisation of one person-one vote in South Africa would never be heeded while Castro's forces remained in Angola, propping up Angola's one-party Marxist autocracy, and while multi-party democracy was forbidden in Cuba itself.

The bottom line was that necessary reforms and new thinking throughout southern Africa could not begin while Cuba stayed; but for Castro to be persuaded to leave, the War for Africa and its consequences were a necessary catalyst.

The concluding battles of the war provided the opportunity for diplomats, civil servants and senior military leaders to get to work on integrated solutions for the region under the patient prodding, pleading and patient guidance of Chester Crocker.

Crocker's eight years of effort on Namibia, Angola and South Africa has come to be seen as one of the most important, subtle and intellectually coherent diplomatic peace-making exercises in Africa, perhaps anywhere. Fate had condemned governments involved in almost every form of odious behaviour – authoritarianism, terrorist violence, racism, brutal oppression, Marxism-Leninism, quasi-Marxism, tribalism, appalling Big Man dictatorship, organised butchery of unarmed villagers and gross official corruption – to live side by side in a very rough neighbourhood featuring several interconnected wars. The countries of the region would have continued making war unless they could be brought to make peace, said Crocker. 'To achieve peace,' he said, 'the planets would have to come into perfect alignment.'

Crocker resisted all efforts to deliver high-minded Sermons on the Mount. He instead adopted an unimpassioned, even colourless, strategy that eschewed windy rhetoric and was strong only in content and careful evaluation. Crocker played it long and patiently, working from firm principles and refusing to be diverted by salvoes of partisan abuse from shallow politicians and commentators proposing magical quick or simplistic fixes. Indeed, when Crocker and his team set out on their eight-year odyssey they believed that the ultimate goal of a peace deal was a 'long shot': they compared themselves to vets at Washington's National Zoo who had been striving unsuccessfully for about a decade to get Chinese pandas to breed in captivity.

Crocker despised oversimplified analyses. He suffered criticism from right and left and from within the United States administration, and especially from two prominent hawks, the warlike CIA Director James Casey and the equally hardline Ambassador to the United Nations, Jeane Fitzpatrick, who both sought 'total victory' in Angola. 'Jesus, Chet, I thought *we* had a conservative problem!' South African foreign minister Pik Botha said to Crocker after one of his visits to Washington for talks.[49]

At one point, in 1986, a senior *Washington Post* correspondent David Ottaway, twice a Pulitzer Prize for journalism finalist, wrote a comment piece wondering 'how long Crocker can last' – pegged to Casey's and Fitzpatrick's enmity to him together with the hatred of the extreme rightwing white supremacist Senator Jesse Helms and other conservatives in the Senate. 'Yet to the chagrin of his detractors, he [Crocker] has proven an extraordinarily good bureaucratic infighter,' said Ottaway. 'And he is a master of the linguistic ambiguity that is his trademark. His double-edged or round-about replies to questions have been known to drive congressmen and reporters to despair, leaving nagging doubts about whether he really said "yes" or "no" to a delicate question.'

To which Crocker responded: 'Actually, it was all very clear. I had a goal.' And, he added, he had full support, through thick and thin, of US Secretary of State George Schultz.[50]

Crocker felt genuine sympathy with those black African states that were trying to build their futures but who had only sets of clichés for their pasts. But he never patronised them by refusing to criticise them. He lamented instead the paternalism they were subjected to by many in the West: 'The attention they receive is not like the attention received by successful societies. Instead, they become theme parks, Disney Worlds of barbarity and deprivation, places for which funds are raised by rock concerts. Saddest of all, these countries lose their best and brightest citizens.'

One of his most important principles was cold realism. Thus, although ostensibly his first and main task was to achieve the independence of Namibia to satisfy international posturing and demands over that sparsely populated but intensely beautiful territory, he recognised that the problem could not be isolated from its regional context.

'So we decided to link the intractable problem in Namibia to the seemingly intractable problem in Angola,' he said. 'This radically altered the structure of negotiations, expanding the range of trade-offs and the numbers of parties.' Crocker's game plan was christened 'constructive engagement.' It was despised as a sell-out plan by supporters of Cuba, Angola, the Soviet Union, SWAPO and the ANC: it was regarded with utmost wariness by South Africa and UNITA.

Crocker's 'linkage' first principle led him to a second negotiating principle – 'that one must give in order to get. No one capitulated in the Namibia-Angola settlement. Everyone gained.'

His third principle was that solutions to difficult problems tended to emerge when all the parties involved in a conflict had reached a rough balance in the power equation. It was also clear that the chance of a solution increased the longer the level of mutual pain increased and the longer the conflict went unresolved.

The fourth principle was that mutually advantageous negotiation occurs as a process, not an event. 'Our experience (i.e. that of the US mediators) demonstrates conclusively that creative diplomacy can create new facts. The very process of negotiation can enable the parties to understand accurately each other's interests and priorities so that deals can be struck.'

Fifth, successful negotiation requires strong parties, not weak ones. 'When people seek to hold or acquire power by forcing their enemy's capitulation they end up working harder and harder to get less and less. Such logic leads not to victory but to a wasteland. Our diplomacy in the 1980s ultimately succeeded when the top authorities in Luanda, Pretoria and Havana realised how much of a stake they had in the unity and cohesion of their negotiating partners.'

Finally, Crocker emphasised the necessity of local responsibility for decisions. The US did *not* impose or dictate the Namibian and Angolan settlements, he said. 'Yes, we offered the concepts and stuck with them through good times and bad. And we also provided a legitimate vehicle of communication and mediation. And it is true that Moscow at a certain point ceased its efforts to discredit our diplomacy and actually developed its own brand of constructive engagement.

'But the three signatories (South Africa, Cuba and Angola) to the New York Accords took the tough decisions, recognised their stalemate and hammered out a new common language and shared principles.

'The Angolans, Cubans and South Africans wanted assurances that an "honourable" settlement could be achieved. No one had won on the ground: therefore, everyone would have to win at the table [and have it] fully reflected in the language, symbols and political imagery of the deal.'

★ ★ ★

The South African government and the SADF learnt a number of lessons while participating in the negotiations that resulted in the New York Accords. First, they realised that there was no such thing as a total military victory or solution. At some point political problems could only be resolved by the creation of fair and just conditions for *all*. In one of his early speeches, soon after his National Party had won the last whites-only general election, in September 1989, South Africa's new State President, F W de Klerk,[51] said the SADF could probably enforce white minority rule by military means for another 80 years, but it would be at a dreadful cost to future generations, both black and white. Therefore another way forward had to be found in which the legitimate aspirations of every South African would be respected and constitutionally guaranteed.

Second, the Pretoria government had obtained in the New York Accords the complete neutralisation of the ANC's military wing, *Umkhonto we Sizwe*. ANC fighters were expelled progressively northwards from Angola, far from any front line with South Africa. The ANC itself announced an official end to the armed struggle on 7 August 1990. With the Cubans also returning home from Angola, it meant there was no possible external threat to the Nationalist government. This reinforced the conclusion reached by 'moderate' Nationalists, as a result of taking part in negotiations about a regional peace settlement, that Crocker's techniques could be applied to internal problems. The black opposition, which had in the past been demonised, could be talked to and solutions allowed to emerge, given sufficient time and incentives for all. Foreign Minister Pik Botha and the Director-General of Foreign Affairs, Neil van Heerden, were particularly keen for the Crocker technique to continue into internal South African negotiations once the main pillars of the regional settlement were in place. In fact, the Crocker system, which had at its heart the production of an endless series of 'synthesis papers' setting out the latest positions of the antagonists, was based on a process developed by Roger Fisher, Professor of Law at Harvard University and director of the Harvard Negotiation Project, and first used successfully at the Camp David negotiations of 1977 which produced the Israeli-Egyptian peace settlement.[52]

President de Klerk embraced the idea that an internal negotiation, along Fisher-Crocker Lines, leading to a peaceful settlement of South Africa's grave political and constitutional problems, was possible. Therefore, on 10 February 1990, he made his historic announcement that the 30-year ban on the ANC and the 40-year ban on the South African Communist Party would be lifted and that the ANC's veteran leader Nelson Mandela would be freed after serving 27 years of his life sentence for planning the violent overthrow of the white government. Mandela made his sweet walk to freedom the following day from Victor Verster Prison in Paarl, 60 kilometres from Cape Town.

In May and August 1990 'talks about talks' between the government and the newly legalised ANC-Communist Party alliance were held in Cape Town. Full-scale constitutional negotiations between 19 political parties began in Johannesburg on 21 December 1991.

The New York Accords were also a blessing in disguise for the ANC, which, despite the clarity of its early democratic ideals under such leaders as Chief Albert Luthuli and Oliver Tambo, subsequently got itself entangled in many ideological contortions and moral contradictions. Its armed struggle against the South African government was stronger on rhetoric than action, a failure publicly acknowledged in February 1990 in Lusaka by the then Acting President of the ANC, Alfred Nzo, who said *Umkhonto we Sizwe* had insufficient numbers to wage an armed struggle to any significant degree inside South Africa.

Following the Luanda government's obligation under the New York Accords to expel the ANC from its main bases in Angola, another so-called African Frontline State, Zambia, came in line and in mid-1988 expelled about two thousand ANC officials and fighters to Uganda and Tanzania.[53]

The sojourn of the ANC in Angola was a particularly shameful chapter in the history of the movement. Its leaders in the ANC training and prison camps, such as Quatro, Viana, Pango, Quibaxe, Villa Rosa, Kangandala, Caculama and Nova Catengue, subjected the guerrillas to all manner of humiliations, torture and even executions.

Umkhonto we Sizwe fighters were ordered into battle against UNITA in Angola in late 1983 by Chris Hani, the political commissar of *Umkhonto*. In their first encounters with UNITA the South African guerrillas, eager for battle, performed well, said Stephen Ellis and Tsepo Sechaba in their book *Comrades against Apartheid: The ANC and the South African Communist Party in Exile*.[54] 'While demoralised Angolan government conscripts broke and ran in the face of UNITA attacks, abandoning their equipment to the enemy, the ANC fighters did well enough to impress the Soviet military advisers who helped plan their campaigns,' wrote Ellis and Sechaba.

'The increasingly confident ANC brigade began to make forays deep into UNITA territory. It was then that they started taking losses and falling into ambushes. The more the casualties mounted, the more the troops asked themselves why they were fighting black Angolans, hundreds of miles away from South Africa, in a war which was not theirs, and why they could not fight their real enemies in South Africa.'

It is not a purpose of this book to examine in depth the ANC crisis in Angola, but dissatisfaction turned into insubordination, and insubordination into a pro-democracy mutiny by hundreds of guerrillas which, in turn, escalated into killings, public executions and torture in hideous conditions presided over by *Umkhonto*'s security organ, *Mbokodo*, 'The Boulder That Crushes.'

The author Paul Trewhela, imprisoned for three years in the 1960s in South Africa for his membership of the then banned Communist Party, describes near-endless atrocities in the Angolan camps by ANC commissars and guards in his book *Inside Quatro: Uncovering the exile history of the ANC and SWAPO*.[55] Some of the mutineers, once captured, were subjected to beatings and tortures under interrogation, 'with melted plastic dripped on their naked bodies and private parts, whipped while tied to trees and forced under torture to exhume the bodies of the ANC loyalists who had died several days before and wash them for a heroic burial.'[56]

Mwezi Twala, an ANC guerrilla who had fought against UNITA and then joined the mutiny, demanding to be permitted to fight in South Africa, recalled his experience as a prisoner in Quatro: 'People were removed from amongst us and disappeared for ever without reason. We heard rumours of execution by being buried alive.' Twala went on: 'At Quatro all actions were designed to subdue prisoners ... With the arrival of each new day, doubt and fear would grow in me as the guards continued their orgy of sadistic beating ... The death rate grew to horrific proportions, some by suicide but mostly by murder. Others went insane under the constant stress from everlasting pain ... The dehumanisation of the detainees damaged, as it was intended to, the very core of the men. I watched healthy young men disintegrate into cabbages with no will to live. They became little more than robots, morons.'[57]

Amnesty International in 1992 published a 24-page report on torture and executions in the ANC's Angola camps. Describing conditions in Quatro, Amnesty said security officials who ran the camp used the language of 'rehabilitation', but they were in fact responsible for a regime of extreme brutality and degradation. 'Torture and other ill-treatment of Quatro inmates appears to have been routine,' said Amnesty. 'Many former prisoners describe being severely beaten on arrival at the camp, particularly on the buttocks and the soles of the feet. Prisoners also suffered random beatings and other ill-treatment throughout their time there. In one incident described by two former inmates, guards poured boiling water on the head of a prisoner. The wound blistered and became purulent. A sympathetic medical orderly shaved the prisoner's head to help the wound heal, but the guards repeatedly banged his head against a tree to reopen the wound.

'The systematic nature of the abuses makes it clear that these were no isolated excesses by undisciplined guards but represented a deliberate regime of ill-treatment. The reality was in grotesque contrast to Quatro's stated purpose of rehabilitation.'[58]

In September 1991 Nelson Mandela, against the opposition of other ANC leaders, announced the establishment of an ANC commission of inquiry into allegations of abuses committed against guerrillas in the Angolan camps. The commission's creation was prompted by the return to South Africa the previous month of 32 exiles who alleged that they had been tortured while they were prisoners of the ANC. The focus of the inquiry was on those specific cases, although its investigations ranged more broadly. Despite many weaknesses and flaws in its terms of reference, the three-member commission concluded that within the ANC in exile for the greater part of the 1980s 'there existed a situation of extraordinary abuse of power and lack of accountability.' The commission described as 'staggering' the extent of brutality by the ANC security department.[59]

The full story of the problems and abuses in the ANC's Angola camps may never be told. But without the New York Accords that spread détente throughout southern Africa, perhaps nothing would have come to light. It was necessary for people to know just how easily idealism can transmogrify into barbarity and for the leadership of the ANC to be obliged to address and admit these atrocities if, in the future, it was to be able to govern wisely and humanely.

★ ★ ★

It would of course be absurd to argue that the motivation for the intervention by the SADF in Angola in 1987–88 was to promote democracy and peace throughout an arc of states from Angola to South Africa. The teenage soldiers who fought on the banks of the Lomba and Cuito Rivers came from every point on the broad spectrum of white South African opinion as it existed just before negotiations began with Nelson Mandela for a transformation to all-race, one person-one vote democracy. The main objective of the SADF was largely pragmatic, to give South Africa security against the threat posed by Cuba and the Soviet Union, whose ideologies were a negation of the democracy they espoused for South Africa. Captain Reg van Eeden of the South African Air Force once told me prophetically: 'Because of our strange political situation, we can do nothing right as far as the rest of the world is concerned. They [the Cubans, MPLA, SWAPO and the ANC] know they can't beat us militarily, but I'm not too sure at this stage that we're going to beat them politically.'

But whatever the motivation of the SADF, the final outcome of the War for Africa was to break the diplomatic impasse and open up new possibilities for prosperity and degrees of liberty throughout southern Africa. Eventually, as the guns became silent and ceased to roar, it became possible for Chester Crocker to secure his regional peace agreement and say of South Africa's past and future: 'South Africa is richly endowed with great men and women in its political, cultural, religious and economic life. They have built political movements, corporate giants, labour unions, churches, newspapers and marvels of engineering.

'Every racial and cultural group in this great country has produced heroes and heroines. The best known are heroes of domination and resistance. The time has come to celebrate your peacemakers and reconcilers – and they are many. But your great political leaders have never been wholly free: some have been held literally behind bars. Others have been imprisoned by the limited dogmas and institutions of exclusive nationalism and racism. When they become free, they will show the world why this is a land of hope.'

Nelson Mandela walked free 19 months after the final shots were fired in the War for Africa. He was elected South Africa's first black head of state on 27 April 1994 and set a fine example to Big Men elsewhere in Africa by standing down voluntarily from power after five years. Four more all-race general elections have been held successfully since that first historic poll in 1994. The country seems likely to survive a period of current turbulent and scandal-ridden rule under Jacob Zuma, state president since 2009, the worst of whose African Big Man predilections are contained, thanks to the strong democratic constitution negotiated by the National Party, the ANC and several other parties between 1991 and 1994.

Namibia, one of the world's most spectacularly beautiful countries, has held five multi-party elections since independence in 1990. SWAPO has won every presidential and parliamentary poll. The country is one of the most peaceful and prosperous in Africa. Inter-racial reconciliation encouraged the country's white minority population to remain and they still play a major role in farming, wildlife conservation and other economic sectors. However, civil rights activists, led by Phil Ya Nangolo, continue to campaign about human rights abuses perpetrated by SWAPO's leaders when they were in exile in Angola and Zambia.[60]

Angola has held two more presidential and National Assembly elections since the killing in 2002 of Jonas Savimbi, and the country is due to go to the polls again in August 2017. Angola is a country of immense wealth – oil, diamonds, many other minerals, fantastic water resources and abundant fertile soils. The MPLA, now hardline capitalist, has won every election and UNITA, which before Savimbi's death challenged the MPLA tightly, has been reduced to just 32 members in the 200-seat National Assembly. After 25 years of carnage in the most horrendous civil war, the country is at peace, but corruption is rife and there is a spectacular gap between an extremely rich elite and the poor majority. Civil rights, constantly threatened, are upheld by such courageous activists as Rafael Marques, recipient of several international awards for the work of his anti-corruption watchdog *Maka Angola.*

Cuba is the lone participant in the War for Africa not to have embraced multi-party democracy since the guns fell silent. It continues to be a one-party Marxist state, but freedoms are being expanded slowly. Roughly 500,000 Cubans were self-employed as of December 2015, and accounted for 11 percent of the workforce: in 2009, by contrast, there were only 148,000 self-employed workers on the island. Since Raúl Castro assumed power from his ailing brother, cellphones have become legal, unused state land has been turned over to small private farmers and for the first time in half a century ordinary Cubans have been allowed to buy and sell property, if they can afford to do so on fixed salaries for 70 percent of the workforce of 600 pesos, about US$ 25 a month, rising to US$ 67 for doctors.

Human rights concerns persist, particularly over the issue of arbitrary short-term detentions of regime opponents who plan meetings or demonstrations. But Cuba has freed most political prisoners in recent years. The government released 53 imprisoned dissidents as a result of negotiations with the United States in early 2015, and in October that year authorities freed graffiti artist Danilo Maldonado, who was identified in some press accounts as the last 'prisoner of conscience' in Cuba. For a while there were special detention camps for homosexuals and Seventh Day Adventists, but these have been disbanded.

Although he stepped down from power in 2008, Fidel Castro cast a vast shadow over his tropical island. The Cuban novelist Wendy Guerra who, as a small girl, used to be taken by her mother to Havana's Plaza de la Revolución to listen to Castro's hours-long speeches, asked at the age of 12, 'Mommy, is Fidel the king of Cuba? Is that why we don't have elections?'[61] Castro's supporters were publicly adulatory, giving rise to what some commentators described as a faith around him they christened *Fidelismo*; his doubters mainly kept quiet.

Then, on 25 November 2016 the man who took supreme power died in his 91st year. It removed the single biggest obstacle to change and opened an era of uncertainty for Cuba. Whether, or when, multi-party democracy will creep over the horizon is difficult to predict. Cuban commentator Peter Campos, who lives in Havana, observed: 'The vast majority of the population of the island, desiring change, is expectant.'[62] The question is: How will the Cuban state, without Fidel, manage such expectations?

Notes

1 An aphorism attributed to the Ancient Greek dramatist Aeschylus (525–456 BC) and later plagiarised in 1917 by a US Republican Senator, Hiram Johnson, and innumerable others.

2 Vladimir Shubin, of the Soviet (now Russian) Academy of Sciences, in an article, 'War in Angola: a Soviet Dimension', *Review of African Political Economy* (Routledge, London, 2001).

3 A BBC-TV Four documentary, as repeated on You Tube, 17 December 2015. The term 'mulattoes' referred to people of mixed race and would probably have been regarded as racist if used in South Africa. In Angola people of mixed race are referred to as 'mestiços' in Portuguese.

4   Speech as delivered in Havana, 2 December 2005.

5   See Prologue.

6   Author's italics.

7   Author's italics.

8   See later in this Epilogue.

9   Chester Crocker, *High Noon in Southern Africa: Making Peace in a Rough Neighbourhood* (W W Norton, New York, 1992), p.355.

10   *High Noon in Southern Africa: Making Peace in a Rough Neighbourhood*, p.426.

11   Interviews with author, December 1989 and February 1990.

12   Author's italics.

13   South African, Cuban and MPLA delegations met on Sal in the Cape Verde Islands on 22–23 July 1988.

14   See Chapter 38, 'Fidel's last hurrah!'

15   Leopold Scholtz, *Africa@War 26: The Battle for Cuito Cuanavale* (Helion and Company, Solihull, UK, 2016), p.54.

16   See Chapter 38, *Fidel's Last Hurrah!* Also Crocker, *High Noon in Southern Africa: Making Peace in a Rough Neighbourhood*, p.372; Edward George, *The Cuban Intervention in Angola, 1965–1999 – From Che Guevara to Cuito Cuanavale* (Routledge, London and New York, 2005), pp.241–246; Scholtz, *Africa@War 26: The Battle for Cuito Cuanavale*, pp.50–53.

17   Leopold Scholtz, *The SADF in the Border War 1966–1989* (Helion, Solihull, UK, 2015), pp.53–54.

18   Crocker, *High Noon in Southern Africa: Making Peace in a Rough Neighbourhood*, p.433.

19   Crocker, *High Noon in Southern Africa: Making Peace in a Rough Neighbourhood*, pp.348, 422.

20   Pik Botha at peace negotiations in New York, 11–13 July 1988.

21   Marius Scheepers, *Striking Inside Angola with 32 Battalion* (Helion, Solihull, UK, 212).

22   Allister Sparks, *The Mind of South Africa* (Heinemann, London, 1990), p.305.

23   David Mannall *Battle on the Lomba: A Crew Commander's Account* (Helion, Solihull, UK, pp.276-277).

24   Public lecture by Professor Gary Baines, *Secrets, Silences and Stories of South Africa's Border War*, Budapest, 2007.

25   Rocky Williams, *Cuito Cuanavale: For Gary, 1987*, as delivered by Gary Baines in a lecture at the Grahamstown National Arts Festival, 1 July 2008.

26   Of course, Techipa was not the "*only* scrap" in the southwest. The Cuban Air Force and armour responded with an attack that took 12 South African lives and largely destroyed the Calueque Dam on the Cunene River. Most of the dead at Techipa were Fapla soldiers. *Africa Confidential* reported that the number of Cuban dead may have been 140. The Cubans conceded the loss of ten men: see Crocker, *High Noon in Southern Africa: Making Peace in a Rough Neighbourhood*, p.372.

27 Crocker, *High Noon in Southern Africa: Making Peace in a Rough Neighbourhood*, p.372.
28 Crocker, *High Noon in Southern Africa: Making Peace in a Rough Neighbourhood*, p.427.
29 Crocker, *High Noon in Southern Africa: Making Peace in a Rough Neighbourhood*, p.428.
30 Jannie Geldenhuys, *At the Front: A General's Account of South Africa's Border War* (Jonathan Ball, Cape Town, 2009); Author's interviews with Geldenhuys; Crocker, *High Noon in Southern Africa: Making Peace in a Rough Neighbourhood*.
31 I conducted two extensive interviews with General Geldenhuys in December 1989 and February 1990.
32 Hayward Alker, Ted Robert Gurr and Kumar Rupesinghe, *Journeys Through Conflict: Narratives and Lessons* (Rowman and Littlefield International, London, 2001), p.181.
33 For detailed accounts of the post-1992 MPLA–UNITA conflict, see a report by the New York-based Human Rights Watch, titled *Angola: Arms Trade and Violations of the Laws of War since the 1992 Elections* (New York, 1994); and a 9 March 2015 article by Paul Trewhela, a commentator and former political prisoner in South Africa, 'Angolan horror reveals threat of flawed South African law', on 'Politicsweb', a Johannesburg-based website focussed on southern African news and politics.
34 Crocker, *High Noon in Southern Africa: Making Peace in a Rough Neighbourhood*, p.402.
35 Crocker, *High Noon in Southern Africa: Making Peace in a Rough Neighbourhood*, p.400.
36 Leroy Binns, 'The Demise of the Soviet Union and its Effects on Cuba', *Caribbean Quarterly* (March 1996). For one period in 1985 Moscow was buying Cuban sugar at more than eleven times the world market price.
37 Lee Hockstader, reporting for the *Washington Post* from Cuba (30 July 1990).
38 Peter Baker, 'US to Restore Full Relations With Cuba, Erasing a Last Trace of Cold War Hostility', *New York Times* (17 December 2014).
39 Julia Preston 'The Trial that Shook Cuba', *The New York Review of Books* (7 December 1989).
40 For details of Ochoa's career, see Prologue.
41 Edward George, *The Cuban Intervention in Angola, 1965–1999 – From Che Guevara to Cuito Cuanavale*, p.260.
42 Preston, 'The Trial that Shook Cuba'.
43 *New York Times* (14 July 1989).
44 Edward George, *The Cuban Intervention in Angola, 1965–1999 – From Che Guevara to Cuito Cuanavale*, p.237.
45 Preston, 'The Trial that Shook Cuba'.
46 *Wikipedia* (16 October 2016).

47 Tripartite Agreement Among the People's Republic of Angola, the Republic of Cuba and the Republic of South Africa, signed in New York, 22 December 1988.

48 Crocker, *High Noon in Southern Africa: Making Peace in a Rough Neighbourhood*, p.442.

49 Crocker, *High Noon in Southern Africa: Making Peace in a Rough Neighbourhood*, p.281.

50 Crocker, *High Noon in Southern Africa: Making Peace in a Rough Neighbourhood*, pp.302–303.

51 Appointed on 14 August 1989 after P W Botha was forced from power in an internal cabinet coup.

52 The most famous book by Professor Fisher, who died in 2012, was *Getting to Yes* (Penguin, London, 1981).

53 Gavin Maasdorp and Alan Whiteside, *Towards a Post-apartheid future* (Palgrave Macmillan, New York, 1992), p.50.

54 Stephen Ellis and Tsepo Sechaba, *Comrades against Apartheid: The ANC and the South African Communist Party in Exile* (James Currey, London, 1992), p.131.

55 Paul Trewhela, *Inside Quatro: Uncovering the exile history of the ANC and SWAPO* (Jacana Media, Johannesburg, 2010).

56 Trewhela, *Inside Quatro*, p.28.

57 Mwezi Twala, *Mbokodo. Inside MK – A Soldier's Story* (Jonathan Ball, Cape Town, 1994), pp.87, 90, 94.

58 *Torture, ill-treatment and executions in African National Congress camps* (Amnesty International, London, December 1992).

59 *The Skweyiya Commission Report: Report of the Commission of Enquiry into Complaints by former African National Congress Prisoners and Detainees* (ANC publication, Johannesburg, 1992).

60 *Accountability in Namibia: Human Rights and the Transition to Democracy* (Human Rights Watch, August 1992); Sue Armstrong, *In Search of Freedom: The Andreas Shipanga Story* (Ashanti Publishing, 1989); Bernard Moore, 'SWAPO in Exile and After: Dilemmas of Pragmatic Nationalism', *Southern African Digital History Journal* (Michigan State University, 2015).

61 Wendy Guerra, 'Welcome to Savage Capitalism', *New York Times* (3 December 2016).

62 Peter Campos, in the Havana-based online newspaper *14ymedio*, as quoted in the *Washington Post* (28 November 2016).

POSTSCRIPT: UNITA

This book, as first written, was essentially about the part played by the ordinary fighting men of the South African Defence Force in the War for Africa. There was neither time, nor money, nor opportunity to garner the stories of individual MPLA or Cuban soldiers. Their stories are beginning to be told, but as yet only in a limited and fragmentary way.

Some analysis of the contribution of UNITA is, however, necessary. Its name runs like a thread through the whole story. Since UNITA claimed the entire credit for victory in the War for Africa and denied that it was in military alliance with the South Africans, its own analyses were, to say the least, somewhat misleading. I therefore turned to Colonel Fred Oelschig of Chief of Staff Intelligence (CSI), the senior SADF liaison officer with the leader of UNITA, Jonas Savimbi, throughout 1986–89, for his assessment of how the Angolan liberation movement had performed in battle. The following are extracts from his account.

★ ★ ★

'UNITA is a total guerrilla army which is well motivated and well disciplined. But in 1985, when it was faced by a full Fapla conventional offensive involving great numbers of troops and advanced Soviet weapons, UNITA was most decidedly trounced. It was saved then from disastrous setbacks by SADF intervention.

'I had fought extensively in Angola, notably in Operation Savannah in 1975 and in Operation Protea in 1981. In 1986 I was appointed as the chief SADF liaison officer working with UNITA. My job was twofold. First to liaise between Savimbi and the SADF general staff. Second, to give UNITA some training in how to fight a conventional war. My team taught UNITA to realise the limitations of possibilities in conventional warfare. We made them get into captured T-54 tanks and BRDM armoured cars to see how little their commanders and gunners could actually see of the surrounding terrain. UNITA is one of the most remarkable foot-slogging armies since the Romans. It meant that they thought in terms of four kilometres an hour; to enable them to carry out a conventional offensive we had to get them to think in terms of 40 km an hour, and that wasn't easy.

'I left towards the end of 1986, but was back again in May 1987 with two other CSI liaison teams under my command, led by Colonel Bert Sachse and Commandant Les Rudman, to help UNITA to organise to meet the coming offensive.

'I was also required to report back on the ability of UNITA to counter the offensive.

'The eight conventional brigades put into the offensive by Fapla were more than anyone had expected. A guerrilla army and the two multiple-rocket-launchers I had with me weren't enough to stop them.

'So we agreed with the general staff to pursue delaying tactics with UNITA, the aim being to ensure that the Fapla forces arrived at the Lomba River in a position of weakness rather than strength, by which time our conventional forces would be ready to deal with them.

'Les Rudman and Commandant James Hill of 5 Recce Commando organised the delaying tactics, working mainly with three UNITA generals, Demostenes Chilingutila, Ben-Ben Arlindo Pena and Bok Sapalalo. Ben-Ben was a particularly active thinker on how to disrupt the advance. Savimbi frequently came up to the front lines, so there was constant interaction and joint decision-making. Savimbi conducts a nine-week course for his commanders every year, putting great emphasis on the use of their own discretion on the battlefield. He grants a lot of autonomy in the conduct of warfare.

'At that time we were fighting a real guerrilla war. We would hit and then run in every direction. UNITA performed very well, but the enemy's tanks and BM-21 Stalin Organs on tracked vehicles won a lot of space. At the very beginning, when tanks appeared on the horizon I ran and the UNITA men ran. The tanks were being used in a long-range pre-emptive role, firing into the bush from considerable distances and keeping the BM-21s firing throughout the night. We were often nailed down by Migs too.

'But we quickly worked out ambush tactics to delay them. With UNITA we laid mines across their lines of advance. As they moved, we hammered them with 120 mm mortars, US Law anti-tank missiles and Apilas anti-tank missiles which were delivered to UNITA by the French at the beginning of 1987. At night, when they laagered, we kept them busy all the time with 81 mm and 128 mm mortars. They lost a lot of sleep and suffered a lot of damage to their soft-skin trucks.

'It was a really interesting period. One of the UNITA soldiers was captured. He escaped and told us that a Cuban officer had ordered a Fapla soldier to shoot him. The Fapla soldier took him away and then told him to run for his life.

'There were probably about 8,000 UNITA fighters opposing 10,000 Faplas. We used the 1st, 2nd, 3rd and 4th UNITA Regular Battalions, with the 5th Battalion in reserve. There were also eight semi-regular battalions, with much lighter weapons. And there were five penetration groups, infiltrating enemy lines in co-operation with our 5 Recce teams and laying anti-personnel mines. In the last analysis, the results that UNITA achieved were what we were looking for. They delayed the enemy advance. It took the enemy brigades eleven days to travel the 50 km from the source of the Cunzumbia to the Lomba, by which time our forces were ready for them.

'We were reorientating UNITA all the time. They hadn't fought on such a massed scale before, so we had to teach them how to control and manage a full battalion. And the UNITA generals' staff had to know the tactics and systems and be well-informed. It is difficult to control a thousand men in battle.

'I found them to be dedicated and extremely proud. It was on my advice that our teams were called liaison rather than advisory teams. That was important.

★ ★ ★

'When Fapla reached the Lomba UNITA took responsibility for certain sectors and the SADF others to prevent the enemy crossing. By then I was keeping direct contact between the top structure of UNITA and Colonel Deon Ferreira. We asked UNITA to identify all potential crossing points, and there was disappointment among some South African officers when Savimbi's people failed to point out some of the crossing points that Fapla used. But it was a matter of perception, which was not appreciated by some of our officers. Many of the UNITA guerrillas, good fighters but often with no education, had no conception of the kind of modern Russian mobile bridging equipment used by Fapla at places that UNITA soldiers would not have considered to be a crossing. So when some of our officers held it against UNITA, I think some of the blame might have lain with me for failing to explain. The fact is that there were disappointments with the defensive reconnaissance role of UNITA on the Lomba. It became doubtful whether they were playing their part properly. But you can't cover 120 km of river with only 8,000 men.

'There was severe criticism of UNITA again when Robbie Hartslief's Combat Group Bravo encountered 21 and 47 Brigades on the south bank of the Lomba on 13 September 1987. Hartslief had to confront enemy tanks, and when they appeared UNITA upped and ran. That infuriated the SADF commanders. But I accepted that UNITA was not up to tackling tanks. Some of the commanders had too great expectations of UNITA at times. After all, it was we who had taught them to run from tanks at the beginning. From then onwards, the policy was: Let's involve UNITA, but only within the limits of their capabilities. Anything that they achieve beyond that is a bonus.

'One result was to concentrate our training on two UNITA battalions in particular, the 3rd Regular Battalion and the 1st Regular Battalion. The 3rd was to be combined as infantry with 61 Mech and the 1st with 4 SAI. The liaison and cooperation between 61 Mech and the 3rd Regular Battalion before the battle on the Lomba of 3 October 1987 were particularly well done during a training period of several days. However, there was some disappointment when UNITA failed to cut off a small detachment from 47 Brigade which retreated to the west with Russian advisers.'

★ ★ ★

'One of the great achievements of UNITA was in maintaining a regular flow of information that we needed about the enemy. It was high-quality information. Soon they were emulating our own recces and giving us ten-minute warnings of Mig attacks. UNITA penetration groups continually harassed the rear of the enemy brigades, and one of the reasons why the Russians with 47 Brigade moved out by land was that UNITA made it impossible for helicopters to come in and get them.

'Despite the marrying-up exercises, their sense of timing continued to disappoint us. It was the four-kilometres-an-hour versus 40 km per hour factor. If our mechanized forces decided to start at 4 am and move 20 km before the sun rose, it was very frustrating if UNITA was not in position as agreed. But it wasn't through lack of willingness. This is Africa, and notions of time were very different. I tried to explain that to our commanders who had different degrees of tolerance and understanding. It became part of my liaison job to try to bring together compatible personalities from UNITA and the SADF.

'In August I was deeply involved in the attack on the Cuito bridge by 4 Reconnaissance Regiment. Les Rudman did all the advance recce work with UNITA. A team of about 120 UNITA Special Forces men acted as guides and porters for our six recces who blew the bridge. Those UNITA men were bloody excellent. The operation was a model of liaison.'

★ ★ ★

'In the three attacks on Tumpo I frankly feel that UNITA was mismanaged. By then Bert Sachse had been badly wounded and Les Rudman and I had been withdrawn because liaison with UNITA was by then well established at all levels. In the Tumpo attacks UNITA were used as infantry riding on the tanks. In the course of the three Tumpo attacks they were simply shot off the tanks. More than 1,200 of them were killed. To their credit, by then they no longer ran. But there were so many UNITA dead that the Olifants were riding over their bodies, which were crunching between the sprockets. It was a horrific job to clean the tracks back at the laagers.'

★ ★ ★

'Those of us who worked closely with UNITA analysed their soldiers in accordance with the guerrilla doctrines of Mao Tse-tung. We found that they scored well on many points. And although they also had many faults, that is true of all armies.

'Mao said that an army that could not adapt itself to prevailing conditions would not be successful. From its inception UNITA has proved its ability to adapt itself to a wide range of conditions and changing circumstances, many of them unfavourable. In 1990 UNITA acquired 30 T-54/55 tanks and several batteries of D-30 guns. They held the tanks and guns back in reserve and gradually incorporated them into their guerrilla operations. Few guerrilla forces can adapt themselves in that way unless they are a very good army.

'Their ability to adapt themselves was shown by their victory at Mavinga in May 1990 when they beat off yet another Fapla conventional offensive by themselves. That was an out-and-out UNITA victory. The SADF had long been gone. It was pure General Ben-Ben. Ben is a thinker. He has a very quick analytical brain, but he's not impulsive. He's got foresight, and he's not afraid to react. He has a sense of humour, and he is very human, a sound, solid leader who keeps good personal contact with his troops. The only thing that surprises me about him is that he took so long to reach the top.[1]

'As a guerrilla army, UNITA is excellent, a very strong force in the context of Africa. Its soldiers are well motivated, well disciplined and well organised. They have good training and equipment. The ability that Savimbi has shown in building up UNITA from just his original eleven recruits makes him potentially a very powerful African leader.'

Notes

1   A full profile of Ben-Ben Arlindo Pena is contained in the author's book *Jonas Savimbi: A Key to Africa* (Coronet Books, London, 1987).

TIMELINE

10 December 1956	MPLA formed in Luanda to demand independence for Angola from Portugal.
February 1965	Che Guevara meets Jonas Savimbi in Dar es Salaam.
12 March 1966	UNITA founded in eastern Angola to fight the Portuguese.
25 April 1974	Carnation Revolution in Portugal. Dictatorship overthrown by military officers who favour rapid decolonisation from Portugal's African empire.
15 January 1975	Agreement signed at Alvor, on Portugal's Algarve coast, setting Angola's Independence Day as 11 November 1975.
9 August 1975	A 30-man South African Army patrol moves more than 50 km into southern Angola and occupies the Ruacana-Calueque hydro-electric complex and other installations on the Cunene River.
21 August 1975	Some 500 Cuban instructors begin arriving in Angola to set up MPLA military training camps in Cabinda, Salazar (N'Dalatando), Benguela and Henrique de Carvalho (Saurimo).
23 September 1975	South African Paratroop Colonel Willem Van der Waals arrives in the central Angola town of Silva Porto to begin training UNITA guerrillas.
14 October 1975	Several columns of armoured South African soldiers, encouraged by the CIA and US Secretary of State Henry Kissinger, secretly cross Angola's southern border and advance northwards. The South Africans overrun Fapla and Cuban defences and enter Benguela and Lobito. Cuba officially recognises its first losses: four killed, seven wounded and thirteen missing in action.

7 November 1975	Cuban troop reinforcements and warplanes begin arriving in Luanda.
11 November 1975	Angolan Independence Day. The MPLA in Luanda proclaims itself the government of the People's Republic of Angola.
12 November 1975	South Africa's invasion force reaches Novo Redondo, more than 800 km inside Angola and within 320 km of Luanda.
14 November 1975	Reuter's Central Africa correspondent publishes a detailed report exposing South Africa's secret invasion of Angola.
19 December 1975	US Senate cuts off covert aid to forces fighting the MPLA in Angola. The South African Army, following the United States' decision not to back the Angolan invasion publicly, begins a strategic retreat from Angola which is completed on 26 March 1976.
13 March 1976	Heavily reinforced Cuban armoured forces complete recapture of southern Angola. UNITA's Jonas Savimbi leads a Long March of his guerrillas back into the forests of eastern Angola to begin a prolonged post-independence civil war.
March 1981	Chester Crocker, the new US Under-Secretary of State for Africa, begins an eight-year-long 'constructive engagement' peace process to link Cuban withdrawal from Angola to South African withdrawal from Namibia.
23 August 1981	South Africa re-enters southern Angola with 5,000 soldiers supported by tanks and armoured cars, hitting SWAPO guerrilla bases. Training and supply of UNITA begins again.
March 1985	Chester Crocker presents 'basis for negotiations' to Angolan and South African governments. The pre-negotiations quickly collapse.
5 July 1985	The US government restores covert military aid to UNITA.
28 May 1987	General Rafael Del Pino, commander of the Cuban Air Force in Angola, defects to the USA, criticising Fidel Castro for his Angolan operation which he says is riven by corruption and incompetence.
4 August 1987	The South African Defence Force initially deploys 2,000 men, armoured cars and heavy artillery into Angola to assist UNITA to defend Mavinga against a huge Soviet-backed Fapla assault from the town of Cuito Cuanavale.
3 October 1987	In Africa's biggest land battle since the battle of El Alamein in North Africa between the British and the Germans in October–November 1942, the South African Defence

	Force destroys the Fapla advance on Mavinga, annihilating Fapla's 47 Brigade and driving three other brigades into headlong retreat towards their starting point at Cuito Cuanavale.
30 January 1988	General Arnaldo Ochoa Sánchez, commander of Cuba's armed forces in Angola, is summoned to Havana by Fidel Castro and ordered to begin a strategic retreat from Cuito Cuanavale, leaving only one Fapla brigade in the small town. Ochoa does not comply with Castro's orders and leaves four brigades in the town and across the river to the east.
23 March 1988	The SADF's counter-offensive against Cuito Cuanavale stalls on the eastern bank of the Cuito River, opposite the town, as South African tanks are crippled in a massive minefield. Cuban troops capture three South African tanks.
27 June 1988	A big SADF armoured unit attacks a Cuban and MPLA garrison in southwest Angola at Techipa, about 40 miles inside Angola. Some 300 Fapla troops and a number of Cubans are killed. Eight Cuban Air Force Mig-23 fighter-bombers immediately retaliate, attacking the South Africa-occupied Calueque Dam on the Cunene River in southwest Angola. Twelve South African soldiers are killed and permanent damage is inflicted on the dam infrastructure.
28 June 1988	Hostilities suddenly end. The War for Africa is over.
30 August 1988	Last South African soldiers withdraw over border from Angola into Namibia, ending a quarter-century of military involvement in Angola.
22 December 1988	The Angolan, South African and Cuban governments sign the historic New York Accords which provide for the withdrawal of all Cuban troops from Angola, the withdrawal of all South African troops from Namibia and Angola, and the disarming and expulsion of South African ANC guerrillas from Angola.
10 January 1989	First 3,000 Cuban troops leave Angola.
13 July 1989	Ochoa Sánchez, the Cuban general who commanded the defence of Cuito Cuanavale, is executed by firing squad in Havana after being denounced for four hours by Fidel Castro at a 'Court of Honour'.
7 November 1989	Namibia holds a pre-independence general election. SWAPO wins.
9 November 1989	The Berlin Wall comes down, triggering the collapse of Soviet Union and socialist bloc.

11 February 1990	Nelson Mandela released from prison in South Africa after serving 27 years of a life sentence.
21 March 1990	Namibia becomes independent.
31 May 1991	The MPLA and UNITA agree to end their civil war and hold free multi-party elections.
14 June 1991	The last Cuban troop ship from Luanda docks in Havana, officially ending the Cuban intervention in Angola.
29–30 September 1992	Angola's first multi-party general election is held since independence 17 years earlier. The MPLA wins 54 percent of the votes and 129 seats in the Luanda parliament. Jonas Savimbi declares the election rigged and takes his UNITA movement back to war against the wishes of some of his senior military officers.
27 April 1994	The ANC wins a large majority in South Africa's first all-race general election and Nelson Mandela becomes the country's first black State President.
2 February 2002	Jonas Savimbi is killed, aged 67, in an ambush planned by one of his former and finest generals, Geraldo Nunda. UNITA's surviving leaders immediately sign a ceasefire agreement with the ruling MPLA and agree to their followers being disarmed, ending a civil war that lasted more than a quarter-century.
5 December 2013	Nelson Mandela dies at the age of 95.
25 November 2016	Fidel Castro dies at the age of 90.

GLOSSARY

While I have tried to keep the number of acronyms used in this book to a minimum, some are unavoidable. To help readers those most commonly used are listed here, together with names with which some may be unfamiliar.

4 SAI — Fourth South African Infantry battalion, one of the main SADF units involved in the War for Africa.

Alouette — French-built light helicopter used by the SAAF (see below) mainly in search-and-rescue and reconnaissance roles.

ANC — South Africa's ruling African National Congress, banned during the War for Africa and based in exile in Angola, Zambia and Tanzania.

Anhara — A word used by the Ovimbundu tribe of central Angola to denote wide-open grassland. Used here to specify grass and marsh lining the banks of Angola's rivers, and to make a distinction from *shona* (see below).

Anhara Lipanda — An important physical feature in the War for Africa: an area of flat, featureless, sparsely vegetated land, fanning out eastwards from the Cuito River to the Chambinga High Ground (see below).

Antonov-12, Antonov-22, Antonov-26 and Antonov-30 — Soviet-built transport planes used by the Cubans and Russians to supply Fapla with weapons and ammunition during the War for Africa.

Armscor — The Armaments Corporation of South Africa, the state weapons production industry set up in the wake of the international arms embargo. Until the war ended, Armscor had more than 20,000 employees and some 1,000 subcontractors. Under the post-apartheid ANC government, Armscor remains the procurement arm of the new South African National Defence Force.

BMP-1 — A Soviet armoured infantry combat vehicle that was in service in Angola with the Cuban and Fapla forces. Mounted with a 73 mm gun and wire-guided anti-tank missiles.

Bosbok — Italian-made single-piston-engined light aircraft used by the SAAF in a spotter/reconnaissance role in Angola. Able to land in an emergency on cleared space only 65 metres long.

BRDM-2 — Soviet-made light armoured car supplied to Fapla in great numbers. Eight-wheeled and amphibious, it carries 14.5 mm and 7.62 mm machine-guns. It attains a top speed of some 100 km per hour only because its armour is very light.

BTR-60 — Soviet armoured personnel carrier in service in great numbers with Fapla. The Soviet Army itself subsequently replaced the model with updated BTR-60s and BTR-72s.

Buccaneer — A British-made, low-level strike aircraft with a radius of action in excess of almost 1,000 kilometres. Delivered to the SAAF from the late 1960s in spite of the developing international arms embargo. Served with distinction in the War for Africa, but was phased out in 1990 because the ageing airframes were succumbing to metal fatigue.

Buffalo Battalion — One of the key SADF (see below) battalions in the War for Africa. Made up of Angolan refugees and their descendants who fled their country in 1976 after the MPLA (see below) established a single-party, Marxist-Leninist state. Initially, a wild bunch of brigands, they were welded into a tough, well-disciplined South African Army unit by Colonel Jan Breytenbach, a Special Forces officer whose late brother was Breyten Breytenbach, the exiled ANC poet. The Buffalo Battalion, officially known as 32 Battalion, got its name from the great herds of wild buffalo which roamed the forests of its training base in Namibia's Caprivi Strip. From 1976 until 1988 some unit of the Buffalo Battalion was nearly always deep inside Angola on some clandestine military mission. Foreign journalists usually attach the adjective 'notorious' to the battalion, almost wholly on the basis of allegations by an English mercenary who deserted the unit to run a hamburger restaurant on a motorway outside London and accused 32 Battalion of committing atrocities against Angolan villagers. Buffalo Battalion, most of whose soldiers now have South African citizenship, moved to a new base in South Africa in 1989 and served in 1990 in the black townships of Natal and Transvaal in keeping the peace between the ANC and the rival Zulu Inkatha Freedom Party.

Canberra — British-built jet bomber aircraft dating from the mid-1950s used by the SAAF in the early stages of the War for Africa but later grounded in the face of far superior enemy aircraft. Permanently taken out of service in 1990.

C-130 Hercules — Troop transport aircraft of the SAAF, built by the American Lockheed Company.

C-160 Transall — A French-built turbo-prop transport aircraft in service with the SAAF. Lower cargo capacity than the C-130 Hercules, but has a quicker 'turn-around' time on the ground.

Casevac — Slang for 'casualty evacuation'. Wounded soldier on the battlefield awaiting removal, usually by helicopter, for medical treatment.

Casspir — High-bodied mine-protected armoured personnel carrier, with 12 seats for infantrymen. It was highly regarded by the old SADF for its cross-country mobility and reliability, but its armour was proof only against infantry weapons.

CSI — Chief of Staff Intelligence, the SADF supremo who oversaw military intelligence in the Army, Navy and Air Force.

D-30 — A highly regarded piece of light artillery that was widely used by Fapla and increasingly by UNITA as more and more of the guns fell into the guerrillas' possession. Highly manoeuvrable, it can fire 21.8 kg shells over a distance of more than 15 km. It also fires a deadly HEAT (see below) round in a shorter range anti-tank role.

EW — Electronic warfare, the ability to intercept or jam enemy communications. Armscor's EW electronics in the apartheid era were on the secret list, especially its family of transmission and transceiver equipment. During the War for Africa certain items of South African EW equipment were used to jam enemy tank communications.

Fapla — *Forces Armadas Popular de Angola*, or the People's Armed Forces for the Liberation of Angola, the military wing of the former Marxist-Leninist MPLA which seized government power by force, with Cuban, Soviet and East German military support, following Angola's independence from Portugal in November 1975.

FNLA — The National Front for the Liberation of Angola, one of two liberation movements which fought the totalitarian takeover of Angola by the MPLA. Strongly supported by the American Central Intelligence Agency and Zairean President Mobuto Sese Seko, the FNLA was nevertheless the weakest militarily of the three main Angolan political traditions.

G-2 — A World War II vintage heavy artillery gun with a range of more than 16 km. Was used by the South African Army as back-up for its state-of-the-art G-5s and G-6s (see below).

G-5 — The pride of Armscor at the time of the War for Africa, many experts ranked the G-5 at the time as the world's finest modern heavy artillery piece. It was developed from technology provided to South Africa by the maverick American artillery genius Dr Jerry Bull, who was assassinated by persons unknown in Brussels in 1990 after his company, Space Research Corporation, allegedly sold advanced artillery systems to Iraq. The G-5, which entered production in 1978, has a range of 45 km. The gun, which fires a range of different function computer-guided 'base-bleed' 45 kg shells, was the most outstanding SADF weapon during the War for Africa. It has also been an export success. Both Iran and Iraq purchased G-5s. It has also been sold to Oman and the United Arab Emirates.

G-6 — A self-propelled spin-off from the tractor-pulled G-5.

HEAT — High explosive anti-tank shell, used by both Fapla and the South African Army. A typical HEAT shell has a core of super-hard metal, such as tungsten, which penetrates tank armour on impact.

Ilyushin-76 — Giant Soviet transport plane diverted from strategic role in Europe to Angola in 1987–88 to ferry military supplies to Fapla troops fighting the SADF and UNITA.

M-46 — A highly praised Soviet artillery piece supplied to the MPLA. Fires a 33 kg shell with great accuracy up to 27 km.

MI-24 — A Soviet state-of-the-art helicopter gunship, known as the 'Hind', which put the fear of God into anti-government guerrillas in both Afghanistan and Angola. Heavily armed with cannons, machine-guns and anti-tank missiles. Several were shot down by UNITA.

Mig-21 — All-purpose Soviet fighter-bomber and air-to-air interceptor supplied to the MPLA. Top speed of 2,230 km per hour.

Mig-23 — Successor to the Mig-21, it was the main air superiority 'top-gun' fighter of the Angolan Air Force, leaving the Mig-21 to fill the fighter-bomber role. With a top speed of 2,500 km per hour, the Mig-23 is not only fast but has impressive acceleration power. Its sophisticated short-range radar systems make it a formidable opponent in dogfights.

Mirage F-1AZ — The former SAAF's main ground attack aircraft. Built by the French Dassault company, it was delivered to South Africa from late 1975 onwards. With Israeli assistance its electronics were updated several times by Armscor after it entered service.

Mirage F-1CZ — The SAAF's principal fighter and interceptor during the War for Africa, delivered from Dassault in 1975. Despite several upgrades of its systems, its top speed of 2,335 km per hour meant it was easily outmatched by the MPLA's Mig-23.

Mirage III — Another French Dassault aircraft of early 1970s vintage that was used by the SAAF for photographic reconnaissance.

MPLA — The Popular Movement for the Liberation of Angola, the Marxist-Leninist movement which, with Cuban, Soviet and East German collusion, came out on top in 1975–76 and established a government which declared a one-party state.

MRL — Used in the text mainly to describe the South Africa Army's Valkirie multiple rocket launcher (MRL), developed by Armscor in response to the Soviet BM-21 Stalin Organ used to devastating effect during the 1975–76 Angolan independence war. The 24 truck-mounted tubes of the Valkirie MRL fire 127 mm, 60 kg rockets out to a maximum range of 22 km. A more advanced version of the weapon was produced in 1990; it has 40 tubes.

Olifant — The South African Army's main battle tank in the 1980s, upgraded with British, West German, American and Israeli technology from 1950s-vintage British Centurion tanks. Its powerful 105 mm gun is a direct copy of a successful British tank gun and its laser range finder is of Israeli origin. In 1990 Armscor unveiled the Olifant 1B, which has a more powerful V-12 turbo-charged engine and special armour.

OP — Military observation post.

Passive night vision equipment — Night-vision technology, used in binoculars and weapons sights, in service with the SADF. It works on the principle of capture and intensification of light that it is always present during darkness. It compares with active night vision equipment, which is dependent on an infra-red transmitter. Active equipment has the grave disadvantage that its infra-red component emits a faint green glow, which can be picked up by the enemy. Fapla was equipped with Soviet active equipment, which gave the SADF – whose passive equipment does not glow – a distinct advantage in night fighting.

PT-76 — A Soviet amphibious tank carrying a 76 mm gun. Supplied in large numbers to Fapla.

Puma — The SAAF's primary transport helicopter during the war. French-built, it is used in trooping, assault, supply and casevac roles.

R-4 — SADF assault rifle, the South African version of the Israeli Galil manufactured in South Africa under licence.

Ratal Command — An adaptation of the Armscor Ratel mechanised infantry combat vehicle. Main command features are internal map tables, specialised communications equipment, air conditioning and a public address system.

Ratel-20 — The South African Army's standard mechanised infantry combat vehicle in the 1980s and 1990s, it is armed with a 20 mm cannon and a 7.6 mm machine-gun. It can carry a crew of three and a nine-man infantry section. Its light armour provides protection only against small arms fire, shell fragments and mine blasts. Its main strengths lie in its rapid fire power and manoeuvrability.

Ratel-60 — Ratel adapted so that a 60 mm mortar replaces the 20 mm canon as the main weapon.

Ratel-81 — Ratel adapted to carry an 81 mm mortar mounted on a central turntable.

Ratel-90 — Carries the biggest gun, 90 mm with a range of 1,200 metres, in the Ratel series. Performs in anti-tank and 'bunker busting' roles. Like the other infantry carrier vehicles in the range, the Ratel-90 is highly manoeuvrable.

Ratel-ZT3 — Ratel series carrying anti-tank missiles. Four ZT3s were sent into action during the War for Africa. The missile is probably developed from the NATO Milan missile, great quantities of which have been supplied to the SADF.

Ratpac — Ration packs, food packs supplied to soldiers in the field, consisting mainly of lightweight, dehydrated high protein items.

RP — Rendezvous point.

RPG-7 — Shoulder-held Soviet anti-tank rocket launcher supplied to Fapla. Captured in great numbers by the SADF and UNITA, becoming part of their weapons inventories.

RPV — Remote Piloted Vehicle. The SADF deployed these pilotless planes to excellent effect in surveillance and deception roles during the War for Africa.

RV — Map reference point.

SAAF — South African Air Force.

SADF — South African Defence Force, comprising Army, Navy and Air Force. Medical Services is the fourth component of the SADF.

Sam-3 — Soviet medium-altitude surface-to-air missile, with a range of 29 km and a ceiling of 15,000 metres, used mainly in short-range defence.

Sam-6 — Powerful Soviet computer-controlled missile with a range of 60 km which can also lock on to aircraft as close as 100 metres to the ground and up to a height of 18,000 metres.

Sam-7 — Early Soviet man-portable, shoulder-launched surface-to-air missile. Has limited range and its infra-red seeker is prone to easy distraction by the sun or decoy flares.

Sam-8 — Self-propelled Soviet medium-range missile system with acquisition and fire-control radars aboard which can guide two missiles simultaneously. Can knock out targets only 10 metres above the ground at a minimum range of 1,600 metres.

Sam-9 — Short-range Soviet surface-to-air missiles mounted on BRDM-2 armoured car.

Sam-13 — Updated Sam-9 mounted on a PT-76 chassis.

Sam-14/Sam-16 — Improved version of the Sam-7.

Shona — A word used by the Ovambo tribe of northern Namibia to denote wide-open grassland. Used here to specify big patches of open grassland within Angola's forests away from the rivers, and to make a distinction from *anhara* (see above).

SWAPO — South West African People's Organisation, the Ovambo-dominated liberation movement which fought a prolonged guerrilla war against South Africa and became the first elected government of independent Namibia in 1990.

Stinger — American shoulder-launched surface-to-air missile which is reputed to be the world's most effective man-portable Sam. Details of the missile are classified, but the US Central Intelligence Agency supplied the weapon in large quantities to UNITA, South Africa's Angolan ally in the War for Africa. Stinger production began in 1978 but UNITA was supplied with an updated 1983 unit.

T-54/T-55 — Standard battle tanks of the Soviet Army until the 1960s. Supplied in large numbers to Fapla.

UNITA — The National Union for the Total Independence of Angola, the main guerrilla opposition to Angola's MPLA government. Close ally to the United States and South Africa and received considerable support from many other countries, including France, Zaire and West Germany.

ZU-23 — Widely admired Soviet radar-controlled 23 mm light anti-aircraft gun with a vertical range of 2,500 metres. Captured by UNITA and the SADF in great numbers from Fapla and integrated into their own weapons systems.

SELECT BIBLIOGRAPHY

The central account in this book, which remains unchanged from the original, was almost entirely based on interviews with soldiers who fought in the War for Africa. Since nearly all of the material came from 'rockface' interviews, no extensive source notes were provided. However, a wide range of books, publications and newspaper articles were read as background research, and much more has been written, and read, in the intervening years. Of the publications that have appeared since the original book appeared, I found Chester Crocker's *High Noon in Southern Africa: Making Peace in a Rough Neighbourhood* (W W Norton & Company, New York, 1992) particularly fascinating and especially enlightening. The following is a partial but not exhaustive list of references:

James Adams, *Israel and South Africa: The Unnatural Alliance* (Quartet Books, London, 1984).

Sue Armstrong, *In search of freedom: the Andreas Shipana Story* (Ashanti Publishing, Gibraltor, 1989). This book is unfortunately mistitled because it is the most authentic and rigorous inside story of SWAPO in exile yet to be published.

Amnesty International, *Political Imprisonment in the People's Republic of Angola* (Amnesty International, London, 1984).

Gerald Bender, *Angola under the Portuguese: The Myth and The Reality* (London, Heinemann, 1978).

Fred Bridgland, *Jonas Savimbi: A Key to Africa* (Coronet, London, 1986).

Chester Crocker, with Mario Greznes and Robert Henderson, *Southern Africa – A US Policy for the 80s* (Africa Report, Washington DC, February 1981).

Francis Deng and William Zartman, *Conflict Resolution in Africa* (Brookings Institution, Washington DC, 1991).

Jannie Geldenhuys, *At the Front: A General's Account of South Africa's Border War* (Jonathan Ball, Cape Town, 2008).

Edward George, *The Cuban Intervention in Angola, 1965–1991, from Che Guevara to Cuito Cuanavale* (Routledge, London, 2005).

Richard Gibson, *African Liberation Movements: Contemporary Struggles Against White Minority Rule* (Oxford University Press, 1972).

Piero Gleijeses, *Visions of Freedom: Havana, Washington, Pretoria and the Struggle for Southern Africa, 1976–1991* (University of North Carolina Press, 2013). A comprehensive analysis of the Cuban role in Angola and the War for Africa from the Cuban viewpoint by a pro-Castro academic. Gleijeses is Professor of US foreign policy at Johns Hopkins University, Baltimore. He is the only foreign scholar to have been allowed access to Cuba's Castro-era government archives. Gleijeses refused to condemn the Cuban intervention in Ethiopia on behalf of the Marxist dictator President Mariam Mengistu who between 1974 and 1991 ran a 'Red Terror' campaign in which an estimated half a million to 1.5 million of his fellow countrymen died. Mengistu is now in his 80s. He fled Ethiopia and lives under high security in Robert Mugabe's Zimbabwe. In absentia, he was found guilty of genocide by Ethiopia's High Court and sentenced to death. President Mugabe has refused to extradite Mengistu.

Helmoed-Römer Heitman, *South African Arms and Armour* (Struik, Cape Town, 1988).

Helmoed-Römer Heitman, *War in Angola: The Final South African Phase* (Ashanti Publishing, Gibraltar, 1990). This book, based on official SADF records, was an excellent guide to the thinking of the top brass.

Lawrence W Henderson, *Angola: Five Centuries of Conflict* (Cornell University Press, Ithaca and London, 1980).

Tony Hodges, 'How the MPLA Won in Angola,' in Colin Legum and Tony Hodges, eds., *After Angola: The War Over Southern Africa*, (London, Rex Collings, 1976).

Jane's Armour and Artillery, *Jane's Infantry Weapons, and Jane's Weapons Systems* (Jane's Information Group, Coulsdon, UK).

Colin Legum, *The Western Crisis Over Southern Africa* (African Publishing Company, New York and London, 1979).

Mao Tse-tung [Zedong], *Guerrilla Warfare*, translated by Brigadier General Samuel B Griffith (Anchor Press/Doubleday, New York, 1978).

David Mannall, *Battle on the Lomba 1987: A Crew Commander's Account* (Helion Books, Solihull, UK, 2015).

John Marcum, *The Angolan Revolution, Volume 1: The Anatomy of an Explosion, 1950–1962* (The MIT Press, Cambridge, Massachusetts, 1969).

John Marcum, *The Angolan Revolution, Volume 2: Exile Politics and Guerrilla Warfare, 1962–76* (The MIT Press, Cambridge, Massachusetts, 1978).

Gabriel García Márquez's Cuban account of the 'internationalist military mission' to Angola, in the Havana magazine *Proceso* in January 1977. It was also serialised in three issues of the *Washington Post*, 10–12 January 1977, under the title 'Cuba in Africa: Seed Che (Guevara) Planted'. The account by Marquez, the Colombian winner of the Nobel Prize for Literature and close friend of Fidel Castro, is an extraordinarily entertaining, boastful and sensationalistic piece of work, patronising and racist in tone. In one passage Marquez laments the 'cultural backwardness' of the MPLA Africans the

Cubans found themselves working with, and goes on: 'Old African supersititions not only complicated daily life but also hindered the war effort. The Angolans had been convinced that the bullets would not penetrate white skin. They feared the magic of airplanes and refused to go into trenches because tombs were only for the dead ... It was a dirty war in which Cubans had to watch out as much for snakes as for mercenaries, as much for cannibals as cannonballs. A Cuban commander, in the midst of battle, fell into an elephant trap. Many times Cuban scouts felt betrayed by the primitive telegraph of the talking drums, whose thumping could be heard for as much as 20 miles.' This cliché-ridden nonsense is unrecognisable to anyone who has spent any length of time in the tragic territory known as Angola. It reflected the general inaccuracy of the Marques account. But such was his reputation that the Cuban 'truths' he asserted became incontrovertible ones in many minds far beyond Cuba.

Gabriel García Márquez, 'Operation Carlota,' New Left Review (January–April 1977). The official account of Cuba's initial involvement in the Angola conflict.

Lara Pawson, In the Name of the People: Angola's Forgotten Massacre (I.B. Tauris, London, 2014). An outstandingly brave account by a former BBC correspondent of atrocities perpetrated by Angola's ruling MPLA.

Leopold Scholtz, The Battle of Cuito Cuanavale (Helion and Company, Solihull, UK, 2016).

Vladimir Shubin, The Hot 'Cold War' (Pluto Press, London, 2008).

Willem Steenkamp, South Africa's Border War 1969–1989 (Ashanti Publishing, Gibraltar, 1989).

John Stockwell, In Search of Enemies: A CIA Story (Andre Deutsch, London, 1984). This is an account by the former head of the CIA Task Force in Angola of how the Americans first got deeply involved in the Angolan civil war in 1974 and then withdrew at the end of 1975. When the American effort failed, Stockwell resigned from the agency and threw his support behind the MPLA.

Hugh Thomas, The Cuban Revolution (Weidenfeld and Nicolson, London, 1986).

Paul Trewhela, Inside Quatro: Uncovering the exile history of the ANC and SWAPO (Jacana Media, Johannesburg, 2010), an account of the African National Congress' activities in exile in Angola, a history the ANC would probably prefer to forget, by an author and journalist who was imprisoned for three years in South Africa in the 1960s for his anti-apartheid activism.

Jiri Valenta and Frank Cibulka, eds., Gorbachev's New Thinking and Third World Conflicts (Transaction Books, New Brunswick, New Jersey, US, 1990).

Al J Venter, Challenge: South Africa Within the African Revolutionary Context (Ashanti Publishing, Gibraltar, 1989).

Michael Wolfers and Jane Bergerol, Angola in the Front Line (Zed Books, London, 1983). This is a book on the Angolan war written from the MPLA perspective by two British sympathisers who worked for the movement in Luanda.

Magazine and newspaper articles from newspapers in Europe, Africa and North America are too numerous to list. But I found the following particularly valuable:

The Johannesburg Sunday Star's eight-page supplement, entitled 'Mission Impossible: The Long Search for a Namibian Settlement' (9 April 1990). This is an excellent account, full of human insights, into the Chester Crocker-brokered negotiations on Namibia and Angola between Cuba, the MPLA and South Africa through 1987 and 1988 right up to the signing of the New York Accords in December 1988.

Military Technology, a high-quality monthly magazine on weapons innovation published by the Monch Group, Bonn, West Germany.

Africa Confidential, an excellent monthly newsletter published in London on African politics rich in facts and informed speculation. The editor in the 1980s and 1990s, the late Stephen Ellis, managed to upset all sides in every country, so *Africa Confidential* must have been getting a lot right.

International Defence Review, probably the best of the multinational monthly journals on weapons, military developments worldwide and conflict; part of the Jane's Information Group and carried outstanding coverage of the Angolan war.

ACKNOWLEDGEMENTS

Many people gave me help during my research for *The War for Africa*. Not all can be listed, but most of them were generous with their time and refreshingly straightforward. The following gave me particularly rich interviews: Commandant Jan Hougaard, Sergeant Mac da Trinidada, Lieutenant Tshisukila Tukayula ('TT') de Abreu, Captain Herman Mulder, Commandant Robert Hartslief, Commandant Mike Muller, Major Tinus van Staden, Captain Arthur Piercey, Commandant Gerhard Louw, Colonel Deon Ferreira, Captain Piet van Zyl, Colonel Dick Lord, Major Laurence Maree, Sergeant Piet Fourie, Major Pierre Franken, Colonel Jean Lausberg, Captain Reg van Eeden and General Jannie Geldenhuys.

I also drew heavily on my personal interviews with Cuban Air Force General Rafael Del Pino Diaz.

The wisdom and insights of Paul Trewhela, the writer and polemicist who was a prisoner of the apartheid government in Johannesburg and Pretoria for three years in the 1960s for his membership of the banned South African Communist Party, was invaluable.

I owe special thanks also to my original publisher, Al Venter, for his constant encouragement and his determination that I should meet my deadline. For this new edition I greatly enjoyed working with Casemate commissioning editor Ruth Sheppard.

The debt I owe to Tito Chingunji, the former foreign secretary and number three in the hierarchy of UNITA, is beyond measure. He was an unusually kind man and close friend who taught me most of what I know about Angola. Tito, his wife, Raquel, their four small children and Tito's entire extended family of about 50 people were executed on the orders of UNITA leader Jonas Savimbi for the most bizarre of reasons. I miss Tito badly to this day.

Finally, the author Sue Armstrong was an unpaid critic and sub-editor to whom my debt is very great.

INDEX

Adamishin, Anatoly 397–401, 443
African 'Frontline' States 398
African National Congress (ANC) 12,
    34, 352, 392, 389, 442, 447, 456,
    461–4, 465
AIDS 50
Aldana, Carlos 44, 450–1
Alvor Accord, 1975 46
Amnesty International 156, 463
ANC see African National Congress
Andropov, Yury Vladimirovitch 40
Angola:
    Angolan Air Force 38, 68, 305–6,
    336, 356, 363
    Civil War mid–70s 20
    Civil War mid–80s 36–7
    economy 37
    intervention of SADF in 68, 471–6
    Marxist regime in 20
    scheduled independence 19
Anhara Lipanda 317, 318, 320, 322,
    327, 328, 345, 347, 348, 350, 355,
    364, 381, 382, 383, 394
apartheid 12, 30, 402, 447, 456
Armacost, Michael 400
Armaments Corporation of South Africa:
    Armscor 98, 149, 185, 194, 218,
    223, 224, 234, 315–6, 394, 418

indigenous weapons 194
classified weapons 98, 315
development of HEAT shells 111,
    328
military equipment developed by 98,
    149, 185, 194, 223, 315
Auret, Derek 375, 400–1

Badenhorst, Sapper Johannes Jacobus 392
Baixo Longa 283, 340, 381
Bambi, Sergeant 122
Barnard, Dr Niël 13, 397, 442, 451
Barrientos, General René 47
Batista, Sergeant Fulgencio 35, 43, 410
    the Batista regime 35, 371
Ben-Ben see Pena, General Arlindo
Beneke, Lance-Corporal 143, 145
Benitez, Colonel Tomas 51
Bittersoet training area 81, 152
Borsao, Brigadier-General Francisco
    Crus 405, 409
Botha, P W, State President of South
    Africa 33, 62, 63, 156, 162–3, 247,
    289, 375
Botha, Roelof 'Pik', Foreign Minister
    of South Africa 267, 269, 289, 295,
    374–6, 380, 397, 401–3, 435, 444,
    447, 448, 458, 461

Branco, Corporal 275–6
Breytenbach, Breyten 352
Breytenbach, Colonel Jan 352, 482
Breytenbach, Lieutenant Koos 259,
    260
Breytenbach, Wynand 162
Brezhnev, Leonid 20, 21, 34
    death in 1982 40
    forward policy for scientific
    socialism 20
Britain:
    MI-6 Intelligence Agency 296
    permitted mercenary recruitment by
    FNLA 22
Buffalo Battalion (aka 32-Battalion)
    57–9, 65–6, 70, 72, 74, 81, 86,
    87, 91–2, 97, 100–1, 106, 115,
    119, 140, 141, 143, 145, 151, 152,
    161–2, 186, 187, 189, 197, 206,
    212, 227, 238, 240–2, 245, 250,
    252, 276, 282–3, 284, 289, 313,
    314, 333, 334–7, 338, 339, 347–8,
    350–1, 352, 355, 357, 361, 364,
    369, 381, 382, 408, 414–7, 424,
    425, 427, 429, 430, 431
Bull, Dr Jerry 483

Cabinda 156
Cacadas, Captain Ramos 214
Cahama airfield 407, 432
Calueque 409, 411, 414, 415, 416, 418,
    419, 420, 422, 423, 424, 425, 430,
    431, 432, 433, 434, 441, 442, 443,
    454, 468, 477, 479
Camp David negotiations 461
Candonga 236
Caprivi 65, 352–3, 482
Castenada, Lieutenant Raul Quiala 50
Castro, Fidel 34–5, 42, 43–9, 51, 63,
    267, 268, 312, 375, 398, 404, 405,
        409–10, 436, 437, 450, 453, 454–5,
        467
Castro, Raúl (Defence Minister) 49,
    312, 452, 454–5, 466
Chambinga High Ground 66–7, 236,
    251, 252, 259, 261, 269–70, 271,
    300, 301, 307, 310, 317–8, 319–20,
    326, 330, 336, 347, 348, 351, 354,
    356, 364, 378, 381, 382, 392, 392
Chambinga River 66, 67, 207, 222,
    236, 251, 254, 255, 259, 262, 263,
    271, 273, 300, 303, 304, 355, 356,
    391
chemical weapons 93–4
Chilingutila, Brigadier Demostenes 59,
    103, 159, 187, 193, 307, 327, 472
China, role in Angolan war 35
Chingunji, Samuel Kafundanga 10,
    260
Chingunji, Tito 10, 11, 492
CIA:
    Angolan Task Force 24–5, 29
    covert aid to UNITA 24
Claiborne, William 42
Clark, Dick, US Senator 34
Coetsee, Kobie 12, 13
Coetzee, Lance-Corporal 145
Coutinho, Admiral Rosa 48, 103
Crocker, Dr Chester 33, 370, 371–6,
    398–403, 439, 442–3, 446–7, 450–1,
    456–61, 465
Cuatir 66, 67, 205, 252, 283, 286, 288,
    300, 301, 302, 306, 307, 311, 319,
    333, 337, 338, 341, 391, 393
Cuba:
    Cuban revolution 41
    forces to depart from Angola 371,
    404
    strength of forces in Angola 34, 37,
    371

Cuito Cuanavale 57, 59, 62, 77, 95, 99, 127, 130, 131, 164, 178, 204, 205, 207, 213, 214, 219, 222, 224, 245–6, 250, 252, 266–7, 268, 270, 273, 281, 283, 287, 299, 300, 303–4, 312, 318, 323, 333, 334, 340, 357, 381, 383, 385, 391, 394, 405, 436, 437–40, 445, 446, 448, 455

Cuito River 57, 58, 62, 66, 67, 77, 127, 199, 203, 207, 214, 250, 263, 266, 269, 270, 271, 273, 274, 281, 284, 297, 299, 311–2, 313–6, 318, 328, 330, 345, 347, 358, 363, 380–1, 383, 391, 393, 464

Cunene River 406, 407, 411, 412, 414, 415, 422, 423, 434, 441

Cunzumbia River 59, 67, 87, 86, 93, 129, 159, 186, 204, 274

Cuvelai 246

Cuzizi River 67

Da Trinidada, Sergeant Mac 66, 70–4, 106–7, 115, 120, 123, 126, 140–4, 146, 159, 164, 166, 183, 195, 196, 274, 277

De Abreu, Lieutenant Tshisukila Tukayula ('TT') 427

De Klerk, President F W 460–1

De Vries, Colonel Roland 247–8

De Waal, Thielman 223–4

De Wet, Sergeant-Major Jacques 306

Del Pino Diaz, General Rafael 16, 42, 43–52, 62, 404, 409–10, 438, 478
   defection from Cuba 45, 62

Del Toro, General Ulysses Rosales 397, 399, 446, 448

Delport, Colonel Michau 419, 423

Delville Wood 362

Devangulo Mountains 408, 410

Devenish, Captain Maurice 416–8

Dos Santos, Captain Carlos 42

Dos Santos, President Eduardo 312, 405, 449

Du Plessis, Major Lourens 206, 208, 210, 211, 253

Du Randt, Commandant Johan 86, 88, 89

Du Toit, Corporal 406

Du Toit, Captain Wynand 156

Dumeni, Bishop Cleophas 363

East German Army units 37, 41, 304

Every, Major Ed 129, 337–8, 341

Fapla 14, 17

Ferreira, Colonel Deon 91–2, 99, 140, 147, 158, 185, 186, 196, 198, 203, 234, 260, 266, 273, 312, 319, 326, 334, 391, 474

Fisher, Professor Roger 461

FNLA 21, 22, 32

Font, Brigadier-General Patricio De Laguardia 405

Fort Buffalo base 352, 354

Fouché, Colonel Paul 274, 310, 318, 319, 370, 377, 379, 380, 388, 389, 393

Fourie, Lieutenant Hein 'Mieliepap' 230

Fourie, Sergeant Piet 87–8, 103, 123–4, 125, 130, 212, 253, 277, 284–5, 408, 410–3, 425

Franco, General Antonio Dos Santos 397

Franken, Major Pierre 70–1, 72, 73, 93, 108–9, 120, 130, 140, 142, 145, 155–6, 157–8, 159–60, 163, 164–5, 166–7, 168, 172, 173, 176, 177, 179, 181–4, 185, 186, 195–6, 196, 197, 198, 212, 301, 336, 339, 425–6

Fraternidade, Captain Banca Armindo 364

'Frenchie', Sergeant 74, 126, 141, 144, 146, 210–1, 253, 277, 285

Frias, Major-General Leopoldo Cintra
    385, 405
Fuch, Lieutenant Charles 314

Garcias, Lieutenant-Colonel Manuel
    Rocas 214
gas masks 94
Geldenhuys, General Jannie 9, 10, 58,
    91, 92, 121–2, 140, 147, 158, 162,
    168, 263, 370, 374, 391, 397, 398,
    399, 401, 402, 414, 422, 436, 439,
    440, 441, 442, 445–6, 447, 448, 451
'Gharra' (South African Remote Piloted
    Vehicle) 150
Gimbe 286, 333–8
glasnost, policy of 44, 45, 267, 453
Glynn, Lieutenant 87, 89
Gorbachev, Mikhail 40, 44, 267, 268,
    374, 400–1, 443, 447, 451
Grigoryev, Valeriy 268
Grobler, Major Vim 297
Grootfontein 14, 82, 83, 128, 133, 213,
    287, 290, 303, 304, 316, 337, 339, 382
Guevara, Che 35, 43, 47–8, 371

Hani, Chris 462
Harris, Colonel Jock 59
Hartslief, Commandant Robert 65,
    66, 67, 70–1, 72, 73, 74, 93, 96,
    98, 100, 101, 102, 105–6, 107–8,
    109–11, 112, 113, 114, 119, 141,
    151, 156, 158, 162, 206, 245, 247,
    249–50, 252, 256–7, 267, 271, 273,
    274, 277, 283, 289, 319, 333, 334,
    335, 336–7, 338–9, 340–1, 352, 474
Hastings, Max 33
Heartbreak Hill 318, 320, 364, 381, 382
Heliopolis, British Commonwealth War
    Cemetery at 402
Hendricks, Corporal 349
hepatitis 298, 311, 317, 347

Highpoint 1251: 329–30, 345
Hill 1208: 355, 357, 358
Hill, Commandant James 472
Hind, Lieutenant Adrian 15, 178
Hoedspruit 82, 91, 92
Honey, Peter 394
Hornsby, Michael 39
Hougaard, Commandant Jan 57, 58,
    64, 68–9, 7–5, 77, 86–8, 90, 94–5,
    99, 100, 101, 123, 131, 147–9, 150,
    151, 162, 185, 186, 189, 190–3, 196,
    203–4, 212, 281, 283, 284, 285–6,
    288–9, 313, 333, 340, 346, 406–7,
    408–9, 410, 413–6, 418, 419–21,
    423, 427–8, 431, 434
Human, Lieutenant Jurg 221, 242, 256
Hungary 20, 452

Inkatha Freedom Party 482
International Committee of the Red
    Cross 156

Jamba 10, 39, 63, 140, 296, 297, 346,
    439, 443

Kissinger, Henry 20, 33, 477
Kock, Major Piet 392
Koekemoer, Sergeant 351
Kooij, Lieutenant Johannes 114, 180
Kundera, Milan 20–1

Labuschagne, Sergeant Willem 257–8
Lake St Lucia, Natal 315
Lausberg, Colonel Jean 214–5, 219, 222–4,
    233, 236, 248, 260, 298, 314, 318
Lehman, Major Johan 187, 188, 191
Liebenberg, Lieutenant-General Kat 58,
    94, 121, 122, 162, 203, 263, 297,
    298, 346, 389, 439
Liebenberg, Commandant Koos 307,
    310, 317

Lima, General Pedro Benga 222
Lobito 28–9, 30, 41, 189, 466
Lomba River 14, 38, 39, 59, 63, 67,
   70–1, 72, 74, 75, 76, 77, 81, 82, 83,
   86–7, 88–9, 90, 93–4, 96, 97, 98,
   99, 100, 101, 103–15, 119, 120, 122,
   123, 129–30, 131, 134, 139–40, 141,
   142, 145, 149, 157, 158, 159, 162,
   163, 164, 169, 174, 175, 180, 181–3,
   186, 189, 195, 197, 198, 204–5, 213,
   222, 228, 246, 283, 301, 303, 327,
   437, 440, 443, 444, 464, 472, 474
Lombard, Major Florentine Aztilloga
   435
Longa River 240
Lord, Colonel Dick 85, 90, 92, 132,
   138, 159, 220, 303, 408, 432, 492
Lotter, Major Dawid 113–4, 162, 163,
   164, 175, 179, 180, 195
Louw, Commandant Gerhard 377–90
Louw, Lieutenant Louwtjie 350
Luanda 15, 29, 41, 42, 48, 156, 221,
   222, 263, 303, 316, 371, 374, 375,
   399, 400, 449, 454, 459, 462
Luassinga 283, 286, 333, 341
Lubango air base 336, 363, 407
Luta Contra Banditos troops 103
Luthuli, Chief Albert 461

Macallum, Captain 'Mac' 106–7, 115,
   119, 228
Machel, Samora 40
Malan, Commandant Jan 306, 301, 317
Malan, Defence Minister Magnus 162,
   223, 289, 295–6, 346, 401
malaria (cerebral) 298, 311, 314
Mandela, Nelson 12–3, 15, 461, 464,
   465, 480
Mannall, David 14–5, 444–5
MAOT see South African Air Force
   'Mobile Air Operations Teams'

Mao Tse Tung 476
Maquelengue River 220, 222
Marais, Commandant Leon 219, 229,
   230, 234–5, 237, 238, 239, 243, 251,
   252, 253, 257, 258, 266, 273, 307
Marais, Commandant Piet 223
Maree, Major Laurence 152, 153–4,
   157–8, 168, 174–81, 208, 209, 247
Maria, Major Afonse 92
Maria, Delida 46
Mavinga 38–9, 40, 63, 65–7, 76, 77,
   81, 86, 87, 93, 96, 115, 119, 134,
   140, 149, 152, 153, 154, 191, 198,
   212, 214–5, 218–9, 220, 221, 222,
   236, 245–9, 313, 346, 347, 354, 439,
   443, 446
May, Lieutenant Hans 159, 164, 196
Mbinda, Afonso van Dunem see Van
   Dunem, Afonso
McLoughlin, Colonel Pat 319–20, 325,
   326, 335, 351, 354, 361, 363, 364,
   370, 380
Meier, Karl 341
Meiring, Lieutenant Muller 430, 432, 441
Mendes, Sergeant 276
Menongue 41, 77, 99, 205, 246, 286,
   287, 289, 290–1, 299, 303, 305, 311,
   319, 333–41, 352, 406
Meyer, Major-General Willie 159, 162,
   311
Mickey, Major 106, 107, 110
Mitton, Rifleman M J 239
Morocco 35
MPLA 10, 14, 17, 21, 22, 29, 30–1,
   32–9, 40–2, 48–9, 58, 63, 221, 234,
   263, 267, 268, 303, 328, 334, 335,
   340, 371–5, 397, 400, 401, 404, 405,
   442, 443, 449, 450, 451, 456, 457,
   466
Mucobolo Hill 159, 163, 164, 166,
   168, 181, 195, 196

Mulder, Captain Herman 59, 76, 89, 90, 94, 96, 105, 161–2, 163–5, 168, 333–4, 336, 337, 340, 421, 425
Muller, Commandant Mike 227, 229, 237, 243, 251, 259, 260, 261, 265, 267, 270–1, 273, 274, 275, 307, 317, 318, 325, 327, 329, 345–61, 363–8, 378, 383, 414, 423, 425, 429–30, 433, 434
Muller, Colonel Piet 59

Namibe 41
Namibia 14, 24, 34, 36, 38, 59, 62, 65, 81, 82, 93, 127, 151, 217, 265, 267, 295, 304, 352, 372, 372, 375, 382, 398, 399, 407, 408, 409, 413, 414, 434–5, 441, 442, 443, 444, 446, 447, 448, 459, 466
   general elections 435, 466
   independence of 435, 466
   SADF troops left 435
Netherlands, the: role in Angolan war: 22
Neto, Dr Agostinho 32
New York Accords, the 435, 439, 443, 449, 450, 456, 460, 461, 462, 464, 479, 491
Ngueto, Major 224
Nguleica, Captain 255
Nicholson, Mike 26, 29, 52
Nortmann, Major Hannes 97–8, 100, 110, 111, 112–3, 119, 247, 248, 255, 256–7, 261, 294, 402, 424, 430, 434
Nova Lisboa (Huambo) 27–8, 450
Nzo, Alfred 461

Oelschig, Colonel Fred 12, 59, 68, 69, 75, 471–6
Omuthiya 414, 423
Ondangwa 408, 422, 427
Operation Askari (1983–4) 405

Operacion Camilo Cienfuegos (1988–9) 409
Operation Displace (1988) 393, 394, 402
Operation Hooper (1988) 273, 295–306, 370
Operation Moduler (September 1987) 92, 151, 269, 271, 272, 273, 290, 303, 304
Operation Packer (1988) 370, 393
Operation Perfect Lemon (1982) 92
Operation Protea (1981) 92, 354, 402, 407, 471
Operation Savannah (1975) 29, 327, 471
Organisation for African Unity (OAU) 372
Oshakati 407, 408, 414, 423
   Swapo bomb attack 1st Nat. Bank 363

Papenfus, Private John 406, 409, 417
Patton, General George 152, 423
Peace talks: Angola–Cuba–South Africa 391
   in Cairo, June 1988 401–3
   in Geneva, February 1988 374–5
   in London, May 1988 375, 397–9
   in Luanda, January 1988 370–71
   in New York, July–December 1988 435, 451
   on Sal Island, July 1988 441
Pena, General Ben-Ben Arlindo 159, 186, 187, 192, 206, 472, 476
Peoli, Isidor Malmierca 435
Perestroïka, policy of 44, 267
Pestretsov, Sergeant-Major Nikolai 354
Piercey, Captain Arthur 132–9
plofadder mines 240–1, 255, 350, 383–4, 385, 386
Potgieter, Captain Jako 276
Pretoria, seat of high command 203–4, 263

propaganda pamphlets 302, 306
psychological warfare 148, 302
Putter, Admiral Dries 121, 141, 159, 162, 263

Rankin, Commandant Johan 139
Reagan, President 372, 374, 400, 447
Redelinghuis, Lance–Corporal 257–8
Redman, Charles 371
Retief, Major André 228, 231, 232, 238–9, 241, 242
Revolutionary Armed Forces, the 51, 405, 435, 437
Risquet, Lieutenant Jorge 'Oom Kaspaas' 371, 374, 397, 402, 447, 448, 450
Ruacana 408, 414, 418, 420, 421, 422, 427, 428, 431, 432, 477
Rudman, Commandant Les 122, 141–2, 144, 145, 215–6, 472, 475
Rundu 27, 59, 65, 68, 86, 87, 88, 92, 93, 132, 133, 137, 138, 194, 269, 281, 287, 334, 339, 354, 362, 377, 378, 380, 407
Rupping, Sergeant Rian 112–3

Sachse, Colonel Bert 111, 472, 475
Sanchez, Major–General Arnaldo Ochoa 42–4, 312, 385, 405, 441, 443, 453–6
Savimbi, Jonas 10–12, 16, 23–4, 26–32, 33, 34–6, 39, 40, 43, 46, 47–8, 63, 115, 159, 187, 191, 193, 194, 206, 216, 234, 296–7, 298, 373, 402, 448, 449, 450, 466, 471, 472, 476
Schoeman, Commandant Cassie 317–8, 319, 320–1, 325, 326, 327, 347
Serfontein, Brigadier Chris 407, 414, 417, 418, 419, 423, 431
Setti, Lieutenant-Colonel 169
Shaganovitch, General Konstantin 53, 93

Shevardnadze, Eduard 374
Sierra Maestra campaign 43, 47, 48, 371
Silva, Commander 164, 173–4
Silva Porto (Kuito) 23–24, 25, 27, 29, 477
Sinclair, Captain John 132
'Skip' 24–5
Smit, Commandant Bok 152, 154, 156–8, 162, 163–4, 169, 170–1, 172, 174, 177, 179, 182, 186, 197–8, 205, 206, 208, 209, 210, 212–3, 227
Smit, Brigadier Fido 213, 362, 380
South Africa:
    Chief of Staff Intelligence (CSI) 121, 188, 397, 471
    international arms embargo 74, 98, 131, 149, 218, 390
    policy of secrecy, denial of involvement 63, 247
    presence of forces in Angola 28–9, 464–5
    proposed reform of internal politics 376
    victim of sanctions, boycotts and disinvestment 62
South African Air Force:
    critical role 148, 152, 155, 286–90, 299, 316, 337, 346, 363–4, 381, 419–22
    mobile air operations teams (MAOT) 303
South African Communist Party 461–3
South African Defence Act 391
South African Defence Force:
    Army Battle School at Lohatla, Cape 217–8, 377
    Commando forces 34
    deception exercises 364, 393
    De La Rey Citizen Force Battalion 379–80
    HQ in Pretoria 68, 147, 302
    liaison with UNITA in Angolan War 14, 471–6

Potchefstroom University Artillery Regiment 370, 380
Pretoria Regiment 297, 301, 309
Regiment Groot Karoo 380–1
Regiment Mooi Rivier 370, 380, 385, 389
Regiment President Steyn (OFS) 377–80, 385
School of Armour in Bloemfontein 217, 377
School of Artillery in Potchefstroom 214, 217
secret weapons 98, 199, 315
structure of Army 263–5
South African Department of Foreign Affairs 269
South African National (State) Security Council 375, 391
South West Africa 24, 28, 34
  see also Namibia
South West African Territorial Force 394
Soviet Union see Union of Soviet Socialist Republics
Steenkamp, Willem 433
Steyn, Brigadier Jan 131
Stockwell, John 32
Strauss, Lieutenant Abrie 'Sirkuslecu' 230, 240
Strauss, Prime Minister Franz Josef 374
Strydom, Sergeant 144
SWAPO 27, 34, 36, 37, 66, 68, 91, 92, 139, 246, 265, 354, 363, 392, 405, 406, 407, 409, 413, 414, 415, 447, 449, 459, 466
Swawek 434

Tambo, Oliver 461
Tarzan, Colonel 190, 193, 194
Techipa 407, 408, 409, 410, 411, 412, 413, 414, 415, 416, 419, 420, 421,
422–5, 426, 427, 430, 433, 441, 442, 446
Terblanche, Captain Christo 'Spikkels' 320, 321, 323
Theron, Thai 221, 242, 256, 381
Tobias Hanyeko Training Centre 363
Tortolo, Colonel Redro 49
Trautman, Major Robert 301–2, 311
Tsumeb HQ 307
'TT' see de Abreu, Lieutenant Tshisukila Tukayula
Tucker, Lieutenant Noah 432
Tumpo Triangle 250, 269, 270, 300, 303, 307, 310, 312, 317, 321, 324, 326, 328, 330, 345–68, 377–94, 405
Tunney, John 34

Umkhonto We Siswe 456, 460, 462
Union of Soviet Socialist Republics:
  advisors in Angola 42
  Aeroflot transport planes 42, 291
  financial aid to MPLA 41–2
UNITA 10–52:
  role in Angolan War 471–7
  liaison with SADF 14, 471–6
United Nations 63, 375, 401, 450
  role in Namibia general elections 435
United Nations Resolution 435: 373, 398, 401, 448
United Nations Security Council 295
United States:
  financing of arms 32, 193, 373
  recruitment of FNLA mercenaries 22

Van Coppenhagen, Major Willie 381
Van den Bergh, General Frans 223–4
Van der Merwe, Major Cassie 236, 314
Van der Waals, Commandant Willem Kaas 26, 477
Van der Westhuizen, Commandant Jan 190, 214

Van Dunem, Afonso 371, 374, 397, 402, 435, 447
Van Dunem, Fernandes 371, 397
Van Eeden, Captain Reg 82, 83, 84–5, 128–9, 132, 339, 465
Van Heerden, Brigadier Carl 440
Van Heerden, Neil 379, 374, 375, 397, 398–400, 401, 402, 403, 442, 451
Van Staden, Major Tinus 347, 352–62, 369, 381
Van Tonder, General Neels 397
Van Zyl, Captain Piet 119–21, 122, 129–30, 187–92, 195, 206, 208, 211, 212–3, 219, 220–2, 227–9, 230, 231, 232, 235, 238, 238–9, 240, 241, 242, 244, 249, 252–3, 255, 258, 260, 261, 262, 273
Venter, Lance-Corporal Henrik Jacobus 406
Venter, Lance-Corporal Johan 145

Ventura, Lieutenant 71–2
Villegas, Colonel Harry 'Pombo' 46–7
Vimpulo River 208, 210, 211, 246, 249, 251, 252–3, 254, 274, 275, 324
Viposto High Ground 208, 210, 254, 255, 355–6, 362
Vlasev, Vladilen 403
Vos, Lieutenant Tobias de Villiers 229, 241, 242, 276–7

Waterkloof Air Force Base 82, 132, 133, 138, 139
weapons captured/destroyed 199, 392
Wessels, Corporal 'Wessie' 233, 242, 256
Wilken, Major Theo 109–10

Xangongo 407, 413, 415, 419, 425, 454

Zaire 35, 37, 50, 51, 63, 487